SOARING

—— on ——

EAGLE'S WINGS

When the
Supernatural
Becomes
Natural

366 Devotional Readings

BY J. DAVID ESHLEMAN

SOARING ON EAGLE'S WINGS

Supernatural Becomes Natural, 366 Devotional Readings

Copyright © 2018
by **J. David Eshleman**

Library of Congress Number: 2018946833
International Standard Book Number: 978-1-60126-587-6

Published by

Masthof Press

219 Mill Road | Morgantown, PA 19543-9516
www.Masthof.com

DEDICATION

This book is dedicated to all who hunger and thirst
for more of the fullness of life in Jesus.
"Just as you received Christ Jesus as Lord,
continue to live in him, as you were taught,
rooted and built up in him, strengthened in the faith
and overflowing with thankfulness" (Col. 2:6-7 NIV).

It's also dedicated to my loving wife,

Helen,

for her prayers, encouragement,
helpful suggestions and many hours of proofreading.

"To the only God our Savior be glory,
majesty, power and authority,
through Jesus Christ our Lord,
before all ages, now and forevermore! Amen."
JUDE 25

PREFACE

Soar with the eagles! Eagles soar on the winds of the storms of life. God designed us to overflow with love, to live with great joy and peace that's beyond our understanding. There are trials but as we allow Jesus to live his life through us, he enables us to ride on the winds of the storm.

These daily readings will enable you to live victoriously bringing honor to God and new life to others as you become involved in God's exciting and joyful adventure—seeing lives transformed through Jesus' resurrection power! They will challenge and equip you to be an encouragement to everyone. Jesus' final words give you both the authority (Matthew 28:18-20) and the power to be his witnesses (Acts 1:8).

I have used different translations to make God's word more understandable for our culture. When there is no abbreviation after the Scripture it is from the NIV (New International Version) or it is not a direct quote. Occasionally I inserted words in the text for clarification which appear in parenthesis. Other abbreviations are:

AMP	Amplified Bible
CEV	Contemporary English Version
LB	Living Bible
JKV	King James Version
Msg.	Message Bible
NLT	New Living Translation

I have abbreviated many of the longer names of the books of the Bible: Psalms – Ps., Proverbs – Pr., Isaiah – Is., Jeremiah – Jer., Matthew – Matt., Romans – Ro., Corinthians – Cor., Galatians – Gal., Ephesians – Eph., Philippians – Phil., Colossians – Col., Thessalonians – Thess., Timothy – Tim., and Revelation – Rev.

Much of this book is a revision of my earlier devotional books: *Living with Godly Passion, Daily Readings for those with a Passion to Share Jesus,* 2010 and *Power Scriptures for Successful Living, 366 Timely Devotions,* 2012 both published by Masthof Press.

Eagles' Wings

Isaiah 40:29-31

"Have you not known? Have you not heard? The everlasting God, the Lord, the Creator of the ends of the earth, does not faint, or grow weary . . . He gives power to the faint and weary, and to him who has no might. He increases strength—causing it to multiply and making it abound. Even youths shall faint and be weary, and the selected young men shall feebly stumble and fall exhausted; But who those wait for the Lord—who expect, look for and hope in Him—shall change and renew their strength and power; they shall lift their wings and mount up [close to God] as eagles [mount up to the sun]; they shall run and not be weary; they shall walk and not faint or become tired" (Is. 40:28-31 AMP).

There comes a time when the mother eagle pushes her young from the nest. Sometimes God takes our lives and pushes us out of our comfort zone. The test from the doctor reveals stage four cancer. The principal calls informing you your child was found carrying drugs. You discover your car needs major repairs but there's no money. Worst of all your spouse shocked you with the news he or she is filing for divorce. God is shaking your nest. (Heb. 12:6).

Why would God push you out of your nest? Is it because he no longer loves you? No, as the eaglets would never learn to fly unless pushed out of their nests, so it is with us. God has to push you out of your lethargic mind set so you learn to trust him and soar to new heights. God is at work in those painful changes. We were not made to grovel in the dust; we were made to soar in the heights.

"He gives power to the faint and weary, and to him who has no might. He increases strength—causing it to multiply and making it abound" (Isaiah 40:29). As I look back over my life it was the times that God pushed me out of my nest that I grew the most.

Lord Jesus, thank you for pushing me out of my nest so I can soar to new heights. Amen.

You Can Create a Party in Heaven

Luke 15:3-24

When the shepherd finds a sheep that has wandered away he calls together his friends and neighbors saying, "Rejoice with me; I have found my lost sheep." Jesus says, "I tell you that in the same way there will be more rejoicing in heaven over one sinner who repents than over ninety-nine righteous persons who do not need to repent" (Luke 15:6-7). In vv. 9-10, when the woman finds her lost coin she says, "Rejoice with me, I have found my lost coin." Jesus says, "In the same way, I tell you, there is rejoicing in the presence of the angels of God over one sinner who repents."

In verses 22-24, the father rejoices when the lost son returns: "The father said to his servants, 'Quick! Bring the best robe and put it on him. Put a ring on his finger and sandals on his feet. Bring the fattened calf and kill it. Let's have a feast and celebrate. For this son of mine was dead and is alive again; he was lost and is found.' So they began to celebrate."

I expect there is joy in heaven whenever God's people walk in faithfulness to their Lord but the only time the Bible explicitly states we cause rejoicing in heaven is when a person repents and accepts Jesus as their Lord and Savior. What a privilege we have to bring joy to the angels in heaven.

Someone said, "Witness 24/7, if necessary use words." That's like saying, "Be sure to wash, if necessary use water." We need to employ both words and deeds. If Jesus would have come and not informed us that he was the Son of God to pay for our sins we would still be lost. Share Jesus so others can be transferred from the kingdom of darkness to the Kingdom of God's Son. (Col. 1:14).

Father, I thank you for sending Jesus who paid our debt making it possible to enter the family of God. Lord, enable me to be a faithful and fruitful witness and cause a party in heaven. Amen.

Fullness of Joy

Psalm 16:11

"In your presence is fullness of joy and at your right hand are pleasures forever more" (Ps. 16:11 JKV).

Everyone strives for fulfillment and joy. This verse promises fullness of joy. When the disciples returned from their first missionary journey they were joyful because of the power Jesus gave them to drive out demons. Jesus informed them they were to rejoice not because of the power to cast out demons but because their names were written in heaven. Joy comes from a right relationship with Jesus. (Luke 10:20).

We are a pleasure-seeking society. At God's right hand are pleasures forever. Living in his presence brings joy. Think of David's problems. King Saul wanted to kill him. His own son was seeking to annihilate him. David had to run for his life. His infant son died in spite of David's fasting and prayers. Yet he writes: "I have set the Lord always before me . . . I will not be shaken. Therefore my heart is glad and my tongue rejoices; . . . You have made known to me the path of life; you fill me with joy in your presence" (Ps. 16:8-11).

Joy comes from abiding in Jesus. "As the Father has loved me, so have I loved you. Now remain in my love. If you obey my commands, you will remain in my love, just as I have obeyed my Father's commands and remain in his love. I have told you this so that my joy may be in you and that your joy may be complete" (John 15:9-11). Jesus gives us his joy. His joy is perfect!

Paul experienced Jesus' joy and writes, "We are close to death, but here we are still alive. We have been beaten within an inch of our lives. Our hearts ache, but we always have joy" (II Cor. 6:10 NLT).

Jesus said you are blessed when you are mocked, and persecuted. You are to rejoice and leap for joy because a great reward awaits you in heaven. (Matt. 5:11-12).

Lord Jesus, enable me to experience your presence in my life. Thank you for your presence and your joy. Amen.

Thirsty for God

Psalm 42:1-2

David was thirsty for God. "O God, you are my God, earnestly I seek you; my soul thirsts for you, my body longs for you, in a dry and weary land" (Ps. 63:1). "As the deer pants for streams of water, so I long for you, O God. I thirst for God, the living God" (Ps. 42:1-2a NLV). "One thing I have asked of the Lord, that will I seek after, inquire for and [insistently] require, that I may dwell in the house of the Lord—in his presence—all the days of my life" (Ps. 27:4 AMP). God will reward you if you earnestly and diligently seek him. (Heb. 11:6).

Jesus said that you will be completely satisfied if you thirst for righteousness. (Matt. 5:6 AMP). Again he says, "If you are thirsty come to me! If you believe in me, come and drink! For the Scriptures declare that rivers of living water will flow out from within" (John 7:37-38 NLT).

"If you will look for me in earnest you will find me when you seek me. I will be found by you" (Jer. 29:13-14 NLT).

Why does God seemingly make it hard to find him at times? He wants us to be sincere in our desire for him. God demands our allegiance. He must be first. He will not share his glory with another.

When you got up this morning were you thinking about all the things you needed to do today? Or was your heart longing for the streams of living water? Did you say, "Good God, morning!" or "Good morning, God?"

Ask God to give you a single-minded focus—a focus desiring to please him with every thought. Oswald Chambers writes, "Once we see Jesus, the impossible things He does in our lives become as natural as breathing." Practice spiritual breathing: exhale any thought or image that appears in your mind that would be displeasing to God. Then inhale his love, forgiveness, grace and power.

Father, I confess that I need a greater passion to love and serve you. Draw me to yourself. May your streams of living water flow from me to thirsty people. Amen.

Do You Love God's Word?

Psalm 119:20

"I am overwhelmed continually with a desire for your laws" (Ps. 119:20 NLT). "My soul is starved and hungry, ravenous!—insatiable for your nourishing commands" (Msg). Do you love the word of God? God's word is a lamp and light throughout the day. Walk in his light. You will not stumble or fall. (Ps. 119:105).

"Oh, how I love your law! I meditate on it all day long" (Ps. 119:97). Is your mind focused on the news or on the Good News? David was a man after God's own heart. He loved the Lord and he loved his word. He writes: "Your commands make me wiser than my enemies for they are ever with me. I have more insight than all my teachers, for I meditate on your statutes. I have more understanding than the elders, for I obey your precepts" (Ps. 119:97-100). How can this be? "In Christ are hidden all the treasures of wisdom and knowledge" (Col. 2:3).

If your hunger for God's word grows cold, sincerely ask him to give you a love for his word. I assure you he will answer that prayer. In answering that prayer your day will be transformed. The supernatural will become natural. You will move from one degree of glory to another. (II Cor. 3:18 KJV).

Good things are often the enemy of God's best. You will find time for what is most important to you. Beware of the barrenness of a busy life! God's word is a lamp and light throughout the day. Walk in his light. You will not stumble or fall. (Ps. 119:105).

It's the word of God that points us to Jesus the living word. (Luke 24:44, Heb. 1:1-3). We don't worship a book. We worship Jesus. Jesus said, "You diligently study the Scriptures because you think that by them you possess eternal life. These are the Scriptures that testify about me, yet you refuse to come to me to have life" (John 5:39-40).

Father, give me a fresh love for your word so I can know you more intimately. Amen.

Eyes to See

Psalm 119:37

"Divert my eyes from toys and trinkets, invigorate me on the pilgrim way" (Ps. 119:37 Msg.). The NIV reads, "Turn my eyes away from worthless things; preserve my life through your word." "My eyes are fixed on you. O Sovereign Lord; in you I take refuge" (Ps. 141:8).

Children are drawn to toys and trinkets. As adults most of us have a lot of childishness in us. The average person in the U.S. watches TV a couple hours a day plus spends another hour or two on the internet. How many commercials and TV programs promote "worthless, toys and trinkets?" Someone said TV is chewing gum to the eyes. Many programs are thoroughly evil promoting violence, immorality and filthy language. A verse a day or five minutes a day in God's word will not offset hours of TV. Jesus said, "Your eye is a lamp for your body. A pure eye lets sunshine into your soul. But an evil eye shuts out the light and plunges you into darkness" (Luke 11:34 NLT).

From prison Paul reminds us to set our mind on things that are, "true and honorable and right. Think about things that are pure and lovely and admirable. Think about things that are excellent and worthy of praise" (Phil. 4:8 NLT). On more than one occasion Jesus used hyperbole to get his point across, "If your eye causes you to sin, gouge it out and throw it away. It is better for you to enter life with one eye than to have two eyes and be thrown into the fire of hell" (Matt. 18:9).

David wrote in Psalm 23 the shepherd leads me in green pastures. Green pastures provide satisfying nourishment. Growing up on a dairy farm I observed cows lying down in contentment after feeding on the green pastures. They chewed their cud—a picture of meditation. As you feed on the nourishing word of God and meditate on it throughout the day you will become a new person.

Father, give me pure eyes and a love for your word like David who said, "My soul is consumed with a longing for your word." Amen.

You Are Commissioned

Matthew 28:18-20

Choosing Scripture selectively is a temptation. We like Jesus' invitation. "Come to me, all you who are weary and burdened, and I will give you rest" (Matt. 11:28), or John 10:10, Jesus came to give us life even abundant life. But taking up our cross, loving our enemies or obeying the Great Commission that's different. Jesus wants us to obey all his commands. (John 14:14, 23).

Jesus says: "All authority in heaven and on earth has been given to me. Therefore go and make disciples of all nations, baptizing them in the name of the Father and of the Son and of the Holy Spirit, and teaching them to obey everything I have commanded you. And surely I am with you always, to the very end of the age" (Matt. 28:18-20). This is his commission to every child of God.

Jesus gives us authority to invite people to become his fully devoted followers. The key to fulfilling the Great Commission is your relationship to him. Do you know the risen Lord? Jesus said, "I am the Vine, you are the branches. When you're joined with me (know me) and I with you, the relation intimate and organic, the harvest is sure to be abundant" (John 15:5 Msg.).

He says, "Apart from me you can do nothing" (John 15:5b). We have the mind of Christ. (I Cor. 2:16). It's not our wisdom that will make disciples. It is his Spirit living in and through us that draws people to Jesus.

Jesus said, "When I am lifted up from the earth I will draw all men unto me" (John 12:32). Only those who know him can lift him up. Paul's supreme goal in life was: "I want to know Christ and the power of his resurrection and the fellowship of sharing in his suffering, becoming like him in his death" (Phil. 3:10-11). It must be our goal, too. The Greek word for "knowing" is experiential knowledge: a personal intimate relationship with Jesus. Jesus commissions you to be his disciple maker.

Lord, forgive me for being selective with your word. Enable me to represent you well today. Amen.

Jesus' Father Our Father

Mark 3:31-35

"A crowd was sitting around Jesus, and they said to Him, 'Your mother and Your brothers and Your sisters are outside, asking for you.' He replied, 'Who are My mother and My brothers?' Looking around on those who sat in a circle about Him, He said, 'See! Here are My mother and My brothers, for whoever does the things God wills is My brother, and sister, and mother!'" (Mark 3:32-35 AMP).

"Jesus and the ones he makes holy have the same Father. That is why Jesus is not ashamed to call them his brothers and sisters. For he said to God, 'I will declare the wonder of your name to my brothers and sisters. I will praise you among all your people.' He also said, 'I will put my trust in him.' And in the same context he said, 'Here I am—together with the children God has given me'" (Heb. 2:11-13 NLT).

"God knew his people in advance, and he chose them to become like his Son, so that his Son would be the firstborn among many brothers and sisters" (Ro. 8:29 NLT).

Jesus is not ashamed to call us his sibling. With our older brother, Jesus, on our side nothing can defeat us! Until we know Jesus, God is merely a concept. We don't have faith in a concept; our faith is in a person, Jesus. Jesus brings God to us. We walk and live by faith in Jesus. We do not rely on our feelings. (Ro. 1:17).

One thing that will help us walk in this reality is to remember that others who name the name that is above every name, are also our brothers and sisters. "In Christ we who are many form one body and each member belongs to all the others" (Ro. 12:4). We have experienced the same blood washed cleansing from the Lamb of God who was slain before the foundation of the world. Let's build bridges to all God's children. Then the world will know that Jesus is God's Son who gives life to all who come to him. (John 17:21).

Lord Jesus, I can't comprehend how you can be my brother or how your Father can be my Father but by faith I claim that relationship today. Thank you! Amen.

Everyone Is a Worshipper!

Since the beginning of time every tribe and people group worships something or someone. For those who don't know God their worship is focused on themselves, their needs, their wants and pleasures. Our worship is focused on God, our Father, the Creator of the cosmos and his Son, our Messiah and Lord.

"You will worship me with all your heart and I will be with you and accept your worship" (Jer. 29:13 CEV). Notice the word "all?" God wants more than your time, talents and treasure. He wants your heart. (Matt. 22:37-39). Your heart is the same as your will. Jesus wants our wills. "The true worshippers will worship the Father in spirit and truth for they are the kind of worshippers the Father seeks" (John 4:24b).

The dictionary defines worship as expressions of reverence toward God—extravagant respect or admiration of God. How wonderful it is that we have a God who is worthy to receive our worship. The false gods of materialism, power, or pleasing people will never satisfy. Jesus alone satisfies. He hears our every plea and knows our every thought, as well as our joys and disappointments. Let's thank him for his greatness, his compassion and faithfulness which is new every morning. (Lamentations 3:23). Take time to see Jesus in creation, and in your circumstances. Take time to hear his voice. He is there whether you discern his presence or not. "I can never get away from your presence!" (Ps. 139:7 NLT).

Thank God that he is with you. That is worship! Pray for grace to recognize him in each person you meet. He is at work in every situation and in every person. We work with God rather than for God. As the Spirit gives you eyes to see and ears to hear, thank Jesus and worship Him! As you focus on Jesus, he will put a spring in your step, a smile on your face and a song of joy in your heart.

Lord I love you, I give myself to you, I worship you. I praise you. You are all I want. You alone satisfy. Amen.

You Are Greater Than . . .

Matthew 11:11

One of the most unbelievable verses in the Bible is: "I assure you, of all who have ever lived; none is greater than John the Baptist. Yet even the most insignificant person in the Kingdom of Heaven is greater than he is!" (Matt. 11:11 NLT).

It sounds blasphemous to say that I am greater than Abraham, Jacob, Moses, David, Isaiah, Jeremiah or Daniel. How can that be? According to Luke 10:23-24 and I Peter 1:10-11 the Kings and prophets longed to see our day. "It is all so wonderful that even the angels are eagerly watching these things happen" (I Peter 1:12 NLT).

How blessed we are to live after the resurrection. The resurrection of Jesus changed everything! We have a new DNA, a new nature. "He has given us his very great and precious promises, so that through them you may participate in the divine nature and escape the corruption in the world caused by evil desires" (II Peter 1:4). "If anyone is in Christ, he is a new creation; the old has gone the new has come" (II Cor. 5:17). No wonder Paul writes that the gift of Jesus is too wonderful for words. (II Cor. 9:15).

When Moses returned from Mt. Sinai after receiving the Ten Commands his face was so bright that the people insisted he wear a veil. Moses' glory faded. Our glory doesn't fade; it increases continually as we walk with Jesus. "All of us have had that veil removed so that we can be mirrors that rightly reflect the glory of the Lord. And as the Spirit of the Lord works within us, we become more and more like him and reflect his glory even more" (II Cor. 3:18 NLT). "Our lives gradually becoming brighter and more beautiful as God enters our lives and we become like him" (Msg.).

If you are not becoming more like Jesus examine your heart. With David pray: "Search me, O God, and know my heart; test me and know my anxious thoughts. See if there is any offensive way in me, and lead me in the way everlasting" (Ps. 139:23).

Lord, thank you for the cross and your resurrection. I want to reflect your glory becoming more and more like you. Amen.

Scale a Wall!

Psalm 18:29

Are you up against a wall? "With my God I can scale any wall" (Ps. 18:29b NLT). "I pray that out of his glorious riches he may strengthen you with power through his Spirit in your inner being" (Eph. 3:16). Paul prays for the Colossians to be strengthened with all power according to God's might so that they may have great endurance and patience and joyfully give thanks to God. (Col. 1:11-12).

Is your life filled with discouragement, frustration, and seemingly impossible circumstances? David writes: "With my God"—notice the three secret code words. "With my God" I can scale a wall! With God I can do anything. Paul writes from prison, "I can do everything with the help of Christ who gives me the strength I need" (Phil. 4:13 NLT). Don't be discouraged, defeated or feel dejected for "the joy of the Lord is your strength" (Nehemiah 8:10). The Lord's strength and joy was there for Nehemiah and for David. It can be your strength too! Jesus reminds us to abide in him and obey him so that our joy is full. (John 15:11).

You say, "No one understands how high my walls are!" "Remember that the temptations that come into your life are no different than what others experience. God is faithful. He will keep the temptation from becoming so strong that you can't stand up against it. When you are tempted, he will show you a way out so that you will not give in to it" (I Cor. 10:13 NLT).

Every day thank the Lord for his many blessings. One of my closest friends was an unwanted child, shuffled from one foster home to another. Most every community has a need for foster parents. Even in America some children roam the city streets often getting involved in drugs and become slaves of evil men. Pray about adopting a child who needs a home. Open your heart, God will give you special grace and strength.

You can bring the light of Jesus into their lives so they too can have hope enabling them to rise above their indescribable circumstances.

Lord, enable me to remember no wall is too high for you to overcome. Amen.

In the Desert/Wilderness

Psalm 6:6-7

Yesterday we focused on Psalm 18:29 NLT, "With God I can scale a wall." David did not feel this way every day. "I am worn out from sobbing. Every night tears drench my bed; my pillow is wet from weeping. My vision is blurred by grief; my eyes are worn out because of all my enemies" (Ps. 6:6-7 NLT). Then in the next verses he says, "The Lord has heard my crying and my plea; the Lord will answer my prayer." David is realistic. He is honest. He owns his feelings.

David said, "My whole world is coming unglued" (Ps. 82:5c Msg.), and then he adds in v. 8 "You've got the whole world in your hands!"

"Day and night I have only tears for food. . ., My heart is breaking as I remember how it used to be: I walked among the crowds of worshipers, leading a great procession to the house of God, singing for joy and giving thanks - it was the sound of a great celebration!" (Psalm 42:3-4 Msg.)

David tells us the solution to his depression: v. 5, "I will put my hope in God! I will praise him again—my Savior and my God!" Then he talks about his tears, his enemies, running from Absalom his son, and running from King Saul and his army who sought to kill him. Don't be afraid to confess your pain and anguish before God. Even Jesus did in Gethsemane. ". . .he began to be filled with anguish and deep distress . . . my soul is crushed with grief to the point of death . . ." (Matt. 26:37-38 NLT).

Paul says, "We are hard pressed on every side, but not crushed; perplexed, but not in despair; persecuted, but not abandoned; struck down, but not destroyed. We always carry around in our body the death of Jesus, so that the life of Jesus may be revealed in our body. (II Cor. 4:8-9).

Father, look upon my pain and my sorrow. Grant me faith to believe you are with me in this valley of testing. Enable me to keep my eyes fixed on you. "Get me out of this mess and up on my feet." (Ps. 71:2 Msg.). Amen.

I'm OK, You're OK, Really?

Jeremiah 17:9

Check the headlines or watch the evening news and you know we are not OK. Crime is increasing. Our prisons are full. "The heart is deceitful above all things and beyond cure. Who can understand it?" (Jer. 17:9). When we don't get our own way we want to take revenge. We're never satisfied. (Jer. 17:9). We inherited a sin nature.

Philosopher Blaise Pascal is credited as saying: "There is a God shaped vacuum in the heart of every person which cannot be filled by any created thing, but only by God the Creator."

"God knows the secrets of our hearts" (Ps. 44:21). When we compare ourselves with others we often pick persons who we perceive as "worse" than we are. "There is no one righteous, not even one; there is no one who understands; no one who seeks God. All have turned away; they have together become worthless; there is no one who does good, not even one . . . " (Ro. 3:10-18).

However, "If we confess and renounce our sins, God will forgive and purify us from all unrighteousness. If we walk in the light of Jesus as he is in the light, the blood of Jesus cleanses us from all sin. If we claim to be without sin, we deceive ourselves and the truth is not in us. If we confess our sins, he is faithful and just and will forgive us our sins and purify us from all unrighteousness" (I John 1:7-9).

"Search me, O God, and know my heart; test me and know my anxious thoughts. See if there is any offensive way in me, and lead me in the way everlasting" (Ps. 139:23-24). "He who conceals his sins does not prosper, but whoever confesses and renounces them finds mercy" (Prov. 28:13). We are as sick as our secrets.

The good news is, "God demonstrated his own love for us . . . while we were still sinners" (Ro. 5:8). We are free from condemnation when we are in Christ Jesus. (Ro. 8:1). When Jesus is in us and we are in him we are OK! (John 15:10).

Lord create in me a clean heart and renew a right spirit within me. Amen.

Pray with Perseverance and Resolve

Luke 11:5-13

When the disciples asked Jesus to teach them to pray he gave this pattern: "Father, hallowed be your name, your kingdom come. Give us each day our daily bread. Forgive us our sins, as we also forgive everyone who sins against us. And lead us not into temptation" (Luke 11:2-4). Jesus continues "Suppose you have a friend, who comes at midnight and says, 'Friend, lend me three loaves of bread, because a friend of mine on a journey has come to me, and I have nothing for him.' Then the one inside answers, 'Don't bother me, the door is locked.'. . . Because of the man's boldness (persistence) he will get up and give it to him . . . "So I say to you: Ask (and keep on asking) and it will be given to you; seek (and keep on seeking) and you will find; (knock and keep on knocking) and the door will be opened to you. For everyone who asks receives; he who seeks finds; and to him who knocks, the door will be opened. "Which of you fathers, if your son asks for a fish, will give him a snake instead? . . . If you . . . know how to give good gifts to your children, how much more will your Father in heaven give the Holy Spirit to those who ask him!" (Luke 11:5-13).

"The Hebrews groaned in prayer." (Exodus 2:23). "Give God no rest." (Isaiah 62.7). "Listen to my cry, for I am in desperate need." (Psalm 142:6). "I am again in the pains of childbirth until Christ is formed in you." (Gal. 4:19).

As parents give good gifts to their children, God will give us himself in the person of the Holy Spirit. (v. 13). God's Spirit is greater than the spirit in the world. (I John 4:4). He equips us to overcome the world. Our prayers of faith and persistence give permission for God's Spirit to answer our prayers.

Someone reported at Billy Graham World Congress of Evangelism, that it was easy to tell who was from the United States. After the long days of inspirational messages, those from other nations were asking, "Where can we go to pray?" while the Americans were asking, "Where is the nearest restaurant?"

Lord, too often my prayers are casual. Forgive me and teach me to pray! Amen.

All In

Luke 7:36-39

A Pharisee invited Jesus to his home for a meal. As they were eating an immoral woman brought an alabaster jar filled with expensive perfume. Then she knelt at his feet, weeping. Her tears fell at his feet, and she wiped them off with her hair . . . (Luke 7:36-39).

The perfume which she likely used in her profession as a prostitute would become the symbol of her extravagant expression of faith. By breaking this jar she is shouting her full commitment to Jesus. She is repentant—she is saying no to her former life and giving her allegiance to Christ. This is radical repentance in front of these self-righteous Pharisees.

Perhaps this jar represented her life savings, likely more than a year's wages. Would you be willing to give Jesus your 401(K) to extend his Kingdom? Jesus speaks more about money than any other subject because it is so easy to let money and possessions take first place. Our bank statement does not lie. It reveals our priorities. If we are giving two percent to God can we say we are sold out to God's Kingdom? What about five percent?

"If we withhold the tithe, can we really say 'in God we trust'? If we give God our leftovers instead of the firstfruits, can we say we're seeking first His kingdom? God doesn't need our money, but He does want our heart. Where our treasure is there our heart will be also. Happiness is not the byproduct of making more money. It's the by-product of giving more money." (As Mark Batterson writes in *All In*, (p. 68).)

"They joyfully accepted the confiscation of their property, because they knew that they had better and lasting possessions? (Heb. 10:34). What is most precious to you? Can you pour it out trusting your life and your future to Jesus?

Jesus, I give you my all. I give you my treasure, my time, my talent but I know you want more than that: I give you my heart. I want to love you with all my heart. Amen.

January 16

How Big Is Your Faith?

Psalm 2:8

"Ask of me, and I will make the nations your inheritance, the ends of the earth your possession" (Ps. 2:8). While this is speaking prophetically of Jesus, Paul reminds us, "Since we are his children, we will share his treasures—for everything God gives to his Son, Christ, is ours, too" (Ro. 8:17 NLT).

"Ask for the nations,"—have you asked God for the salvation of your next door neighbor? Few Christians feel a responsibility for their neighbors or peers. On the judgment day will your friends or neighbors turn to you and say, "Why didn't you tell me I needed to be born into God's Kingdom? I saw you and talked with you hundreds of times. You never once told me about Jesus?" What will you say?

Jesus said, "As the Father sent me I am sending you into the world" (John 17:18 and 20:21). Why did the Father send Jesus—"to seek and save the lost" (Luke 19:10). Just as Jesus was sent you are sent!

You are sent to your office, to your classroom, to your neighbors. How can we work at the same place, live beside our neighbors for years, go to school for a semester, sit or work beside people and not pray or share the Good News with them?

Ask God to give you a compassion for your unchurched friends. He will open the door for you to share the Good News if you sincerely ask him. The apostles were bold. They went everywhere sharing Jesus. The Holy Spirit will give you the same boldness if you cry out to God for a fresh anointing of his Spirit.

Don't let guilt overwhelm you for not sharing Jesus. He will forgive you. However, repentance means we will change our ways. We can't change except through his power. Trust him. He will surprise you today as you seek to be a witness for him. I know this from daily experience!

Lord, empower me by your Holy Spirit to witness for you today. Amen.

Do You Want More Faith?

Matthew 9:29

When the blind man came to Jesus for healing, Jesus said, "According to your faith it will be done to you" (Matt. 9:29). Perhaps we don't have faith because our concept of Jesus is not big enough. Remember, he knows the hairs on our head. (Matt. 10:30). He knows our thoughts. (Psalm 139:2). He counts the stars and calls them by name. (Psalm 147:4).

"The sun is one of 100 billion stars in our galaxy, the Milky Way . . . there are 100 billion galaxies!" That's 10 trillion stars for every one of the 7 billion people on planet earth. Some say when God told Abraham, "I will multiply your descendants into countless millions, like the stars of the sky and the sand of the seashore" (Gen. 22:17 NLT); He was saying that there are as many stars as there are grains of sand on the sea shore. God is incomprehensible. Why do we doubt God's greatness?

David writes: "You keep track of all my sorrows. You have collected all my tears in your bottle. You have recorded each one in your book" (Ps. 56:8 NLT). If he can call the stars by name it's nothing for him to collect all our tears in a bottle.

The longer we walk with Jesus the fewer questions we have because we learn to trust our all-knowing Father even though we can't understand or comprehend his ways. (Is. 55:8-9).

As I was writing the phone rang with the news that a godly man whom scores of people had prayed for was just admitted to intensive care. While I have experienced many direct and dramatic answers to prayer and scores of answers to physical healing, this man is in God's care just as much, or even more so than the persons who experienced dramatic physical healing.

Jesus never leaves us nor forsakes us. (Heb. 13:5). He never makes a mistake. He always does what is right. (Gen. 18:25). Greater is he that is within us than he that is in the world. (I John 4:4). You can trust him!

Father, increase my faith today. Amen.

Does God Get Angry?

John 1:14

God's mercy and grace are the predominant themes of the bible. "The Day of the Lord" depicts terrific suffering but God's mercy is always presented. He will recreate our world. It will be perfect.

We have rightly focused on God's love and forgiveness but we have forgotten he is a God of justice, truth and righteousness. Jesus was "full of grace and truth." (John 1:14). "The law was given through Moses, grace and truth came through Jesus Christ." (John 1:17). Grace and truth are couplets. Emphasize grace along and you have lawlessness. Emphasize truth alone and you can have legalism and bondage.

Today forgiveness is too often offered without repentance. It is wonderful that Jesus freely forgives us but his forgiveness is in the context of our seeking to live in an authentic relationship with Him. There is a relationship between our unbalanced theology and the moral slide both within the church and the world? The world has lost its way because the church has lost its fire. We have lost our respectful fear of the Lord.

Paul and Jude remind us the O.T. was written to keep us from setting our hearts on evil things as they did. Paul illustrated this with the account of God punishing his people as 23,000 died in one day. (I Cor. 10:6-10). Jude gives several illustrations of God's judgement from the O.T. and concludes, "They serve as an example of those who suffer the punishment of eternal fire." (5-7).

God wrath is mentioned more than 200 times in the Bible with 30 appearances in the New Testament. God's wrath is not uncontrolled anger. it is his righteous and just reaction to our sin. "God is a righteous judge, a God who displays his wrath every day." (Ps. 7:11). Why? Because we sin every day. Habakkuk writes, "Your eyes are to pure to look on evil; you cannot tolerate wrong. . ." (Habakkuk 1:13).

God gave his Son so that when we trust him we will not perish. (John 3:16). A few verses later (3:36), "Whoever believes in the Son has eternal life, but whoever rejects the Son will not see life, for God's wrath remains on him."

Lord enable me to keep a balance between your love and my need to express reverential fear or respect. Amen.

We are God's Children

I John 3:1-3

"See what [an incredible] quality of love the Father has given (shown, bestowed on) us, that we should [be permitted to] be named and called and counted the children of God! And so, we are! The reason that the world does not know (recognize, acknowledge) us, is that it does not know (recognized, acknowledge) Him. Beloved, we are [even here and] now God's children; it is not yet disclosed (made clear) what we shall be [hereafter], but we know that when He comes and is manifested we shall [as God children] resemble and be like Him, for we shall see Him just as He [really is. And everyone who has this hope [resting] on Him cleanses (purifies) himself just as He is pure—chase,undefiled, guiltless." (I John 3:3 AMP).

God is perfect, therefore when he says we are his child we can be sure we are loved. We know he will do only what is best for us. Doing what is best for us includes discipline.

The book of Hebrews explains why we often have problems, trials, and frustrations in our life even though we are God's child. "Do not think lightly or scorn to submit to the correction and discipline of the Lord, nor lose courage and give up and faint when you are reproved or corrected by Him; For the Lord corrects and disciplines every one whom He loves, and He punishes, even scourges, every son whom He accepts and welcomes to His heart and cherishes. You must submit to and endure [correction] for discipline. God is dealing with you as with sons; for what son is there whom his father does not train and correct and discipline? . . . if you are exempt from correction . . . , then you are illegitimate offspring and not true sons [at all]. . . . For the time being no discipline brings joy but seems grievous and painful, but afterwards it yields peaceable fruit of righteousness to those who have been trained by it—a harvest of fruit which consists in righteousness, [that is, in conformity to God's will in purpose, thought and action, resulting in right living and right standing with God.] (Heb. 12:5-8 AMP).

Lord, thank you that you love me enough to discipline me. Do whatever is needful to make me more like you. Amen.

Worship

John 4:24

Jesus said we are to worship him in spirit and in truth. (John 4:24). What does it mean to worship God in spirit? I think it is similar to Jesus' command to love God with all our heart. (Matt. 22:37). The heart is the executive center of our lives.

If I were writing John 4:24 I would want to place "truth" before "spirit." We who are cultural products of the western world emphasize the rational. Jesus is just as concerned for our spirit. He said he will send the Holy Spirit to guide us into all truth. The Contemporary Bible is helpful: "God is Spirit and those who worship God must be led by the Spirit to worship him according to the truth." Jesus said, "When the Spirit of truth, comes, he will guide you into all truth" (John 16:13).

Spirit and truth are both essential. But many Christians, including myself, have emphasized the letter of the word and neglected hearing the Spirit's interpretation and intent of the word.

Jesus came to fulfill the law. (Matt. 5:17 and Ro. 8:1-4). When we emphasize the letter as the Pharisees did and neglect the spirit our worship becomes legalistic and dead. It's the Spirit that brings life. Are we afraid of the Spirit because we can't control the Spirit? Our desire to control things reduces our faith and trust. Jesus said the Spirit is like the wind. (John 3:8). Our worship must be founded and lined up with the truth.

One reason Christians lack the joy of the Lord is that we grieve the Spirit by our ritualistic and formal worship. We like to worship with our mind more than our heart. Let's not be afraid to follow our heart and of course check to see that our actions do not contradict the word of truth which "teaches us what is true and makes us realize what is wrong in our lives. It straightens us out and teaches us to do what is right" (II Tim. 3:16-17 NLT).

Father, May I be led by the Spirit to worship you according to the truth. Amen.

Real Life

Colossians 3:3-4

"For [as far as this world is concerned] you have died, and your new, real life is hid with Christ in God. When Christ Who is our life appears, then you will also appear with Him in (the splendor of His) glory" (Col. 3:3-4 AMP).

Can we be any more secure? We are hid securely in Christ. This is beyond the natural mind; therefore we must accept it by faith. Activating our faith is not always easy. If you are hidden with Christ in God you do not need to worry. If you put him first he will supply your needs. He will never let you fall. He will give you wisdom for every decision. He will give you strength to do what he wants you to do. You are secure in Him.

As a result of being hid with Christ in God, Paul says: (vv. 5-6), "We kill (deaden, deprive of power the evil desire lurking in our members— those animal impulses and all that is earthly in you that is employed in sin; sexual vice, impurity, sensual appetites, unholy desires, and all greed and covetousness . . . [the deifying of self and other created things instead of God]. It is on account of these [very sins] that the [holy] anger of God is ever coming upon (those who are obstinately opposed to the divine will) the sons of disobedience.")

When our life is hidden with Christ in God we will linger in his presence so we recognize his voice. (John 10:3). We will be holy as he is holy. (I Peter 1:16). We go only where he wants us to go, do only what he wants us to do, say only what he wants us to say. Is such life possible? Yes, but only if our life is hidden with Christ in God.

Can you remember today that your life is hidden with Jesus in God? That nothing, absolutely nothing will hurt or even touch you without God's permission as long as you stay with Christ in God.

Father it is not my life any longer but your life in me. Amen.

Not Condemnation

Romans 8:1

"There is now no condemnation for those who are in Christ Jesus" (Ro. 8:1). Two hundred times the New Testament informs the Christian that he or she is in Christ. Why this constant repetition? Is it because we forget? One of my favorite verses is, Galatians 2:20, "I have been crucified with Christ and I no longer live, but Christ lives in me. The life I live in the body, I live by faith in the Son of God, who loved me, and gave himself for me." The Message says, "Christ lives in me. The life you see me living is not 'mine,' but it is lived by faith in the Son of God, who loved me and gave himself for me."

There is only one person who can live the Christian life and that is Christ. I have been a Christian seventy years. When I live in that reality, life has purpose, meaning, joy and peace beyond description. I am a new creation. (II Cor. 5:17). Hallelujah! No more struggling except the struggle of faith. That's what Paul meant when he said we are to fight the good fight of faith. The fight is to have the faith to believe that we are in Christ. It's his life lived in us and not our life lived in the power of the flesh.

What area of your life needs to change? Is it holding your tongue? Is it being ashamed to speak up for Jesus? Is it your thought life? Perhaps you struggle with feeling inferior? What about envy, jealousy or pride? The Good News is that if we confess our sins he will forgive us and cleanse us from all sin.

Thank Jesus for living in you and through you. We are becoming who Jesus says we are. He changes our "want to." We no longer want to get revenge. We no longer have jealous feelings when others get promoted ahead of us, even though we were in the office longer than they were. We show love to those who would be our enemies. Only Jesus by his Holy Spirit abiding in us can give us this life of victory.

Father, thank you I am not under condemnation but living in your loving presence. Amen.

Servants or Friends

John 15:12-15

"My command is this: love each other as I have loved you. Greater love has no one than this that he lay down his life for his friends; you are my friends if you do what I command. I no longer call you servants, because a servant does not know his master's business. Instead, I have called you friends, for everything that I learned from my Father, I have made known to you" (John 15:12-15).

How many friends do you have? A friend is someone who knows you intimately. They accept you. You are free to talk things over with them. You feel comfortable in their presence. If you need money you are free to ask. If you have an emergency you are free to call even in the middle of the night. They are available 24/7.

Jesus is our friend. We usually think of Jesus as our Lord and Savior. But remember Jesus is our friend. Abraham was the only person in the Old Testament who was called the friend of God. How privileged we are to know that we are friends of Jesus if we love him and keep his commandments. In a healthy marriage your spouse is your best friend. We will give our "right arm" for them without a second thought.

Friendship takes time. Friendship develops as you learn to know and understand each other. Jesus wants you to be his best friend. Do you spend quality time with Jesus? Do you share your deepest desires, longings, and disappointments with him? Do you share your pain and your joys with him?

When you have a friendship relationship with Jesus you can say like Oswald Chambers (Feb. 29th Devotional), "Once we see Jesus, the impossible things He does in our lives become as natural as breathing. The agony we suffer is only the result of the deliberate shallowness of our own heart."

A servant does not have the deep level of relationship of a friend. Move from being a servant of Jesus to being his friend.

Jesus, how blessed I am to be your friend. May I never take your friendship for granted. Amen.

Why Did Jesus Come?

Luke 19:10

Fifty times in the Gospels we are told why Jesus came and how he spent his time.

Jesus came to seek and save those who are lost. (Luke 19:10 TEV).

His very name, Jesus, means "The Lord saves" (Matt. 1:21 NIV footnote).

Jesus came not to condemn the world but to save it. (John 3:17).

Jesus came to give sight to the blind and to show those who think they see that they are blind. (John 9:39b and 12:47-48).

Jesus says, "I have not come to call the righteous, but sinners" (Mark 2:17).

"The Spirit of the Lord . . . has anointed me to preach good news to the poor. He has sent me to proclaim freedom for the prisoners and recovery of sight to the blind, to release the oppressed, to proclaim the year of the Lord's favor" (Luke 4:18-19).

"Jesus had great pity for the crowds that came, because their problems were so great and they didn't know where to go for help" (Matthew 9:36). "As he approached Jerusalem and saw the city, he wept over it" (Luke 19:41).

Jesus said, "We must go on to other towns as well, and I will preach to them, too, because that is why I came" (Mark 1:38 NLT).

Luke sums up Jesus' activities: ". . . He went around doing good and healing all who were under the power of the devil, because God was with him" (Acts 10:38).

These many scriptures make it clear Jesus came to save the lost and minister to the needs of those who were marginalized. Since he sends us, John 17:18 and 20:21, just as the Father sent him, we don't need to wonder about our assignment. Jesus will give you opportunities every day if you have open eyes and hearts to trust him to use you as his representative.

Lord Jesus open my eyes and heart today to see the opportunities you give me and to trust your Holy Spirit to empower me and speak through me. I desire with all my heart to be a fisher of men. Amen.

Faith, Hope and Love

1 Cor. 13:13

"These three remain: faith, hope and love. But the greatest of these is love" (I Cor. 13:13). Love is eternal. "God is love" (I John 4:16). "God so loved the world that he gave his one and only Son, that whoever believes in him shall not perish but have eternal life" (John 3:16).

"We love because he first loved us" (I John 4:19). "The goal of our faith is love, which comes (springs) from a pure heart and a good conscience and a sincere faith" (I Tim. 1:5).

"Love the Lord your God with all your heart... soul... and mind (intellect). This is the great (most important, principle) and first commandment. And the second is: You shall love your neighbor as [you do] yourself. All the Law and the Prophets hang on these two commandments" (Matt. 22:37-40 Amp).

"Let no debt remain outstanding, except the continuing debt to love one another, for he who loves his fellow man has fulfilled the law. The commandments, 'Do not commit adultery,' 'Do not murder,' 'Do not steal,' 'Do not covet,' and whatever other commandment there may be are summed up in this one rule: 'Love your neighbor as yourself...' Love is the fulfillment of the law'" (Romans 13:8-10). "God's royal command is: "Love your neighbor as yourself" (James 2:8 NLT).

"Be imitators of God as dearly loved children and live a life of love, just as Christ loved us and gave himself up for us" (I John 5:1-2). "The most excellent way is love" (I Cor. 12:31). "Love each other deeply, because love covers a multitude of sins" (I Peter 4:8).

Rick Warren reminds us that we are commanded to love one another fifty-five times in the New Testament. "My command is this: 'Love each other as I have loved you. Greater love has no one than this, that one lay down his life for his friends. You are my friends if you do what I command'" (John 15:12-13).

"The fruit of the Spirit is love, joy, peace, patience, kindness, goodness, faithfulness, gentleness and self-control" (Gal.5:22). Notice "fruit" is singular. If we have love we will have joy, peace, patience, etc..."

Lord, enable me to love as you loved me.

Let's Empower Our Youth!

Mark 3:17

"These are the twelve Jesus appointed: . . . James son of Zebedee and his brother John (to them he gave the name Boanerges, which means Sons of Thunder)" (Mark 3:16-17).

How old were the disciples when Jesus called them? I believe Jesus called John when he was in his teens and the other disciples in their twenties. In their culture you were not recognized as a teacher until you were thirty. (Luke 3:23). Jesus broke the cultural traditions by calling young men. Let's call and empower our youth. Yes they will do things differently. Jesus referred to James and John as "sons of thunder" (Mark 3:17 NLT) or "thunderbolts" as the Contemporary English Version states. That can be frightening but Jesus took the risk. We too must take the risk. Empowering youth and young adults will bring new life to our traditional congregations.

We need their enthusiasm. Ask God to open your eyes to see potential young men and women who have a passion to see people come to Jesus and the ability to relate well with people. Tap them on the shoulder. Believe in them, listen to their concerns. Bless and affirm them in their gifting. Assure them you believe God has gifted them for ministry in extending his Kingdom. As we mentor, pray and walk with them, they will revitalize our churches.

Most people who become Christians accept Christ when they are in their teens or even before. Pray for eyes to see the potential in each youth/young adult and invite them to hear the call of the Lord upon their lives.

The ball is in our court. Jesus said we are to pray to him to send workers into the harvest. (Matt. 9:37-38). Don't be surprised that many of our Christian workers will be found among our own youth and young adults. It happened in Jesus' day. It will happen as we pray and tap people on the shoulder. Offer to disciple them. Encourage them to be zealous for the Lord.

Lord Jesus, make me an encourager to these youth to step out in faith using their gifts in making disciples and planting churches. Amen.

We Are Fruit Bearers!

John 15:16

"You didn't choose me, remember; I chose you, and put you in the world to bear fruit, fruit that won't spoil. As fruit bearers, whatever you ask the Father in relation to me, he gives you" (John 15:16 Msg.).

Paul says he would rather be in heaven but if he continues here he will be fruitful. I love his positive attitude. (Phil. 1:22).

Approximately a dozen times in the first several verses of John 15 we are told to remain in Jesus and he will remain in us. We are to be proactive. We are to draw near to God and he will draw near to us. (James 4:8). Fruit bearing is first of all about our relationship to Jesus. With that relationship in sync we are to love one another. (vv. 12,13,17). God's love in you results in fruit—that lasts for eternity. Jesus tells us this so that his joy might be in us and our joy will be complete. (v. 11).

If we are not remaining in Jesus we can do many things but they amount to nothing of eternal value. (15:5). We need to maintain our appointments to meet with God each day. Meeting with him in the morning will help us cultivate a consciousness of his presence throughout the day. Remaining or abiding necessitates a conscious decision to keep the relationship up to date. Paul says, "Pray continually" (I Thess. 5:17). Fruitfulness begins as we remain in Jesus.

Peter says if you make every effort to add to your faith goodness, knowledge, self-control, perseverance, godliness, brotherly kindness and love these qualities will keep you from being ineffective and unproductive in your knowledge of our Lord Jesus Christ . . . If you do these things you will never fall, and you will receive a rich welcome into the eternal kingdom of our Lord and Savior Jesus Christ. (I Peter 1:5-11).

Lord, enable me to remember you throughout the day. May your Holy Spirit speak deep within my spirit reminding me of your presence. Make me a channel of blessing to others. Amen.

Why Are There Accidents?

Luke 13:1-5

Every day we hear about disastrous situations: car, train, airplane, or motorcycle accidents. Why are there tornados, hurricanes, famines, wars, or fires? Is it fair that people suffer for years while others seem to have it easy?

Jesus answers: "There were some present at that time who told Jesus about the Galileans whose blood Pilate had mixed with their sacrifice. Do you think that these Galileans were worse sinners than all the other Galileans because they suffered this way? I tell you, no! But unless you repent, you too will all perish. Or those eighteen who died when the tower of Siloam fell on them—do you think they were more guilty than all the others living in Jerusalem? I tell you, no! But unless you repent, you too will all perish" (Luke 13:1-5).

People in Jesus' day assumed that all calamities came because of sin. Jesus says these tragedies come to remind us that unless we repent we too will perish. God speaks loud and clear every day. Our response should be, "Jesus that could just as well have been me. I repent, forgive my sin. Lord, cleanse and use me for your glory."

Sue started to come to church. I inquired about her husband. She said, "He will never come to church." He was involved in a car accident. Following the accident he has come every Sunday. These experiences were meant to bring us closer to God. Often we ignore them. People suffered horrifically during the plagues but they refused to repent. (Rev. 9:20-21). There can be no grace without repentance.

In John 11, Mary and Martha sent word to Jesus that their brother, Lazarus was very sick. Jesus did not go immediately to his aid. Lazarus died. When Jesus heard about his death he explained that Lazarus' death happened for the Son of God to receive glory. (v. 4, NLT).

Jesus, enable me to see the tragedies of life as warnings to repent and enable your Holy Spirit to call others to repentance. Amen.

The Generosity of God

John 4:10

In John 4 Jesus being tired stopped to rest at Jacob's well in Samaria. The disciples went to town to buy food. A Samaritan woman came to the well to draw water. In those days Jews and Samaritans did not talk together, but Jesus asked her for a drink of water. She was shocked that Jesus spoke to her. She asked him, "Why are you asking me for a drink?" (v. 9). Jesus answered, "If you knew the generosity of God and who I am, you would be asking me for a drink, and I would give you fresh, living water" (v. 10 Msg.).

Jesus says to you and me, "If you but knew the generosity of God you would ask me for living water for yourself as well as to give to others." Why are we so often running on empty? Where is the living water? Jesus promised in John 7:37-38 Msg., "If anyone thirsts, let him come to me and drink. Rivers of living water will brim and spill out of the depths of anyone who believes in me this way, just as the Scripture says." Soar with wings as eagles. (Is. 40:31).

Do we believe in the generosity of God? The generosity of God is for the prebelievers like this Samaritan woman as well as for you and me! No wonder Paul writes, "I pray that from his glorious, unlimited resource he will give you mighty inner strength through his Holy Spirit" (Eph. 3:16 NLT). Do you believe God has unlimited resources? Let's pray as Paul suggests that he will give us mighty inner strength through his Holy Spirit. Whatever you pray, believe you shall have. Jesus said, we are to ask, seek and knock and he will give us his Holy Spirit. (Luke 11:13). "We can be confident that he will listen to us whenever we ask him for anything in line with his will. And if we know he is listening when we make our requests, we can be sure that he will give us what we ask for" (I John 5:14-15 NLT).

Father, I thank you for your unlimited resources. I repent of self-centeredness. Fill me with your Holy Spirit so I can share the water of life with others today. Amen.

Rejoice in Suffering

Habakkuk 3:17-19

"Though the fig tree does not bud and there are no grapes on the vines,
    Though the olive crop fails and the fields produce no food,
    Though there are no sheep in the pen and no cattle in the stalls,
    Yet I will rejoice in the Lord, I will be joyful in God my Savior.
The Sovereign Lord is my strength; he makes my feet like the feet of a
    deer, he enables me to go on the heights" (Habakkuk 3:17-19).

"We rejoice in our sufferings because we know that suffering produces perseverance; perseverance character" (Ro. 5:3). "Consider it pure joy, my brothers, whenever you face trials of many kinds because you know that the testing of your faith develops perseverance. Perseverance must finish its work so that you may be mature and complete, not lacking anything" (Ja. 1:3-4).

"It has been granted to you . . . to suffer for Christ" (Phil. 1:29).

"In all our troubles my joy knows no bounds" (II Cor. 7:4).

"Trials have come so that your faith . . . may be proved genuine and may result in praise, glory and honor when Jesus Christ is revealed" (I Peter 1:7).

Many brothers and sisters suffering in prison ask us to pray not for their deliverance but that they may be faithful. Remember Stephen's victorious death. (Acts 6-7). Read the *Martyrs Mirror* or *Foxes Book of Martyrs* and take courage as you read of their joy in the midst of indescribable persecution.

A house church leader in China was imprisoned three different times. He has suffered much over the years. One time he could have escaped but the Holy Spirit told him to stay and witness to the other prisoners. God used him in a mighty way to bring the Good News to many in prison. Now that he is released he continues to be an effective witness for our Lord. Forgive me for not being bold to speak up for you.

Lord Jesus, empower me to rejoice in suffering. Amen.

Real Happiness!

Luke 15:5-7

In Luke 15 Jesus says that all of heaven is joyful when one sinner returns home. The Shepherd leaves the ninety-nine and searches for the one lost sheep. If you pray and ask the Lord to open your eyes to the lost sheep in your sphere of influence, he will reveal to you who that sheep is. Pray for that person. Tell God you will be willing to do anything to bring that person into the fold. If you lack that passion or zeal, ask God to give it to you. Mother Teresa said, "Anyone who imitates Jesus must also share in his passion."

Moses and Paul illustrate that passion: "Please forgive their sin—and if not, then blot me out of the record you are keeping" (Exodus 32:32 NLT). "My heart is filled with bitter sorrow and unending grief for my people, my Jewish brothers and sisters. I would be willing to be forever cursed—cut off from Christ!—if that would save them" (Ro. 9:2-3 NLT).

What would happen if you and I would have the zeal of Moses and Paul? Pray for God to give you a heart of compassion. For most Saturdays of my 50 years of pastoral ministry I visited with one or more unchurched families in the community inviting them to consider Christ and worship with us. During the past 60 years I picked up people with my car and brought them to church.

Whenever you see a U-Haul coming to your area you don't need to pray about going to see the new family and extending a welcome to them. You can pray about when to go, what to say, or to take along as a welcoming gift. Jesus commissioned you to go and be a witness in "Jerusalem." Welcome them to the community. Offer to help them unload the truck. Show them around town. There is no end to the possibilities: invite them to church, introduce the children to their new Sunday school teacher or the adults to a small group that has been praying for the new family moving to that address. You will experience such joy beyond description as you relate to your unsaved friends and new people. I do.

Jesus, give me a passion like Moses and Paul. Give me courage to take the initiative to invite new people to worship and meet you. Amen.

Live With Passion and Compassion

Matthew 9:36

"When Jesus saw the crowds, he had compassion on them, because they were harassed and helpless, like sheep without a shepherd. Then he said to the disciples, 'The harvest is plentiful but the workers are few. Ask the Lord of the harvest to send out workers into the harvest field'" (Matt. 9:36-37).

Imagine walking along the woods when you hear someone crying. Your eyes see a man who has a little girl pinned down as he molests her. Jesus sees lost souls harassed and helpless, molested and pinned down by the enemy. No wonder Jesus wept when he saw the crowds as sheep without a shepherd.

I thank God for his passion in giving his only Son for me. I thank Jesus for his willingness to leave heaven and live among sinful men and die a cruel death. I thank the Holy Spirit for living in my sinful heart made holy by his power. That morning prayer has made a profound difference in my life.

The primary emotional response of Jesus for our world was compassion. Jesus is perfect. If anyone would be turned off by the sin in our world it would be the sinless Jesus. Yet instead of looking or reacting with disdain at sinful people he reacted with compassion. Jesus saw people as sheep that had been bruised, beaten and confused. They needed a shepherd.

Jesus is perfect yet sinners crowded around him. The more mature we are spiritually the more sinners should feel comfortable with us. It was true with Jesus. He exemplified love. He was approachable. Both sinners and children were drawn to him. They knew he was genuine. They felt loved.

Ask God to give you the heart of Jesus toward those who are lost and have no understanding of God's indescribable love for them. God will whisper, "Now is the moment to speak for me."

Lord enable me to see people as you see them—sheep without a shepherd. Fill me with your love and compassion. Amen.

Wisdom

Proverbs 19:27

"If you stop learning you will forget what you already know" (Prov. 19:27 CEV).

"Wisdom is sweet to your soul. If you find it, you will have a bright future, and your hopes will not be cut short" (Prov. 24:14 NLT).

If you lack wisdom ask God who gives generously. (James 1:5).

Wisdom from heaven is pure, peace loving, gentle, willing to yield to others. It's full of mercy and good deeds, shows no favoritism and is always sincere. (James 3:17).

In Christ are hidden all the treasures of wisdom and knowledge. (Col. 2:4).

One of my definite joys in life is gaining a new insight. This was true for David as well. Consider these verses from the longest chapter in the Bible, Psalm 119 in the NLT: "I am overwhelmed continually with a desire for your laws" (20). "Your laws are all I want in life" (39b). "Your law is my delight" (77b). "I have more insight than my teachers, for I am always thinking of your decrees" (97, 99). "Your decrees are my treasure; they are truly my heart's delight" (111). "I open my mouth, panting expectantly, longing for your commands" (131). Once David started talking about God's Word he couldn't get stopped.

Ask God to give you a love for his word. I often get up in the morning thinking what a privilege it is to read and feast on God's eternal word. Ask God for a holy passion for his Word, especially the living Word, who is Jesus. He will answer your prayer.

Paul prayed for wisdom more than anything else. There is a huge difference between wisdom and knowledge. "While knowledge may make us feel important, it is love that really builds up the church. Anyone who claims to know all the answers doesn't really know very much. But the person who loves God is the one God knows and cares for" (I Corinthians 8:1b-3 NLT). Keep wisdom and love at the top of your prayer list.

Father, I need your wisdom and love. I ask in faith believing you will grant it. Thank you. Amen.

Prayer and Passion

Luke 22:44

When Eastern Mennonite Mission Board representatives asked the Ethiopia leaders why they took a day each week to pray and fast, they said when they stopped this practice the church stopped growing and church planting ceased. However when they gave a day each week to prayer and fasting the work was blessed by God. Lives were changed, churches were planted and God's Kingdom expanded.

The early church devoted themselves to prayer. (Acts 2:42). Paul instructs us: "Devote yourselves to prayer, being watchful and thankful." (Col. 4:2).

Jesus agonized in prayer. (Lk. 22:44). The church was earnestly praying for Peter in prison. (Acts 12:5). Paul writes, "I want you to know how much I am 'struggling' for you and for those in Laodicea, and for all who have not met me personally" (Col. 2:1). Epaphras . . . is always 'wrestling' in prayer for you to stand firm" (Col. 4:12-13).

The persecuted church prays out of desperation. Entire congregations pray aloud; all at once for an extended time fervently begging God for his will to be done.

Is your zeal for the Lord lagging? Come to him in repentance. Ask him to light the fire in your heart for his mission. Our zeal for the lost must come from a heart of obedience to the Great Commission of our Lord. (Matt. 28:18-20). We are told to go, to baptize, to teach and make disciples. It is not primarily the need to see people educated or lifted out of poverty that will keep us giving sacrificial service. It is obedience to Christ's command and the power of the Holy Spirit in us that enables us to serve faithfully and pray without burnout.

Repent of your indifferent attitude. Tell God you are putting him ahead of everything else. God will give you a burning passion to reach a lost world beginning with your peers.

Jesus, forgive me for my indifference. Give me a passion to love you with all my heart.

Open my eyes to the many opportunities I will have today. Amen.

Facing a Mountain?

"Humanly speaking, it is impossible. But not with God. Everything is possible with God" (Mark 11:27 NLT).

As a youth I stuttered. I knew what it was to be humiliated, to be laughed at, to feel inferior. As a boy, life was often discouraging. At age 15, I developed a heart condition that caused me to miss five months of school. It was during that time that I read missionary stories, listened to gospel preachers on the radio and grew in my faith. I felt God wanted to use me in his Kingdom work but I was frustrated because of my poor self image and poor health. How could God use me?

I'm embarrassed to say, as a young pastor I prayed more frequently, "Lord help me talk," than, "Lord give me something to say." I prayed for grace to speak without stuttering. As I walked with the Lord, prayed and did my part in accepting every opportunity to serve him, gradually over the years he has enabled me to overcome this handicap. This is one of the greatest miracles of my life.

Interestingly when the Lord called me to my first pastorate, their former pastor had a very noticeable speech impediment. While we certainly do not rejoice in other's handicaps, it made it easier for me to accept that pastoral position.

Paul prayed for the Lord to remove his "thorn in the flesh. (II Cor. 12:7-10). God's grace was sufficient for Paul. If you live with a "thorn in the flesh" do your part to overcome it, but if God does not see fit to remove it he will use you in spite of it. In fact he will likely use you to a greater advantage than if you did not have the "thorn."

"No sin is worse than the sin of self pity, because it removes God from the throne of our lives, replacing Him with our own self-interests." (Oswald Chambers, My Utmost for His Highest, Devotional Reading, May 16).

Lord Jesus, thank you for the painful difficulties of life. They have helped me to lean on you more. Use, refine, and mold me for your glory. Amen.

Do More Than We Can Imagine!

Ephesians 3:20-22

Our key scripture at Capital Christian Fellowship was Ephesians 3:20-21, "Now to him who is able to do immeasurably more than all we ask or imagine, according to his power that is at work within us, to him be glory in the church and in Christ Jesus throughout all generations, for ever and ever! Amen."

The amazing aspect of this scripture is not that God can do more than we can ask or imagine. The amazing thing is that he does more than we can imagine through us. He is Almighty, the sovereign Lord of the cosmos. The Ephesians had to be reminded of God's mighty power in them. "Finally, be strong in the Lord and in his mighty power" (6:10).

Paul reminds young timid Timothy, "God did not give us a spirit of timidity, but a spirit of power, of love, and of self-discipline" (II Tim. 1:7). "God doesn't want us to be shy with his gifts, but bold and loving and sensible" (Msg.).

After the Resurrection Jesus met the disciples. "He breathed on them and said, Receive the Holy Spirit" (John 20:22). The Holy Spirit came as they prayed. Peter preached with boldness. Three thousand people repented and received Christ. Throughout the book of Acts the apostles and the early Christians were bold for our Lord. Today that same power and boldness is there for each of us. Let's walk in it. "The righteous are as bold as lions" (Prov. 28:1).

Pray with boldness and persistence. Paul prayed as in the pains of childbirth that Christ would be formed in them. (Gal. 4:19). Peter was surprised that the fig tree Jesus cursed had withered. "Have faith in God," Jesus answered, "I tell you if anyone says to this mountain, 'Go throw yourself into the sea,' and does not doubt in his heart but believes that what he says will happen, it will be done for him. Whatever you ask in prayer, believe that you have received it, and it will be yours." (Mark 11:22-24).

Jesus, I forget the promise of Ephesians 3:20-21. I claim by faith your promise to do through me more than I can ask or imagine. Amen.

My Blind Friend

Luke 4:18

My blind friend walks with a white cane. I marvel how he can "see." He loves to travel to "see" many new and wonderful scenes. How is that possible? Lois his wife serves as his eyes, describing everything for him.

You and I have many spiritually blind friends, at least we should have. Like Lois we need to open blind eyes. In fact Jesus says that's why he came. Luke 4:18 NLT, "He has sent me to proclaim . . . that the blind will see."

"The Lord opens the eyes of the blind" (Psalm 146:8 NLT). "When God comes he will open the eyes of the blind and unstop the ears of the deaf" (Isaiah 35:5 NLT). These scriptures point to a new day when all God's children who are blind will see. In the meantime we must open the minds and the eyes that the devil has blinded. "Satan, the god of this evil world, has blinded the minds of those who don't believe, so they are unable to see the glorious light of the Good News that is shining upon them" (II Cor. 4:4 NLT).

Helen Keller said, "The most pathetic person in the world is someone who has sight, but has no vision." Some people have no apparent vision, no goals, no enthusiasm or passion. Life to them is a treadmill of work, pursuing pleasure and sleeping. They are running on empty.

Jesus created us to live with a purpose—to fellowship with him. As God came in the garden looking for a relationship with Adam and Eve he comes knocking on your heart's door to relate to you. Ask him to open your eyes to see him in nature, in other people, in your situation, and listen to hear his voice.

David prayed: "O Lord, you have examined my heart and know everything about me. You know when I stand up. You know my every thought when far away. You chart the path ahead of me. And tell me where to stop and rest. Every moment you know where I am. You know what I am going to say even before I say it, Lord. You both precede and follow me. You place your hand of blessing on my head" (Ps. 139:1-5 NLT). Amen.

February 7

Our Blessed Hope

Titus 2:13

"We wait for the blessed hope—the appearing of the glory of our great God and Savior, Jesus Christ" (Titus 2:13). "We eagerly await a Savior from heaven, the Lord Jesus Christ . . . He will transform our lowly bodies so that they will be like his glorious body" (Phil. 3:20-21). "We live with great expectation . . . a priceless inheritance that is kept in heaven for us . . . beyond the reach of change and decay" (I Peter 1:3-4 NLT). "Let us exult in the hope of the divine splendor that is to be ours" (Ro. 5:2 NEB). "Be joyful in hope . . ." (Ro. 12:12).

A motto in my boyhood home impacted my life: "Go nowhere you would not want to be when Jesus comes; say nothing you would not like to be saying when Jesus comes; and do nothing you would not like to be doing when Jesus comes."

The Corinthians longed for Jesus' return: "You do not lack any spiritual gift as you eagerly wait for our Lord Jesus Christ to be revealed" (I Cor. 1:7). C. S. Lewis states, "Those most conscious of heaven make the most effective Christians on earth."

"Set your hearts on things above, where Christ is seated at the right hand of God. Set your minds on things above, not on earthly things" (Col. 3:1-2). God doesn't ask us to get rich or to make a name for ourselves. A U-Haul never follows the hearse.

Jesus said, "Don't be troubled. You trust God, now trust in me. There are many rooms in my Father's home and I am going to prepare a place for you . . . When everything is ready, I will come and get you so that you will always be with me" (John 14:1-3 NLT).

"Our present troubles are quite small and won't last very long. Yet they produce for us an immeasurably great glory that will last forever! . . . The joys to come will last forever" (II Cor. 5:17-18 NLT).

Lord, I thank you for the blessed hope where I will be with you forever. Amen.

Compel Them to Come!

Luke 14:15-24 & Mark 2:1-12

Someone said to Jesus it would be great to share in God's Kingdom. In response Jesus gave this parable. A Master prepared a great feast and invited guests but they all made excuses: one bought a field, another bought oxen and another just got married. This upset the Master so he told his servant to invite the poor, the crippled, the lame and the blind. The servant reported there is still room. The Master said make anyone you find come, so that my house will be full. (v. 23). The word for "make" in the Greek means "this is an absolute necessity." I checked 19 versions or translations: six said, "make them come in," six "compel," four "urge," two "force," and one "drag them in."

How do we make/compel people to come to the heavenly banquet? We do it just like Jesus did: giving his life, loving sacrificially just as Jesus did, giving our time, money, energy even to the point of being willing to die for others.

In Mark 2 when Jesus came to his home town the people packed out the house where he was. Four men brought a paralytic on a stretcher for Jesus to heal him. Because of the crowd they were unable to get to Jesus so they went up on the roof, removed the tiles and lowered the man down in front of Jesus.

Imagine going to your neighbor's house and taking off part of the roof! These men meant business! They had faith that Jesus would heal this man. They were determined to have him meet Jesus. How determined are we to have our neighbors meet Jesus? Jesus said we are to compel them to come to the heavenly banquet. Jesus suffered on the cross to make it possible for us to come to him for healing, both spiritually and physically.

Do you have this kind of passion? Ask Jesus to give you the passion and the faith of these four men who brought the paralytic to Jesus.

Lord, give me a greater passion for the lost. You proved your love by dying for me. Enable me to love as you loved. Amen.

February 9

You Are Sent

John 20:21-23

Jesus said, "Peace be with you! As the Father has sent me, I am sending you" (John 20:21). As he was praying he said to the Father, "As you sent me into the world, I am sending them into the world" (John 17:18 NLT). Jesus' prayer includes you and me. Notice the word "as." This implies that there is no difference between the Father sending Jesus and Jesus sending us. Does that mean we have the same authority? The next verses in John 20 say, "And with that he breathed on them and said, 'Receive the Holy Spirit. If you forgive anyone his sins, they are forgiven, if you do not forgive them, they are not forgiven'" (vv. 22-23).

Where does Jesus send us? "Into the world!" Forty-five of Jesus' parables were given in the marketplace and all but ten of his conversations were outside the temple. Let your light shine brightly in the world.

As the Holy Spirit leads you, there will be opportunities to invite your friends to receive the forgiveness that Jesus has already provided for them. Instead of condemning them for what they are doing you can ask them to receive the forgiveness Jesus has provided. Say, "Jesus forgives you, I forgive you. Accept the forgiveness offered to you."

Some will say, "Who needs forgiveness? What did I do to need forgiveness?" Share with them that you need forgiveness every day. Sometimes I have thoughts or actions of pride, jealousy, envy, irritability, lust or hate. God says these are all sins. He forgives me if I sincerely ask him. The Bible says First John 1:8-9 NLT, "If we say we have no sin, we are only fooling ourselves and refusing to accept the truth. But if we confess our sins to him, he is faithful and just to forgive us and to cleanse us from every wrong. If we claim we have not sinned, we are calling God a liar."

Lord I thank you for your forgiveness. Enable me to extend that forgiveness to my friend who does not yet understand Jesus loves him and gave his life so he too can be forgiven. Amen.

Our Incredible God

II Peter 3:18

"Grow in grace and knowledge of our Lord and Savior Jesus Christ" (II Peter 3:18). How do you grow in grace? Paul says, I Cor. 15:9, "I am the least of the apostles and do not even deserve to be called an apostle" (I Cor. 15:9). Five years later in AD 60 he writes in Ephesians 3:8, "I am less than the least of all God's people." Finally near the end of his life he writes, "Jesus Christ came into the world to save sinners, of whom I am the worst" (I Tim. 1:15). Note the progression of thought in Paul's journey with Christ: I am the least of the apostles, I am less than the least of all God's people and lastly, I am the worst of sinners.

The longer Paul walked with Jesus the more he saw his need for the grace of Christ. One reason we lack zeal and passion for the lost is that we do not see ourselves as needing more grace.

The closer we come to Jesus the more we realize our sinful nature is still raising its head. When we see ourselves as God sees us outside of Christ we are hopeless. When we come to Christ he forgives and brings us out of darkness into the light, restoring us back to God's family. What an absolutely incredible transfer!

"I am unspiritual, sold as a slave to sin," and "I know that nothing good lives in me, that is, in my sinful nature" (Ro. 7:14 & 18). "All have sinned and fall short of the glory of God" (Ro. 3:23). Sin separates us from God but Jesus bridges the gap in bringing us back to God. What marvelous grace!

"The heart is deceitful above all things and beyond cure. Who can understand it?" (Jeremiah 17:9). "The heart is hopelessly dark and deceitful, a puzzle that no one can figure out" (Msg.). If we understand that we are utterly sinful by nature we will cry out to God for his grace.

Lord you are absolutely incredible! Thank you for your grace. Enable me to love and serve you with your passion, your love and energy. Amen. (Mark 12:30 Msg.).

Endless Treasures

Ephesians 3:8 & 16

"I was chosen for this special joy of telling the Gentiles about the endless treasures available to them in Christ" (Eph. 3:8 NLT). The Message Bible speaks of the "inexhaustible riches and the generosity of Christ." The NIV says, "The unsearchable riches of Christ." In v. 16 NLT Paul writes: "I pray that from his glorious, unlimited resources he will give you mighty inner strength through His Holy Spirit."

Can you remember hunting for something and experiencing the joy of finding it? Maybe it was your wallet, car keys or a passport. When you read the Word of God do you find treasures? David did. Jeremiah, the weeping prophet, also saw the endless riches in God even before Jesus came.

"The thought of my suffering and homelessness is bitter beyond words. I will never forget this awful time, as I grieve over my loss. Yet I still dare to hope when I remember this: The unfailing love of the Lord never ends! By his mercies we have been kept from complete destruction. Great is his faithfulness; his mercies begin afresh each day. I say to myself, 'The Lord is my inheritance; therefore, I will hope in him!' The Lord is wonderfully good to those who wait for him and seek him. So it is good to wait quietly for salvation from the Lord. And it is good for the young to submit to the yoke of his discipline" (Lamentation 3:19-27 NLT).

Have you discovered that Jesus has endless treasures available for you? They are there. All you have to do is claim them. Cry out to Jesus for the fullness of the Holy Spirit (Eph. 5:18) and you will see them. You will need to do this again and again because our heart grows cold. We need his fullness every moment. Learn to operate in this fullness. "In His presence is fullness of joy" (Ps. 16:11 KJV).

That's the secret. Don't go another moment without operating in his endless treasures his inexhaustible riches! It's there for you. Accept and live in it.

Father, thank you for your endless treasures in your Son Jesus and his Word. Open my eyes to see and my heart to live in them. Amen.

Increase My Faith

Matthew 17:17

When the disciples were unable to heal the demon-possessed boy Jesus said, "You stubborn, faithless people! How long must I be with you until you believe? Bring the boy to me" (Matt. 17:17 NLT). When Peter got out of the boat he walked on the water but seeing the waves he began to sink. He shouted for Jesus to save him. Jesus grabbed him and said, "You don't have much faith. Why did you doubt me" (Matt. 14:31 NLT)? When the disciples and Jesus were in the storm they woke Jesus. "Jesus rebuked the wind and the raging waves. The storm stopped and all was calm! Then he asked them, 'Where is your faith'" (Luke 8:24-25)?

When I was sure I needed to resign from a church plant because of organized opposition I was not sure what to do. Like Peter I needed to learn to trust the Lord to save me. After crying out to God the door opened in a way I could not have imagined. We flew to an urban center to a small dying church of less than two or three dozen adults. By God's grace the church grew to four hundred with twenty nationalities.

That was perhaps the greatest miracle of my 50 years of pastoral ministry. God put me in that situation so my faith would grow. The way we grow in faith is to listen to God's promises: "God has said, 'Never will I leave you; never will I forsake you.' So we say with confidence, 'The Lord is my helper; I will not be afraid, what can man do to me'" (13:5-6 AMP)? You can read God's promises every day but they will not become real to you unless you obey him. Don't resist him, say "Yes Lord!"

Jesus cursed the fig tree. Peter was surprised when he saw it had withered. Jesus said, "I assure you that you can say to this mountain, 'May God lift you up and throw you into the sea, and your command will be obeyed. All that's required is that you really believe and do not doubt in your hearts. Listen to me! You can pray for anything, and if you believe, you will have it'" (Mark 11:23-24 NLT).

Lord, increase my faith! Amen.

You Are God's Masterpiece!

Ephesians 2:10

"We are God's masterpiece. He has created us anew in Christ Jesus, so that we can do the good things he planned for us long ago" (Eph. 2:10 NLT).

"God in heaven appoints each person's work" (John 3:27 NLT).

God tells his story through our lives. In Ephesians 2:10, "Poiema" is the Greek word we translate masterpiece, his workmanship. This is the root word for poem. God weaves us into his poem. Poiema is God's awesome plan to conform us to the image of his Son. (Ro. 8:29). He will carry it on to completion. (Phil. 2:6). God is the great craftsman and storywriter who loves to tell his story through our lives as we are being restored and redeemed, moving from one degree of glory to another. He does not overlook any area of our life.

God speaks to you, his child and says, "My child, don't ignore it when the Lord disciplines you and don't be discouraged when he corrects you. For the Lord disciplines those he loves and he punishes those he accepts as his children" (Hebrews 12:5b-6 NLT).

Jesus said, "God cuts off every branch that doesn't produce fruit and he prunes the branches that do bear fruit so they will produce even more" (John 15:2 NLT).

One of our biggest challenges in life is to willingly submit to God's discipline. We are a diamond in the rough. God keeps chiseling off the rough spots so we can shine like stars in the universe. (Phil. 2:15).

We are God's masterpiece in the making. We are created in the image of God. He breathed into us the breath of life, i.e. eternal life. His life enables us to be and do all that he designed for us to be and do. Know that whatever God allows in your life is for your benefit. He is transforming you from one degree of glory to another. (II Cor. 3:18).

Lord, help me to accept with joy whatever comes into my life today. Give me a faithful heart of love as I trust you to design and mold me into your masterpiece. Amen.

I am Shocked . . .

Galatians 1:6

"I am shocked that you are turning away so soon from God who in his love and mercy called you to share the eternal life he gives through Christ" (Gal. 1:6 NLT). With this one exception Paul began all of his letters to the churches thanking them for their faithfulness. Why was Paul so upset? Their legalism nullified God's grace.

When it comes to sins of the flesh the Corinthian church tops them all. Paul writes, "I am afraid that I will find quarreling, jealousy, outbursts of anger, selfishness, backstabbing, gossip, conceit, and disorderly behavior. Yes, I am afraid that when I come, God will humble me again because of you. And I will have to grieve because many of you who sinned earlier have not repented of your impurity, sexual immorality, and eagerness for lustful pleasure" (II Cor. 12:20-21 NLT). We would be embarrassed to be a member of this church.

Why was Jesus more upset with the Pharisees in their legalism than with those in the world living in overt sin as the woman at the well, or the rich man unwilling to give up his riches?

Hypocrites are like play actors, pretending to be something other than themselves. Jesus said in Matthew 23 NLT, "How terrible it will be for you teachers of religious law and you Pharisees, for you cross land and sea to make one convert, and then you turn him into twice the son of hell as you yourselves are" verse 15. "You are careful to tithe even the tiniest part of your income, but you ignore the important things of the law—justice, mercy, and faith" verse 23. "You are so careful to clean the outside of the cup and the dish, but inside you are filthy—full of greed and self-indulgence!" verse 25. "Snakes! Sons of vipers! How will you escape the judgment of hell?" verse 33. The Lord hates hypocrisy.

Lord, search my heart. I want to be authentic and transparent in all I do and say. Amen.

What Greater Cause?

I Peter 4:10

"Each one should use whatever gift he has received to serve others" (I Peter 4:10).

Your lost relatives and neighbors are important to Jesus. The lost need to be found. Believers need to hear and be challenged to do all they can to help others who are lost find hope in Jesus. Jesus came to seek and to save the lost. (Luke 19:10).

When Jesus left heaven he came to serve and to rescue you and me from our sins and give us his life. (Phil. 2:5-7). His life was a life of service. "Jesus went around doing good and healing all who were oppressed by the Devil, for God was with him" (Acts 10:38b NLT).

Jesus washed the disciples' feet—taking the position of a slave. (John 13). We must get outside our four walls and serve our communities. What concerns the people of the community concerns us. We need to be a voice for the voiceless, whether they are abused children, orphans, those without healthcare, those in bondage to drugs, unwed mothers living in poverty or those caught in human trafficking.

Celebrate the joys of serving. When you serve others, your faith is made stronger. When you help those in need, your needs look smaller. Jesus says in serving the "least of these"—we are serving Him. You're never closer to Jesus than when you're serving, loving and helping the poor and hurting—doing all in the name of Jesus.

Oswald Chambers reminds us in his October 3 devotional reading, "We actually slander and dishonor God by our very eagerness to serve him without knowing him." We get burned out if we continually work for Christ. Working with him he carries the load and energizes us continually. Paul says that he strives with all God's energy to present others perfect in Christ. (Col. 1:28-29).

Lord Jesus, I dedicate my life to working with you in serving others. Amen.

Fickle Praise

Luke 4:14-32

"Jesus taught in their synagogues and was praised by everyone" (Luke 4:15 NLT).

Jesus came to his hometown and as was his custom he went to the synagogue. The leaders gave him the Isaiah scroll to read. He chose Isaiah 61:1-2: "The Spirit of the Lord is upon me, for he has appointed me to preach Good News to the poor. He has sent me to proclaim that captives will be released, that the blind will see, that the downtrodden will be freed from their oppressors, and that the time of the Lord's favor has come" (Luke 4:18-19 NLT).

Jesus reminded them that during the time of famine Elijah was sent not to Israel but to the widow of Zaraphath and that he healed Naaman, a Syrian, rather than the lepers in Israel. This angered these "good church people." (vv. 25-27). They wanted to kill him but he slipped away through the crowds. Why did their praise turn so quickly to rage? They believed the Messiah was coming to benefit only the Jews. They forgot that through Abraham all the families of the earth would be blessed.

Jesus' focus was on people who were needy and far from God. There are nearly 4,000 Scripture passages demonstrating God's concern for orphans, widows, prisoners, immigrants, homeless, the poor, hungry, disabled, and sick. (Eze. 16:49). Jesus spent considerable time with those on the margins. Only two percent of Christians in the United States work with or even know the poor. We isolate ourselves from the poor even though they are in most every community. How many friends do you have in these categories?

The more spiritually mature we are the more approachable we need to be. Everyone is created in God's image. That's reason enough to love everyone.

Dear Lord, give me a heart of compassion like you had for those who are oppressed and needy. Amen.

Perseverance

I Timothy 4:16

"Watch your life and doctrine closely. Persevere in them, because if you do, you will save both yourself and your hearers" (I Tim. 4:16). "May the Master take you by the hand and lead you along the path of God's love and Christ's endurance" (II Thess. 3:5 Msg.). "We pray that you will be strengthened with his glorious power so that you will have all the patience and endurance you need" (Col. 1:11 NLT).

Human nature wants immediate results. Some red lights test my patience. We want high speed internet. We get frustrated when the fast food restaurant order is delayed more than ten seconds.

"Consider it pure joy...whenever you face trials of many kinds, because you know that the testing of your faith develops perseverance. Perseverance must finish its work so that you may be mature and complete, not lacking anything" (James 1:2-4). Perseverance is a characteristic of maturity.

Life is not a 100-yard dash; it's a marathon. Paul writes: "I discipline my body like an athlete, training it to do what it should. Otherwise, I fear that after preaching to others I myself might be disqualified" (I Cor. 9:27 NLT). Paul is not implying that he will lose his salvation but he is concerned that he will not be qualified to preach to others.

My neighbor prayed for more than thirty years before her parents came to Christ. Noah waited 120 years for the flood. Abraham had to wait 25 years for his promised son. Moses was on the back side of the desert for 40 years before God called him to deliver his people. Joseph waited 17 years before he was raised to a position of leadership. I prayed many years before the door opened to write books.

"For the light, momentary afflictions that we bear are producing in us an eternal weight of glory far beyond all comparison" (II Cor. 4:17 NLT). We endure as we focus on the eternal perspective rather than our current situation. God will answer our prayers even though we may not see the answer in our lifetime. He is faithful.

Lord, enable me to I persevere and be patient in all things. Amen.

Hidden Treasures

Colossians 2:3

In Christ are hidden all the treasures of wisdom and knowledge. (Col. 2:3).

Why does God seem to hide from us? There are times when the Scriptures don't seem to speak to us. "You will seek me and find me when you seek me with all your heart" (Jer. 29:13). "Yes, when you get serious about finding me and want it more than anything else, I'll make sure you won't be disappointed" (Jer. 29:13 Msg.). "If you seek God, you will find him. But if you forsake him, he will reject you" (I Chron. 28:9 NLT). "Blessed are those who seek, inquire for and of Him and crave Him with their whole heart" (Ps. 119:2 AMP).

Eight times the Psalmist writes: "Do not hide your face from me." Moses instructs Aaron and his sons to bless the people: "The Lord make his face shine upon you and be gracious to you; the Lord turns his face toward you and gives you peace" (Numbers 6:25-26).

Ask God to search your heart to see if there is anything displeasing to him. (Ps. 139:23-24). Pray, "Lord open my blind eyes to see anything that displeases you and I will do whatever you say." David writes, "Be silent and know that I am God" (Ps. 46:10 NLT). Accept the silence and praise him for who he is. Thank God that he promised to never abandon you. (Heb. 13:5).

The more intense and determined we are to find something that is hidden, the greater our joy when we find it. The longer we search the greater our celebration when we find it. Our faith grows as we search the Scriptures to find hidden treasures. Our joy knows no bounds. We are overcome with joy and gladness. (Isaiah 35:10). Share these new discoveries and once hidden treasures with others so they too can rejoice with you.

I remember when my eyes were opened as I read Ro. 5:1 where we stand in his grace. I don't need to struggle to get there. Jesus has placed me there. Wow!

Jesus, I thank you for revealing hidden treasures. They give me great joy. Amen.

Every Family on Earth

Genesis 12:3

"All the families of the earth will be blessed through you" (Gen. 12:3b NLT).

"I pray that these words, 'all the families of the earth,' may be written on our hearts. It is this expression more than any other that reveals the living God of the Bible to be a missionary God. It is this expression too that condemns all our petty parochialism and narrow nationalism, our racial pride (whether white or black), our condescending paternalism and arrogant imperialism. How dare we adopt a hostile or scornful or even indifferent attitude to any person of another color or culture if our God is the God of 'all the families of the earth'! We need to become global Christians with a global vision, for we have a global God." (John R. W. Scott in *The Living God is a Missionary God*.)

One of the weaknesses of the American Church is that Sunday morning is the most segregated hour of the week. Jesus prayed four times in John 17 (verses 11, 21, 22, and 23) that we would be one. He knew that unity would be a great challenge for us. He taught us to pray that his Kingdom would be realized on earth just as it is in heaven. In heaven we will be one. John saw, "a crowd, too great to count, from every nation and tribe and people and language, standing in front of the throne and before the Lamb" (Rev. 7:9 NLT).

One of my greatest joys was pastoring Capital Christian Fellowship in Lanham, Maryland, with 20 nationalities represented throughout the congregation and in all levels of leadership. It was a foretaste of heaven. Whenever a church through the power of the Gospel breaks down the dividing walls of hostility the Gospel is a beacon light of healing.

There are various nationalities in most every community. Include them in your congregation. You will be enriched and experience a new perspective of the greatness of our God.

Lord, enable me to love people of all classes and cultures, to worship together and demonstrate your love with practical acts of God's generosity. Amen.

You Are Sent

John 17:18 & John 20:21

Dedicated disciples of our Lord believe and know they are called by God to serve others. After all, Jesus came to serve, not to be served. (Mark 10:45). Jesus lived with a consciousness of being sent. He refers to it forty times in John's Gospel. He says in John 17:18 NLT, "As you sent me into the world, I am sending them into the world." And again 20:21 NLT, "As the Father has sent me, so I send you." He didn't send Jesus with a clear command and you and me with a "if you feel like it" command. Just as the Father sent Jesus he sends us!

Are you conscious of being sent? When you get up in the morning do you realize that Jesus is sending you today to a lost world? You have a responsibility to represent the one who sends you. You need to hear and obey what he has outlined for your day. Not only are we to be faithful we are to be fruitful: "This is to my Father's glory, that you bear much fruit, showing yourselves to be my disciples" (John 15:8).

Jesus then adds: "You didn't choose me. I chose you. I appointed you to go and produce fruit that will last, so that the Father will give you whatever you ask for, using my name" (John 15:16 NLT). We are sent and also chosen to produce fruit that will last for eternity. Ask in Jesus' name for the fruit which he promised you.

What is the fruit? Is it the fruit of the Spirit: "Love, joy, peace, patience, kindness, goodness, faithfulness, gentleness, and self-control" (Gal. 5:22-23 NLT)? Or is it the fruit of people coming to Christ? "When the Holy Spirit has come upon you, you will receive power and will tell people about me everywhere—in Jerusalem, throughout Judea, in Samaria, and to the ends of the earth" (Acts 1:8 NLT). It is both character and witness, maturity and souls. Both are necessary. Both bring glory to the Father.

Lord, help me to realize that just as you were sent by the Father, you send me into the world to be a light and a fruitful witness for you. Amen.

February 21

All I Want

Psalm 16:5

"You Lord are all I want! You are my choice and you keep me safe" (Ps. 16:5 CEV). "Your laws are all I want in life" (Ps. 119:39b NLT). "You're all I want in heaven! You're all I want on earth" (Ps. 73:15 Msg.).

David wanted one thing more than anything—the presence of God. People want a lot of things. Their credit card debt is proof. For Christians, earthly things need to take a back seat. The Lord must be first. In fact Jesus said, "If anyone comes to me and does not hate his father and mother, his wife and children, his brothers and sisters—yes, even his own life—he cannot be my disciple" (Luke 14:26). We know we are not to hate anyone so what does Jesus mean? Anyone who comes to me but refuses to let go of father, mother, spouse, children, brothers, sisters—yes, even one's own self!—can't be my disciple" (Luke 14:26 Msg.).

Paul writes, "Everything else is worthless, when compared with the priceless gain of knowing Christ Jesus my Lord. I have discarded everything else, counting it all as garbage, so that I may have Christ and become one with him" (Phil. 3:8-9a NLT).

"This one thing I ask of the Lord—the thing I seek most—is to live in the house of the Lord all the days of my life, delighting in the Lord's perfections and meditating in his Temple" (Ps. 27:4 NLT). Do you desire more than anything to live in his presence?

Jesus promised, if we keep his Kingdom ahead of everything else the "everything else" will be given to us. (Matt. 6:33). Paul writes, "I want to know Christ and the power of his resurrection and the fellowship of sharing in his sufferings, becoming like him in his death" (Phil. 3:10).

Have you come to the place where you can say: Lord, you are all I want?

Lord, I surrender my all to you. I give you my time, my allegiance, my family, my money, my job, my will, my life. It is yours to use as you see fit. So help me Lord. Amen.

February 22

Who Will Be in Charge?

Romans 7:18-20

"I know that nothing good lives in me, that is, in my sinful nature. For I have the desire to do what is good, but I cannot carry it out. For what I do is not the good I want to do; no, the evil I do not want to do—this I keep on doing. Now if I do what I do not want to do, it is no longer I who do it, but it is sin living in me that does it" (Ro. 7:18-20).

We have two levels of processing going on in our lives. On the conscious level I desire to do what is right but there is the subconscious old nature who wants control. As God's child we choose to live on the conscious level.

Focus on Jesus' Holy Spirit's power at work within you to overcome the subconscious messages. For example, I don't want to raise my voice at my wife or children but if I am tired and stressed when they do something that irritates me my subconscious voice automatically causes me to speak in an angry voice. My subconscious tells me they should know better than to bother me now, or answer all their questions because I had a difficult day.

When I pause to pray in faith, "Lord help me respond as you would respond," then I can overcome the subconscious message and respond appropriately. When we fail, and we fail many times, we come to the cross, die to self, repent and ask God for his strength to do better next time.

Paul continues: "In my inner being I delight in God's law; but I see another law at work in the members of my body, waging war against the law of my mind and making me a prisoner of the law of sin at work within my members. What a wretched man I am! Who will rescue me from this body of death? Thanks be to God—through Jesus Christ our Lord!" (Ro. 7:22-25).

Lord Jesus, help me to be aware of the power of your Holy Spirit living within me giving me the ability to respond as you would in each situation. Amen.

53

Overcomers

Luke 10:3-4, 19

Jesus said to the 70 disciples, "Go now, and remember that I am sending you out as lambs among wolves. Don't take along any money, or a traveler's bag, or even an extra pair of sandals." "I have given you authority over all the power of the enemy and you can walk among snakes and scorpions and crush them. Nothing will injure you" (Luke 10:3-4, 19 NLT).

What do wolves do with lambs? Devour them!

Jesus sends you but that does not mean you will find it comfortable and easy. He sent the disciples in a boat and a furious storm arose. Jesus was driven by the Spirit into the wilderness and was deluged with temptation.

A Christian facing martyrdom said, "I am near death, but I'm not in danger." Is this what Jesus meant when he said that nothing can harm you? (v. 19).

Do you believe your security is in Christ even though the wolves may eat you alive? "Do not be afraid of those who kill the body but cannot kill the soul. Rather, be afraid of the One who can destroy both the soul and body in hell" (Matt. 10:28). Are you at peace with the thought of going home to be with Jesus even though it involves suffering? If you hesitate because of unfinished business like an unforgiving spirit, make peace now. If your hesitancy is that you believe your work on earth is not finished, tell God and let the results in his hands.

Paul writes, "To me, living is for Christ, and dying is even better. Yet if I live, that means fruitful service for Christ . . . I'm torn between two desires: Sometimes I want to live, and sometimes I long to go and be with Christ. That would be far better for me, but it is better for you that I live . . . I will continue with you so that you will grow and experience the joy of your faith" (Phil. 1:21-25 NLT).

Lord, enable me to be faithful so that one day I will hear: "Well done, good and faithful servant, enter into the joy of the Lord." Amen.

A Plentiful Harvest

Luke 10:1-12 & John 4:35

Jesus informed his disciples in Luke 10:2, that the harvest is plentiful. Do you experience a plentiful harvest? If the harvest is not plentiful Jesus says we are to pray for more workers. Do your children and the children in your church know you pray that they become workers? Or are you hoping your children will strive for a lucrative position, make a name for themselves and have a comfortable nest egg for retirement?

Jesus said the harvest is ripe. John 4:35, "Do you not say, 'Four months more and then the harvest.' I tell you, open your eyes and look at the fields! They are ripe for harvest. Even now the reaper draws his wages; even now he harvests the crop for eternal life, so that the sower and the reapers may be glad together.'" Jesus says, we are to be urgent, and zealous. Bring in the harvest while it is ripe.

In Luke 10:4 Jesus instructs the 70 not to greet anyone on the road. In that culture greetings could easily take several hours. We are not to stop on the way and dilly-dally around. The time is short. Jesus at this point was focusing on the Jewish people. Night comes when no one can work. (John 9:4). We go where Jesus sends us (v. 4), not necessarily where we want to go or where we will feel safe. Our mission is to go where he sends us.

We want our lives to count for something. We want to make a difference. People are motivated more by a great cause than by comfort. We want to know we are doing something worthwhile, be it costly or painful. This is what caused the disciples to face the wolves. Jesus called them to a vision. He calls you as well.

Isaiah's prophecy paints a picture of God's Kingdom where the wolves and the lambs will lie down together. (Is. 11:6). Jesus sends us into the harvest field to help fulfill that fantastic prophecy.

Jesus open my eyes to see the ripe fields about me. I pray for more workers to gather in the harvest. Enable me to be a harvester today. Amen.

Person of Peace

Matthew 10:13 & Luke 10:5

"Whatever town . . . you enter, search for some worthy person there and stay at this house until you leave. As you enter the home give it your greeting. If the home is deserving, let your peace rest on it; if it is not, let your peace return to you" (Matt. 10:11-13).

Ask the Holy Spirit to help you find persons of peace, persons of respect. If we can't find them Jesus says, "Don't stay there." Paul and Jesus found those people: Lydia (Acts 16:14-15), Cornelius (Acts 10, 11), the woman at the well (John 4), the demoniac (Mark 8:20) and others. At least four different times in the book of Acts when one person met Jesus the whole household came to the Lord. (Acts 11:14, 16:15, 31, 18:8).

In my fifty years of pastoral ministry God led me to many persons of peace. One man came and over the next couple years was influential in bringing 30 others. Another man, an alcoholic for 26 years, brought his buddies, family and friends to Jesus. A schoolteacher brought her extended family. An international person from Cameron opened the door for many internationals to come to Christ and the church.

Don't be surprised that the Lord uses those with a background of overt sin in a great way. I wonder how many churches were planted from the demoniac's witness of the work of Jesus in his life as he went through the Decapolis? The Decapolis was composed of ten cities, each it is estimated with a population of five thousand or more. This opened the door in a dramatic way to those in the Greek culture.

Pray that you can find persons of peace. When they open their hearts to the Lord, build faith in them by telling them how God will use them to reach their lost relatives and peers. Disciple and empower them to reach into their world. Great will be your joy as you see them reach out in faith. Remember the righteous are as bold as lions. (Prov. 28:1).

Lord, open my eyes to see persons of peace so your Gospel can penetrate into their culture. Amen.

"Do Not Take a Purse, or Bag or Sandals."

Luke 10:4

As Jesus sent them out he instructed the 70 not to take a purse, bag or sandals (v. 4). "Travel light—comb and toothbrush and no extra luggage" (Msg.).

Why no extra clothes or shoes? We are not to depend on our ingenuity, our money, possessions or our training. By allowing the people we meet to help us it opens the door enabling them to hear us. Why did Jesus ask the woman at the well for a drink? He could have performed a miracle to get the water for himself. Why did Jesus use the boy's five loaves to feed the 5,000? Why did Jesus asked more than 150 questions? He knew the answers. Jesus humbled himself. He invited others to assist him. He listened as he reached across to them. We must do the same so people can hear us.

What do we do? We heal their sick. (v. 9). We assist the needy. Maybe we feel more at home in the middle or upper class. We like the country club atmosphere. Granted they too need to meet Jesus. Go wherever Jesus sends you. There are 4,000 biblical passages demonstrating God's concern for orphans, widows, prisoners, aliens, homeless, poor, hungry, sick and the disabled. "God gives justice to orphans and widows. He shows love to the foreigners living among you and gives them food and clothing. You too, must show love to foreigners for you yourselves were once foreigners in the land of Egypt" (Deut. 10:18-19). Jesus says we are to invite these persons into our homes. (Luke 14:12 and 21).

We reach across, not down. Be humble and accept their gifts with gratitude. This makes it easier for them to hear the Good News. Listen to their life's story. People will not hear until they have been heard. They don't care how much we know until they see how much we care. We bless people, and they bless us.

Lord Jesus, I will not depend on my education, or my wallet but I look to you for your love and power to meet the needs of those I see today. Amen.

Rejoice Because Your Name Is Written in Heaven

Luke 10:17-20

The disciples returned from their mission trip full of joy with a triumphant report but Jesus said don't rejoice just because evil spirits obey you; rejoice because your names are recorded in heaven. The Message Bible reads: "The great triumph is not in our authority over evil, but in God's authority over you and his presence with you. Not what you do for God but what God does for you—that's the agenda for rejoicing" (Luke 10:18-19).

Rejoice because of your great salvation. Rejoice that your name is written in the Lamb's Book of Life. Do you find it difficult to sincerely thank God for his daily blessings? His mercies are new every day. (Lam. 3:22-23).

Why did Jesus feel it was necessary to warn his disciples about being excited over casting out demons? Jesus is the source of all his gifts to you. Be excited over Jesus. We are apt to believe that his gifts are more important than knowing him. We are simply tools in the hands of the potter. Anything we do is only as a result of abiding in him. (John 15:4).

The Lord told Zerubbabel: "Not by (our) might nor by power, but by my Spirit, says the Lord Almighty" (Zechariah 4:6).

"Who do you think Paul is, anyway? Or Apollos, for that matter? Servants, both of us—servants who waited on you as you gradually learned to entrust your lives to our mutual Master. We each carried out our servant assignment. I planted the seed. Apollos watered the plants, but God made it grow. It's not the one who plants or the one who waters who is at the center of this process but God, who makes things grow. Planting and watering are menial servant jobs at minimum wages. What makes them worth doing is the God we are serving" (I Cor. 3:5-8 Msg.).

Give God the credit for everything you accomplish since you cannot make one hair white or black. (Matt. 5:36).

Lord, I delight in your gift of salvation through Christ Jesus my Lord. Amen.

Do You Need Courage?

Luke 10:17-20

"When the seventy-two returned with joy and said, 'Lord, even the demons submit to us in your name.'" He replied, 'I saw Satan fall like lightening from heaven. I have given you authority to trample on snakes and scorpions and to overcome all the power of the enemy; nothing will harm you. However, do not rejoice that the spirits submit to you, but rejoice that your names are written in heaven'" (Luke 10:17-20).

You will not see Satan fall in your church unless you claim the authority Jesus gave you in his great commission. (Matt. 28:18-20). Satan rejoices as we spend hours trying to solve an internal squabble or form another committee to help squelch yet another controversial issue. If we put our energy into our mission of making disciples the internal problems will dissipate. Too often the "kitchen worker" issues or the "color of our carpet" issues in our churches become more important than our mission. As long as we think we must get our petty differences settled in our churches before we can go to our peers and neighbors with the Good News, we will not see Satan fall.

Is conflict in our churches more comfortable for us than going where Jesus wants us to go? Jesus sends each of us into our world just as the Father sent him. (John 20:21). When Jesus commissioned us he gave us all authority in heaven and on earth to go and make disciples. How much clearer can Jesus be? Paul said, "I am not ashamed of the Gospel of Christ for it's the power of God for salvation." Are we ashamed?

The early church was far from perfect but the Good News spread because the Good News was the priority of the apostles and early church. If we love God's salvation we will continually magnify the Lord. (Ps. 40:16).

Father, help me not to allow Satan to defeat me by spending all my time on internal differences. Enable me to make your Great Commission my priority. Amen.

Take Inventory

II Corinthians 13:5-6

"Test yourself to make sure you are solid in the faith. Don't drift along taking everything for granted. Give yourselves regular checkups. You need first hand evidence, not mere hearsay, that Jesus Christ is in you. Test it out. If you fail the test, do something about it" (II Cor. 13:5-6 Msg.).

"Be . . . eager to make your calling and election sure. For if you . . ., add to your faith, goodness, knowledge, self-control perseverance, godliness, brotherly kindness and love you will never fall, and you will receive a rich welcome into the eternal kingdom of our Lord and Savior Jesus Christ" (II Peter 1:5-11).

"Examine your motives, test your heart, come to this meal (communion) in holy awe" (I Cor. 11:28 Msg.). "Take the plank out of your own eye, and then you will see clearly to remove the speck from your brother's eye" (Matt. 7:5). "Search me, O God, and know my heart: test me and know my anxious thoughts. See if there is any offensive way in me, and lead me in the way everlasting" (Ps. 139:23-24). "Examine me from inside out, surprise me in the middle of the night—You'll find I'm just what I say I am. My words don't run loose" (Ps. 17:3 Msg.).

Focusing only on our own holiness makes us self-centered. "We must desire to know God. God can't deliver us while our interests are merely on our own character. Paul was not conscious of himself. He was reckless, abandoned, totally surrendered and separated by God for one purpose—to proclaim the Gospel of God." (Oswald Chambers). Paul's passion was to "know Christ, the power of his resurrection and the fellowship of sharing in his sufferings, becoming like him in his death" (Phil. 3:10). "I consider my life worth nothing to me if only I may complete the task the Lord Jesus has given me, the work of telling others the Good News about God's wonderful kindness and love" (Acts 20:24).

Dear Lord, search my heart and thoughts. Forgive my sins. I want to know you and serve you with all my heart. Amen.

Pride—the President of Hell

First Chronicles 21

Pride is the president of hell, the root of all sin. Pride raised its ugly head in the garden when Eve thought she knew better than God. We are self absorbed. When you look at a group picture who do you look for first? If your picture is lousy you don't like the picture. "The heart is deceitful above all things and beyond cure" (Jer. 17:9).

David insisted on taking a census. (I Chron. 21). Joab, with better judgment, resisted strongly but reluctantly obeyed King David. God punished Israel for David's "substituting statistics for trust" (v. 7 Msg.). God disciplined David by giving him three choices: three years of famine, three months of being overrun by the enemy or three days encountering the sword of the Lord. David chose the latter and 70,000 died. (v. 14). David repented saying, "I am the one who sinned and done wrong. . . . O Lord my God, let your hand fall upon me and my family, but do not let this plague remain on your people" (v. 17).

"Pride goes before destruction and a haughty spirit before a fall" (Prov. 16:18). "If you think you are standing firm, be careful that you don't fall" (I Cor. 10:12). "God opposes the proud but gives grace to the humble" (James 4:6).

Much of my life I prayed before I preached that I would be humble. Later in my church consulting work as I was praying before I was to speak, the Lord seemed to say look in *Strong's Concordance*. How often does the New Testament tells us to be humble and how often does it remind Christians to be bold, confident or courageous. Boldness appears more frequently. Satan is delighted when we believe if we are humble we can't be bold. Paul writes, "Pray that I may declare the Gospel boldly and courageously" (Eph. 6:20 AMP).

We are nothing. Jesus is everything. But at the same time Jesus has redeemed us and chosen to use us. Speak confidently and boldly so people can leave the broad way that leads to destruction and come to Jesus. (Matt. 7:13-14).

Father give me your Holy Spirit's boldness that I may serve you. Amen.

Are You a Fanatic?

Mark 2:1-12

"After a few days, Jesus returned to Capernaum, and word got around that he was back home . . . A crowd gathered, jamming the entrance so one could not get in or out. They brought a paralytic to him, carried by four men. When they were unable to get in because of the crowd, they removed part of the roof and lowered the paralytic on his stretcher. Impressed by their bold belief, Jesus said to the paralytic, 'Son, I forgive your sins'" (Mark 2:1-5 Msg.).

Apparently the people heard about the miracles Jesus performed and came to see and hear him. The testimonies of the healed people raised the faith level of the four men who brought the paralytic to Jesus.

As Jesus was preaching these men came carrying a stretcher with the paralyzed man. Since the house was packed there was no way they could get through the door. Determined to bring him to Jesus they climbed the stairs to the roof. They removed the tiles and lowered the paralyzed man in front of Jesus. On seeing the faith of the four men He said to the paralyzed man, "My son, your sins are forgiven."

These four men were fanatics. Maybe their roofs were easier to patch than ours but who of us would think of going to our neighbor's house and tearing off part of the roof to bring someone into the presence of Jesus? Our neighbors would think we were crazy. We might end up in prison or a mental hospital for such a crime.

You know people in need. Are you taking risks to bring them to Jesus? How serious are you in helping others come to Jesus?

Our zeal needs to be according to knowledge. Paul in speaking about his Jewish brothers says, "I know what enthusiasm they have for God but it is misdirected zeal" (Ro. 10:2 NLT). We need to pray for wisdom so our zeal is according to God's will.

Dear Lord Jesus, when I compare my zeal with the zeal of these four men I fall short. Forgive me. Give me greater faith. Show me who I need to bring to you today. Amen.

Teamwork

Mark 2:3-5

Four men brought a paralytic to Jesus. Since they could not get him to Jesus because of the crowd, they made an opening in the roof above Jesus and, after digging through it, lowered the mat the paralyzed man was lying on. (Mark 2:3-5).

Did all four men have the gift of evangelist? One had to start by saying to the others, "This paralytic man must meet Jesus. Will you help me take him to Jesus?" Likely he had the gift of leadership or mercy. Someone had to take the initiative to get this man to Jesus. We need people to take leadership.

Perhaps the other three had the gift of service or helps, or maybe a mix of other gifts. Could the leader do it alone? No, he needed others to assist him. Perhaps those with the gift of craftsmanship helped repair the roof.

To bring someone to Jesus usually takes many people with various gifts. God designed us to learn to work together, to be a model of his love and caring. Others were involved in discipling this man. Perhaps they had the gift of teaching and exhortation. I believed others used their gift of hospitality so his family and relatives could find Christ.

Others prayed. Prayer is a vital gift that releases the power of God. God gifts certain persons with the gift of intercession. Faith, mercy and healing are also evident in this encounter.

"Each one should use whatever gift he has received to serve others" (I Peter 1:10). Invite others to help you bring people to Jesus. Paul took others along on his missionary journeys. Jesus sent people out two by two. Jesus called others to go with him. (Mark 3:14). By taking others with you, you are participating in the discipling process as they observe how you relate so they in turn can make disciples. Disciples must reproduce or they are not true disciples. (Matt. 28:18-20). This is the process Jesus outlined for us to extend his Kingdom.

Lord, enable me to use whatever gifts you have given me. Show me who to invite to work with me so others can come to Jesus and be healed. Amen.

Keep the Cross Central

I Cor. 2:2

If the devil can't squelch our evangelistic enthusiasm he will do his best to misdirect it. He may have us focus on some good psychological principles that we have learned from the latest book or seminar. God can use these principles but these principles do not have the power to deliver a person from death to life. Only Jesus can do that. Usually the more training we have the more we are tempted to trust our training rather than to trust Jesus for deliverance. Too often we trust in our learning when Jesus' power is the only source of genuine healing and deliverance.

The reason the psychological principles fall short is because they usually do not deal with the root of the problem. We can take people through many good and helpful psychological steps and still not deal with their sinful self-centered nature. As long as that self-centered nature is not dealt with we are spinning our wheels. We may see some progress but we will not see victory that lasts.

Take people to Jesus. Keep the cross central. Paul wrote, "I decided to concentrate only on Jesus Christ and his death on the cross" (I Cor. 2:2).

"I have laid a foundation as an expert builder, and someone else is building on it. But each one should be careful how he builds. For no one can lay a foundation other than the one already laid, which is Jesus Christ" (I Cor. 3:10-11). "Everything else is worthless when compared with the priceless gain of knowing Christ Jesus my Lord . . . I want to know Christ and experience the mighty power that raised him from the dead" (Phil. 3:10).

"We preach Christ crucified: a stumbling block to Jews and foolishness to Gentiles, but to those whom God has called, . . . Christ is the power of God and the wisdom of God. For the foolishness of God is wiser than man's wisdom, and the weakness of God is stronger than man's strength" (I Cor. 1:23).

Take people to the cross. The cross is God's plus sign that makes life add up. Jesus is our bondage breaker.

Lord, thank you for the cross where you paid for our sin so we can be set free. Amen.

Holy Spirit Power

John 20:21-23

After the resurrection Jesus spoke to the disciples and said, "Peace be with you." Then be breathed on them and said to them, "Receive the Holy Spirit" (John 20:23).

If you feel you need more courage, boldness or power and authority ask Jesus to "breath on you" and fill you with his Spirit as Paul admonishes us in Ephesians 5:18. The Greek New Testament indicates this is a continuous filling. We lose the fullness of God's Spirit unless we go back to the source again and again to be refilled, reenergized by his Holy Spirit.

We may enjoy a great meal today but tomorrow we need to eat and be filled again. So we need to be filled continually with the Holy Spirit.

Jesus says: "Ask and keep on asking and it shall be given you; seek and keep on seeking, and you shall find; knock and keep on knocking and the door shall be opened to you. For everyone who asks and keeps on asking receives, and he who seeks and keeps on seeking finds and to him who knocks and keeps on knocking the door shall be opened. What father among you if his son asks for a loaf of bread, will give him a stone; or if he asks for a fish will instead of a fish give him a serpent; or if he asks for an egg, will give him a scorpion? If you then, evil-minded as you are, know how to give good gifts—gifts that are to advantage—to your children, how much more will your heavenly Father give the Holy Spirit to those who ask and continue to ask Him!" (Luke 11:9-13 AMP).

Don't be afraid or hindered by the various interpretations concerning the filling of the Holy Spirit. Don't for one minute get hung up on such controversial terms as baptism of the Holy Spirit, or second work of grace. Simply cling to the Lord asking for His resurrection power and the fullness of his Holy Spirit.

Father, I need you. I am helpless without you. You alone have the power to draw people to yourself. Lord, fill me with your Holy Spirit. Amen.

Not Ashamed

Romans 1:14-17

"Everyone I meet—it matters little whether they're mannered or rude, smart or simple—deepens my sense of interdependence and obligation. And that's why I can't wait to get to you in Rome, preaching this wonderful good news of God. Its news I'm most proud to proclaim, this extraordinary Message of God's powerful plan to rescue everyone who trusts him" (Ro. 1:14-17 Msg.).

Paul was anxious to go to the world's capitol. Why? Because the Gospel has power to change lives, power to transfer people from one kingdom to another. Some who have been born in "Christian homes" believe they have inherited their parents' faith while others are merely content with their religious rituals and good works. They say we love God. Yet they talk about their love for their kids or their favorite sports team but never share Jesus because he's an add-on like another club or activity in their life.

They've never experienced salvation in Jesus. As Jim Morgan writes: "Our passion for the Lord should be evident to all those around us. 'Private Christian' should be an oxymoron—our faith should pour out through every fiber of our being. That passion should extend to a sincere concern for those who don't know the Lord. The fate awaiting those dying without Christ should compel Christians to set off on a rescue mission—to bring their family, friends, neighbors and coworkers toward Christ before it's too late. That sense of urgency should drive us to risk our reputations or even lives for the sake of sharing something we value with those at such great risk."

If you found a doctor or a mechanic you could trust or even a terrific diet, you would be glad to tell your friends. Since you've found the One who forgives sin and provides everlasting life. Isn't that something you would want to share?

Don't be discouraged if people don't respond immediately. Build a relationship with many people. It usually takes a variety of contacts before a person comes to Jesus.

Lord, enable me to share the powerful plan of salvation to someone today. Amen.

Wounded Healers

Matthew 18:23-35

Peter asked Jesus how many times he must forgive a brother when he sins against him. Jesus answered with a parable. A man owed the king a million dollars. He begs the king to have mercy on him by giving him more time to pay. The King forgave the huge debt but the debtor never "heard" the king's answer. At least he lived as if he was in debt because he didn't apply this forgiveness to a fellow servant who owed him a few dollars.

When the king heard about this man's actions Jesus said: "In anger his master turned him over to the jailers to be tortured, until he should pay back all he owed. This is how my heavenly Father will treat each of you unless you forgive your brother from your hearts" (Matt. 18:34-35).

We are all servants in a debt far more than we could ever pay. In fact when you consider the wages of this servant he would have needed more than 27,000 years to pay back the million dollars. He was hopelessly in debt. We too are hopelessly in debt. Until we realize our indebtedness we will never be as grateful as we should be to our Lord who paid the debt for us on the cross.

"For you know that it was not with perishable things such as silver or gold that you were redeemed from the empty way of life handed down to you from your forefathers, but with the precious blood of Christ, a lamb without blemish or defect" (I Peter. 1:18-19).

Thank God for his great sacrifice in forgiving us so we can go free. (Ro. 8:1). In response to this freedom let us gladly serve him with all our heart, soul, mind and strength. Who does God want you to serve today? Remember, by loving and serving others you are serving Jesus. (Matt. 25:35-46).

Lord, thank you for the gift of your Son, a gift too wonderful for words. I'll serve you as long as I live. Amen.

Mary and Martha

John 11:17-44

After Lazarus died Mary and Martha were grieving. When they learned that Jesus had finally come they both said to Jesus: "If you had been here, my brother would not have died" (vv. 21 and 32). Note how differently Jesus responded to them.

To Martha who was more cognitive, more left brain, than Mary he said, "Your brother will rise again . . . I am the resurrection and the life. He who believes in me will live, even though he dies; and whoever lives and believes in me will never die. Do you believe this?" (vv. 23-26). To Mary who is more feeling-oriented and emotional Jesus was deeply moved in spirit and troubled. Jesus wept with Mary. (v. 33).

To reach people with the Good News it's necessary to identify on a deep level. As you pray God will give you insight into their heart and soul. God will help you to be sensitive so they feel God's love flowing through you.

People tell you how you are to witness to them by the way they share their hurts and by their actions. We give our attention to them in listening and observing their body language. They feel loved when they know we understand. God will answer your prayer as you make a sincere effort to understand each person.

Most persons I have the joy of bringing to Jesus need someone to understand and accept them like Mary. They feel lonely and insignificant. If people ask questions, like Martha, we need to provide answers.

Jesus drew the seeker to himself. Seekers need to feel your love; if they don't like you, they will have a difficult time loving your Savior. Persevere, pray and share the Good News. How wonderful it is that God has chosen to use us in bringing others to too Jesus.

Lord, give me a heart of wisdom and insight to love and understand others. Amen.

The Priority of Relationships

Luke 10:38-42

Jesus was on his way to Jerusalem but stopped in Bethany about two miles from Jerusalem where Martha and Mary lived. Martha welcomed him. "Her sister, Mary, sat at the Lord's feet, listening to what he taught. But Martha was worrying over the big dinner she was preparing. She came to Jesus and said, 'Lord, doesn't it seem unfair to you that my sister just sits here while I do all the work? Tell her to come and help me.' But the Lord said to her, 'My dear Martha, you are so upset over all these details! There is really only one thing worth being concerned about. Mary has discovered it—and I won't take it away from her" (Luke 10:38-42).

Jesus knew he was headed for the cross. The last thing he wanted was a banquet meal. He desired quiet. Jesus preferred a relaxed conversation with someone like Mary whose heart was set on learning from her Master. Martha, on the other hand, wanted to love Jesus in the way she thought best. She did not take time to think of Jesus' needs. How often do we show love to people in the way we like to be loved rather than show love in the way they can feel our love?

Jesus saw the heart of Mary as one who was a listener and a learner. While Martha's heart desired to give sacrificial service, she was self-motivated doing things her way. My wife wants my heart more than my service. If she has my heart she will have my service. Take time to think, pray and discover your approach to others so they feel loved and can receive God's love.

Jesus desires our relationship more than our service. He desires and seeks worshippers (John 4:23). After Mary sat at Jesus feet, I believe she could have served Jesus very well meeting his physical needs. Let's love others the way they need to be loved.

Lord, help me to fellowship with you, to know you more intimately, to love and serve you with a heart of love and a life of service. Amen.

Love and Works Must Go Together

I Corinthians 8:1 & 3

Paul wrote, "You think that everyone should agree with your perfect knowledge. While knowledge may make us feel important, it is love that really builds up the church" (I Cor. 8:1 & 3 NLT).

He writes, "If I could speak in any language in heaven or on earth, but didn't love others, I would only be making meaningless noise. If . . . I knew all the mysteries of the future . . . but didn't love others, what good would I be? And if I had the gift of faith so that I could speak to a mountain and make it move, without love I would be no good to anybody. If I gave everything I have to the poor and even sacrificed my body, I could boast about it; but if I didn't love others, I would be of no value" (I Cor. 13:1-3 NLT).

Jesus' number one emotional response is compassion! Jesus saw people as sheep that had been bruised, beaten and confused. He was filled with love. (Matt. 9:36).

As spiritual maturity increases, love and approachability should increase. Do we really love and accept others? They can tell if we are genuine. How can we increase our love level? The fruit (singular) of the Holy Spirit is love. (Gal. 5:22). Be filled with the Spirit. (Eph. 5:18).

Along with God's love we must use words. Francis of Assisi preached five times a day. He did not say, as is commonly believed, "Witness 24/7 and if necessary use words." The Gospel is naturally and essentially verbal. Paul writes, "How can they believe in him if they have never heard about him? And how can they hear about him unless someone tells them?" (Ro. 10:14 NLT).

If Jesus would have come and not told us who he was we would all be lost. His perfect life was not enough. We can live a pure and holy life before our neighbors but that will not translate into their salvation unless we tell them how they can find eternal life through Jesus Christ.

Lord, enable me to love others with my demeanor and my tongue. Amen.

Sacrifice Is the Price

II Corinthians 4:11-12

"We live under constant danger of death because we serve Jesus, so that the life of Jesus will be obvious in our dying bodies. So we live in the face of death but it has resulted in eternal life for you" (II Cor. 4:11-12).

There is no progress without sacrifice, little or no growth without suffering. When things go well we often forget to depend on God. As we suffer and rise above difficult circumstances through the Holy Spirit Jesus is lifted up. The church grows in many countries where there is persecution. In other countries where persecution is so intense the Christian church is almost wiped out, at least for a time. Persecution drives the church to imploring and pleading prayer. They say "no" to what the world calls pleasures and sacrifice time in prayer and service. The early church devoted themselves to prayer. (Acts 2:38).

Just before Jesus went to the cross he prayed: "As you sent me into the world. I have sent them into the world. For them I purify myself, that they too may be truly pure" (John 17:18-19). Not only did Jesus die on the cross but he modeled a lifestyle for us. (I John 2:6 and 4:17).

"Don't let any part of your body become a tool to wickedness . . . give yourselves completely to God since you have been given new life. Use your body as a tool to do what is right" (Ro. 6:13 NLT).

"I plead with you to give your bodies to God. Let them be a living and holy sacrifice—the kind he will accept. When you think of what he has done for you, is this too much to ask? Don't copy the behavior and customs of this world, but let God transform you into a new person by changing the way you think. Then you will know what God wants you to do and you will know how good and pleasing and perfect his will really is" (Ro. 12:1-2 NLT).

Father, I say "no" to the world and "yes" to all you want for me. Amen.

Riches of God's Grace (Part I)

II Corinthians 8:9

"You know the generous grace of our Lord Jesus Christ. Though he was rich yet for your sakes he became poor, so that by his poverty he could make you rich" (II Cor. 8:9 NLT).

Our worst days are never so bad that we are beyond the reach of God's grace, and our best days are never so good that we are beyond the need of God's grace.

We can't earn grace, nor do we deserve it. No effort can obtain it because it comes only from God's unselfish love. To receive his grace we must acknowledge that we cannot save ourselves (repent) and give our allegiance to Jesus.

"Mercy is not getting what you deserve—the wrath of God. Grace is getting what you don't deserve—the righteousness of Christ. Everything you've done wrong is forgiven and forgotten. And everything Christ did right—His righteousness—is transferred to your account. Then God calls it even." (Mark Matterson in *All In*, p. 25.)

Paul admonishes Timothy to "be strong in the grace that is in Christ Jesus" (II Tim. 2:1). Peter concludes his final letter: "Grow in the grace and knowledge of our Lord and Savior Jesus Christ" (II Peter 3:18).

Peter asked Jesus how often he should forgive—offer grace? Jesus said, "Seventy times seven" (Matt. 18:22). Jesus forgave our sin debt by paying with his life on the cross. That's grace! As forgiven servants of Jesus we must extend grace and forgiveness to others. Have you extended grace and forgiven everyone who treated you unjustly? Unless we forgive others our heavenly Father will not forgive us. (Matt. 6:14-15).

Father thank you for your grace and forgiveness. I chose to forgive others as you forgave me. Amen.

Riches of God's Grace (Part II)

Ephesians 1:7-8

"In him (Christ) we have redemption through his blood, the forgiveness of sins, in accordance with the riches of God's grace that he lavished on us ..." (Eph. 1:7-8). Grace is a gift. But to receive any gift you need to humble yourself. We must bow before the cross of Christ so we can receive his grace.

Bonhoeffer warned that "cheap grace is the deadly enemy of the Church. Cheap grace is the preaching of forgiveness without requiring repentance, baptism without church discipline, communion without confession, absolution without personal confession. Cheap grace is grace without discipleship, grace without the cross, grace without Jesus Christ, living and incarnate." Bonhoeffer calls us to "costly grace" which "is costly because it cost a man his life, and it is grace because it gives a man the only true life."

To keep Paul from becoming proud after he received a special revelation, he says, "I was given a thorn in my flesh, a messenger from Satan to torment me ... Three different times I begged the Lord to take it away. Each time he said, 'My grace is all you need. My power works best in weakness.' So now I am glad to boast about my weaknesses, so that the power of Christ can work through me. That's why I take pleasure in my weaknesses, and in the insults, hardships, persecutions and troubles that I suffer for Christ. For when I am weak, then I am strong" (II Cor. 12:7-10 NLT).

"Grace is all you need" or "My grace is sufficient." This may sound hollow until we realize Paul's trials: "whipped times without number, faced death again and again. Five different times the Jews gave me 39 lashes. Three times I was beaten with rods. Once I was stoned. Three times I was shipwrecked. I have faced danger from flooded rivers and from robbers ... I have faced dangers on the stormy seas ... Often I have been hungry and thirsty and have done without food. Often I have shivered with cold, without enough clothing to keep me warm" (II Cor. 11:23-27 NLT).

Lord, I can't thank you enough for your supernatural gift of grace! Amen.

Riches of God's Grace (Part III)

Romans 6:12-18

God gives us grace not only concerning the forgiveness of our sins but so we can live faithfully for him. We are to bring every thought in line with Christ Jesus and do only what pleases him carrying out his will in all we say and do. (John 5:30 and 12:49-50). He gives us grace and power to live in conformity to Christ. When we fail, as we all do, he gives us grace to receive his forgiveness. This way we move from one degree of glory to another in Christ letting him produce the fruit of his Holy Spirit in us. (II Cor. 3:18).

"Do not give in to sinful desires. Don't let any part of your body become an instrument of evil to serve sin. Instead give yourselves completely to God, for you were dead, but now you have new life. So use your whole body as an instrument to do what is right for the glory of God. Sin is no longer your master . . . You live under the freedom of God's grace. Since God's grace has set us free from the law, does that mean we can go on sinning? Of course not! Don't you realize that you become the slave of whatever you choose to obey? . . . Once you were slaves to sin but now you wholeheartedly obey this teaching we have given you. You are free from your slavery to sin and you have become slaves to righteous living" (Ro. 6:12-18 NLT).

Corrie Ten Boom asks us why we wade around in our backyard mud puddle and not swim in the vast ocean of God's grace?

God gives us grace and power to do his will. "It is God who works in you to will and to act according to his good purpose" (Phil. 2:13). "All glory to God, who is able to keep you from stumbling, and who will bring you into his glorious presence innocent of sin and with great joy. All glory to him who alone is God our Savior through Jesus Christ our Lord. Yes, glory, majesty power, and authority belong to him, in the beginning, now, and forevermore. Amen" (Jude 24-25 NLT).

Thank you God for your gift of grace to me! Amen.

Riches of God's Grace (Part IV)

Ephesians 1:8

I tell God often that every heart beat and breath is yours Lord, for you gave them to me. I pray for God to search me, and know my heart, my thoughts. Point out anything in me that offends you (Ps. 139:23-24 NLT).

Because of God's grace David writes, "When I look at the night sky and see the work of your fingers—the moon and the stars you have set in place—what are mortals that you should think of us, mere humans that you should care for us? For you made us only a little lower than God, and you crowned us with glory and honor" (Ps. 8:3-6 NLT). That's why David can say, "With my God I can scale a wall" (Ps. 18:29 NLT). With Paul I say, "I can do everything with the help of Christ who gives me the strength I need" (Phil. 4:13 NLT).

When Christ is our life we are so immersed in Christ that we become one with him. (Col. 3:4). It is as if you are no longer living but he is living through you. (Gal. 2:20). The joy this brings is beyond description! I think so often, if only I could share this joy with those who are depressed, those taking drugs because life has no meaning, joy and purpose. This is why those in prison for Christ often say, "Don't pray for my release, pray that I be faithful." Their joy exceeds their pain! (Luke 2:10). Paul writes from prison, "Always be full of joy in the Lord. I say it again—rejoice!" (Phil. 4:4 NLT).

Joni Eareckson Tada in her book, *A Spectacle of Glory*, March 27 devotional reading: "I wish I could adequately describe what it's like when I'm aware of the overwhelming presence of power of God's grace in my life. It's like 'living above' my wheelchair in a strata of heart-splitting joy that comes with God-breathed courage to tackle whatever lies ahead! Frankly, I believe that the more aware you are of God's grace, the more joy and courage you will have . . . When are we more aware of God's grace? It's when we are needy and feeling spiritually impoverished."

Lord, thank you for your lavish grace giving us overwhelming joy. Amen.

Encouragement

I Thessalonians 5:11, 14

Everyone needs encouragement. "Encourage one another and build each other up, just as, you are doing" (I Thess. 5:11 NLT). "Encourage the timid" (v. 14). "May our Lord Jesus Christ himself and God our Father, who loved us and by his grace gave us eternal encouragement and good hope, encourage and strengthen you in every good deed and word" (II Thess. 2:16-17).

Someone said there are three things people need: "Encouragement, encouragement, encouragement and if that doesn't work try encouragement." Paul writes, "Encourage each other" (II Cor. 13:11 NLT). "You know that we treated each of you as a father treats his own children. We pleaded with you, encouraged you and urged you to live your lives in a way that God would consider worthy" (I Thess. 2:11-12 NLT). Just as a father encourages his children we need to encourage each other.

In the New Testament, "encourage" in its several forms appears 46 times. Luke depicts Paul as an apostle of encouragement: "Paul sent for the believers and encouraged them. Then he said good-bye and left for Macedonia. Along the way, he encouraged the believers in all the towns he passed through" (Acts 20:1-2 NLT).

"Think of ways to encourage one another to outbursts of love and good deeds. And let us not neglect our meeting together, as some people do, but encourage and warn each other, especially now that the day of his coming back again is drawing near" (Hebrews 10:24-25 NLT).

Be an encourager as you relate to people. Be conscious of your language, your tone of voice, your faith in building others up. Encouragement will help open the door for you to share the Good News of Jesus. Who will you encourage today?

Dear God, make me an encourager especially as I meet others who are discouraged. Give me words to say that point them to Jesus—the greatest encourager of all. Amen.

Desperate Times

Matthew 24:11-14

"Lying preachers will come forward and deceive a lot of people. For many others, the overwhelming spread of evil will do them in—nothing left of their love but a mound of ashes. Staying with it—that's what God requires. Stay with it to the end. You won't be sorry . . . All during this time, the good news . . . will be preached all over the world, a witness staked out in every country. And then the end will come" (Matt. 24:11-14 Msg.).

"When this Gospel of the Kingdom is preached to the whole world then the end will come." According to the "Joshua Project" there are 6,700 people groups who have never heard the Good News. That's 3 billion persons out of the 7.2 billion in our world.

Jesus' final words were: "The Holy Spirit will come upon you and give you power. Then you will tell everyone about me in Jerusalem . . . and everywhere in the world" (Acts 1:8 CEV). The Holy Spirit has come which means the power to tell everyone is in us.

Do your children hear you pray for workers to spread the Gospel? Do you model sharing the love of Jesus with others? Does your budget reflect the priority of sharing the Good News?

Do you encourage your children to be missionaries in their chosen vocation here or in a foreign country? Even small children can be great missionaries. Start a Bible story time and let them invite their friends.

As you are obedient to share God's love with one person it will become easier to make sharing God's love your lifestyle. Build relationships with your unsaved friends.

Lord, so many never heard the Good News. Enable me to be faithful in prayer and faithful in sharing your love with my family and friends. Raise up workers to reach the 6,700 groups who have never heard. Amen.

Does Jesus Get Disgusted With Us?

Matthew 17:17

When James and John came down the mountain after seeing Jesus transfigured . . . , they were immediately inundated by a huge crowd. A father brought his demon possessed son to the other disciples but they were unable to cast out the demon. Jesus responded, "Unbelieving and perverse generation . . . How long shall I stay with you? How long shall I put up with you?" (Matt. 17:17). They asked Jesus why they couldn't cast the demon from the boy. (v. 19). He replied, "Because you have so little faith. I tell you the truth, if you have faith as small as a mustard seed, you can say to this mountain, 'Move from here to there' and it will move. Nothing will be impossible for you'" (vv. 20-21). Your faith may be very small like a mustard seed. Exercise your mustard seed faith and it will grow.

What disappoints Jesus is our lack of faith. How do we increase our faith? Jesus said we need to pray and fast (Mark 14:29). Paul writes, "Faith comes from hearing the message and the message is heard through the word of Christ" (Ro. 10:17). Faith and love springs from hope. (Col. 1:5). Pray and feast on the word so your faith can grow— the supernatural becoming natural. We are to add to our faith: goodness, knowledge, self-control, perseverance, godliness, kindness and love (II Peter 1:5-9). As we do this our faith grows.

Jesus encourages our faith with this promise, "If you remain in me and my words remain in you, ask whatever you wish, and it will be given you. This is to my Father's glory that you bear much fruit, showing yourselves to be my disciples" (John 15:7-8).

"Without faith it is impossible to please God, because anyone who comes to him must believe that he exists and that he rewards those who earnestly seek him" (Hebrews 11:6). You will have only one battle in life, i.e. fighting the good fight of faith. (I Tim. 6:12).

Lord, forgive my unbelief. As your disciple enable me to pray and feast on your Word so I can bear much fruit. Amen.

Witness and Martyr Are the Same Greek Word

Acts 1:8

The final words of Jesus were: "You will receive power when the Holy Spirit comes on you; and you will be my witnesses in Jerusalem, and in all Judea and Samaria and to the ends of the earth" (Acts 1:8).

Final words are important words. Here Jesus states our purpose for life: to be witnesses. The Greek word is "martures," which means martyrs. This implies that we are commissioned by Jesus to share the Good News even to the point of death.

This was not the first time the disciples heard this message. In Luke 10 Jesus told the seventy disciples he was sending them out as lambs among wolves. He had explained more than once that if they were going to be his followers they must take up their cross, an instrument of death.

When Jesus commissions you to make disciples (Matthew 28:18-20) he promised that he will be with you every day until he returns. That should remove all fear. Trust Jesus to take care of you even if your witness leads to your death. Jesus said, "Don't be afraid of those who want to kill you. They can only kill your body; they cannot touch your soul. Fear only God who can destroy both soul and body in hell. Not even a sparrow worth only half a penny, can fall to the ground without your Father knowing it. And the very hairs of your head are all numbered. So don't be afraid, you are more valuable to him than a whole flock of sparrows" (Matt. 10:28-31 NLT).

In the early 20th century some missionaries did not pack a suitcase. They built their own caskets and used them as suitcases believing they would not return. In the Great Commission Jesus told us to go. He didn't promise we would return. He did promise he would never forsake us. As Job says, "Though he slay me yet will I put my trust in him" (Job 13:15 KJV). Thousands give their life for the witness of the Good News each year.

Lord, enable me to be faithful to the point of death. Amen.

March 20

Follow Me

Luke 5:27

"Jesus saw a tax collector by the name of Levi sitting at his tax booth. 'Follow me,' Jesus said to him, and Levi got up, left everything and followed him" (Luke 5:27).

A church spent hours planning and preparing for a community evening at the park, providing food and drink, games, a movie, welcoming material but no one mentioned anything about follow up. The welcoming people never thought about getting people's names or how they might keep in touch. When I mentioned this it was clear they did not want to offend anyone by being that assertive.

Joe, a golfer, invited Sam to go golfing Sunday morning. Sam said, "Sunday, I'm in church." Joe said, "Give up that nonsense. You know you don't believe it." Sam replied, "What do you mean?" "I can prove you don't believe," replied Joe. "I worked with you every day for twenty years. The Bible says I'm headed for hell, but you never urged me to consider changing my life." What will Joe say to Sam on Judgment Day? Ask yourself, "Am I like Sam?"

Jesus was assertive. He said to Levi, "Follow me." Are we more concerned about offending people than we are about their eternal destiny? Ask your friends who are prebelievers to go with you to a ball game or a backyard picnic. As you build a relationship with them but sense they are not yet ready to come to a worship service, invite them to a church social function. Introduce them to your friends. Timothy was shy but Paul wrote, "God doesn't want us to be shy with his gifts, but bold, and loving and sensible" (I Tim. 1:7 Msg.).

Often we are too shy, or fearful of offending people. We say, "It is not politically correct to invade another's territory." Coming to Jesus is a life and death issue. At the judgment our neighbors may look at us and say, "I talked with you many times. You never told me I needed to follow Jesus. Why didn't you tell me I would need to give an account to him?"

Lord, help me to be sensitive to your Holy Spirit. Enable me to be bold, loving and sensible. Amen.

The Necessity of the Holy Spirit

Acts 1:8 & John 20:19-23

"You will receive power when the Holy Spirit comes on you; and you will be my witnesses in Jerusalem, and in all Judea and Samaria, and to the ends of the earth" (Acts 1:8).

After the Resurrection his disciples were gathered with the doors locked. Jesus appeared to them and said, "Peace be with you." Then he showed them his hands and side. The disciples were overjoyed when they saw the Lord. Again Jesus said, "Peace be with you! As the Father has sent me, I am sending you." And with that he breathed on them and said, "Receive the Holy Spirit. If you forgive anyone his sins, they are forgiven; if you do not forgive them, they are not forgiven" (John 20:19-23).

In Back to Jerusalem, Paul Hattaway, (Gabriel Publishing, 2003 p. 68) writes: "I have come to understand that it is completely impossible for even a single lost person . . . to become a Christian unless a great miracle takes place. Lost human souls are firmly chained prisoners of Satan and his demonic forces. They cannot be argued into the kingdom of God because their problem is not an intellectual one. Nor is there any point in trying to change their outward behavior if they do not have the inward spiritual power that only Jesus can give. The Bible clearly says that every person outside of Christ is spiritually dead, and a battle needs to be waged for his or her soul. People living outside the grace of Jesus Christ are trapped by the devil, . . . (II Tim. 2:26).

He continues, "The demonic forces that hold souls captive are far more powerful than we are, in our own strength. There is not the slightest possibility that we can lead anyone to the foot of the cross unless Jesus himself becomes involved. Only his power can save a sinner. The good news is that we can be completely sure that Jesus will help us to reach the lost for him, for the word of God says, 'He is patient with you, not wanting anyone to perish, but everyone to come to repentance'" (II Peter 3:9).

Lord, help me to depend on the Holy Spirit as I witness to others. Amen.

March 22

Converts or Disciples?

Matthew 28:18-20

Jesus says we are to make disciples. The reason the church in the United States is so anemic is because we have made converts rather than disciples. This is like a mother who is about to give birth. She goes to the hospital and is blessed with a healthy child. After a short stay she is dismissed with her baby but instead of taking the baby home she leaves it on the street in front of the hospital to take care of itself.

That is often how we treat new Christians. Jesus commands us to make disciples. It is much more time consuming and demanding to grow mature Christians. Jesus spent most of his time with the disciples, training them so they could reproduce.

Paul worked diligently with the churches he started so they would grow to the fullness of the stature of the Lord. "I proclaim Christ Jesus, admonishing and teaching everyone with all wisdom, so that we may present everyone perfect (mature) in Christ. To this end I labor, struggling with all his energy which so powerfully works in me" (Col. 1:28-29). "Remember the three years I was with you—my constant watch and care over you night and day, and my many tears for you" (Acts 20:31 NLT). Paul says he is in the pains of childbirth until Christ is formed in them. (Gal. 4:19).

Too often we have people pray the sinner's prayer: "Lord Jesus I believe you are the Son of God, that you died and rose again. I invite you to come into my life and make me what you want me to be. Amen." Some improve this prayer by including repentance which is absolutely necessary. "Unless you repent you will perish" (Luke 13:3). "If you lvoe me keep my commandments" (John 14:15).

I have often asked a spouse if their partner was a Christian. Their response is that he/she believes in God. Even the devil believes and trembles. (James 2:19). True belief in Jesus results in a new lifestyle. "Old things are pasted away and behold all things become new" (II Cor. 5:17).

Lord Jesus enable me to be diligent in following through with those I introduce to salvation, so they in turn become faithful disciples who make disciples. Amen.

Don't Neglect One-Fourth of the Bible

II Peter 3:1-2

Can we say we take the Bible seriously when we neglect the 18 books of prophesy? The prophets comprising twenty-five percent of our Bible have a vital and urgent message for today. Peter says, "I want you to recall the words spoken in the past by the holy prophets" (II Peter 3:1-2). Apparently, like today, the early church was neglecting the message of the prophetic books.

By ignoring the message of the prophets we have lost a respectful fear of the Lord. The prophets warned that disobedience results in God's judgment. But in their warning hope is never lost. God's plan is not to obliterate the world, but to create a new world. "The Day of the Lord" depicts terrific suffering thus allowing God's mercy to shine even brighter.

Today many Christians focus on God's love and forgiveness through Jesus but neglect God's warning of justice. God is just. (II Thes. 1:8-9). Both judgment and God's new creation are certain. "The law was given through Moses, grace and truth came through Jesus Christ" (John 1:17). Grace and truth are couplets. One without the other is incomplete. Emphasize grace alone and you have lawlessness. Emphasize truth alone and it can so easily degenerate into legalism and bondage.

The Old Testament was written to keep us from setting our hearts on evil. Paul illustrates this with the account of God punishing his people as 23,000 died in one day. (I Cor. 10:6-10). Jude gives several illustrations of God's judgment from the Old Testament and concludes, "They serve as an example of those who suffer the punishment of eternal fire" (5-7). The author of Hebrews writes: "Our God is a consuming fire" (12:29). Unless we return to a balanced Gospel which includes the prophetic message our moral slide will continue.

Father, thank you for your love for me in Jesus, but help me remember if I turn my back on you I will suffer consequences. I pledge my allegiance to you. Amen.

My Life Is My Witness

I Peter 3:15

"Always be prepared to give an answer to everyone who asks you to give the reason for the hope that you have. But do this with gentleness and respect, keeping a clear conscience . . ." (I Peter 3:15-16).

Some Christians never talk about their faith. They have the philosophy: my life speaks for Christ—my life is my witness. In one sense this is the most egotistical philosophy anyone could have. In essence they are saying my life is perfect. Just look at what I do, or how I act and you will see Jesus and who he is. It's true that we are Christians, i.e. little Christs, modeling the life of Christ. The problem is none of us are perfect models. James writes: "We all stumble in many ways" (James 3:2).

People need more than models. They need a Lord and Savior. They need power to overcome sin. Our life, as imperfect as it is, must point people to Jesus but there are times when we are ineffective as a model. We need to verbalize our faith. We do this by reminding them that we all need forgiveness for our sins, a daily cleansing through the blood of Christ. John reminds us, "If we say we have no sin, we are only fooling ourselves and refusing to accept the truth. But if we confess our sins to Jesus, he is faithful and just to forgive us and to cleanse us from every wrong" (I John 1:8-9 NLT).

Helen is often asked about her faith. "With five chronic medical conditions how can you be so happy?" Do people ask you about your faith? Are you letting your life shine so they are attracted to you? At these times you must be ready to give an answer pointing them to Jesus who is the only way, the truth and the life. What a wonderful opportunity you have to open their eyes to the abundant life in Jesus. (John 10:10). Share Jesus both in word and deed.

Lord, enable me to live faithfully for you and to boldly and confidently share the Good News of salvation. Amen.

Chosen by God

Ephesians 1:4

Who is chosen? Jesus said many are called or invited but few are chosen. (Matt. 11:22). The "many" includes everyone. "The Lord is patient with you, not wanting anyone to perish, but everyone to come to repentance" (II Peter 3:9).

"You didn't choose me . . . I chose you and put you in the world to bear fruit, fruit that won't spoil. As fruit bearers, whatever you ask the Father in relation to me, he gives you" (John 15:15-16 Msg.).

In elementary school we chose sides to play games. It felt good to be chosen. If you were a poor player you were chosen last. That did not feel good. God chose you before the world was created. We were not an afterthought with God. We were not last or even close to the end of the line. "He chose us in him before the creation of the world to be holy and blameless in his sight" (Eph. 1:4).

He not only chose you to be his child, he chose you to be blameless in his sight! That is only possible through Jesus Christ. He is our righteousness, holiness and redemption. (I Cor. 1:30). We were chosen to bear eternal fruit. God could have created robots but robots can't receive or give love. God created you with a free will. This explains the evil in our world. We turned our backs on God and are suffering the consequences every day.

God wants a reciprocal relationship. Not only did he choose you to be in his family but he chose you to do good works which he prepared beforehand for us to do. (Eph. 2:10). How privileged we are to be chosen by God for his wonderful work of helping to extend his Kingdom.

Thank you for choosing me and giving me the privilege of working with you to make disciples who in turn make disciples. Amen.

Live in the Fullness of the Spirit

Ephesians 5:18

"Let the Holy Spirit fill and control you" (Eph. 5:18 NLT). "Jesus full of the Holy Spirit, left the Jordan River. He was led by the Spirit to go out into the wilderness where the Devil tempted him for forty days" (Luke 4:1-2 NLT). "Then Jesus returned to Galilee, filled with the Holy Spirit's power" (v. 4). On the day of Pentecost they were all filled with the Holy Spirit. (Acts 2:4).

The early church saw the absolute necessity of the Holy Spirit. The Spirit is spoken of 27 times in the Gospels, 43 times in the book of Acts and 30 or more times in the remaining books of the New Testament. Jesus was conceived (Matt. 1:18-20), baptized (Matt. 3:16), led (Lk. 4:1), empowered (Lk. 4:14, 18), and raised from the dead by the Spirit (Ro. 8:11).

By the Spirit you are born from above (Jn. 3:3-6), led (Ro. 8:14), liberated (Ro. 8:2), empowered (Lk. 24:49), baptized (Jn. 1:23-34), sealed (Eph. 4:30) and anointed for service (Lk. 4:18). The Holy Spirit molds our character and produces fruit. (Gal. 5:22-23). He intercedes for us (Ro. 8:26). He interprets Scripture. (I Cor. 2:13 & Eph. 1:17). He convicts of sin. (Jn. 16:9 & 14). He teaches, inspires our prayers, calls and commissions, gives gifts, and guides the believer. By his power you put to death the habits and evil practices of the flesh. (Ro. 8:2).

We have a Holy Spirit deficit disorder. Is the Holy Spirit too mystical for American Christians who are "scientifically oriented?" We make plans and figure everything out. No wonder we don't pray more. We don't need the Holy Spirit if we always say, "This is just common sense." There is a difference between common sense and God's sense. Does it make sense to drive an older car so you can give more to building God's Kingdom? Why would you move, leave a good job to help plant a church or assist a struggling pastor? Why would you spend money to send your children to a Christian School, or adopt a handicapped child or a refugee family, take a vacation helping others instead of sightseeing?

Father, fill me with your Holy Spirit so people see Jesus in me. Amen.

Stench or Perfume?

II Corinthians 2:14-16

"Thanks be to God, who made us his captives and leads us along in Christ's triumphal procession. Now wherever we go he uses us to tell others about the Lord and to spread the Good News like a sweet perfume. Our lives are a fragrance presented by Christ to God. But this fragrance is perceived differently by those being saved and those perishing. To those who are perishing we are a fearful smell of death and doom. But to those who are being saved we are a life-giving perfume. And who is adequate for such a task as this?" (II Cor. 2:14-16 NLT).

Can you name persons that are a sweet perfume? The Holy Spirit's joy, peace and patience radiates from them. You don't want to leave their presence. By the time you leave, your spirit is transformed. You wish every day could be like this.

Then there are those who are not receptive to anything that is pure and of good report. If you have to work beside them they resent your presence and joke with others about your faith and pure life. They wish you were not there so they could live their life without being reminded and convicted of their sin. Some may smell of alcohol, nicotine or drugs. Their speech may be filthy. Love them. Pray for God's Spirit to soften their hearts. When you "hug" them you will receive some of their smell but they will receive a bit of God's loving fragrance through you. His fragrance will linger with them throughout the day.

Paul reminds us that Jesus leads us in his triumphal procession. Wherever we go his Spirit shines through our life. The triumphal procession was the march of victorious soldiers returning from battle with their loot and the captives marching in submission. Picture yourself with Jesus marching and leading his triumphal procession as your life radiates the fragrance of our Lord everywhere you go. Begin your day like Jesus did by spending time with his Father.

Lord, may my life be a sweet fragrance to those I meet today. Amen.

Are You Tired?

II Corinthians 4:14-18 & Luke 15

"We know that the same God who raised our Lord Jesus will also raise us with Jesus and present us to himself along with you . . . . And as God's grace brings more and more people to Christ there will be great thanksgiving and God will receive more and more glory. That is why we never give up. Though our bodies are dying, our spirits are being renewed every day. For our present troubles are quite small and won't last very long. Yet they produce for us an immeasurable great glory that will last forever! So we don't look at the troubles we can see right now, rather we look forward to what we have not yet seen. For the troubles we see will soon be over, but the joys to come will last forever" (II Cor. 4:14-18 NLT).

"Let us not become weary in doing good, for at the proper time we will reap a harvest if we do not give up. Therefore, as we have opportunity let us do good to all people" (Gal. 6:9-10). Isaiah says if we wait on the Lord we can soar like eagles. (40:31).

"Always give yourself fully to the work of the Lord, because you know that your labor in the Lord in not in vain" (I Cor. 15:58). God's mercies are new every morning so why shouldn't we be renewed every day? (Lamentation 3:22).

Are you tired? Nehemiah says, "The joy of the Lord is your strength" (Neh. 10:8). Jesus said, "Come to me and I will give you rest." (Matt. 11:28-29).

Paul admonishes the slaves: "Serve wholeheartedly, as if you were serving the Lord, not men. Because you know that the Lord will reward everyone for whatever good he does, whether he is slave or free" (Eph. 6:7-8).

Fix your focus on Jesus, "who for the joy set before him endured the cross, scorning the shame, and sat down at the right hand of the throne of God. Consider him who endured such opposition from sinful men that you may not grow weary and lose heart" (Heb. 12:2-3).

Thank you Lord that as I look to you I regain my strength. Amen.

Joy in Parting

John 16:7-11

"It is actually best for you that I go away, because if I don't, the Counselor won't come. If I do go away, he will come because I will send him to you. And when he comes he will convince the world of its sin, and of God's righteousness, and of the coming judgment. (The Message reads: "He will expose the error of the godless world's view of sin, righteousness and judgment. He will show them that their refusal to believe in me is their basic sin"). The world's sin is unbelief in me. Righteousness is available because I go to the Father, and you will see me no more. Judgment will come because the prince of this world has already been judged" (John 16:7-11 NLT). When Jesus rose from the dead he defeated satan.

When our best friend moves away or dies there is sorrow, not joy. How could Jesus tell the disciples they should be joyful because he is leaving? Most of us would love to have Jesus' physical presence instead of the mystical presence of the Holy Spirit. Jesus is sending the "Paraclete" (one who stays with you or beside you) which means he is sending the Comforter, Encourager, Advocate and Counselor. The Paraclete or Holy Spirit is all of these and more. In his body Jesus was confined by human limitations of place and time. The Spirit has no limitations. Now the promise that Jesus will be with us always is a reality. (Matt. 28:19). We have continual fellowship with the great God of the universe. That's the reason for the joyful parting.

The Spirit is with us all the time but he is with us in a special way when we share the Good News. (Acts 1:8). Our responsibility is to share the Good News of eternal life through Jesus. It's the Spirit's work to bring conviction of sin.

Lord, thank you for sending the Holy Spirit to stand beside me, to live in me and give me his, comfort, encouragement, wisdom and power. Teach me to tune into his continual guidance. Enable me to obey your voice today. Amen.

Come

Revelations 22:17 & Matthew 11:28-29

"The Spirit and the bride (the true Christian church) say, 'Come.' Let each one who hears them say, 'Come.' Let the thirsty ones come—anyone who wants to. Let them come and drink the water of life without charge" (Rev. 22:17 NLT).

The word "come" appears approximately 2,300 times in the Bible. One of our greatest needs is for relationship and community. Misbehavior in prison is often punished by placing people in isolation. We are meant to live in relationship with others and with God. It was not good for Adam to be alone so God created a helper for him. (Genesis 2:18). Jesus longs for our fellowship and our worship. (John 4:23).

"Are you tired? Worn out? Burned out on religion? Come to me. Get away with me and you'll recover your life. I'll show you how to take a real rest. Walk with me and work with me—watch how I do it. Learn the unforced rhythms of grace. I won't lay anything heavy or ill-fitting on you. Keep company with me and you'll learn to live freely and lightly" (Matthew 11:28-29 Msg.).

"If anyone is thirsty, let him come to me and drink. Whoever believes in me, . . . streams of living water will flow from within him. By this he meant the Spirit, whom those who believed in him were later to receive" (John 7:37-38). James writes: "Come near to God and he will come near to you" (James 4:8).

"Come, all you who are thirsty, come to the waters; and you who have no money, come, buy and eat! Come, buy wine and milk without money and without cost. Why spend money on what is not bread, and your labor on what does not satisfy? Listen, listen to me, and eat what is good, and your soul will delight in the richest of fare" (Is. 55:1-2).

"You diligently study the Scriptures because you think that by them you possess eternal life. These are the Scriptures that testify about me, yet you refuse to come to me to have life" (John 5:39-40). Come and invite others to come.

Jesus, I accept your invitation with deep gratitude! Amen.

Keep Your Focus

John 12:32

"When I am lifted up from the earth I will draw all men to myself" (John 12:32). "All that the Father gives me will come to me, and whoever comes to me I will never drive away" (John 6:37). Do you lift up Jesus?

Jesus draws people to himself when we lift him up. Some wear a cross but unless we take up our cross and live as he designed for us to live we are not lifting him up. There is no other name whereby we must be saved. However there is no other name that is more offensive to the world than the name of "Jesus." It is powerful, beyond any other name! Be bold and reverently use the name of Jesus.

We lift up Jesus so the world will see our good works and give glory to God. (Matt. 5:14-16). We lift up Jesus by loving one another: "Your love for one another will prove to the world that you are my disciples" (John 12:35 NLT). We lift up Jesus as we renounce a life of darkness and live as people of light! (Eph. 5:8). "Be careful to live properly among your unbelieving neighbors. Then even if they accuse you of doing wrong, they will see your honorable behavior, and they will give honor to God when he judges the world" (I Pet. 2:12 NLT).

Jesus alone is the answer to our needs. You can point people to helpful psychological principles, common sense, logic, reason with them, and warn them of the consequence of their poor decisions but unless you bring them to Jesus they will not move from the Kingdom of darkness into the Kingdom of light. Only Jesus can give us a full, purposeful and meaningful life.

People in need of life are everywhere. Pray for eyes to see their pain, their frustration and emptiness. Pray for God's courage and wisdom to know what to do to help them and how to encourage them. Most of all point them to Jesus. Jesus will never drive anyone away. (John 6:37).

Father enable me to lift up Jesus by my words and actions. Amen.

April 1

My Will *or* His Will?

John 6:37-40

"For I have come from heaven to do the will of God who sent me, not to do what I want" (John 6:38 NLT). We are to be like Jesus. (I John 2:6 and 4:17).

God made us with the ability to choose our thoughts and actions. You are not a robot. There is no fellowship with robots. God desires fellowship that's why he gave Jesus to atone for our sin so we can have fellowship with him. (I John 1:6). Since the Garden of Eden we chose to do our will instead of God's will. Evil entered our heart in our fallen world.

God's will is revealed to us in the Bible. "Every Scripture is God-breathed—given by His inspiration—and profitable for instruction, for reproof and conviction of sin, for correction of error and discipline in obedience, and for training in righteousness [that is, in holy living, in conformity to God's will in thought, purpose and action], so that the man (or woman) of God may be complete and proficient, well-fitted and thoroughly equipped for every good work" (II Tim. 3:17-18 AMP).

As you saturate your mind with Scripture you can bring your thoughts and actions into obedience to Christ. Two hundred times in the New Testament we are reminded that we are in Christ and he is in us. (John 15). You have God's Spirit in you to interpret the Scripture for daily living. "We are setting these truths forth in words not taught by human wisdom but taught by the (Holy) Spirit, combining and interpreting spiritual truths with spiritual language [to those who possess the (Holy) Spirit]" (I Cor. 2:13 AMP).

Does this mean we are perfect? No we are learners: Paul learned to be content in every situation. (Phil. 4:12). "I don't mean to say that I have already achieved these things or that I have already reached perfection! But I keep working toward that day when I will finally be all that Christ Jesus saved me for and wants me to be" (Phil. 3:12-13 NLT).

Lord Jesus, help me to bring my will in line with your will. Amen.

The Joy of Work

II Thessalonians 3:6-13

Jesus said, "If you love me you will keep my commandments" (John 14:15 and 23).

If we ask our children to clean their room today and they do not do it today that is disobedience. They may say, "I'll do it tomorrow." We may give grace but how much more pleasing it is to the parent if obedience is immediate. Delayed obedience is disobedience. Putting off what God wants us to do is disobedience.

Persons near death were asked what do you wish you could have changed in your life. Eighty-four percent wished "they would have done what they always wanted to do but didn't do it" while sixteen percent said "they regret doing what they did." God made us to do good works which God has planned for us from eternity. (Eph. 2:10).

The lazy servant in the parable of the three servants said, "Master, I knew you to be a harsh and hard man, reaping where you did not scatter seed, and gathering where you had not winnowed [the grain]; so I was afraid, and I went and hid your talent in the ground. Here you have what is your own." But his master answered him, "You wicked and lazy and idle servant! Did you indeed know that I reap where I have not sown, and gathered grain where I have not winnowed? Then you should have invested my money with the bankers, and at my coming I could have received what was my own with interest. So take the talent away from him and give it to the one who has the ten talents . . . Throw the good-for-nothing servant into the outer darkness; there will be weeping and grinding of teeth" (Matt. 25:24-30 AMP).

"Stay away from any Christian who lives in idleness and doesn't follow the tradition of hard work we gave you . . . We were never lazy . . . We never accepted any food without paying for it. We worked hard day and night so that we would not be a burden to any of you . . . Whoever does not work should not eat" (II Thess. 3:6-13 NLT).

If we know what God wants us to do and do not do it, that is disobedience. (James 4:17).

Jesus, enable me to work with you in serving others. Amen.

April 3

Worship Jesus

John 12:32 & Revelation 7:9-12

"When I am lifted up from the earth I will draw all men to myself" (John 12:32).

Recently I attended a celebration designed to highlight the long history of a church. One person after another talked about relationships that encouraged them through the years. No one mentioned Jesus. No one thanked Jesus for his faithfulness throughout the many years. We sang about Jesus. We did not sing directly to him but about him. To me there is a big difference in worship if I sing about him or sing to him. It's like saying to you, "My wife is wonderful," instead of saying to my wife, "Honey, you are wonderful."

Maybe Jesus doesn't mind when we talk about all the wonderful times we have when we come together at church but wouldn't it be appropriate to thank him personally and for the congregation to express thanks directly to him. Isn't that what we are going to do in heaven? Let's do it now. Enjoy the power that flows from this kind of heart—worship. Worship from our spirit to his Spirit. (John 4:24). We can learn from John's vision of worship in heaven.

"I looked and there before me was a great multitude that no one could count, from every nation, tribe, people and language, standing before the throne and in front of the Lamb. They were wearing white robes and were holding palm branches in their hands. And they cried out in a loud voice: 'Salvation belongs to our God, who sits on the throne, and to the Lamb.' All the angels were standing around the throne and around the elders and the four living creatures. They fell down on their faces before the throne and worshiped God, saying: 'Amen! Praise and glory and wisdom and thanks and honor and power and strength be to our God for ever and ever. Amen!'" (Rev. 7:9-12).

Worship God directly. "Come boldly to the throne of grace that you can find help in time of need" (Hebrews 4:16).

Lord Jesus, you are everything to me. I worship you today! Amen.

Criticism Often Comes From Within the Church

Acts 11:1-3

"The apostles and the brothers throughout Judea heard that the Gentiles also had received the word of God. So when Peter went up to Jerusalem, the circumcised believers criticized him and said. You went into the house of uncircumcised men and ate with them" (Acts 11:1-3).

When you love people and witness to them the Holy Spirit will open their hearts to receive the Word of God. As you introduce them to your church family there will likely be some who are uncomfortable because these new Christians will be different. They have not been trained in the church traditions, customs, liturgy and protocol. Their music tastes are different. Their lifestyle is different. This will make some church people very uncomfortable.

If these new people are shy and stay in the background, not rocking the boat all may be well. Most older traditional congregations can accept new persons as long as they sit quietly in the pew and give in the offering but if they make suggestions or are moved into church leadership, then the tension begins to rise. One church authority reports that the crisis comes when new believers number about fifteen percent of the congregation. At that point the new people become a threat.

The best way to confront this evil is for the leadership to keep the Great Commission the driving force of our lives and the life of our congregation. As long as we have a passion to see new people born into God's family and become disciples much of the criticism will be abated. The first thing is to keep the first thing, i.e. to make disciples of all ethnic groups. (Matt. 28:18-20).

Healthy congregations are those with persons of many backgrounds and cultures, a foretaste of heaven!

Lord, help me to welcome, accept and love new believers even when they have different traditions, opinions and lifestyles. Mold me and the members of my congregation into a powerful witness for you. Amen.

April 5

Perseverance

Romans 5:3-5

"We rejoice in our sufferings, because we know that suffering produces perseverance, perseverance, character; and character, hope" (Ro. 5:3-5).

"Let us run with perseverance the race marked out for us. Let us fix our eyes on Jesus. . . . Who for the joy set before him, endured the cross, scorning its shame, and sat down at the right hand . . . . of God. Consider him who endured such opposition . . . so that you will not grow weary and lose heart" (Heb. 12:1-3).

"Make every effort to add to your faith goodness, knowledge, self-control, perseverance. . . . For if you possess these qualities in increasing measure, they will keep you from being ineffective and unproductive" (II Peter 1:5-8).

"Among God's churches we boast about your perseverance and faith in all the persecutions and trials you are enduring" (II Thess. 1:4). The testing of our faith develops perseverance which results in maturity. (Ja. 1:3-4).

"We are pressed on every side by troubles, but we are not crushed and broken. We are perplexed, but we don't give up and quit. We are hunted down, but God never abandons us. We get knocked down, but we get up again and keep going . . ." (II Cor. 4:8-10 NLT). We so often pray for God to remove us from our trial when he wants to improve us through the trial.

From John Wesley's diary . . . "Sunday, A.M. May 5: Preached in St. Anne's. Was asked not to come back anymore. May 5 P.M. Preached in St. Jude's. Can't go back there either. Sunday, A.M. May 19 Preached in St. Somebody Else's. Deacons called a meeting and said I couldn't return. Sunday, P.M. May 19, Preached on street, kicked off street. Sunday, A.M. May 16, Chased out of meadow as bull was turned loose during service. Sunday, A.M. June 2, Preached . . . kicked off the highway. Sunday, P.M. June 2, Afternoon, preached in a pasture. Ten thousand people came out to hear me."

Lord, help me to be persevere in my situation. Thank you. Amen.

Love Begins at Home

I Corinthians 13:4-8

"Love endures long and is patient and kind; love never is envious nor boils over with jealousy, is not boastful, does not display itself haughtily. It is not conceited—arrogant and inflated with pride; it is not rude (unmannerly), and does not act unbecomingly. God's love in us does not insist on its own rights or way, for it is not self-seeking; it is not touchy or fretful or resentful; it takes no account of the evil done to it—pays no attention to a suffered wrong . . . It rejoices when right and truth prevail. Love bears up under anything and everything that comes, is ever ready to believe the best of every person, (its hopes are fadeless under all circumstances and it endures everything) [without weakening]. Love never fails—never fades out or becomes obsolete or comes to an end" (I Cor. 13:4-8 AMP).

It's impossible for anyone to live up to this definition of love. Only one person can live the Christian life and that is Jesus. We must have Jesus living in us, via God's Holy Spirit!

Of the fifteen characteristics of love perhaps the most difficult is that love keeps no record of the wrong. I have used this verse in scores of weddings reminding the couple that it is only through God's Holy Spirit living in them that they can fulfill this command.

A husband and wife were "fighting" until finally the husband said, "I wish you would become hysterical and forget the historical." Every time they got into a spat she brought up his past. His past was forgiven by God since he confessed his sins. "As far as the east is from the west, so far has He removed our transgressions from us" (Psalm 103:12 AMP). "Their sins and their lawbreaking I will remember no more" or "I will remember their deeds of unrighteousness no more" (Heb. 8:12 and 10:17 AMP). That is good news! (I John 1:9).

Father, enable me to remember to forgive and forget the mistakes and sins of others. I choose to love them as you love and forgive me. Amen.

April 7

Dandelions

I Corinthians 9:21

"When I am with the Gentiles who do not have the Jewish law, I fit in with them as much as I can. In this way, I gain their confidence and bring them to Christ. But I do not discard the law of God; I obey the law of Christ . . . I try to find common ground with everyone so that I might bring them to Christ. I do all this to spread the Good News, and in doing so I enjoy its blessings" (I Cor. 9:21-23 NLT).

Find common ground with those around you to win their respect. Jesus identified with rich people as well as those who were poor or shunned by others. He knew what it was to be a refugee and homeless. (Matt. 2:13-23 and 8:20).

The other day I was in the home of a pastor. He was lamenting the fact that he tried to relate to his neighbors but they were not receptive or even hospitable. One would not come to the door and yet he and his wife tried to take gifts to them. Before I entered his house I was very conscious of the dandelions with their tall seed heads growing profusely throughout his lawn. All the neighbors' lawns were basically free of weeds and very well manicured.

Chatting later in the evening he commented that he waits to mow his grass until it is worthwhile. Why mow so often? I have little question in my mind that his weedy, overgrown lawn affected his witness to his neighbors.

When Paul writes that we become all things to all people so we can by all means save some he was saying that we make every effort not to offend people. In this pastor's context a well kept lawn is important to gain the respect of his neighbors. They will not hear the Good News of the Gospel from him until they respect him.

Paul writes, "I'd be more than happy to empty my pockets, even mortgage my life, for your good" (II Cor. 12:15 Msg.). I am obligated to everyone I meet. (Ro. 1:14).

Lord help me to be sensitive to cultural differences so I can share the Good News to everyone I meet. Amen.

Enoch Walked With God

Genesis 5:24

"When Enoch was sixty-five years old, he had Methuselah. Enoch walked steadily with God. After he had Methuselah, he lived another 300 years, having more sons and daughters. Enoch lived a total of 365 years. Enoch walked steadily with God. And then one day he was simply gone: God took him" (Genesis 5:21-24 Msg.).

The Amplified Bible reads that Enoch walked in habitual fellowship with God.

It's interesting that Enoch went to heaven at a young age. Of the deaths recorded in this chapter seven lived over nine hundred years, one other died at age seven hundred seventy-seven. Enoch was taken by God at the young age of three hundred sixty-five. Although I cannot be certain I believe the Lord took him because of the increasing evil in the world at that time. (Jude 14-16). Genesis 6:1-3 informs us that because of the evil in the earth God shortened the life span to one hundred twenty years.

Paul informs us that if we partake of the communion service, unworthily, not honoring the body of Christ, we are eating and drinking God's judgment upon ourselves. That is why many of you are weak and sick and some have even died" (I Cor. 11:29-30 NLT).

God may choose to shorten one's life to relieve their pain because of a sinful culture as in Enoch's situation. (Read Lot's situation as described in Second Peter 2:7-8). Or, he may shorten people's lives because of their sinful practices.

As we pray and witness remember the principle Paul gives in Galatians 6:7 NLT: "Don't be misled. Remember that you can't ignore God and get away with it. You will always reap what you sow!" Jude writes: "Show mercy to those whose faith is wavering. Rescue others by snatching them from the flames of judgment. There are still others to whom you need to show mercy, but be careful that you aren't contaminated by their sins" (Jude 22-23 NLT).

Lord, I want to walk with you continually like Enoch. Amen.

April 9

Cracked Pots

II Corinthians 4:7

"We have this treasure in jars of clay to show that this all surpassing power is from God and not from us" (II Cor. 4:7). It's amazing that God uses us whether clay jars or cracked pots. We are God's channel of his treasure to the world. The treasure is the Good News that Christ is the light of the world.

"Our Message is not about ourselves; we're proclaiming Jesus Christ, the Master. All we are is messengers, errand runners from Jesus for you. It started when God said, 'Light up the darkness!' and our lives filled up with light as we saw and understood God in the face of Christ, all bright and beautiful. If you only look at us, you might well miss the brightness. We carry this precious Message around in the unadorned clay pots of our ordinary lives. That's to prevent anyone from confusing God's incomparable power with us. As it is, there's not much chance of that. You know for yourselves that we're not much to look at. We've been surrounded and battered by troubles, but we're not demoralized; we're not sure what to do, but we know that God knows what to do; we've been spiritually terrorized but God hasn't left our side; we've been thrown down, but we haven't broken. What they did to Jesus, they do to us—trial and torture, mockery and murder; what Jesus did among them, he does in us—he lives! Our lives are at constant risk for Jesus' sake, which makes Jesus' life all the more evident in us. While we're going through the worst, you're getting in on the best" (II Cor. 4:5-12 Msg.).

We are messengers, errand runners for Jesus! I love that. It's not about us. It's about him. At Capital Christian Fellowship where I pastored I frequently had the congregation repeat: "It's not about me, it's not about you, it's all about Jesus!"

Let's remember it's not about us but God chooses to use us as his instruments. We are his beloved allowing the all surpassing power of God to flow from our lives.

Lord, use me, clay pot that I am. Thanks for the privilege of being a messenger of your Good News. Amen.

Vision

Proverbs 29:18

"Without A Vision the People Perish" (Prov. 29:18 KJV). "Where there is no revelation, the people cast off restraint; but blessed are those who keep God's law" (Prov. 29:18 NIV). This is why America is perishing. "If people can't see what God is doing they stumble all over themselves. But when they obey his laws they are most blessed" (Msg.).

Can you imagine a ship in the ocean drifting alone without a destination? Many people are in the midst of the ocean of life but have no destination, no direction, no vision, and no eternal goals. They live for themselves, seeking fulfillment but never finding it.

Many Christians including pastors are maintenance oriented. They are content year after year with a plateaued or declining congregation even though new people move into their community each month. Even though a U-Haul just unloaded its contents they have no motivation to welcome the new family or invite them to church. It seems that often pastors and church members are content as long as the church bills are paid. With this lethargic and visionless attitude Christians are not being the salt, light or leaven for Jesus. (Matt. 5:13-16).

You receive your vision from the Lord. His Holy Spirit places a desire in your heart to know him, serve him and proclaim him. You pray, you search the word, and seek him. You ask God for eyes to see and for your heart to discover his will for you. His will becomes your passion.

Your vision will line up with your gifts. Jesus gifted every one. (Ro. 12:3-6 and I Cor. 12). He expects you to develop your gifts to serve others. (I Peter 4:10). God has a specific work for everyone. (Eph. 2:10). We have a responsibility to discover our ministry, attend to it and walk in it. As we do this we become a blessing to others.

Lord, enable me to see what you are doing and work with you in fulfilling your vision bearing fruit for you. Amen.

April 11

Preaching or Teaching?

Acts 8:4

"The believers who had fled Jerusalem went everywhere preaching the Good News about Jesus" (Acts 8:4 NLT).

Most church people desire for their pastor to be a preacher rather than a teacher. As Paul lists the gifts that build up the church he doesn't list the gift of "preacher" but apostles, prophets, evangelists, pastors and teachers. (Eph. 4:11). Preaching in the New Testament is to persons who have not yet responded to the Christian faith. Once we become followers of Jesus we need teachers. Whenever the word "preach" is used in the New Testament it implies the presentation of the Gospel, the Good News which is mainly for prebelievers.

One reason our churches are anemic is that we want preachers rather than teachers. Teachers give lessons and expect accountability. If people are not growing, teachers are frustrated. They feel they are not doing their job. It's easier for Christians to listen to preaching and go home and forget about the message because there is no accountability. They say, "I believe in Jesus." James says the devil believes in Jesus too. (2:19). Belief must affect our life as the Amplified Bible reads: "trust in, cling to and rely on Jesus." Our lack of accountability fits well with our American individuality focused culture: "No one will tell me what to do." Until teaching becomes our preferred style we will have anemic Christians, not disciples.

This is why accountability groups, whether in small congregations or in mega churches are important. "You can only go so far in rows—Jesus used circles." In other words Jesus and the early church had face to face encounters with their house church structure where there was more accountability. Around the world where disciples are being formed they focus on teaching.

Since Jesus sends each of us (John 17:18 and 20:21) we first preach, i.e. share the Good News, and then as people respond, we teach, i.e. make disciples.

Lord, help me be to not only share the Good News but to make disciples. (Matt. 28:18-20). Amen.

Resurrection Power

Ephesians 1:18-23, 2:6

Paul prays that the Ephesians will know Christ better. Then he writes: "I pray also that the eyes of your heart may be enlightened in order that you may know the hope to which he has called you, the riches of his glorious inheritance in the saints, and his incomparable great power for us who believe. That power is like the working of his mighty strength, which he exerted in Christ when he raised him from the dead and seated him at his right hand in the heavenly realms, far above all rule and authority, power and dominion, and every title that can be given, not only in the present age but also in the one to come. And God placed all things under his feet and appointed him to be head over everything for the church which is his body, the fullness of him who fills everything in every way" (Eph. 1:18-23).

There is absolutely nothing that can defeat Christ. We are seated beside him in a position of authority. I have many favorite verses but I think Ephesians 2:6 means more to me than any other in my daily walk with Jesus. "He raised us up together with Him and made us sit down together—giving us joint seating with Him—in the heavenly sphere [by virtue of our being] in Christ Jesus, the Messiah, the Anointed One" (Eph. 2:6 AMP).

In that seat beside Jesus you have incomparable great power—even resurrection power. Are your eyes open to see where you are sitting? Are you daily operating from that perspective? If you are there is no need for despair. There is no need for worry. There is no need to be shy about sharing your faith.

Pray with Paul that the eyes of your heart will be open to see your position of being seated with Christ—to make his power applicable to you in your experience. The Holy Spirit did it for Paul and he will do it for you as you believe and act upon it.

Lord Jesus, you tell me that your incomparable great power is for me. Enable me to believe and operate from that position of security, confidence and boldness. Amen.

April 13
Anxious or Fearful

Isaiah 41:10

People are anxious. Fear is easier to deal with than anxiety. Fear has an enemy we can identify. Anxiety is a general feeling of uncertainty, insecurity, and vagueness that we can't identify.

Peace is the opposite of anxiety. Jesus said, "Peace I leave with you; my peace I give you. I do not give to you as the world gives. Do not let your hearts be troubled and do not be afraid" (John 14:27). The Holy Spirit brings peace. (Gal. 5:22). "You will keep in perfect peace him whose mind is steadfast because he trusts in you" (Isaiah 26:3). "Don't worry about anything; instead, pray about everything. Tell God what you need and thank him for all he has done. Then you will experience God's peace" (Phil. 4:6-7).

"Do not fear, for I am with you; do not be dismayed, (anxious) for I am your God I will strengthen you and help you, I will uphold you with my righteous right hand" (Isaiah 41:10). Our fears come from lack of faith in God.

It's been stated that there are 365 "Fear Nots" in the Bible; one for each day of the year. But there are some things we must fear. We must reverence God. "Fear God and keep his commandments, for God will bring every deed into judgment, including every hidden thing, whether it is good or evil" (Ecclesiastes 12:13-14). "This is love for God: to obey his commands. And his commands are not burdensome" (I John 5:3). "There is no fear in love. But perfect love drives out fear, because fear has to do with punishment. The one who fears is not made perfect in love" (I John 4:18).

For those who live with anxiety Jesus says, "Come to me, all you who are weary and burdened, and I will give your rest. Take my yoke upon you and learn from me, for I am gentle and humble in heart, and you will find rest for your souls. For my yoke is easy and my burden is light" (Matt. 11:28-29).

Father, help me to cast all my fears and anxieties on you because you care for me. (I Peter 5:7). Amen.

Ambassadors

II Corinthians 5:20

"We are . . . Christ's ambassadors, as though God were making his appeal through us. We implore you on Christ's behalf: Be reconciled to God" (II Cor. 5:20).

Ambassadors are privileged people. The greater the dignitary you represent the more prestigious the position. We are ambassadors of the King of Kings, who is "far above any ruler or authority or power or leader or anything else in this world or in the world to come" (Eph. 1:21 NLT). What an honor!

Do we see our privileged position as an honor? Too often Christians see it as a burden. Someone said: Many Christians would rather have a root canal than share their faith. Why is that? Is it because we feel we are invading someone's private realm? Is it because we do not really believe we are ambassadors? Is it because we are not excited about what Jesus has done for us? How can we not be excited when we read the next verse: "God made Jesus who had no sin to be sin for us, so that in him we might become the righteousness of God" (I Cor. 5:21).

When I invited Jesus into my life I made an exchange—my sin for his righteousness and his righteousness for my sin. He takes my worthless sin and gives me something of indescribable worth. How grateful I am for his exchange. Being in Jesus is more than a changed life it is an exchanged life, i.e. Jesus living in us.

You are an instrument he uses to change the eternal destiny of others. Jesus has no plan "B." When he left he commissioned you to be his disciple maker.

It's a joy to set aside our own desires and walk in the desires of the one we represent. He promises us great rewards. (Matt. 10:41-42). "When I am with those who are oppressed, I share their oppression so that I might bring them to Christ. Yes I try to find common ground with everyone so that I might bring them to Christ. I do all this to spread the Good News, and in doing so, I enjoy its blessings" (I Cor. 9:22-23 NLT).

Lord, enable me to be your faithful ambassador. Amen.

For Such a Time as This

Esther 4:14

"Who can say but that you have been elevated to the palace for just such a time as this?" (Esther 4:14b NLT). She stood alone and saved her nation. She said, "If I perish I perish" (Esther 4:16). If we are faithful to Jesus there will be times when we need to stand alone.

Do you believe in God's providence? God knows your thoughts, where you are, what you do, what you are going to say even before you say it. (Psalm 139:1-4). God will use you as his instrument in the place where you are if you let him control your life. In that place you will find complete fulfillment. I'm sure Esther did not want to be where she was—a Jew in the palace of a Gentile King. Her life was in grave danger. But God used her to save her people.

Jesus underscores this, "If you remain in me and I in you, you will bear much fruit ... You did not choose me, but I chose you and appointed you to go and bear fruit—fruit that will last ..." (John 15:5, 16). Peter says, "You are a chosen people ... God's holy nation, his very own possession. This is so you can show others the goodness of God, for he called you out of the darkness into his wonderful light" (I Peter 2:9 NLT).

The Message Bible states: "You are the ones chosen by God chosen for the high calling of priestly work, chosen to be a holy people, God's instruments to do his work and speak out for him, to tell others of the night-and-day difference he made for you—from nothing to something, from rejected to accepted."

Is Jesus changing your life? If so, share your story. If you pray in the morning for him to guide you and cultivate the habit of conversing with him throughout the day you will find God opening the door to share his love. The Holy Spirit will use you as his tool of blessing both in your words and in your actions. You'll find yourself often serving others by going the second mile. Out of you will flow rivers of living water to the thirsty souls you meet. Claim his presence and his power each morning to stand alone.

Lord, enable me like Esther to stand alone. Amen.

Set Your Heart on Things Above

Colossians 3:1-3

Sometimes Christians are accused of being so heavenly minded they are no earthly good. "Since you have been raised with Christ, set your hearts on things above, where Christ is seated at the right hand of God. Set your minds on things above, not on earthly things. For you died, and your life is now hidden with Christ in God" (Col. 3:1-3).

"Don't shuffle along, eyes to the ground, absorbed with the things right in front of you. Look up, and be alert to what is going on around Christ—that's where the action is. See things from his perspective. Your old life is dead. Your new life, which is your real life—even though invisible to spectators—is with Christ in God. He is your life" (Col. 3:1-3 Msg.). "Anyone united with Christ gets a fresh start, is created new. The old self has gone, the new has come!" (II Cor. 5:17 Msg.).

As followers of Jesus we have the mind of Christ. (II Cor. 2:16). "Do not be conformed any longer to the pattern of this world, but be transformed by the renewing of your mind. Then you will be able to test and approve what God's will is—his good, pleasing and perfect will" (Ro. 12:2). Self-centered goals go out the window, it's all about him. "Don't think only about your own affairs but be interested in others and what they are doing" (Phil. 2:5 NLT).

"I am crucified with Christ and I no longer live, but Christ lives in me" (Gal. 2:20). Christ's life, lived through us is the most exciting life we can have. No more worries—he's in charge, no more shame over our sins. He cares for the sparrows he will certainly take care of us. (Matt. 6:25-34). "The old way of life was nailed to the Cross with Christ, a decisive end to that sin-miserable life" (Ro. 6:6 Msg.).

Jesus does not merely sympathize with us. He enters into our life. He identifies with us. He is our very life. (Col. 3:1).

Lord, enable me to live for things that are eternal, those things that honor and please you. Amen.

April 17
Start Where You Blew It
Acts 1:8

"You will receive power when the Holy Spirit comes on you; and you will be my witnesses in Jerusalem . . ." (Acts 1:8). We begin in Jerusalem i.e. at home. A church leader "must manage his own family well, with children who respect and obey him. For if a man cannot manage his own household how can he take care of God's church?" (I Tim. 3:5 NLT).

Just a few weeks before going to the cross the disciples had denied Jesus. Jesus is saying go back to where you made your biggest mistake, back to where you blew it. Go back to where they really know you.

If you yelled at your spouse when you're expecting people for a back-yard cookout and the neighbor heard you, ask God to give you courage to go to the neighbor and say, "You heard me yell at my spouse. I blew it. I asked her to forgive me. Things are OK again." God can use your confession. The neighbor will think these people are different but real. Transparency and vulnerability are the materials the Holy Spirit will use to bring conviction.

The woman at the well went back home and the whole village responded. The man among the tombs met Jesus and wanted to go with him but Jesus said, "Go home to your family and tell them how much the Lord has done for you" (Mark 5:19b-20). They knew him in the surrounding towns. That's where he was most effective.

Levi invited his peers to a banquet when he met Jesus. They knew his past life as a tax collector. He risked ridicule from those who knew him but God used him in a mighty way. People need to connect with you before you can bring them to Jesus. Jesus said, "Anyone who welcomes you is welcoming me" (Matt. 10:40 NLT).

Jesus will use you even when you blow it. Model God's forgiveness to your family and others by your willingness to admit your mistakes and ask for forgiveness.

Lord, help be to be vulnerable and transparent so others see you in me. Amen.

Now!

Ephesians 2:12-22

Before we were Christians we were without hope and without God in the world. But NOW through Jesus' blood we are brought into God's family. The walls of hostility are gone. Take the walls down between you and your extended family. Remove the walls that divide your church members, remove the walls between you and Christians who don't agree with you, between you and your unfriendly neighbor, between you and the enemies of our nation.

"If it is possible, as far as it depends on you, live at peace with everyone. Do not take revenge . . . 'It is mine to avenge, I will repay,' says the Lord. On the contrary, If your enemy is hungry, feed him; if he is thirsty, give him something to drink . . . Do not be overcome with evil, but overcome evil with good" (Ro. 12:18-21).

"Remember . . . you were separate from Christ . . . , without hope and without God in the world. But now in Christ Jesus you who once were far away have been brought near, through the blood of Christ. For he himself is our peace, who has made the two one and has destroyed the barrier, the dividing wall of hostility . . . His purpose was to create in himself one new man out of the two, thus making peace, and in this one body to reconcile both of them to God through the cross, by which he put to death their hostility. He came and preached peace to you who were far away and peace to those who were near. For through him we both have access to the Father by one Spirit" (Eph. 2:12-18).

Jesus said, "Blessed are the peacemakers" (Matthew 5:9). "Peacemakers" remove walls. "Peacekeepers" may keep the walls but we are to be proactive and remove walls. Jesus says, "If you enter your place of worship and . . . remember a grudge a friend has against you, abandon your offering, leave immediately, go to this friend and make things right. Then . . . come back and work things out with God" (Matt. 5:23-24 Msg.).

Lord, enable me to remove walls in my family, workplace, church and community. Amen.

Share Your "Bread" with the Hungry

II Kings 7:3-10

King Benhadad of Aram mobilized his army and surrounded Samaria. The result was a great famine in Samaria. Four lepers sat at the entrance of the city gates. They said, "Why should we sit here waiting to die? We'll starve here. Let's surrender to the Arameans. If they let us live, great. But if they kill us, we would have died anyway." God caused the army to flee. They ate and drank. They found silver and gold and hid it in the ground. Finally, the lepers said to each other, "This is not right. This is wonderful news, and we aren't sharing it with anyone! If we wait until morning, some terrible calamity will certainly fall upon us. Come on, let's go back and tell the people at the palace." So they went back to the city and told the gatekeeper what had happened. (II Kings 7:3-10a, Free Translation).

The lepers shared the good news! We have the Bread of Life. People are starving for the Bread of Life. Will we share this Bread with them?

Our son, Chet introduced his message at LifeBridge Church saying, "My desire is that we represent Jesus proudly and well, so others can experience the awesome privilege of becoming part of God's family. His greatest, most urgent message for us is to communicate his Good News, joyfully, persuasively and effectively. It's incredible that we are partners with God, we can witness to new life in Jesus, coming along-side others so that, by his grace, we can not only dramatically change people right here and now today, but make the difference in where and how they will spend eternity. There is no greater call, privilege or opportunity."

If you had the cure for cancer and did not share it you would be guilty of a crime. Our Good News cures the cancer of sin. If all you have gained from your salvation is something you hold onto without passing it on, then it is not Good News. God's Good News is meant to be shared with others.

Lord, enable me to share the Bread of Life with the starving people. Amen.

Satan's Greatest Fear

I John 4:4

Satan's greatest fear is that you believe he is real and that you know Jesus who lives in you is more powerful than Satan. "God's Spirit is in you and is more powerful than the one that is in the world" (I John 4:4 CEV).

"Submit yourselves . . . to God. Resist the devil, and he will flee from you. Come near to God and he will come near to you" (James 4:7-8a). Johnny's parents had to be away for a few minutes so they said to their son, "Don't go across the street to play with Joe. We'll be back soon." They returned and saw he disobeyed. When questioned Johnny said, "Satan pulled on one leg and God on the other but Satan pulled harder."

Satan whispers to you: "You can't control your tongue. You know you hate your brother. You worry continually. You are bound to fail. You are jealous and full of pride. You'll never amount to anything."

How do we resist the devil so he flees from us? 1. Admit you have a problem you cannot overcome on your own. Repent and confess your need of the Lord's help. 2. State you faith in God's almighty power. 3. Recognize God lives in you in the person of his Holy Spirit. He's greater than any problem. (I John 4:4). 4. Claim the promise: "God is working in you giving you the desire to obey him and the power to do what pleases him" (Phil 2:13 NLT). 5. Claim God's power and resolve in your heart to walk in obedience. 6. Thank God for his saving grace. 7. Ask others to pray for you and share with them the joy of victory.

"God is faithful. He will keep the temptation from becoming so strong that you can't stand up against it. When you are tempted, he will show you a way out so that you will not give into it" (I Cor. 10:13 NLT).

Father, thank you for defeating Satan. Thank you for giving me your Holy Spirit who is greater than any temptation I will face. Thank you for giving me the will to obey and the power to overcome. Amen.

Seeing God's Perspective

II Kings 6

The King of Aram was constantly frustrated because everywhere he planned to attack, Israel was already armed for battle. The King thought there were traitors in his ranks never realizing the God of Israel was giving Elisha inside information. The King sent a great army to capture Elisha. When Elisha's servant got up early the next morning he saw this huge army. "Ah, my Lord, what will we do now?" he cried out to Elisha. "Don't be afraid!" Elisha told him, "For there are more on our side than on theirs!" Then Elisha prayed, "O Lord, open my servant's eyes and let him see!" "The Lord opened his servant's eyes, and when he looked up, he saw that the hillside around Elisha was filled with horses and chariots of fire" (II Kings 6:15-17 NLT).

Billy Graham said this is one of the most encouraging stories in the Bible. When it feels like everyone is against you, look to the Lord. As God's children he provides us with a special insight and knowledge into life's dilemmas. God wants to give us a new perspective. Pray faith prayers asking God to open your spiritual eyes to see what he sees. Seeing from God's perspective will make all the difference.

We are often like the two disciples on the seven-mile walk to Emmaus after Jesus had arisen from the grave. They were in grief. Jesus came and walked with them but they did not recognize him. He explained to them the writing of Moses and all the prophets how it was clearly stated that the Messiah would suffer all these things before he entered into his glory. "They begged him to stay the night with them, since it was getting late. So he went home with them. As they sat down to eat, he took a small loaf of bread, asked God's blessing on it, broke it, and gave it to them. Suddenly their eyes were opened, and they recognized him" (Luke 24:29-31 NLT).

Pray with David, "Open my eyes to see the wonderful truths in your law" (Ps. 119:18 NLT).

Lord, open my eyes to see things from your perspective. Amen.

Seed Sowers

Matthew 13:8

"Some seeds fell on fertile soil and produced a crop that was thirty, sixty and even a hundred times as much as had been planted" (Matt. 13:8 NLT).

Helen, my wife, spends time with our neighbors showing love and sharing the difference Jesus makes in her life. However she felt checked by the Holy Spirit that now was not the time to confront one neighbor concerning her relationship with God. My wife found out later that someone had knocked on the neighbor's door and asked if she was a Christian. She said, "No." He told her she was going to hell. She said, "When I heard that a preacher was moving across the street I was so angry. But you are different. No matter what I say you accept me." Over the next weeks she and her family came to our church and became new creations in Christ Jesus. They have moved out of state but she remains in contact with Helen forty years later.

Paul writes: "Put into action God's saving work in your lives, obeying God with deep reverence and fear. For God is working in you, giving you the desire to obey him and the power to do what pleases him . . . Do everything without complaining or arguing, so that you may become blameless and pure, children of God without fault in a crooked and depraved generation, in which you shine like stars in the universe as you hold out the word of life" (Phil. 2:12-14 NLT).

The late Richard Halverson, Chaplain of our United States Senate was a seed sower. in the benediction for the U.S. Senate he prayed: "You go nowhere by accident. Wherever you go, God is sending you there. Wherever you are, God has put your there. He has a purpose in you being there. Christ, who indwells you, has something He wants to do through you wherever you are. Believe this and go in His grace and love and power."

May this prayer be implemented in our government from he president to our town councils. May Christians be seed sowers wherever they find themselves.

Enable me to be a seed sower today. Amen.

April 23

I Can't Speak

Exodus 3:11

God appeared to Moses in the burning bush. Moses said to God, "Who am I that I should go to Pharaoh and bring the Israelites out of Egypt?" (Exodus 3:11). God's response was that he would be with Moses and give him the ability to perform signs so Pharaoh would be convinced. "Moses said to the Lord, 'Pardon your servant, Lord. I have never been eloquent neither in the past nor since you have spoken to your servant. I am slow of speech and tongue . . . Please send somebody else'" (Exodus 4:10 & 13, 6:12).

The word of the Lord came to Jeremiah calling him to be a prophet to the nations. He said, "Ah, Sovereign Lord, I do not know how to speak; I am only a child . . ." The Lord responded, "You must go to everyone I send you" (Jer. 1:3-7).

Elijah had experienced a mighty victory over Baal, Queen Jezebel's god. In a frenzy of rage Jezebel retaliated with a death sentence for Elijah to be carried out within twenty-four hours. In despair Elijah says in essence, "I have had enough, Lord, let me die" (I Kings 19:4 & 10).

As a youth I stuttered. How could I preach with stammering speech? Yet God seemed to be saying, "I want you to prepare to become a pastor." While my deliverance from stuttering coupled with a poor self-image took many years to overcome, God was faithful. As in the Biblical examples there were many times I was tested and still am tested. But God who calls, also promises to equip us for the task. Sometimes God will remove the physical obstacles but he promises to be with us always.

Jesus reminds us that we are all called. God calls you and sends you to speak for him. (John 17:18 and 20:21). Say, "Yes Lord, I am willing to do whatever you say."

Lord, I thank you for calling me. Enable me to be a faithful witness for you. Amen.

Enthusiasm

Romans 12:11-12

Enthusiasm translated from the Greek simply means: "In" "God" = in God. "Never be lacking in zeal, but keep your spiritual fervor, (be enthusiastic), serving the Lord. Be joyful in hope" (Ro. 12:11-12a).

As Christians grow older many seem to lose their enthusiasm. Paul writes to Timothy a shy young pastor who needed encouragement: "I remind you to fan into flame the gift of God which is in you . . . For God did not give us a spirit of timidity, but a spirit of power, of love, and of self-discipline" (II Tim. 1:6-7). The Message reads: "The gift of ministry you received—keep that ablaze! God doesn't want us to be shy with his gifts, but bold and loving and sensible."

To Christians at Ephesus, a church with thirty or more years of history, Jesus says, "You have lost your first love" (Rev. 2:4). To the church at Laodicea: "You are neither cold nor hot, I wish you were either one or the other! So, because you are lukewarm . . . I am about to spit you out of my mouth" (Rev. 3:15-16). Jesus says, "Because of the increase of wickedness, the love of most will grow cold" (Matt. 24:12).

How do we move from cold to hot? We come back to the cross. Jesus is the source of life. We confess our sins. He forgives and heals us. (I John 1:9). Even the lukewarm, indifferent, and discouraged persons will be transformed into his likeness. (Ro. 8:29).

We fight the good fight of faith. (I Tim. 6:12). We bring every thought into obedience to Christ. (II Cor. 10:5). We come to Jesus and drink. He said, "If anyone thirsts, let him come to me and drink. Rivers of living water will brim and spill out of the depths of anyone who believes in me this way" (John 7:37-38 Msg.).

Father, forgive me for my lack of zeal. I come to you thirsty. I drink of you knowing you give living water that transforms me from indifference to an enthusiastic servant. Amen.

April 25

You Can Hear His Voice

John 10:3-4

"The gatekeeper opens the gate for the shepherd, and the sheep hear his voice and come to him. He calls his own sheep by name and leads them out. After he has gathered his own flock he walks ahead of them, and they follow him because they recognize his voice . . ." (John 10:3-4, 27 NLT).

Many times Jesus said, "He who has ears [to hear], let him be listening and consider and perceive and comprehend by hearing" (Matt. 13:9 AMP). The Message reads: "Are you listening to me? Really listening?"

"Here I am! I stand at the door and knock. If anyone hears my voice and opens the door, I will come in and eat with him, and he with me" (Rev. 3:20). The church at Laodicea became lukewarm. They said, "I have acquired wealth and do not need a thing. Jesus said, 'But you do not realize that you are wretched, pitiful, poor, blind and naked'" (Rev. 3:17). They were not tuned into the voice of God.

God directed Elijah to stand before the mountain. The Lord passed by in the windstorm, the earthquake and the fire but after the fire there was a gentle whisper. (I Kings 19:11-12 NLT). Quiet yourself so you can hear God's whisper. God gave us two ears and one mouth. That should tell us something. We don't learn when we're talking unless God is speaking through us.

God speaks primarily through his word. Five minutes a day will not give you time to quiet your heart to hear his still small voice. It takes meditation time, concentration and devotion to hear rather than a mere rushing into God's presence and exiting quickly. "Be silent and know that I am God" (Ps. 46:10 NLT). Surveys indicate that we spend more than three hours a day viewing TV and two hours on our Iphones and the internet. If we fill our minds with trivia we will miss God's voice.

God also speaks through nature. As you see his beauty thank him. "Thanks" opens your ears since your mind is on God not yourself.

Father, I will live in your presence and listen for your voice. Amen.

Tears Are Liquid Prayers

Hebrews 5:7

"While Jesus was here on earth, he offered prayers and pleadings, with a loud cry and tears, to the one who could deliver him out of death. And God heard his prayers because of his reverence for God" (Heb. 5:7 NLT).

"Remember that for three years I never stopped warning each of you night and day with tears" (Acts 20:31). "I am in the pains of childbirth until Christ is formed in you (Gal. 4:19). "I wrote . . . in great anguish, with a troubled heart and many tears. I didn't want to grieve you, but I wanted to let you know how much love I have for you" (II Cor. 2:4 NLT). This is the same Paul that sang hymns in prison and wrote, "Rejoice in the Lord always" (Phil. 4:4). David who suffered much reminds us that in "God's presence is fullness of joy" (Ps. 16:11).

"I have done the Lord's work humbly—yes, and with tears" (Acts 20:19 NLT). "My heart is filled with bitter sorrow and unending grief, for my people, my Jewish brothers and sisters. I would be willing to be forever cursed—cut off from Christ!—if that would save them" (Ro. 9:2-3 NLT).

"Those who sow in tears will reap with songs of joy. He who goes out weeping carrying seed to sow, will return with songs of joy, carrying sheaves with him" (Ps. 126:5-6).

Jesus wept over Jerusalem. (Luke 19:41). Have we wept before the Lord for our lost friends? I spoke at a church where there was paper tissues at the end of each row of chairs. That's extreme but if we have passion like Jesus and Paul there will be tears.

Surveys say eighty percent of intercessors are women. Have we men lost our passion? Are we so Western that we have buried our emotions?

God is moved by our tears: "You keep track of all my sorrows. You have collected all my tears in your bottle. You have recorded each one in your book" (Ps. 56:8 NLT).

Thank you Lord for your joy in me. (John 15:11). Amen.

April 27

Never Stop Praying

First Thessalonians 5:17

"Pray continually" (NIV). "Keep on praying" (NLT). "Pray at all times" (Msg.). (I Thess. 5:17). "Look to the Lord . . . seek his face always" (I Chronicles 16:11).

Jesus said, "Always pray and do not give up" (Luke 18:1). "Devote yourselves to prayer, being watchful and thankful" (Col. 4:2). Friends love to spend time together. Jesus is our best friend. F.B. Meyer believed that "the greatest tragedy of life is not unanswered prayer, but unoffered prayer."

The early church met daily and was devoted to prayer. (Acts 2:42, 46). Jesus said, "My house shall be a house of prayer" (Mark 11:19).

Pray for the Spirit to open the mind of your heart as you read and study God's Word. "Call to me and I will show you great and mighty things" (Jer. 33:3).

We hear God's voice through the guidance of the Holy Spirit. The Spirit would not allow Paul to preach in Asia or Bithynia. (Ac. 16:6-7). Then Paul had a vision of a Macedonian begging him to come. (v. 9; also 20:22-23). Isaiah prophesied, "Whether you turn to the right or to the left, your ears will hear a voice . . . , saying, 'This is the way; walk in it'" (Is. 30:21).

Prayer requires faith. As we exercise our faith, prayer becomes more natural. Peter commands us to pray for kings and all in authority. (I Tim 2:1-3). Often our faith is too small to believe our prayers will make a difference. Do you pray for missionaries, for the refugees and others who live and suffer under repressive governments? It's easier to pray when we learn that our friend has just received word she has terminal cancer because the need is obvious. It is easier for most Christians to pray for physical healing than to pray for the salvation of their lost neighbors. We all know which is more important.

Lord, help me to make prayer as natural as breathing. Amen.

Trials Make You Partners with Jesus

I Peter 4:12-13

"Do not be surprised at the fiery trials you are going through . . . Be glad about trials because trials will make you partners with Christ in his suffering, and afterwards you will have the wonderful joy of sharing his glory . . ." (I Peter 4:12-13 NLT).

Paul's desire was that he might know Christ and the power of the resurrection and the fellowship of his suffering becoming like him in his death. (Phil. 3:10). Fellowship is positive. Suffering too can be positive as we partner with Jesus through the suffering.

"We continue to shout our praise even when we're hemmed in with troubles, because we know how troubles can develop passionate patience in us, and how that patience in turn forges the tempered steel of virtue, keeping us alert for whatever God will do next. We can't round up enough containers to hold everything God generously pours into our lives through the Holy Spirit" (Ro. 5:3-5 Msg.).

Sometimes we need to let people suffer. God did not run after the prodigal son. He did go after the lost sheep. The prodigal was rebellious; the lost sheep was not mature enough to understand the consequences of wandering off. Sometimes the shepherd breaks the leg of a sheep that is rebellious so they learn to follow the shepherd. Often God allows us to suffer to teach us to trust him.

"Although Jesus was God's Son, he learned trusting obedience by what he suffered" (Heb. 5:8 Msg.). We are granted to suffer for Christ. (Phil. 1:29). Suffering is as much a gift as trusting. (Msg.).

"In this all-out match against sin, others have suffered far worse than you, to say nothing of what Jesus went thorough—all the bloodshed! So don't feel sorry for yourselves. Or have you forgotten how good parents treat children, and that God regards you as his children? . . . Don't be crushed by God's discipline. It's the child he loves that he disciplines, the child he embraces, he also corrects" (Heb. 12:4-6 Msg.).

Lord, help me to remember trials are meant to help me become more like you. Amen.

God Will Give You a New Name

Revelation 2:17

If you don't like your name now you will like the one God gives you for eternity. (Rev. 2:17). Before Jesus was born he was named Jesus, meaning "God saves" (Matt. 1:21).

Our name gives us an identity. God named the trillions of stars. (Ps. 147:4). He had Adam name the animals. When someone calls us by name we know they have made an effort to remember us. One particular chain of restaurants makes it a point to call its customers by name. The waiter or waitress says, "My name is . . . and he or she writes their name so the customer can see it. Then they turn the paper and ask your name and write it so they can see it. Throughout the meal they call you by name indicating they care.

Jesus didn't say, "Hey you, come follow me." He called the disciples by name. He knew us before we were born. (Psalm 139:13).

A family from Africa came to church regularly for more than a year but I could not persuade them to become members although they had a definite faith in Jesus. Finally in the privacy of their home they revealed to me their problem. "When you are baptized you must have a new name. We can't decide on our names." In their culture you received a new name at baptism.

A new name means you have a new identity. Your name affects the way you see yourself, the way you act and live. Those who are faithful followers of Jesus have their names written in the book of life. (Rev. 3:5)

One practice that will help you remember people's names is to repeat their name as soon as it is said and throughout the conversation. This helps you remember their name.

Lord, you know my name. Enable me to love people and remember their name. Amen.

Positive People

I Corinthians 13:7

"Love never gives up, never loses faith, is always hopeful, and endures through every circumstance" (I Cor.13:7 NLT). This week I met an old friend who put a positive twist on everything. I left with a spring in my step and a smile on my face.

God is a positive God. Of all the trees in the Garden only one was forbidden. Even the Ten Commandments begin with the positive affirmation: "I am the LORD your God, who rescued you from slavery in Egypt" (Exodus 20:1 NLT). This positive word was the first "commandment" for the Hebrew people. We number the commandments differently beginning with verse three which starts with the negative statement, i.e. "You shall not . . ."

In the New Testament Jesus states that the Old Testament is summed up in these words: "'You must love the Lord your God with all your heart, all your soul, and all your mind. . . . A second is equally important: 'Love your neighbor as yourself.' All the other commandments and all the demands of the prophets are based on these two commandments'" (Matt. 22:37-40 NLT). Jesus begins the Sermon on the Mount with nine ways to be blessed of God. (Matt. 5:3-12).

Paul began all his letters with the exception of Galatians by complementing the Christians. The Christian message is positive. The Gospel is Good News. Contrast this with the daily news on TV. The message of the early church, especially in the book of Acts, focuses more on the Resurrection than on the Cross of Christ. Of course there couldn't have been a Resurrection without the cross. Without the cross there is no forgiveness of sins.

From his prison cell Paul encourages you to think of things that are: "true and honorable and right . . . pure and lovely and admirable, excellent and worthy of praise" (Phil. 4:8 NLT). "In everything you do stay away from complaining and arguing" (Phil. 2:14 NLT).

Lord, thank you that you know my name. Enable me to remember the importance of calling people by name. Amen.

Slave—a Name of Honor

II Peter 1:1

The Greek word "doulos" is the word we translate servant or slave. The greatest men adopted this name as a title of honor: Moses (Deut. 34:35), Joshua (Josh. 24:19), David (II Sam. 3:18), and Paul (Ro. 1:1). James and Jude both begin their letter identifying themselves as slaves. The prophets are slaves of God. (Amos 3:7). We are Christ's slave. (Acts 2:18; II Tim. 2:24).

This means we are possessed by God. The slave has no rights. As servants or slaves we surrender everything to God. We have no time off, no vacation, and no leisure. Every moment is God's. The command of God is our only law.

"If any of you want to be my followers, you must forget about yourself. You must take up your cross each day and follow me. If you want to save your life, you will destroy it. But if you give up your life for me, you will save it. What will you gain, if you own the whole world but destroy yourself or waste your life? If you are ashamed of me and my message, the Son of Man will be ashamed of you when he comes in his glory and in the glory of his Father and the holy angels" (Luke 14:23-26 CEV).

In the days of slave auctions there was a slave of unusual physical build. When he was being auctioned the bidding kept going higher and higher. He was frightened to meet his new master. He thought he could never earn enough to cover his price. His new master greeted him with the words, "I have bought you to set you free!" Falling to his knees in gratitude he said, "I will gladly serve you as long as I live."

Jesus paid his all, his life for us. We are set free! We can have only one response. I will gladly service you as long as I live. It's an honor and a great privilege to serve the King of Kings with our heart, soul, mind and strength.

Jesus, thank you for the privilege of serving you. Amen.

Hunger and Thirst for Righteousness

Matthew 5:6

"Blessed are those who hunger and thirst for righteousness, for they shall be filled" (Matt. 5:6). "God blesses those who are hungry and thirsty for justice, for they will receive it in full" (NLT).

The Greek word "dikaiosune" is usually translated "righteous" but it can also be translated "justice." Jesus says we are to hunger and thirst for a right relationship with God and with others.

The hunger and thirst described here is the hunger of one starving for food and of one who will die unless he/she has water. Therefore Jesus is asking: "How much do you want righteousness or justice?" Do we want it as much as one wants it if they are starving or dying of thirst? Can you imagine what our world would be like if we desired righteousness and justice to that degree? There is so much injustice. Think of the poverty, the multitudes born in repressive governments, the millions born who are unwanted. Think of the two billion who have never heard the name of "Jesus" and have no hope.

If we long for righteousness and justice as Jesus desires, we'll work to bring injustice to an end in our world. There are about 4,000 scriptures encouraging us to not neglect the widow, the orphan, the immigrant or foreigner and the less fortunate. Think of Jesus' example as he identified with the lepers, the hated tax collectors, the Samaritans, the Pharisees, the prostitutes, and those who were ill and oppressed.

In our own strength we can never attain righteousness. Jesus gives us a righteous status: "It is because of God that you are in Christ Jesus, who has become for us wisdom from God—that is, our righteousness, holiness and redemption" (I Cor. 1:30). (Isaiah 61:10).

Father, thank you for Jesus who places us in this position of righteousness. I long with all my heart to put into practice righteousness and justice to my fellow man. Work through me to that end. Amen.

Filled with God's Spirit

Luke 4:18-19

After Jesus was tempted in the wilderness he returned to Galilee, filled with the Holy Spirit's power. (v. 14). Arriving in Nazareth . . . he went to the synagogue and read from Isaiah (61:1-2): "The Spirit of the Lord is upon me, for he has appointed me to preach Good News to the poor. He has sent me to proclaim that captives will be released, that the blind will see, that the downtrodden will be freed from their oppressors, and that the time of the Lord's favor has come" (Luke 4:18-19 NLT).

We are commanded to be filled with the Holy Spirit. (Eph. 5:18). Jesus read from Isaiah that the Spirit of the Lord was upon him. He spent forty days in the wilderness praying and fasting before he was filled. (Luke 4: 1-13). Since Pentecost the Holy spirit has come. We don't need to wait 40 days (Acts 2).

We have the same Holy Spirit as Jesus. If we do not have the Spirit we are not Christians. (Ro. 8:9). It's the Spirit who brings power to our witness. (Acts 1:8).

Jesus calls us: (1) to announce the Good News to the poor, (2) to proclaim release to the captives, (3) to give sight to the blind, (4) to free the downtrodden from their oppressors and (5) to declare the time for the Lord to act is now.

In the Roman world, unwanted babies were placed on the doorsteps and left to die. The Christians rescued the unwanted children. If every church would take in one needy child, the poverty and crime of our nation would be greatly reduced. Jesus was intentional in his outreach.

Learn to know those who are poor, sick and depressed. Jesus said we are to extend hospitality to those who can't afford to invite us back. (Luke 14:12-14). Be intentional. Learn their names; listen to their stories. You may feel uncomfortable at first. When we serve the least of these we are serving Jesus. (Matt. 25:31-46).

Father, as you anointed Jesus to preach and to set people free, enable me to be an instrument of healing and hope today. Amen.

Jesus Chose the Disciples to Be With Him

Mark 9:30-31

"Jesus tried to avoid all publicity in order to spend more time with his disciples and teach them" (Mark 9:30-31 NLT). Jesus was building relationships.

A pastor died. At the memorial service many people shared how they appreciated his ministry and how he had helped them. No one mentioned his good messages. He impacted people by the quality of the relationship they had with him. Sometimes we are more concerned about imparting facts and being sure our "sermons" are perfect, than we are about the quality of our relationship with others.

Jesus chose the disciples to be with him, i.e. to build a trusting relationship with them and to teach them. People view our lives and are influenced more by our demeanor than by what we say. Actions speak louder than words. Think about the people who influenced you. Was it because they were so brilliant or was it their relationship with you?

In the Old Testament God sent a manuscript. Angels gave the law to Moses who was the mediator between God and the people. (Gal. 3:19). That was not satisfactory. We need a priest who understands us, who desires a relationship with us. (Heb. 4:14-16). Jesus understands us because he was tempted in all points as we are.

You are God's priest. God uses your life's experiences so you can identify with others and comfort them. "He comforts us in all our troubles so that we can comfort others. When others are troubled, we will be able to give them the same comfort God has given us. You can be sure that the more we suffer for Christ, the more God will shower us with his comfort through Christ" (II Cor. 1:4-5 NLT).

There is no substitute for relationships—relationships with Jesus and relationship with others. The love relationship sums up all the law and the prophets—loving God and loving others. (Matt. 22:37-39).

Lord, help me to keep relationships supreme in my schedule today. Amen.

Jesus' Passion

Matthew 23:37

"O Jerusalem, Jerusalem, the city that kills the prophets and stones God's messengers! How often I have wanted to gather your children together as a hen protects her chicks beneath her wings, but you wouldn't let me" (Matt. 23:37 NLT).

Jesus often longed to reach the people of Jerusalem. He grieved over Jerusalem. How many times is often? Paul said he had a great sorrow and unceasing anguish in his heart for his people. (Ro. 9:1-2). Both Jesus and Paul had a continual burden for lost people. Jesus want us to compel, to make them come, urge or force them to come to the heavenly banquet. (Luke 14:23).

While Jesus expresses this strong emotion for his people does that mean he was driven? He held a perfect balance between passion for the lost and at the same time he was not overwhelmed. He was gentle and peaceful so that even the children loved to be with him. (Matt. 18:16) "Come to me, all you who are weary and heavy burdened, and I will give you rest . . . I am gentle and humble in heart" (Matt. 11:28-29).

Jesus lived with a clear purpose and direction: He was driven to go through Samaria (John 4:4), to cleanse the temple (Luke 19:45), to confront the Pharisees (Matt. 23). He got up before sunrise to pray and prayed all night (Luke 6:12), he was driven with compassion for the multitudes denying himself food and rest (Mark 3:20) and he was driven to give his life on the cruel cross for sinful persons like myself. Seventeen times the Gospel records that Jesus must do this or that, yet his life was characterized by calmness and gentleness. (II Cor. 10:1, and Phil. 1:8).

As you abide in Jesus he will give you perfect rest as well as a passion and cause a fire to burn in your heart that will move you to action in helping to fulfill his Great Commission to make disciples.

Lord Jesus you had both passion and gentleness. Enable me to be like you. Amen.

Don't Be Distracted

I Corinthians 9:26

"I run straight to the goal with purpose in every step" (I Cor. 9:26 NLT).

"In a race everyone runs, but only one person gets the prize. You also must run in such a way that you will win. All athletes practice strict self-control. They do it to win a prize that will fade away, but we do it for an eternal prize. So I run straight to the goal with purpose in every step. I am not like a boxer who misses his punches. I discipline my body like an athlete, training it to do what it should. Otherwise, I fear that after preaching to others I myself might be disqualified" (I Cor. 9:24-37 NLT).

Paul's goal was to "become a servant of everyone so that I can bring them to Christ" (9:19 NLT). Paul says he became a servant to everyone. Do you and I see ourselves as servants to our neighbors?

Jesus came to serve. "Jesus did not come to be served but to serve" (Matt. 20:28). He took the form of a slave as he stooped to wash the disciple's feet. (John 13). Ultimately he gave his life on the cruel cross. Again he says he came "to seek and save the lost" (Luke 19:10). "I have come to call sinners to turn from their sins, not to spend my time with those who think they are already good enough" (Luke 6:32 NLT).

Now he says, "Come with me! I will teach you how to bring in people instead of fish!" (Matt. 4:19 CEV). They give up everything to follow Jesus. "Take up your cross daily and follow me" (Luke 9:23).

What can you cut out of your busy schedule so you have time to be a servant? It is often the good things that remove us from doing what's best. It's amazing how acts of kindness reach the heart. My father took a load of hay to a young struggling farmer. Fifty years later he still thanks me for my father's act of kindness.

Lord I want to be a servant like you. Amen.

God Is Sorry He Made Man

Genesis 6:6

"The Lord observed the extent of the people's wickedness, and he saw that all their thoughts were consistently and totally evil. So the Lord was sorry he had ever made them. It broke his heart" (Genesis 6:6 NLT).

If he knew we were going to fail him why did he create us? He was grieved that we chose sin and death instead of a relationship of life with him. He created us because he could see down through time when he would give us his only Son to redeem us. The redemption would cost him indescribable pain and suffering but he thought we were worth the cost. Do you dare question your value when you see the price tag God places on you!

"The ransom God paid was not mere gold or silver. He paid for you with the precious life blood of Christ, the sinless, spotless Lamb of God. God chose him for this purpose long before the world began, but now in these final days, he was sent to the earth for all to see. And he did this for you" (I Peter 1:18-20 NLT). "Thank God for his Son—a gift too wonderful for words!" (II Cor. 9:15 NLT). Our redemption cost us nothing but it cost God everything. Don't let God's precious gift become trite to you. Thank God every day that he rescued you from the kingdom of darkness and translated you to the kingdom of his dear son. (Col. 1:14).

No wonder the hymn writer states: "Such love demands my soul, my life, my all." Horatius Bonar wrote: "Toil on, faint not, keep watch, and pray; Be wise the erring soul to win; Go forth into the world's highway, Compel the wonderer to come in." Knowing the value God places on us should give us a passion to win people for our Lord. Along with Jesus we say, "I give myself entirely to you so they also might be entirely yours" (John 17:19 NLT).

Father, I thank you for giving your very best, your only son Jesus to pay for my sins. I give you my life, my soul, my all. Amen.

Complete Joy

John 15:11

"I have told you this so that my joy may be in you and that your joy may be complete" (John 15:11). James Montgomery gives his account:

Over Christmas vacation Lyn worked in a department store. Her boss was the nastiest, meanest human being. She loved to come up to her sales people and criticize and royally chew them out in front of the customers. Nothing Lyn did pleased her boss. Lyn cried herself to sleep. "Lord," she prayed . . . "I can't go back."

God seemed to be saying to Lyn: "You will go back tomorrow morning, and you will stay there . . . you will love Miss Alma." "Impossible," cried Lyn. "I cannot love that woman." "You're right, you can't love her," the Lord plainly said. "But, I can. In fact I already love her. I died for her."

Lyn thought going back would be impossible, but it wasn't. "Because I now saw Miss Alma in a different light—as someone who needed the Lord. I began to learn what it meant to turn the situation over to Jesus and let him work through me. The woman was just as nasty, but I had changed. Now when she corrected me, I smiled and thanked her for straightening me out. I never tried to excuse my behavior."

The other employees couldn't understand how Lyn could take all the guff. Lyn had the opportunity to witness to every woman in that department. Miss Alma's attitude changed. She invited Lyn to come back and work for her full time in her department.

"In my own strength I couldn't have done it. Even the stock boy was amazed, and I got a chance to witness to him . . . . just love people for the sake of loving them because Jesus commanded us to."

Many times the Holy Spirit's joy and gladness overtakes me. (Isaiah 35:10). "I think, I don't deserve this joy. I wish I could share it with others."

Father, enable me to live in the power of your Holy Spirit. May your joy and love flow through me today. Amen.

You Have an Older Brother

Romans 8:29-30

"God chose his people to become like his Son, so that his Son would be the firstborn, with many brothers and sisters. Having chosen them, he called them to come to him. He gave them right standing with himself, and promised them his glory" (Ro. 8:29-30 NLT).

"Jesus and the ones he makes holy have the same Father. That is why Jesus is not ashamed to call us his brothers and sisters. Jesus said to God, 'I will declare the wonder of your name to my brothers and sisters. I will praise you among all your people.' He also said, 'I will put my trust in God'" (Hebrews 2:11-13 NLT).

It's overwhelming to think that Jesus is our older brother. We are holy because we have the same Father. Oh, that the Holy Spirit would open our spiritual eyes to this truth. How can we go through the day with downcast eyes?

A few years ago there was a fad to wear a wrist band with the letters: WWJD which stood for: "What would Jesus do?" This is a great way to remind ourselves that Jesus, our older brother, is our model and guide for all our actions.

"Follow God's example (model) in everything you do, because you are his dear children" (Eph. 5:1 NLT). Modeling is miles ahead of an instruction manual. You "watch," "observe," "question," and "imitate." You "watch" what God and Jesus do. By the power of God's Holy Spirit you do what they do. Why do we make this so complicated? We cause ourselves pain when we say: "I can't trust God on this." "I know what he wants me to do but I don't have the faith to do it." "I know I should take time to help my neighbor but . . ." "I know God wants me to encourage my friend but. . ." "I know I should read my Bible and have daily devotions but . . ." "I know I should give a tithe but . . ." "I know I don't need this new car but . . ."

Father, help me to remember that I am your child and that Jesus is my older brother. Remind me to ask WWJD and then do it. Amen.

Jacob Wrestled with God

Genesis 32

After being away for many years, cheating his twin brother Esau out of his birthright and fleeing for his life, Jacob is returning home. He sent messengers ahead to inform Esau he was coming. The messengers returned informing Jacob that Esau was on his way to meet him with an army of 400 men. In desperation Jacob prayed, "O Lord, you told me to return to my land and to my relatives, and you promised to treat me kindly. I am not worthy of all the faithfulness and unfailing love you have shown to me, your servant . . . O Lord, please rescue me from my brother, Esau. I am afraid that he is coming to kill me" (Genesis 32:9-11 NLT).

Jacob sent hundreds of animals as gifts to appease Esau. That night while Jacob was alone a man wrestled with him until dawn. He told Jacob he had struggled with both God and men and had won. (v. 28) He blessed Jacob. Jacob named the place Penile—"face of God"—for he said, "I have seen God face to face, yet my life has been spared" (v. 30). Jacob was desperate for God! "You will seek me and find me when you search for me with all your heart" (Jer. 29:13).

Like Jacob we are often fearful to do what God wants us to do. Jacob had to come to the end of himself. As we give our fears to God and wrestle with Him, he will bless us with his wisdom. His Holy Spirit emboldens and empowers us.

Jesus said the first step into the Kingdom is to be poor in spirit. (Matt. 5:3). The Message Bible reads: "You're blessed when you're at the end of your rope." Unless you take up your cross, (an instrument of death), denying yourself you cannot be my disciple. (Luke 9:23). The NLT reads: "If any of you wants to be my follower, you must put aside your selfish ambition, shoulder your cross daily, and follow me."

Lord, I am desperate to do your will. With your help I will put aside my selfish ambitions, take up my cross and serve you. Amen.

Get Involved

Ezra 3

When the children of Israel returned from captivity the first thing they did, even though they were afraid of the local people, was to build an altar to the Lord. They had learned to put first things first. It was expected they would first build a wall to keep their enemies out but they were learning to give God his rightful place. They offered sacrifices every day, morning and evening, as Moses had commanded.

Later they bought materials for the building of the temple. Everyone got involved. They appointed leaders, age twenty and older, from the tribe of Levi to direct the building. When the foundation was laid the priests and Levites with their trumpets and cymbals praised God in the tradition of King David.

"All the people boomed out hurrahs, praising God as the foundation of the Temple of God was laid. As many were noisily shouting with joy, many of the older priests, Levites, and family heads who had seen the first Temple . . . wept loudly. (The new temple was inferior to Solomon's temple.) People couldn't distinguish the shouting from the weeping. The sound of their voices reverberated for miles around" (Ezra 3:11-13 Msg.).

Helen walked into the bank on Friday. She was greeted with, "Are you doing anything exciting this weekend?" She paused a moment and said, "I'm looking forward to worshipping God with my church family. It's the highlight of my week." Church is exciting when people are being transformed by the power of the Good News.

Do the unchurched know we enjoy our worship services? Do we tell them how excited we are to worship and praise the Lord? Emotion is not the primary criteria to prove we love the Lord but showing emotion is certainly one aspect of loving the Lord with all our heart. We're not afraid of getting excited at a ball game. Don't be afraid of worshipping the Lord with excitement privately or in public worship. The world just might catch on to the reality that we love Jesus.

Lord, thank you for the joy I experience in worshipping with God's people. Help me to freely express my praise to you and share my joy with others. Amen.

Open Your Eyes

"As you look around right now, wouldn't you say that in about four months it will be time to harvest? . . . Open your eyes . . . look at what's right in front of you. These Samaritan fields are ripe . . . The Harvester isn't waiting. He's taking his pay, gathering in this grain that's ripe for eternal life. Now the Sower is arm in arm with the Harvester, triumphant. That's the truth of the saying, 'This one sows, that one harvests.' I sent you to harvest a field you never worked. Without lifting a finger, you have walked in on a field worked long and hard by others" (John 4:35-38 Msg.).

The disciples were blind to the harvest around them; blind because they did not have a passion to see the Samaritans come to eternal life. Their mind was on physical food but Jesus had food that really nourished. (v. 34). They had to learn there was something far more important than physical food. They needed to learn to overcome their prejudice and their cultural barriers.

Are we any different? We go past houses in all directions from our home, day after day and don't think to pray for the people, or invite them to meet Jesus. We see a moving van but do we stop to welcome the newcomer to our community and invite them to church. There are fields all around our homes and our churches that are ripe but we are blind. We need eyes to see like Jesus. When we see and show love and acceptance as he does, we too will reap a harvest.

"Many of the Samaritans from that village committed themselves to Jesus because of the woman's witness" (v. 39). What was the woman's witness? "He knew all about the things I did. He knows me inside and out!" (Msg.).

One of the most effective words you can give to your neighbors is that Jesus knows you and me inside and out and still chooses to love and forgive us when we sincerely ask him.

Jesus thank you for crossing the cultural barriers and accepting everyone. Thank you for accepting me. Enable me to share with others what you did for me. Amen.

Beware Eternal Consequences Ahead

Jude 22-23

We live in a time when judgment and eternal hell is pooh-poohed. Many Christians don't believe in eternal hell, however, most Christians believe in an eternal heaven. While hell was not made for humans but for the devil and his angels it is clear that Jesus believed in hell. (Matt. 25:41).

"Show mercy to those whose faith is wavering. Rescue others by snatching them from the flames of judgment. There are still others to whom you need to show mercy, but be careful that you aren't contaminated by their sins" (Jude 22-23 NLT).

People select hell by the choices they make. Seven times Jesus speaks of "outer darkness where there is weeping and gnashing of teeth" (Matt. 8:12, 13:42, 50 etc.). Jesus speaks more about eternal separation, punishment and judgment than any of the New Testament writers. While Christians do not agree on the precise meaning and implication of these terms, it is clear there are very serious consequences for those who reject the Lord Jesus. "Our God is a consuming fire" (Heb. 10:31). Jesus reminds us of judgment to come in more than half of his parables. God's wrath and anger is mentioned 500 times in the Bible with 53 of these in the New Testament. God's wrath is not uncontrolled anger but his righteous reaction to sin.

Knowing this, Jesus' brother, Jude, says we are to rescue others by snatching them from the flames of judgment. Paul writes: "For we must all appear before the judgment seat of Christ, that each one may receive what is due him for the things done while in the body, whether good or bad. Since, then, we know what it is to fear the Lord, we try to persuade men" (II Cor. 5:10-11). "God is just." (II Thess. 11b).

When we come to the judgment day will our unchurched neighbors say to us: "We talked with you many, many times but you never warned us about our need to come to Christ." What will we say?

Lord, forgive me for my lack of urgency to snatch people from the flames. Give me a passion and the power of your Holy Spirit to speak with love, gentleness and urgency to those that don't know you, inviting them to your eternal Kingdom. Amen.

Time—a Most Precious Gift

Psalm 90:12

"These are evil times, so make every minute count" (Eph. 5:16 CEV). We find time for what is important to us. Daily I pray, Lord help me to number my days that I may have a heart of wisdom, teach me to use wisely the time I have so I make the best use of time. (Ps. 90:12). "As long as it is day, we must do the works of him who sent me. Night is coming when no one can work" (John 9:4). Our life is like a vapor, it appears for a short time and then it vanishes. (James 4:14). We have eternity to rest.

"I meditate on your precepts and consider your ways" (Ps. 119:15). "I ponder every morsel of wisdom from you" (v. 15 Msg.). "I will meditate on your wonders and on your promises" (v. 27). "Oh, how I love your law! I meditate on it all day long" (v. 97).

Turn off the TV, go to bed earlier. "I will meditate on your name all night God, treasuring your revelation" (v. 55 Msg.). "I get up in the middle of the night to thank you, your decisions are so right" (v. 62 Msg.). "My eyes stay open through the watches of the night, that I may meditate on your promises" (v. 148).

Use your time to encourage others. "Encourage one another daily as long as it is called Today so that none of you may be hardened by sin's deceitfulness" (Heb. 3:12-14).

"Keep this Book . . . on your lips; meditate on it day and night so that you may be careful to do everything written in it. Then you will be prosperous and successful" (Joshua 1:8).

Jesus said, "I have come to call sinners to turn from their sins, not to spend my time with those who think they are already good enough" (Luke 5:32 NLT). "Don't let me waste my time doing wrong with wicked people" (Ps. 141:4 CEV). "I don't waste my time on impossible schemes" (Ps. 131:1b CEV).

Jesus, I want to use every minute of my time to honor you. Amen.

The Power of One

Jeremiah 5:1-2

"One life totally devoted to God is of more value to Him than one hundred lives which have been simply awakened by His Spirit." Oswald Chambers in *My Utmost for his Highest*, April 24 devotional (1992).

"Run up and down every street in Jerusalem, says the Lord, 'Look high and low, search throughout the city! If you can find even one person who is just and honest, I will not destroy the city'" (Jer. 5:1-2 NLT).

"God looks to see if there is even one with real understanding, one who seeks for God. But no, all have turned away from God; all have become corrupt. No one does good, not even one!" (Ps. 53:2-3 NLT). The Godly people have all disappeared; not one fair-minded person is left on the earth . . ." (Micah 7:2 NLT).

Peter's life (one person) was spared while James was put to death. Sixteen guards were executed because of Peter's "escape." (Acts 12:2-19).

Noah alone was found righteous in the eyes of the Lord. (Genesis 6:9). God used Noah to save humanity from destruction. Daniel would not bow down to the King. The whole nation was affected by his powerful witness. (Daniel 6). God would have spared Sodom if he could have found ten righteous persons. (Genesis 18:32).

"I searched for someone to stand in the gap in the wall so I wouldn't have to destroy the land, but I found no one" (Ezekiel 22:30 NLT). You are called to stand in the gap! You can make a difference in your school, your workplace and in your town or city! Our son, Scott, a civil engineer, has chosen to work with a secular organization to be a witness. Elvin is making a difference because he has chosen to bowl with unchurched men so he could be a witness to them. Jim serves on the school board and makes a definite impact on the school system. Ron sits with the gang whose language becomes decent when he gives his noon hour to them. One person makes a difference! Jesus said, "You are the salt and light of the world" (Matt. 5:14-16).

Father, enable me to be faithful to you even when I stand alone. Amen.

Living God's Way

Galatians 5:22-23

"What happens when we live God's way? He brings gifts into our lives, much the same way that fruit appears in an orchard—things like affection for others, exuberance about life, serenity. We develop a willingness to stick with things, a sense of compassion in the heart, and a conviction that a basic holiness permeates things and people. We find ourselves involved in loyal commitments, not needing to force our way in life, able to marshal and direct our energies wisely" (Gal. 5:22-23 Msg.).

Most versions list the fruits of the Spirit as love, joy, peace, patience, kindness, goodness, faithfulness, gentleness and self-control. Let's compare these with the Message Bible translation and ask ourselves these questions:

Love: Do I have affection for others? Jesus commands us to love others as we love ourselves. (Matt. 22:39).

Joy: Am I exuberant about life? Paul reminds us to be joyful and to rejoice in the Lord always. (I Thess. 5:16 and Phil. 4:8).

Peace: Do I radiate serenity? Throw all our anxiety and care on Jesus. (I Peter 5:7).

Patience: Am I willing to stick with things or do I become irritable and angry? Phil. 2:14 reminds us to do all things without bickering or arguing.

Kindness: Do I possess a compassionate heart? (Eph. 4:32).

Goodness: Do I have a conviction that a basic holiness permeates people? Everyone is created in the image of God. (Genesis 1:27).

Faithfulness: Am I trustworthy and loyal? Do I keep my word? (Col. 3:9).

Gentleness: Can I work along with those who think differently or do I insist on having my way? (Eph. 5:21).

Self-Control: Am I able to marshal and direct my energies wisely? (II Tim. 1:7).

Choose one or two that you need to develop and then pray: Lord Jesus, it is only by your Spirit that I can live as you desire. Enable me to walk in the Spirit's power to please you in all things. Amen.

Tongue Trouble?

Proverbs 21:23

"Watch your words and hold your tongue; you'll save yourself a lot of grief" (Prov. 21:23 Msg.). "Without gossip a quarrel dies down" (Prov. 26:31).

Jesus said, "Let me tell you something. Every one of those careless words is going to come back to haunt you. There will be a time of Reckoning. Words are powerful, take them seriously. Words can be your salvation. Words can also be your damnation" (Matt. 12:36-37 Msg.).

In coaching church leadership teams I come across persons whose tongue has not been tamed. They have to be the first to answer everything. Pretty soon the others draw back and talk very little. Discussion and progress are stymied. The whole church is affected by one person's tongue.

Jesus asked more than one hundred fifty questions. He wanted his listeners to think. James says: "The tongue is a small part of the body, but it makes great boasts. Consider what a great forest is set on fire by a small spark. The tongue is also a fire, a world of evil among the parts of the body. It corrupts the whole person, sets the whole course of his life on fire, and is itself set on fire by hell" (James 3:5-6).

Only God's Holy Spirit can tame your tongue. "No man can tame the tongue. It is a restless evil, full of deadly poison." (v. 8). A common sin among God's people is defensiveness. Why do you need to defend or justify yourself? "When they hurled insults at Jesus, he did not retaliate" (I Peter 2:23). Defending yourself is an indication that your self will is not broken. Take the desire to defend yourself to the cross and confess this sin of pride. Are you so insecure that you can't listen to the other side? Too often when people do listen they come up with a negative response.

Lord Jesus, I come to the cross and confess my defensiveness. Jesus help me to listen and hear what others are saying and then respond with love and understanding. Amen.

Love at Home

I Corinthians 13

"God is love" (I John 4:8). God's very essence is love. First Corinthians 13:4-8 describes God's love. You can't live up to this definition. Only Jesus can. The Good News is Jesus desires to live his life through you.

> Love never gives up. Love cares more for others than for self.
> Love doesn't want what it doesn't have. Love doesn't strut,
> Doesn't have a swelled head, Doesn't force itself on others,
> Isn't always "me first," Doesn't fly off the handle,
> Doesn't keep score of the sins of others, Doesn't revel when others grovel,
> Takes pleasure in the flowering of truth, Puts up with anything,
> Trusts God always, Always looks for the best,
> Never looks back, But keeps going to the end. (Msg.).

Are you courteous or are you unkind in the way you answer? What about your tone of voice? Do you envy? Are you proud or conceited? Do you have to have your own way? Do you think you know best? How is your attitude? Do you blame others? Do you keep track of the sins of others? Do you forgive their sins or do you hold grudges? Do you remind your spouse of their mistakes? Does your love put up with their personal habits or do you constantly complain about habits that annoy you?

We all fall short. What do we do? Live in guilt? No, we confess our sins, i.e. we agree with God that we can't live up to this definition. We come to the cross and ask for his forgiveness. He forgives us of all our sins. (I John 1:9). How often do we need to do this, perhaps many times a day? But we will grow stronger so that there can be more space between our times of confession. We are learning to walk in the light. (I John 1:7). When we walk in the light we have fellowship with each other. Love flows! We are learning to mount up like the eagles.

Lord Jesus, your very essence is love. Only you can give me this selfless perfect love. Forgive me for my lack of love. Cleanse me and enable your love to freely flow through me. Amen.

Great Contrast

John 15:1-17

Six times we are told by Jesus in John 14-16 that if we ask anything in his name he will do it. (14:13). "The Father will give you whatever you ask in my name" (John 15:16). "If you remain in me and my words remain in you, ask whatever you wish, and it will be given you" (15:7).

Jesus explains how these promises are true: "For I did not speak of my own accord, but the Father who sent me commanded me what to say and how to say it. I know that his command leads to eternal life. So whatever I say is just what the Father has told me to say" (John 12:49-50). "The Son can do nothing by himself; he can do only what he sees his Father doing because whatever the Father does the Son also does" (John 5:19). He does only what pleases the Father. (John 8:29).

Jesus has such an intimate relationship with the Father that he does and says only what the Father tells him to say and do. Not only that, but the Father tells him how to say it. We are to have the same relationship with the Father as Jesus had. He says: "You (the Father) are in me and I am in you. May they (you and me) also be in us (in God and Jesus)" (John 17:21). Jesus desires intimacy with us, then whatever we ask he will do since we only ask what is according to his will. We know his voice. (John 10:3-4). Our steps are ordered by the Lord. (Ps. 37:23). He is our life. (Col. 3:4)

When we abide in Christ we begin to experience the joy of prayers that line up with the Father and we will have whatever we ask. Apart from him we cannot do or say anything that has eternal value. This wonderful relationship with the great God of the Cosmos is beyond our imagination. It results in complete joy. (John 15:11).

Jesus, by your Holy Spirit I will remain in you. Your word abides in me. Help me to hear your voice and be obedient to your every command. Thank you for your fantastic promise that whatever I ask in your name, according to your will, you will do it. Amen.

Grow Up!

Hebrews 5:11-14

"I have a lot more to say about this, but it is hard to get it across to you since you've picked up this bad habit of not listening. By this time you ought to be teachers yourselves, yet here I find you need someone and go over the basics on God again, starting from square one—baby's milk, when you should have been on solid food long ago! Milk is for beginners, inexperienced in God's ways, solid food is for the mature, who have some practice in telling right from wrong" (Heb. 5:11-14 Msg.). It's been said, "Maturity is choosing what is right over what is easy."

In speaking to declining and dying churches it seemed their attitude is, we heard this before. Jesus said, He who has ears, let him hear—pay attention and apply what is said. James says, "Do not merely listen to the word, and so deceive yourselves. Do what it says" (James 1:22). John writes: "Let us not love with words or tongue but with actions and in truth" (I John 3:18).

One of the great weaknesses of many American churches is that our members hear hundreds of sermons but are often like the Dead Sea. They continually take in but give out very little and so become stagnant. They think that by coming to church regularly they are doing God and the pastor a favor. This is especially true in the area of evangelism. When you're active in evangelism you are "forced" to grow because you find yourself in situations where you will be challenged to answer questions. Your life must model your answer. "I pray that you may be active in sharing your faith so that you will have a full understanding of every good thing we have in Christ" (Philemon 6). Paul says as you share your faith your understanding of the Gospel will grow!

Growing Christians and churches reach out to their friends and neighbors. Lukewarm Christians and declining churches may be doctrinally sound but empty of spiritual vitality.

Lord Jesus, help me to move from the milk stage to maturity. Whatever it takes Lord, I will serve you. Open my eyes to see someone I can help today. Amen.

Inexpressible Great Joy

I Peter 1:8

"You are filled with inexpressible great joy" (I Pet. 1:8). I wake up with a song in my spirit. I say to myself, "Wow, where did that come from?" My next thought is, "If only I could share this inexpressible great joy to the scores of people who are about to die from a drug overdose. I know my joy far exceeded their high." Joy in Jesus lasts for time and eternity. Isaiah says we are overcome with joy. (Is. 35:12).

Jesus is the source of our joy. "I have told you this so that my joy may be in you and that your joy may be complete" (John 15:11). "Your joy will be a river overflowing its banks!" (John 16:24 Msg.). Do you experience this joy? Church planter Paul writes: "Be joyful always," or "Be cheerful no matter what" (I Thess. 5:16 NIV and Msg.). He writes from prison: "Rejoice in the Lord always. I will say it again: Rejoice!" (Phil. 4:4).

Happiness comes and goes with the circumstances. Joy transcends our circumstances. Paul writes that he is immersed in tears, yet always filled with deep joy. (II Cor. 6:10 Msg.). Paul carried a huge sorrow. He describes it as an enormous pain deep within him. He is never free of it because people don't know Jesus. (Ro. 9:2). Paul learned to carry pain as well as the joy of Jesus all at the same time. If we are filled with the Spirit we are filled with joy. (Gal. 5:22). This is a paradox that you can only understand through experience.

Jesus' joy is a deep feeling of continual contentment and peace that transcends words. It goes much, much deeper than any laughs we might experience from a good joke. It is healing. It is satisfying.

Ask Jesus to fill you with his spirit of joy. Walk in obedience to his every command. "In his presence is fullness of joy. At thy right hand are pleasures evermore" (Ps. 16:11 KJV). "Surely the godly are praising your name, for they will live in your presence" (Ps. 140: 13 NLT).

Thank you Lord for your abiding joy. May your joy overflow in praise within me, so others are drawn to you. Amen.

Accountability

I Corinthians 3:1-3

Jesus was a teacher. He gathered his disciples around him and taught them. A teacher gives a lesson and expects a report. A good teacher is not fulfilled unless you are learning. Teachers ask what you learned and how you are applying it.

Paul taught the people publically and from house to house, i.e. from house church to house church. (Acts 20:20). These were personal, individual encounters. Most of the people Jesus won were converted one on one rather than in a large group. Do you remember what you heard last Sunday? It's so easy to sit in a large group, listen, go home, and forget about it. Jesus commissioned us to make disciples not converts. (Matt. 28:18-20). Jesus taught his disciples as they walked with him and sat with him as he taught them. You can't make disciples without accountability.

Get prebelievers involved in a group where they experience accountability. Jesus modeled as he taught. We teach discipleship to prebelievers by our example. They feel more and more part of the group as the group walks with them and relates closely to them. It takes more than our personal witness to bring people to Jesus. It takes a team. Get others involved as you share Jesus with prebelievers.

One of the reasons the early church was able to turn the world upside down was because their structure was primarily the house church. The larger assembly lends itself to preaching whereas the small group—(circles) lend to teaching and forming disciples. Whether you are in a mega-church or a house church ask yourself: Am I part of a small group of disciples who are making disciples? If not make sure you form a group or find a group so you can make disciples as Jesus commissioned you. Until that happens we will be like the Corinthian church who was worldly—mere infants in Christ, drinking milk when they should have been feeding on solid food. (I Cor. 3:1-3).

Father, my desire is to be accountable to you and to others so I can be a disciple who makes disciples. Amen.

Does Anyone Hate You?

Matthew 10:22

Jesus said, "All men will hate you because of allegiance to me" (Matt. 10:22, Luke 21:17). "Since they persecuted me, naturally they will persecute you" (John 15:20 NLT). "Open Doors" and "Voice of the Martyrs" are working in 68 countries assisting the persecuted. According to The Pew Research Center, "Each month 322 Christians are martyred for their faith, 214 churches and religious properties are destroyed and 722 forms of violence are committed against Christians such as beating, abductions, rapes, arrests and forced marriages" (www.OpenDoors).

In the U.S. efforts are made to remove the "10 Commandments" and the statement "In God we trust" from our currency. Pastors who preach against homosexuality and LGBD lifestyles may receive threats or lawsuits.

The Jewish leaders arrested the apostles, warning them not to teach about Jesus. "They left the Sanhedrin rejoicing because they had been counted worthy of suffering disgrace for the Name of Jesus" (Acts 5:41).

Jesus said, "Blessed are you when people insult you, persecute you and falsely say all kinds of evil against you because of me. Rejoice and be glad, because great is your reward in heaven" (Matt. 5:10-12). "Do not be afraid of those who kill the body but cannot kill the soul. Rather, be afraid of the One who can destroy both soul and body in hell" (Matt. 10:25-31).

Paul says, "Everyone who wants to live a godly life in Christ Jesus will be persecuted" (II Tim. 3:12). We are to expect persecution.

"For you have been given not only the privilege of trusting in Christ but also the privilege of suffering for him" (Phil. 1:29 NLT).

Lord, help me to be faithful to you. Amen.

Faithfulness Plus Fruitfulness

John 15:1-17

We emphasize faithfulness. But God desires faithfulness as well as fruitfulness. Jesus gives us the secret to being fruitful, i.e. to dwell or remain in him. Eleven times the word "remain" appears in John 15:1-10. If we remain in him we will bear fruit.

He cuts off branches that do not produce fruit. He prunes branches that do bear fruit so they will produce more fruit. (v. 2). His "word" prunes us so we will be more fruitful. (v. 3). We can't produce fruit if we are separated from the vine—separated from Jesus. (v. 4). If Jesus remains in us and we remain in him we will bear much fruit. (v. 5). True disciples bear much fruit. (v. 7). He chose us to produce much fruit. (v. 16).

Fruit comes as a result of remaining in Jesus. Bearing fruit is not an option. We can't produce fruit by working up a sweat. Branches don't groan, push, shove or complain. They abide and receive life from the vine. As we receive our life from Jesus we bring forth fruit, much fruit.

What is this fruit? It is Christlikeness. It is the fruit of the Holy Spirit—love, joy, peace, patience, kindness, goodness, faithfulness, gentleness, and self-control. But fruit is also people. Paul wanted to come to Rome so that "I might have some fruit—some results of my labor—among you, as I have among the rest of the Gentiles" (Ro. 1:13 AMP). "You know that the household of Stephanas were the first converts and our first fruits in Achaia . . ." (I Cor. 16:15 AMP). The fruit of a disciple is another disciple.

Jesus commissioned us to bring a harvest of people in order to disciple them, i.e. make them followers of Jesus, so they in turn become fishers of men. (Matt. 28:18-20).

"You didn't choose me, remember, I chose you, and put you in the world to bear fruit, fruit that won't spoil. As fruit bearers, whatever you ask the Father in relation to me, he gives you" (John 15:16 Msg.).

Lord, I choose to remain in you. Enable me to bear fruit that lasts for eternity. Amen.

Catch the Wave

I Corinthians 3:6-11

"I planted the seed, Apollos watered it, but God made it grow. So neither he who plants nor he who waters is anything, but only God who makes things grow. The man who plants and the man who waters have one purpose, and each will be rewarded according to his own labor. For we are God's fellow workers; you are God's field, God's building. By the grace God has given to me, I laid a foundation as an expert builder, and someone else is building on it. But each one should be careful how he builds. For no one can lay any foundation other than the one already laid, which is Jesus Christ" (I Cor. 3:6-11).

It is God who makes things grow. He chooses to use you and me as his instruments to bring in the harvest. Without him we are nothing. As faithful instruments we will be rewarded appropriately. Jesus had more to say about rewards than anyone else. He says, "Anyone who receives a prophet because he is a prophet will receive a prophet's reward, and anyone who receives a righteous man because he is a righteous man will receive a righteous man's reward. And if anyone gives even a cup of cold water to one of these little ones because he is my disciple, I tell you the truth, he will certainly not lose his reward" (Matthew 10:40-42).

God chooses to use us and to reward us. We need to pray for eyes to see where he is working. We can't create a wave—that's God's work. However, he takes into account our prayers in creating waves. He places a burden on the heart of those who are sensitive to him, they pray and God moves. We discern God's movement, we discern God's wave and do our part, whether it is planting or watering. This is the most exciting time in history with more people coming to Christ now than ever before.

Father, I thank you for creating one wave after another, extending your kingdom around the world. May the more than 100,000 who are born into your kingdom each day become faithful disciples bringing your light into this dark world. Amen.

God's Chosen Instrument

Matthew 16:15-19

"Who do you say I am?" Simon Peter said, "You're the Christ, the Messiah, the Son of the living God." Jesus came back, "God bless you, Simon! . . . You did not get that answer out of books or from teachers. My Father in heaven, God himself let you in on this secret of who I really am. And now I'm going to tell you who you are, really are. You are Peter, a rock. This is the rock on which I will put together my church, a church so expansive with energy that not even the gates of hell will be able to keep it out . . . You will have complete and free access to God's kingdom, keys to open any and every door; no more barriers between heaven and earth, earth and heaven. A yes on earth is yes in heaven. A no on earth is no in heaven" (Matt. 16:15-19 Msg.).

No organization, except the church can bring lasting peace to our troubled communities. The local community service clubs and sports organizations can provide some helpful structure to promote cooperation and assist humanity. The military can help bring order. The Red Cross helps in disasters. There is only one organization that God has chosen that can change the heart of humanity, his Spirit working through his body—the church.

Despite all the faults of the church due to our sinfulness it is by far the best concept this world has ever experienced. As Rick Warren writes: "It has been God's chosen instrument of blessing for two thousand years. It has survived persistent abuse, horrifying persecution, and widespread neglect. Parachurch organizations and other Christian groups come and go, but the church will last for eternity. It is worth giving our lives for and it deserves our best."

"Jesus is the head of the church, which is his body" (Col. 1:18 NLT). Love the church! Pray for your church. Encourage the leaders. Work to make it better. It will triumph!!!

Father, forgive us for the sin, the divisions, the carnality within your body. Have mercy upon us and heal us. Amen.

Here Am I, Send Me

Isaiah 6

When Isaiah was in the temple he saw the Lord. The angels praised the Lord saying: "Holy, holy, holy is the Lord Almighty; the whole earth is full of his glory." Then Isaiah saw himself and his people sinful to the core. The angel took a coal from the altar and touched his lips taking his guilt away. Then he heard "Whom should I send as a messenger to my people? Who will go for us?" Isaiah replied, "Lord I'll go! Send me" (Is. 6:8 NLT).

Like Isaiah we too see ourselves in need of cleansing as we come close to the Lord. It's only after we have been cleansed that we can say: "Lord, I'll serve you."

Was this a call directed to Isaiah because he was God's prophet? Notice, someone pointed out that God did not direct His call to Isaiah—Isaiah overheard God saying, . . .who will go for Us? God calls all of us. Isaiah was tuned into God's call. We too will hear God's call if our hearts our open.

Jeremiah writes, "If you look for me in earnest, you will find me when you seek me. I will be found by you" (Jer. 29:13-14 NLT). Jesus says, "Many are called, but few are chosen" (Matt. 22:14 NLT). When the New Testament speaks of the "many" it usually includes everyone. Adam brought death to many through his sin. (Ro. 5:15.)

As you go know that every heart has a desire to know the Lord. "The truth about God is known to them instinctively. God put this knowledge in their hearts. They can clearly see his invisible qualities—his eternal power and divine nature. So they have no excuse whatsoever for not knowing God" (Ro. 1:19-20 NLT). God is no respecter of persons. He is not willing that any perish. (II Peter 3:9).

Let God cleanse you, give you joy, courage and power to go into your world. The Holy Spirit has already planted a desire in everyone's heart to know Jesus Christ.

Lord, I thank you for calling me to yourself to do your work. I pray for others to hear your voice and respond to your call. Amen.

Perfect Conditions?

Ecclesiastes 11:4

"If you wait for perfect conditions, you will never get anything done" (Eccl. 11:4 NLT). "Don't sit around watching the wind . . . Don't stare at the clouds. Get on with your life" (Msg.).

When you sense the Holy Spirit is nudging you to begin building a relationship with another person there will always be some obstacles. You will be too busy or they will be too busy. Unless you are tuned into the Spirit you will come up with a dozen reasons why you cannot relate to the person. You are not perfect and the conditions are never perfect.

As you walk in the Spirit and sense God nudging you to do something, do it—act in faith. Pray for God's guidance and the courage to act. Ask him to give you words to say and how to say them. Ask Jesus for faith to overcome your doubts and fears. Claim the promise, "I will trust in him and not be afraid" (Is. 12:2 NLT). Or claim the verse, "When I am afraid, I put my trust in you" (Ps. 56:3 NLT). There are times when we move out in fear knowing God is calling us. He helps us overcome our fear or works in spite of our fear. Perfect love drives out fear. (I John 4:18).

The early church was far from perfect. The New Testament letters were written to help correct sin in the church yet God used the early church to spread the Good News throughout the world. God works in spite of us. God uses our imperfections when we come to him in humility and repentance. He works in "impossible" circumstances.

When he nudges we must say, "Lord I will trust you. I will serve in your strength and I will go and do what you want me to do." What is God asking you to do today?

Lord Jesus, enable me to obediently step out in faith at your command even though I feel so inadequate and the situation looks impossible. Turn my fears into childlike trust in you. Amen.

Do You Need a Miracle?

John 6:30

"They asked him, 'What miraculous sign . . . will you give that we may see it and believe you? What will you do?"(John 6:30).

In my fifty years of ministry I have experienced many miraculous answers to prayer as well as manifestations of the Holy Spirit's power visibly moving upon people. I have observed in some cases that these supernatural manifestations have little lasting impact. Jesus said, "Do not rejoice that the spirits submit to you, but rejoice that your names are written in heaven" (Luke 10:20). Emotions and feelings come and go. Being committed to Jesus is primarily a matter of our will. "If you love me you will obey what I command." (John 14:15).

Jesus said that many will claim to have cast out demons and performed miracles but he never knew them. (Matt. 7:21-23). False Messiahs will appear and perform miracles to deceive many. (Matt. 24:24-24). (Rev. 12:9).

Jesus says a rich man died. "In hell and in torment, he looked up and saw Abraham in the distance and Lazarus in his lap. He called out, 'Father Abraham, mercy! Have mercy! Send Lazarus to dip his finger in water to cool my tongue. I'm in agony in this fire'" (Luke 16:22-24 Msg.). After Abraham informed him this was not possible the rich man begged Abraham to send Lazarus to warn his five brothers to not come to this place of torment. "Abraham answered, 'They have Moses and the Prophets . . . let them listen to them'" (v. 29). The rich man responded, "They're not listening. If someone came back to them from the dead, they would change their ways" (v. 30). Abraham replied, "If they won't listen to Moses and the Prophets, they're not going to be convinced by someone who rises from the dead" (vv. 31).

While the miraculous is encouraging and has brought many to Christ, focus on Jesus. Paul says: "From infancy you have known the holy Scriptures, which are able to make you wise for salvation through faith in Christ Jesus" (II Tim. 3:15).

Father, thank you for miracles but help us to rejoice that our names are written in heaven. Amen.

Moving Mountains / Faith or Presumption

Mark 11:22-25

"Jesus said to the disciples, 'Have faith in God. I assure you that you can say to this mountain, "May God lift you up and throw you into the sea," and your command will be obeyed. All that's required is that you really believe and do not doubt in your heart. Listen to me! You can pray for anything, and if you believe you will have it. But when you are praying, first forgive anyone you are holding a grudge against, so that your Father in heaven will forgive your sins too'" (Mark 11:22-25 NLT).

"If you stay joined to me and my words remain in you, you may ask any request you like, and it will be granted" (John 15:7 NLT). Staying joined and having faith in God means that we think the way he thinks, his will becomes our will. Since that's true then we can ask anything.

There are some conditions that we must meet: we must forgive others, have genuine faith, and his words must remain in us. Timing is also important. Only God sees all the circumstances. He may choose to move the mountain over time rather than instantly. This is illustrated in John 17 where he prays for his followers to be one. Persistence and earnestness is necessary. (Luke 18:1-8 and James 5:17).

As we forgive everyone, grow in faith/trust, and abide in him our understanding and appreciation of these seemingly broad promises becomes more and more real. Mountain after mountain is moved.

When my wife, Helen, was talking with someone who was crying because she knew her husband, who very seldom came to church would never come since the congregation was moving ten miles from their house. Helen said to her, "I don't know your husband but I know God. He will see that your husband comes." He came and became a committed disciple. God is in the mountain moving business. As we learn to abide in the vine and discern his voice we will find ourselves making bold statements as the Holy Spirit speaks through us.

Father, I thank you for the joy of seeing mountains move. Enable me to trust you more. Amen.

Love Myself?

Galatians 5:13-14

"You . . . have been called to live in freedom—not freedom to satisfy your sinful nature, but freedom to serve one another in love. For the whole law can be summed up in this one command: 'Love your neighbor as yourself'" (Gal. 5:13-14 NLT).

Jesus says, "You must love the Lord your God with all your heart, all your soul, and all your mind. This is the first and greatest commandment. A second is equally important: 'Love your neighbor as yourself.' All the other commandments . . . are based on these two commandments" (Matt. 22:37-39 NLT).

We are to be humble and consider others better than ourselves. (Phil. 2:3-4). Paul says, "I am the worst of sinners" (I Tim. 1:15). The closer we are to God the more we see ourselves in need of his grace. Is it wrong to love myself?

See yourself as God sees you and act accordingly. (Eph. 1:3). We are the crowning work of his creation. (Gen. 1:27). We are his masterpiece. (Eph. 2:10). Jesus presents us to the Father with great joy. (Jude 24). God loves us with an everlasting love. (Jer. 31:3). He gave his Son for us so he could have fellowship with us. (John 3:16).

It is right to love ourselves. Have you accepted yourself concerning things you cannot change. Ninety percent of Hollywood stars wish they were more handsome or more beautiful. Have your accepted your looks, your physical attributes, your intelligence and your personality? Can you thank God for making you the person you are?

This does not mean that you should not work with God to develop your gifts and talents, letting him knock off the rough edges that rub people the wrong way. If we don't love ourselves, we block God's love flowing through us. This negatively affects our witness. Remember we are God's masterpiece. (Eph. 2:10 NLT).

Lord, forgive me for complaining how you made me. Enable me to accept myself as your special creation allowing your love to flow through me. Amen.

What's Your Greatest Challenge?

John 17:17

Christianity is founded on the absolutes of the Bible. Our culture says there are no absolutes although that very statement is an absolute. The Bible answers all the basic questions: Why are we here? Is God who he says he is: The "I AM!" Is Jesus God's only Son divine or just a man like one of us? Is there life after death, and if there is where will I be going? Why is there so much suffering and pain?

Science can't explain our existence, or how or why we are here. Mysteries remain. God says, "My thoughts are not your thoughts. Neither are your ways my ways" (Is. 55:8). "I am of the earth and my understanding is limited to the things of earth, but Jesus has come from heaven. He tells what he has seen and heard" (John 3:31-32 NLT).

"The Message that points to Christ on the Cross seems like sheer silliness to those hell-bent on destruction, but for those on the way of salvation it makes perfect sense . . . It's written, 'I'll turn conventional wisdom on its head, I'll expose so-called experts as crackpots.' Since the world in all its fancy wisdom never had a clue when it came to knowing God . . . , God using what the world considered dumb—preaching, of all things! to bring those who trust him into the way of salvation" (I Cor. 1:18-21 Msg.).

We can study a lifetime in our libraries and universities and never come to a personal relationship with God through Christ. "Whoever believes in the Son has eternal life, but whoever rejects the Son will not see life for God's wrath remains on him" (John 3:36). "God's Word is Truth" (John 17:17). "The word of God is living and active. Sharper than any double-edged sword, it penetrates even to dividing soul and spirit. . .; it judges the thoughts and attitudes of the heart. Nothing in all creation is hidden from God's sight. Everything is uncovered and laid bare before the eyes of him to whom we must give account" (Heb. 4:12-13).

Jesus, your word is true. It speaks to me. Enable me to share it with others. Amen.

"Impossible" Circumstances

Habakkuk 3:17-19

Judah was soon to be swallowed up by Babylon. God's people were on a moral skid. Habakkuk cries out, "How long O Lord must I call for help? But you do not listen! 'Violence is everywhere!' I cry, but you do not come to save. Must I forever see these evil deeds? Why must I watch all this misery? Wherever I look, I see destruction and violence" (Hab. 1:2-3 NLT).

The answer comes in Chapter 2: God will be victorious in the end. God is with us even though our world around us is crumbling. Habakkuk looks the situation in the eye and astonishes us with these words that challenge anyone who has ever read them. (Habakkuk 3:17-19 CEV). "Fig trees may no longer bloom, or vineyards produce grapes; olive trees may be fruitless, and harvest time a failure; sheep pens may be empty, and cattle stalls vacant—but I will still celebrate because the Lord God saves me. The Lord gives me strength. He makes my feet as sure as those of a deer, and he helps me stand on the mountains."

When you receive a pink slip, and there's no food in the cupboard and nothing left in your savings account: Are you able to sing praises to God knowing God will overcome?

Victory is possible because God has given us the will to choose to remember the Lord's faithfulness in the past—to live with despair or to live with faith trusting God for ultimate victory. (Ch. 3). Our will must override our emotions of anguish and hopelessness. Look past your "impossible" situation and know God will give you victory, not only victory but a joyful heart of praise. Greater is he who is in you then he who is in the world. (I John 4:4).

My friend who died with cancer at age 66 had chosen these verses from Habakkuk as his life verses. While he was going through the valley of suffering he found rest and comfort in the prophet's message.

Father, forgive me for my lack of faith. Enable me to trust you in the valleys of my life. Be patient with me as I learn to trust you. Mold me in your image. Amen.

Lift Up Jesus

John 12:32

"But I, when I am lifted up from the earth, will draw all men to myself" (John 12:32).

The sharing of your personal testimony must point directly to Jesus so the listeners see Jesus more than they see you. Jesus said, "The Spirit gives life; the flesh counts for nothing. The words I have spoken to you are Spirit and they are life" (John 6:63).

Lost people may see your passion, your love, your sympathy but this will never save them. No matter how much we show love or elegance of speech, we can't save anyone. When we focus on our disappointments and trials it's easy to detract others from seeing Jesus. It's important to remind people that the only way we are able to overcome disappointment is through Jesus living his life through us.

Paul writes: "My message and my preaching were not with wise and persuasive words, but with a demonstration of the Spirit's power. So that your faith might not rest on men's wisdom, but on God's power" (I Cor. 2:4-5). "We are ... Christ's ambassadors, as though God were making his appeal through us" (II Cor. 5:20). Things that draw attention to ourselves make us a conspirator to Jesus' work. When others see me instead of Jesus they see what I can do but too often do not grasp what Jesus can do.

When Jesus is lifted up the Holy Spirit creates a need in the person for Jesus. Lift Jesus higher. "He must increase and I must decrease" (John 3:30 KJV).

People don't need our sympathy or even the sympathy of Jesus. If sympathy would save us Jesus would not have had to go to the cross. That's why Paul says: "I resolved to know nothing while I was with you except Jesus Christ and him crucified" (I Cor. 2:2). "In him (Christ) we have redemption through his blood, the forgiveness of sins, in accordance with the riches of God's grace that he lavished on us with all wisdom and understanding" (Eph. 1:7-8).

Lord Jesus, I choose to lift you up in all I do and say. All my accomplishments are only because of you. May people see Jesus living through me. Amen.

June 4

Are You a Disciple? (Part I)

John 13:34-35

One reason Christianity in America has not impacted our culture any more than it has is that we focus on calling people to salvation and neglect calling them to make Jesus Christ their Lord. We believe rightly so that Jesus came to seek and save the lost but forget that he commands us to make disciples. Furthermore he promised to send his Holy Spirit especially to carry out this command through us. (Matt. 28:19, Acts 1:8).

Our theology is not based on the number of occurrences of a particular word in the New Testament, but the choice of words can give some indication of their importance. In the N.T. the words "Savior," "saving," and "saved" appear approximately 50 times while the word "Lord" appears more than 600 times. Another related comparison is the word "Christian" which appears three times, "convert" seven times and "disciple" 275 times. We are to make disciples, i.e. fully devoted follows of Jesus!

We urge people to, "Accept Jesus as your Savior," surprisingly, a phrase not found in Scripture. They pray the "sinner's prayer" without true repentance, with little attention to allowing Jesus to transform and control their lifestyle. They live no differently than their secular neighbors. They are not the salt and light Jesus desires. They don't understand the necessity of taking up their cross daily. (Luke 9:23).

The New Testament nearly always puts the word "Lord" before "Savior." If Jesus is Lord, he will be our Savior. If he is not Lord, is he really our Savior? Either he is Lord of all or he is not Lord at all.

Who is a disciple? Jesus said, "A new commandment I give you: As I have loved you so you must love one another. By this everyone will know that you are my disciples, if you love one another" (John 13:34-35). The great commandment of Jesus is to love the Lord with all your heart, soul, mind and strength and your neighbor as yourself. (Matt. 22:37-39). For a disciple love is a verb.

Jesus I want you to be my Lord. You are in charge of my life. I choose to be your fully devoted disciple. Amen.

Who Is a Disciple? (Part II)

II Peter 3:18

A disciple loves God and others 24/7. (Matt. 22:38-39). Jesus said, "By this all men will know that you are my disciples if you love one another" (John 13:34-35).

When we consider making disciples, we think of a "perfect" curriculum. To make disciples we cannot depend on a printed curriculum. Knowledge puffs up while love builds up. (I Cor. 8:1). Head knowledge must be integrated into our daily life.

Ninety percent of the forty-some times the word "knowledge" is used in the New Testament it is translated using the Greek root words, "gnosis" or "ginosko" which is experiential knowledge as compared to cognitive facts. Peter's final words: "Grow in grace (undeserved favor, spiritual strength) and recognition and knowledge and understanding of our Lord and Savior Jesus Christ, the Messiah" (II Peter 3:18 AMP). Peter is speaking of experiential knowledge. Ideas, concepts and principles can be learned through books but to make disciples we need models.

We know people who have studied and memorized God's Word but like the Pharisees their life is not inviting. Jesus said, "You diligently study the Scriptures because you think that by them you possess eternal life. These are the Scriptures that testify about me, yet you refuse to come to me to have life" (John 5:39-40). We worship Jesus. We don't worship a book. The Bible is our manual for knowing and following Jesus.

Disciples are developed primarily through relationships. Disciples have a deep desire to truly love and know Christ and make him known. Paul expresses it well, "I consider everything as loss compared to the surpassing greatness of knowing Christ Jesus my Lord, for whose sake I have lost all things. . . . I want to know Christ and the power of his resurrection and the fellowship of sharing in his sufferings, becoming like him in his death" (Phil. 3:8 & 10). Jesus forgave and prayed for those who persecuted him.

Lord, I want to be your disciple. I surrender my will to you in all things. Amen.

Making Disciples (Part III)

Mark 3:14

Relationship is key. Jesus called the twelve to be with him. (Mark 3:14). You can't make disciples without taking time to get close to people. New Christians see how Jesus lives his life through you and they begin to understand what Jesus wants to transmit to them.

Jesus did most of his ministry outside the temple: he touched the leper, spoke to women, even a Samaritan woman, he ate with sinners, and took time for children. His actions made a deeper impression than merely giving a lecture. Jesus' teachings are in the Bible, but what impacts people is to see his teaching lived daily in the lives of his followers. Actions like forgiveness, kindness, love and peace resonate with people more than our words.

Jesus followers copied his model. Barnabas modeled for Paul; Paul modeled for Timothy; Aquila and Priscilla modeled for Apollos. Silas was a model for John Mark. Paul says, "Follow me as I follow Christ." Until we are willing to give sacrificially of our time to relate to prebelievers we cannot make disciples. After Jesus miraculously healed the demon possessed man he begged to go with Jesus. But Jesus replied, "Go home to your own people and tell them how much the Lord has done for you, and how he has had mercy on you. So the man went and began to tell in the Decapolis how much Jesus had done for him. And all the people were amazed" (Mark 5:19-20).

The woman at the well only met Jesus for an hour or two, but God enabled her to be an evangelist bringing many from her community to Christ. (John 4:41). Levi immediately held a banquet for his fellow tax collectors so he could introduce them to Jesus. (Matt. 9:9-13). We begin to disciple others when there is genuine interest in exploring the Christian faith.

Jesus, I will take time to relate to people like you did so they can see how you work in my life and be drawn to you. Amen.

The Cost of Discipleship (Part IV)

Matthew 10:28-39

Jesus calls for radical obedience to extend God's Kingdom. Being a disciple is not easy. Jesus said there will be a time when, "All men will hate you because of me. . . ." "Do not be afraid of those who kill the body but cannot kill the soul. Rather, be afraid of the One who can destroy both soul and body in hell" (Matt. 10:22, 28).

"I did not come to bring peace, but a sword. For I have come to turn a man against his father, and daughter against her mother, a daughter-in-law her mother-in-law, a man's enemies will be the members of his own household. Anyone who loves his father or mother more than me is not worthy of me; anyone who loves his son or daughter more than me is not worthy of me; and anyone who does not take his cross and follow me is not worthy of me. Whoever finds his life will lose it, and whoever loses his life for my sake will find it" (Matt. 10:28-39).

A man approached Jesus promising to follow him. Jesus said, "Foxes have dens and birds have nests, but the Son of Man has no place to lay his head." Jesus invited another man to follow him, but he wanted to first bury his father. Likely the father was not ill but elderly. Jesus is saying, Life is more important than death. A third man wanted to be a disciple but he thought he first had to get things straightened out at home and then he would follow Jesus. Becoming a disciple means putting Jesus first. God's work is something we must not put off. Seize the day! (Luke 9:57-62).

Followers of Jesus are not guaranteed that even their basic need for shelter will be met. Life is urgent! Share the Good News. Discipleship requires total devotion. Jesus may not literally ask you to live a homeless lifestyle, boycott the family funeral or leave without saying farewell. But a disciple must be ready to do whatever Jesus asks.

Jesus, you counted the cost and said "yes" to the cross. Enable me to take up my cross and follow in your steps. Amen.

Be Sure to Count the Cost—
Discipleship (Part V)

Luke 14:25-33

"Great crowds followed Jesus. He said. 'If you want to be my follower you must love me more than your own father and mother, wife and children, brothers and sisters—yes, more than your own life . . . You cannot be my disciple if you do not carry your own cross and follow me. But don't begin until you count the cost. For who would begin construction of a building without first getting estimates and then checking to see if there is enough money to pay the bills? Otherwise you might complete only the foundation before running out of funds. And then how everyone would laugh at you! . . . So no one can become my disciple without giving up everything for me" (Luke 14:25-33 NLT).

Disciples count the cost and commit their life to Jesus, obeying his teaching. Being a disciple requires total commitment. They consciously work and sacrifice to make more disciples. (Matt. 28:18-20). We choose to take up our cross daily knowing that the cross is an instrument of death. We don't die easily and we don't die once. (Lk. 9:23). "We are crucified with Christ" (Gal. 2:2).

The term "Christian" was a derogatory term given by the antagonists. All Christians should be disciples but today the term "Christian" for many means having an interest in a gathering similar to a club.

A disciple is always asking, "What would Jesus do?" A disciple loves the Lord with all their heart, soul, mind and strength and serves others as he serves himself. A disciple doesn't stay up Saturday night watching TV. He places more emphasis on serving Jesus during his vacation than taking a trip to please himself. He puts his spouse and children ahead of his own self-centered desires. He doesn't need a new car every year. He spends his money and time as Jesus would. What percentage of church attenders in your congregation are disciples?

Jesus, I have counted the cost. By God's grace I will be your disciple. Amen.

Overwhelmed

Ephesians 3:20-21

There are approximately 4000 promises in the bible. First Corinthians 1:19-21 informs us: "Our message is not "Yes" and "No." For the Son of God, Jesus Christ, who was preached among you... was not "Yes" and No," but in him it has always been "Yes." For no matter how many promises God has made, they are "Yes" in Christ. And so through him the "Amen" is spoken by us to the glory of God."

You can't help being overwhelmed as you meditate on these scriptures.

"God is able to do immeasurably more than all we ask or imagine, according to his power that is at work within us" (Eph. 3:20).

"God has raised us up with Christ and seated us with him in the heavenly realms in Christ Jesus" (Eph. 2:6).

"I can do everything through him who gives me strength... My God will meet all your needs according to his glorious riches in Christ Jesus" (Phil. 4:13 & 19).

"God gives strength to the weary and increases the power of the weak. Even youths grow tired and weary, and young men stumble and fall; but those who hope in the Lord will renew their strength. They will soar on wings like eagles; they will run and not grow weary, they will walk and not faint" (Is. 40:29-31).

"Though the fig tree does not bud and there are no grapes on the vines, ... and the fields produce no food, though there are no sheep in the pen and no cattle in the stalls, yet I will rejoice in the Lord, I will be joyful in God my Savior. The Sovereign Lord is my strength; he makes my feet like the feet of a deer, he enables me to go on the heights" (Habakkuk 3:17-19).

"Call to me and I will answer you and tell you great and unsearchable things you do not know" (Jeremiah 33:3).

"I have come that they may have life, and have it to the full" (John 10:10).

Lord, thank you for your many promises. Enable me to claim and implement them today. Amen.

"The Kingdom of God Is . . . Peace."

Romans 14:17

"The kingdom of God is not a matter of what we eat or drink, but of living a life of goodness and peace and joy in the Holy Spirit" (Ro. 14:17 NLT).

"Peace I leave with you; my peace I give you. I do not give to you as the world gives. Do not let your hearts be troubled and do not be afraid" (John 14:27).

In the same discourse Jesus states that he needs to go away but will be coming back: "I have told you all this so that in me you may have peace. In this world you will have trouble. But take heart! I have overcome the world" (John 16:33).

"My peace I give you." Peace is a gift from Jesus. He is the source of your peace. It is his peace he gives you. You must receive it as his gift. You can't work it up from within yourself. That means you must humbly accept it; acknowledging the giver. Peace is not something you earn or deserve. This makes it all the more precious. His peace is a by-product of abiding in him. Isaiah 26:3 reminds us if we keep our mind on God, he will give us perfect peace.

When you receive a gift it makes a difference who gave it. If you love baseball and you receive an autographed baseball from the most valuable player of the major leagues it is valuable to you. If you receive an autographed baseball from someone unknown to you the gift is not as meaningful. Jesus, the King of kings gives us this wonderful gift of peace. He triumphed victorious over death giving him the authority to grant us peace. If we accept his peace there is no need to worry. In fact, if we worry we are rejecting his gift.

Corrie ten Boom said, "Worrying is carrying tomorrow's load with today's strength. Worrying doesn't empty tomorrow of its sorrows, it empties today of its strength."

As long as you experience Jesus' presence you will have peace. It will give you a boldness and confidence. It's the living water that Jesus promised will flow from our inmost being to other thirsty souls around us.

Jesus, may your peace flow through me 24/7 so others are drawn to you. Amen.

"The Kingdom of God Is . . . Joy."

Romans 14:17

"The kingdom of God is not a matter of what we eat or drink, but of living a life of goodness and peace and joy in the Holy Spirit" (Ro. 14:17 NLT). The Message reads: God's Kingdom, "is what God does with your life as he sets it right, puts it together, and completes it with joy." The next verse reads: "Your task is to single-mindedly serve Christ."

It is fascinating that the apostle Paul who suffered much spoke more about joy than any of the other apostles. Writing from prison Paul reminds us: "Rejoice in the Lord always, I will say it again: Rejoice! Let your gentleness be evident to all" (Phil. 4:4-5). Joy comes from the Lord. We rejoice in the Lord. Focusing on Jesus results in joy.

As you relate to older people do they murmur and complain or express a joyful attitude? Unless you are experiencing joy now you will not likely be experiencing joy in your older years. It is interesting that the closer Jesus came to the end of his earthly life the more he spoke of joy.

Where does our joy come from? Joy is rarely mentioned in the Gospels. Mark never uses the word. The infrequency is because the Holy Spirit had not yet come. Joy comes from Jesus. He is made real to us through the work of the Holy Spirit. Jesus gives us his joy. Jesus said if you remain in me your joy will be complete. (John 15:11). "Yes, your joy will overflow!" (NLT).

Jesus explains, "You have sorrow now, but I will see you again; then you will rejoice, and no one can rob you of that joy . . . Ask using my name, and you will receive, and you will have abundant joy" (John 16:22-24 NLT). Peter writes to the persecuted Christians who have inexpressible and glorious joy. (I Peter 1:8). Pray that Jesus' joy in you will be contagious. As Isaiah 35:10 says "everlasting joy will crown their heads. Gladness and joy will overtake them."

Lord Jesus, fill me with your joy so it overflows to those who have no lasting joy. Amen.

June 12

"The Kingdom of God Is Living . . . in the Holy Spirit."

Romans 14:17

"The kingdom of God is not a matter of what we eat or drink, but of living a life of goodness and peace and joy in the Holy Spirit" (Ro. 14:17 NLT).

A majority of Christians can mention God. A few can talk about Jesus. A very few will talk about the Holy Spirit. They are one—the Trinity, Father, Son and Holy Spirit.

The Spirit makes real to me what Jesus did for me. We are born of the Spirit (John 3:5), indwelt by the Spirit (I Cor. 6:19), sealed by the Spirit (Eph. 1:13-14), filled with the Spirit (Eph. 5:18), empowered for witness by the Spirit (Acts 1:8), and anointed for service by the Spirit (Luke 4:18, Acts 10:38). The Spirit produces fruit in us (Gal. 5:22-23). He guides us (Ro. 8:14). He interprets the Scriptures for us. (I Cor. 2:9-14).

"The Spirit of God, who raised Jesus from the dead, lives in you. And just as he raised Christ from the dead, he will give life to your mortal body by this same Spirit living within you" (Ro. 8:11 NLT).

"The Holy Spirit helps us in our distress . . . God's Spirit prays for us with groaning that cannot be expressed in words. The Father who knows all hearts knows what the Spirit is saying, for the Spirit pleads for us believers in harmony with God's own will" (Ro. 8:26-27 NLT).

"The Holy Spirit speaks to us deep in our hearts and tells us that we are God's children. And since we are his children, he will share his treasures—for everything God gives to his Son, Christ, is ours, too" (Ro. 8:16-17 NLT).

Jesus depended on the Spirit. He was conceived and born of the Spirit, led, anointed, crucified and raised to life by the Spirit. He taught in the power of the Holy Spirit and gifts us with his Spirit.

Jesus, I thank you for sending the Holy Spirit to me. Fill me with your Spirit so rivers of living water will overflow to others. Amen.

A Debt to Pay

Romans 1:14

"I have a great sense of obligation to people in our culture and to people in other cultures, to the educated and uneducated alike. So I am eager to come to you in Rome, too, to preach God's Good News. For I am not ashamed of this Good News about Christ. It is the power of God at work, saving everyone who believes . . ." (Ro. 1:14-16 NLT).

Paul is not ashamed to go to the world's capital amidst all its wickedness. In fact he says he is indebted to them. When someone does something for us we feel it is our duty to repay them. The Son of God got us out of the pit we were in, got rid of the sins we were doomed to keep repeating. (Col. 1:14). Paul in prison started thinking about God's blessings (Eph. 1) and couldn't get stopped. No wonder he says he is under obligation to share these blessings with everyone. The more we realize what Jesus has done for us the more we want to share these unearned blessings with others.

Every day we see, read or hear of people in poverty, multitudes living under repressive governments and suffering from violence. We hear warnings of possible pandemics and natural disasters. If we approach these needs in our human sympathy and energy we will eventually experience burnout.

We need divine resources and motivation. Our motivation is not from human sympathy but from our King who commissioned us to make disciples, to do the works that he did. "Jesus arrived from Nazareth anointed by God with the Holy Spirit, ready for action. He went through the country helping people and healing everyone who was beaten down by the Devil. He was able to do all this because God was with him" (Acts 10:38 Msg.). Jesus is our model. Since he came to serve and give his life for others we must do the same. (Matt. 20:28). We are in debt, we are under obligation. "I have an obligation to discharge and a duty to perform and a debt to pay" (Ro. 1:14 AMP).

Lord, I need your Holy Spirit to fulfill my debt and obligation. Make me a faithful witness and servant for you today. Amen.

Quality or Quantity?

John 3:16

"God so loved the world that he gave his only Son, so that everyone who believes in him (trusts in, clings to and relies on him) will not perish but have eternal life. God did not send his Son into the world to condemn it, but to save it" (John 3:16-17 NLT).

God loves the world. That includes everyone. If you or your church say we are not interested in reaching out to others we are saying, "You can go to hell." If you have two children and they become lost you search day and night for them until they are found. If you find one child and not the other, imagine a neighbor saying to you, "You found one child, just forget about the other one." That's what we are saying when we are not making an effort to reach people for Jesus.

Numbers are not our goal, transformed individuals are our goal. As Rick Warren writes: "Anytime someone says, 'You can't measure success by numbers,' my response is, 'It all depends on what you're counting.' If you're counting marriages saved, lives transformed, broken people healed, unbelievers becoming worshipers of Jesus and members being mobilized for ministry and missions, numbers are extremely important. They have eternal significance."

The book of Acts is permeated with numbers. The Gospels frequently inform us that multitudes followed Jesus or that the house was full that others could not enter. The Shepherd left the 99 and sought the one lost sheep. Every person is important! Don't let people deceive you with the idea that numbers are not important.

Those who don't like to talk about numbers frequently state appreciation for their little church where everyone knows everyone else. They need to pray: Father, give me passion like you had in giving your only son for my salvation. Jesus, give me the passion that took you to the cruel cross so I could experience eternal life. Holy Spirit, give me the passion that enabled you to leave heaven in all its splendor to come and live in my sinful heart now made holy by your work.

Father, help me to be passionate about people today. Amen.

Solomon's Prayer

I Kings 8:22-53

Solomon pours out his heart to God in one of the longest prayers in the Bible. (I Kings 8:22-53). His posture of kneeling and holding out his hands to heaven indicates his reverence and allegiance for God. (vv. 22). God's people also hold out their hands in prayer (v. 39). Our posture in prayer can help us in expressing our hearts to God in worship.

Solomon's prayer is missional. He expresses his faith as he entreats God for all the people in the world. (vv. 43 and 60). Do your prayers indicate your faith for the people around the world? God loves the world—all the people of the world. (John 3:16). Your prayers make a difference in the hearts and lives of those thousands of miles away.

Solomon's prayer emphasizes obedience. His words are backed up with action. He sacrificed a hundred and twenty thousand sheep, and twenty-two thousand cattle. (v. 63). Prayer is like putting a car in gear, don't pray unless you plan to move.

Solomon's honesty and transparency is remarkable as he confesses the sins of his people and recognizes God's inevitable punishment for their sin. "If they sin against you—and who has never sinned?—You may become angry with them and let their enemies conquer them and take them to a foreign land. But in the land of exile, they may turn to you again in repentance and pray, 'We have sinned, done evil, and acted wickedly.' Then if they turn to you with their whole heart . . . hear their prayers from heaven where you live. Uphold their cause and forgive your people who have sinned against you. Make their captors merciful to them, for they are your people—your special possession" (I Kings 8:46-51 NLT).

Forgiveness is another theme appearing six times in this prayer. Jesus reminds us that unless we forgive others he will not forgive us. Isaiah says our sin hides God's face from us so that he will not hear. (Isaiah 59:2).

Lord Jesus, teach me how to pray as Solomon prayed. Amen.

Living Gets Better and Better

II Corinthians 3:18

It doesn't matter how long you have been a Christian or how mature you are in your walk with Jesus—there is a higher plain ahead. Growth is exponential. You never reach your potential. "As the Spirit of the Lord works within us, we become more and more like him and reflect his glory even more" (II Cor. 3:18 NLT).

"Always be full of joy in the Lord. I say it again—rejoice! Let everyone see that you are considerate in all you do. Remember, the Lord is coming soon. Don't worry about anything, instead pray about everything. Tell God what you need and thank him for all he has done. Then you will experience God's peace, which exceeds anything we can understand. His peace will guard your hearts and minds as you live in Christ Jesus" (Phil. 4:4-7 NLT).

Today millions of Christians find themselves in prisons or in situations like Paul where physical needs are not being met. We know God promises to be with us even to the point of death. Paul says, "I have learned how to get along happily whether I have much or little. I know how to live on almost nothing or with everything. I have learned the secret of living in every situation. . . . For I can do everything with the help of Christ who gives me the strength I need" (Phil. 4:11-13 NLT).

Paul reminds us the sufferings of this time are not worthy to be compared to our future glory. (Ro. 8:17). God's grace will be with us in the valley of suffering and death. When Corrie ten Boom was forced to leave home realizing she was headed for a Nazi concentration camp she asked her father, what will I do? He reminded her that God's grace will be with her one day at a time. When you need God's grace he will supply it. After horrendous suffering and losing her sister, Betsy and several other family members she said, "You can never learn Christ is all you need, until Christ is all you have."

Lord Jesus, enable me to become more and more like you reflecting your glory. Amen.

Time Is of Essence

Ephesians 5:16

"Be very careful . . . how you live—making the most of every opportunity, because the days are evil" (Eph. 5:15-16). Life is short! David says, "Lord show me my life's end and the number of my days; let me know how fleeting is my life. Each man's life is but a breath" (Psalm 39:5). "Life is like the morning fog" (James 4:14 NLT).

Jesus says, "As long as it is day, we must do the works of him who sent me. Night is coming when no one can work" (John 9:4). Time is precious—you are on probation for only a few short years and then you will meet God, the judge of all the earth. Moses says, teach me to number my days that I may have a heart of wisdom. (Ps. 90:12). We need God's wisdom to live a godly life. I pray every day that I will not waste time. I set my will to do only what God wants me to do and say only what God wants me to say. (John 12:49).

In Psalm 119, David says he will meditate or reflect on God's ways (v. 15, 23, 48, 78, 99). "I ponder every morsel of wisdom from you" (v. 15 Msg.). "I will meditate on your wonders and on your promises" (v. 27). "Oh, how I love your law! I meditate on it all day long" (v. 97). "Seven times each day I stop and shout praises for the way you keep everything running right. For those who love what you reveal, everything fits—no stumbling around in the dark for them" (164-165 Msg.).

"I will meditate on your name all night God, treasuring your revelation" (v. 55 Msg.). "My eyes stay open through the watches of the night, that I may meditate on your promises " (v. 148). Like David, you can meditate on God's promises.

Different times Jesus prayed all night or got up before dawn to pray and meditate. (Luke 6:12; Mark 1:35). Nighttime is a special time to draw near to God. Wisdom comes easier during the night when all is quiet.

Lord enable me to use my time wisely. Amen.

Be Filled with the Spirit

Ephesians 5:18-21

"Do not get drunk on wine, which leads to debauchery. Instead, be filled with the Spirit. Speak to one another with psalms, hymns, and spiritual songs. Sing and make music in your heart to the Lord, always giving thanks to God the Father for everything, in the name of our Lord Jesus Christ. Submit to one another out of reverence for Christ" (Eph. 5:18-21).

The pagan culture tries to find happiness in wine, drugs, sex and worldly pleasures. The Christian finds happiness when he or she is filled with the Holy Spirit. Paul lists three results of being filled with the Holy Spirit.

First, the heart is changed. The Holy Spirit fills it with music—psalms, hymns and spiritual songs. (v. 19). It's wonderful to have a heart filled with praise to the Lord. Most mornings I awake to music of praise in my heart to God. My dad was a whistler. He would whistle hymns in praise to God throughout the day.

The second result of being filled with God's Spirit is giving thanks to God our Father for everything in the name of Jesus our Messiah. (v. 20). How can this be possible? It's possible because we have come to trust him. We know he never makes a mistake or causes us a needless tear. Even when we receive discouraging news we claim the promise that all things will work together for our good. (Ro. 8:28). That is, in everything God works it out for good.

Thirdly, we respect, honor and submit to each other because we reverence Christ. (v. 21). Jesus died for everyone. If he loved them, how can I not love and respect them?

This command to be filled with the Holy Spirit is in the present tense, which means we need to be continually filled. Why, because we leak. Come to Jesus continually requesting his filling. We come, ask and he fills us again and again.

Father fill me with your Holy Spirit. Amen.

Well or Fountains?

John 4:14

"The water I give them takes away thirst altogether. It becomes a perpetual spring within them, giving them eternal life" (John 4:14). Jesus uses the imagery of a fountain rather than a well. There is a huge difference. Jesus said the water is a perpetual spring within. Well water is of value only if you take the effort to bring it to the surface. Fountain water takes no effort. It is free flowing and fresh.

What is the source of this fountain of water? It's from within us. How is that possible? Jesus is the source of living water. Many times we read that Jesus is in us, e.g., "Remain in me and I will remain in you" (John 15:4 NLT). Jesus said in John 7:38 NLT, "Rivers of living water will flow out from within." It flows without effort. Move from struggling to bring water from the bottom of the well to a fountain of water overflowing from within.

Is this your experience? Jeremiah 2:13, "My people have forsaken me, the spring of living water, and have dug their own cisterns, broken cisterns that cannot hold water." Jesus wants his life to freely flow forth from us. If it is not flowing something is obstructing the flow. Sin blocks the flow of the fountain within. Remaining in Jesus is the key. He is our source. Sin separates us from God.

Jesus presents the same principles in John 15:5 NLT, "Those who remain in me and I in them, will produce much fruit." Note it says they will produce much fruit, not they can or might produce much fruit. Whenever the fountain is not flowing, whenever we are not producing fruit; ask, have I removed myself from Jesus? Have I grieved his Spirit? As you wait in his presence and listen to his voice you will find what is blocking the flow. If nothing comes to mind offer praise and thanksgiving to God from your heart. The rivers of water will begin to flow. This attitude of praise will bubble up and overflow through you to others.

Jesus, make me a fountain of blessing to others today. Amen.

Tree Climber Zaccheus

Luke 19:1-10

"Zaccheus ran ahead of the crowd and climbed a sycamore tree so he could get a glimpse of Jesus" (Luke 19:4 NLT).

"Zaccheus was one of the most influential Jews in the Roman tax-collecting business. He was rich" (v. 2 NLT). Being short of statue Zaccheus was so determined to see Jesus he put aside his pride and climbed a tree to catch a glimpse of Jesus among the crowd. Jesus noticing tree-climbing Zaccheus, calls him by name. Jesus said, "Zaccheus, come down immediately. I must stay at your house today" (v. 5). It's important to call people by their name. Jesus knew Zaccheus longed to see him so he invited himself to his home. Zaccheus was excited and full of joy. "The crowds were displeased. 'He has gone to be the guest of a notorious sinner,' they grumbled." (v. 7 NLT).

Among the "crowd" of people you meet today be alert for indications of persons who are open to faith. Times of difficulties such as lost of job, loss of a loved one, illness of someone in their family, or marriage problems often make a person more open to talk about their need for faith. Ask God to give you wisdom and courage to know what to say and how to say it. You may share how in similar circumstances you have found your faith to be most helpful.

You will need to take the risk of being misunderstood when you are obeying Jesus' command to relate to people like Zaccheus. Some people will not appreciate your efforts because you are inviting the wrong kind of people to your church. How sad. Remember that's how they treated Jesus.

Zaccheus' response is clear and concise. He confesses any dishonesty he may have committed. Jesus' response is just as clear, "Salvation has come to this home today, for this man has shown himself to be a son of Abraham. And I, the Son of Man, have come to seek and save those like him who are lost" (vv. 9-10 NLT).

Lord enable me to share the Good News with persons like Zaccheus even though others may ignore or reject them. Amen.

The Heart of the Father Is for the Children

Malachi 4:5-6

"Look, I will send you the prophet Elijah before that great and dreadful day of the Lord comes. He will turn the hearts of the fathers to their children, and the hearts of the children to their fathers; or else I will come and strike the land with a curse" (Malachi 4:5-6).

Research shows when a child grows up in a father-absent home, he or she is four times more likely to live in poverty, have higher levels of aggressive behavior and lower grades. Delinquency is more widespread, abuse and neglect are common. Teen pregnancies are seven times greater when fathers are absent. Children of single parent homes are at a higher risk in the use of alcohol and drugs.

Even in homes where the father is present physically he often is not involved emotionally or spiritually with the family. A prison chaplain, asked the prisoners if they wanted cards to send for Mother's Day. Everyone wanted one. When the same question was asked concerning Father's Day no one desired a card. Less than half of children today grow up living with the same father in the first eighteen years of their life.

Paul gives a good description of a father: "You know that we treated each of you as a father treats his own children. We pleaded with you, encouraged you, and urged you to live your lives in a way that God would consider worthy" (I Thess. 2:11-12 NLT). Our priority as fathers must be to live and share the Good News with our families. As a parent ask yourself, is your heart centered on work, recreation, getting ahead or do you have a heart for your family?

One of the qualifications of church leaders is that, "He must manage his own family well, with children who respect and obey him. For if a man cannot manage his own household, how can he take care of God's church?" (I Tim. 3:4-5 NLT). The world takes notice when they see a godly family.

Lord, enable me to be a godly parent. Give me wisdom to love, guide, nurture and set an example for them in the ways of the Lord. Amen.

Running the Race

I Corinthians 9:24-27

"You've all been to the stadium and seen the athletes race. Everyone runs; one wins. Run to win. All good athletes train hard. They do it for a gold medal that tarnishes and fades. You're after one that's gold eternally. I don't know about you, but I'm running hard for the finish line. I'm giving it everything I've got. No sloppy living for me! I'm staying alert and in top condition. I'm not going to get caught napping, telling everyone else all about it and then missing out myself" (I Cor. 9:23-27 Msg.).

"I do not run like a man running aimlessly; I do not fight like a man beating the air. No, I beat my body and make it my slave so that after I have preached to others, I myself will not be disqualified for the prize" (vv. 25-27). "Train yourself to be godly" (I Tim. 4:7).

Paul uses Olympic imagery here. The runners train for years to win the race. They deny themselves many pleasures for the pleasure of running the race to hear the affirmation of the fans and receive a medal. They deny themselves certain enjoyable foods; they discipline themselves to exercise even when they don't feel like it. They follow the strict rules of their coach. How serious are you in living for Jesus? Are you conscious that you are in training? Are you seeing progress or are you just beating the air? How serious are you in pressing toward the goal?

Paul writes to the Philippians: "I press toward the goal to win the prize for which God has called me heavenward in Christ Jesus" (3:14). When Paul comes to the end of his life he writes: "I have fought a good fight, I have finished the race, I have kept the faith. Now there is in store for me the crown of righteousness, which the Lord, the righteous Judge, will award to me on that day—and not only to me, but also to all who have longed for his appearing" (II Tim. 4:7-8).

Jesus, help me to run with discipline, with determination, my eyes fixed on you. Enable me to keep the faith and receive the crown of righteousness. Amen.

Changed Life or Exchanged Life

Hebrews 12:2

"Throw off everything that hinders and the sin that so easily entangles, and run with perseverance the race marked out for you" (Heb. 12:2). Paul gave up everything for the welfare of others. (II Cor. 12:15). Christ is our life. (Col. 3:4).

Once we enter God's Kingdom our eyes our opened to an entirely new world. He is our Father, Leader, our King! Our own interests are secondary.

What things come between you and Jesus? Are you willing to move to help an overworked pastor or if God calls you to help plant a church in the next town or halfway around the globe? Is there anyone you have not forgiven? Jesus' life becomes our life, his goals become our goals. We live an exchanged life more than a changed life.

I have a close friend who had a high position in a large institution but he gave it up because Jesus wanted him to be a teacher. He sacrificed not only salary but prestige and years of training to be a witness for Jesus in the classroom. Jesus has multiplied his joy and amply provided for his financial needs. He has no regrets! Another friend gave up a medical practice here in the states to serve as a doctor in a very poor country. He has the joy of touching many lives for Jesus.

Perhaps God will ask you to make some sacrifices or he may ask you to remain right where you are and be a witness for him. Do you have reservations in following through in what you know God is asking you to do? To refuse to follow when you know what God is asking you to do will block the free flowing rivers of living water within you. Your life will become stagnant.

Your real test as a Christian is not your willingness to preach the gospel, but your willingness to do whatever Jesus wants you to do, no matter how lowly or seemingly unimportant. Life with Jesus is more than a changed life—it is his life lived through us.

Lord Jesus, search my heart and see if there is any sin that entangles my feet. I surrender my life to you. Amen.

Work Out Your Salvation

Philippians 2:12-13

"Continue to work out your salvation with fear and trembling, for it is God who works in you to will and to act according to his good purpose" (Phil. 2:12-13). "Put into action God's saving work in your lives, obeying God with deep reverence and fear. For God is working in you giving you the desire to obey him and the power to do what pleases him" (NLT).

Salvation is a gift, but we must put our salvation into action. (Eph. 2:8-9). It's God who works in us giving us this desire to obey and the power to perform his purpose through us. Why is it difficult if God's power is performing his will in us? It's difficult if we are not willing to die to self and trust Jesus to lead us. David wrote: "The Lord says, 'I will guide you along the best pathway for your life. I will advise you and watch over you'" (Ps. 32:8 NLT). What a blessed promise!

However, we must yield to his discipline. "Work hard at living at peace with others" (I Peter 3:11 NLT). "Make every effort to apply the benefits of these promises to your life. Then your faith will produce a life of moral excellence" (II Peter 1:5 NLT). "Work hard to prove that you really are among those God has called and chosen. Doing this, you will never stumble or fall away" (II Peter 1:10 NLT). "Make every effort to live a pure and blameless life" (II Peter 3:14 NLT). Many times we are reminded to work hard. We must fight the good fight of faith. (II Tim. 6:12). The Devil is a roaring lion seeking to devour you. (I Peter 5:8).

We are absolutely helpless to earn salvation but once we are born into God's family we need to give ourselves wholeheartedly to our Lord. After all he died for us. We can never repay him for his wonderful gift of eternal life.

Father, I thank you for providing both the will and the power to live the Christian life. I promise by your grace to give every effort to cooperate with your will for me. I choose to please you in all things. Amen.

A Home for Jesus

John 14:2 & 23

Paul prays that, "Out of God's glorious riches he may strengthen you with power through his Spirit . . . , so that Christ may dwell in our hearts through faith" (Eph. 3:16-17). How is it possible for Jesus to dwell in us?

Jesus said, "I am going to prepare a place (home) for you" (John 14:2). In verse 23 we have the same word used when he says, "My Father will love him and we will come . . . and make our home with him." Just as Jesus was going to heaven to prepare a home for us we can prepare a home for him in our hearts.

How can I make a home for Jesus? At Pentecost God came in the form of his Holy Spirit. Through the miracle of the Holy Spirit, God lives in our hearts. He knocks on our heart's door.

Holman Hunt painted a picture of Jesus knocking on the door. There is no handle on the outside. You must open the door for him to come in. "Here I stand at the door and knock. If anyone hears my voice and opens the door, I will come in and eat with him, and he with me" (Rev. 3:20).

Your body is the temple of the Holy Spirit. (I Cor. 3:16). Jesus lives there. "The one who is in you is greater than the one who is in the world" (I John 4:4). If we submit to him we will overcome all sin. "The tools of our trade . . . are for demolishing that entire massively corrupt culture. We use our powerful God—tools for smashing warped philosophies, tearing down barriers erected against the truth of God, fitting every loose thought and emotion and impulse into the structure of life shaped by Christ" (II Cor. 10:4-5 Msg.). Jesus can purify every thought, emotion and impulse into the likeness of himself. That is victory!

Lord Jesus, since you live in my heart, I give you every emotion, desire and thought. My heart and mind are yours, my desires are your desires. Search me and know my heart and see if there is anything displeasing to you. Wash me and make me pure. Amen.

You're a Preacher

Acts 8:4

Don't let the word "preaching" scare you. Preaching in the New Testament means sharing the Good News. "Those who had been scattered preached the word wherever they went" (Acts 8:4). "Wherever they were scattered they preached the message about Jesus" (Acts 8:4 Msg.).

The church gravitates toward staying in salt shakers. The Great Commission should scatter us. It often takes persecution, as in Acts 8, to scatter us. In our salt shakers we do not make people thirsty for the water of life. Too often we hide our light under a bushel rather than allow it to brighten the darkness. Louie Palu says, "The church is like manure, put it on a pile and it stinks, spread it out and it enriches the world."

Why is that? Like the church at Ephesis which was at least thirty years old, we tend to lose our first love. "You have forsaken your first love. Remember the height from which you have fallen! Repent and do the things you did at first. If you do not repent, I will come to you and remove your lampstand from its place" (Rev. 2:4-5). As a general rule the longer we are Christians the less zeal we have.

The church at Laodicea had a similar problem, "I know you inside and out, and find little to my liking. You're not cold, you're not hot—far better to be either cold or hot! You're stale. You're stagnant. You make me want to vomit. You brag, 'I'm rich, I've got it made, I need nothing from anyone,' oblivious that in fact you're a pitiful blind beggar, threadbare and homeless" (Rev. 3:15-17 Msg.).

According to church history there is one sin that will weaken the church every time, i.e. riches. Often when we become Christians God blesses us and then we get our eyes on the blessings and off of Jesus.

Paul admonished the Roman church to serve the Lord enthusiastically. "Never be lacking in zeal" (12:11). "Don't burn out; keep yourselves fueled and aflame" (Msg.).

Lord Jesus, I confess my zeal is lacking. Empower me with enthusiasm by your Holy Spirit as I feed on your word. Use me to witness for you today! Amen.

Find Your Style, Serving

Ephesians 4:7 & 11

We're all are different. "Everything you are and think and do is permeated with Oneness (Godlikeness). But that doesn't mean you should all look and speak and act the same" (Eph. 4:7 Msg.).

It's helpful to realize that Jesus wants us all to share the Good News but he made us so that we express the Good News differently, using different styles. Bill Hybles lists six different styles of evangelism. Each of us has one or more of these styles that we find comfortable. Today we focus on serving.

Serving—How Can I Help? Most Christians believe they are called to serve. We should enjoy serving others. However, too often we have not shared the Good News with those we serve. Dorcas was serving the Lord by helping the poor. (Acts 9:36). Dorcas died. Her friends sent for Peter. When Peter came they showed him the clothing she made. Her deeds of serving impacted many lives.

John and Rhoda continually serve the Lord by helping people move, by lending one of their vehicles to someone when their car lets them sit, by taking food to those in need or fixing a broken pipe under the kitchen sink or providing grocery money. Their sacrificial acts of service impact many lives for Christ inside and outside the church.

Some Christians feel like second-class citizens because "all they can do" is serve others. Serving with joy from a heart of compassion leads people to thank you. Respond by saying, "God has been good to me, I can't help passing on his goodness to others." You can add, "He changed me and made my life wonderfully different. I enjoy helping others. I want you to know you matter to God."

You will plant seeds that others can water and the Holy Spirit can bring to fruition. Many unbelievers need someone like you to soften their hearts through your acts of service. Be that person for them.

Jesus, help me to be your joyful servant today. Enable me to share your love with a life of service and a heart of love. Amen.

Find Your Style, Making Friends

Luke 5:28-29

"Jesus saw a tax collector by the name of Levi sitting at his tax booth. 'Follow Me,' Jesus said to him, and Levi got up, left everything and followed him. Then Levi held a great banquet for Jesus at his house, and a large crowd of tax collectors and others were eating with them. But the Pharisees and teachers of the law who belonged to their sect complained to his disciples, 'Why do you eat and drink with tax collectors and 'sinners'"? (Luke 5:28-29 NLT).

This is friendship evangelism, Jesus' primary style. When Jesus called Levi, Levi left his lucrative business. He immediately hosted his peers at a banquet with Jesus as the guest of honor. The self-righteous Pharisees were turned off with Jesus associating with tax-collector Levi. They were concerned about keeping the "church" pure. Jesus spent time not with these self-righteous leaders, but with people who sensed their need for God and for friendship.

Forty percent of people have no close friend. Identify those in society and in church who have no close friends. Don't neglect those with a poor reputation. They are often open to hearing the invitation of God's love.

If you're an impatient extrovert you will need to exercise patience because relationship building takes time. You don't make a friendship in one encounter. It's easy to be friendly but being a friend demands sacrifice. It will affect your schedule, your priorities, and your finances. There is a million miles between being friendly and being a friend. How many new friends have you made this past year?

Audrey, a beauty salon stylist, shares with her clients how Jesus is transforming her life. She has invited many to church and some have come. Audrey is a relational evangelist. Angie related to her neighbor for several months. Over the course of time her neighbor came to church and brought others with her. New people bring new people and the Kingdom of God grows.

Lord Jesus, help me to love those who need a friend and to lead them to you. Amen.

Find Your Style, Testimonial

John 9

"I know this, I was blind, and now I can see!" (John 9:25 NLT).

In John 9, Jesus healed a blind beggar. The Pharisees were upset that Jesus would heal on the Sabbath. They asked the beggar what he thought of the man who healed him. His answer was straight, "I was blind, now I see!" This experience applies not only to physical blindness but to spiritual blindness. All of us were blind spiritually until Jesus gave us sight. We too can say, "I was blind but now I see! Jesus changed my life. He can change yours too."

Testimonial evangelists usually are not people who became Christians as children and followed a steady path to spiritual maturity. Often they will say they thought they were Christians. "I went to church and tried to live a good moral life. Then I turned control of my life over to Jesus and began to trust Jesus as my Lord. That decision made all the difference in the world. It was the best decision I ever made. If you are interested I would love to tell you more."

A testimony is not preaching; it is basically giving facts about how Jesus has impacted your life. Paul used this approach in Acts 22 and 26 before the multitude in Jerusalem and before King Agrippa. You will find the following questions Paul asked in Acts 26 helpful as you think through your own testimony: Where were you spiritually before receiving Jesus? How did that affect you in your relationships? What caused you to consider Jesus as the solution to your needs? Specifically, how did you receive Christ? How did your life begin to change after you trusted Jesus? What other benefits have you experienced since becoming a Christian? Most of these questions can be answered in a sentence or two.

You have a testimony. Most seekers don't need to hear a sermon: They need a Christian like yourself to share with them how Jesus makes a difference in your life. Your testimony will be one more step the Holy Spirit uses to bring them closer to Kingdom citizenship.

Lord, loosen my tongue. I will share what you are doing for me. Amen.

June 30

Find Your Style, Confrontational

Acts 2:23

"You followed God's prearranged plan. With the help of lawless Gentiles, you nailed him to the cross and murdered him . . . So let it be clearly known by everyone in Israel that God has made this Jesus whom you crucified to be both Lord and Messiah! Peter's words convicted them deeply, and they said to him and to the other apostles, 'Brothers, what should we do?' Peter replied, 'Each of you must turn from your sins and turn to God, and be baptized in the name of Jesus Christ for the forgiveness of your sins. Then you will receive the gift of the Holy Spirit'" (Acts 2:23, 36-38 NLT).

Peter laid it on the line and three thousand responded. (v. 41). Some people must be confronted directly for the Holy Spirit to get through to them. Under the guidance of the Holy Spirit you may have the personality and temperament to confront people with their sin and their need of the Savior.

Billy Graham often used the phrase: "You must be born again!" Charles Stanley repeatedly says in his message: "Listen! Listen!"

Joe was confrontational. Joe embarrassed me at times. We walked up to a home and he abruptly asked, "Is your dog saved yet?" He then shared what Jesus did for him and asked them if they wanted to receive Jesus into their life. When Joe suddenly died because of a heart attack, I had his funeral and gave opportunity for persons to share how Joe touched their life. For more than an hour one person after another spoke of Joe's boldness and how they appreciated his witness. One person flew from another state to attend the funeral and thanked Joe's family for his witness.

"The righteous are as bold as a lion" (Prov. 28:1). In Acts 4 we read, "The members of the council were amazed when they saw the boldness of Peter and John, for they could see that they were ordinary men who had had no special training . . . . Peter and John replied, 'Do you think God wants us to obey you rather than him? We cannot stop telling about the wonderful things we have seen and heard'" (Acts 4:13, 19-20 NLT).

Lord Jesus, help me to be a bold witness for you today. Amen.

Find Your Style, Intellectual

Acts 17:3

In this approach you refer seekers to books and other resources. You'll spend time studying with them. Invite people to follow Jesus in spite of their doubts and questions. All of us have unanswered questions. It's part of being human and expressing our humility, both attitudes are necessary for us to discover God. Questions are good although we need to make a commitment to Christ before we have everything figured out, otherwise there is no need for faith. "As the heavens are higher than the earth, so are my ways higher than your ways and my thoughts then your thoughts" (Isaiah 55:9).

Paul went to the lecture hall of Tyranus and debated daily for two years. (Acts 19:9). He conversed with the intelligentsia and debated with the philosophers of Athens. In his sermon on Mars Hill, he ingeniously used the Athenians' altar to an unknown god as an introduction to his presentation of the true God.

Luke writes, "Paul was explaining and proving the prophecies about the sufferings of the Messiah and his rising from the dead. He said, 'This Jesus I'm telling you about is the Messiah'" (Acts 17:3 NLT).

Don't let persons with a high intellect intimidate you. Often their questions are a smoke screen to hide a guilty conscience. They intuitively know they need salvation. Only the Holy Spirit can break the wall of resistance. On the other hand, honest questions need honest answers.

Once a skeptical journalist, Lee Strobel, freely recognized difficult questions and exposed on them, revealing that faith in Christ is an answer very much worth considering. Josh McDowell, known worldwide for his ministry to university students, uses this approach very effectively. My friend Mike, relates to Jehovah Witnesses and goes on the Internet and debates with those of other faiths. We are not called to win an argument but to share God's love with boldness and respect.

Lord, help me to diligently study and to be able to present the best answers to those who have sincere questions concerning Christianity. Amen.

Find Your Style, Invitational

John 1:41

Someone said, "The measure of love for people is our willingness to tell them they are lost." "When Andrew spent a day with Jesus he went to find his brother Simon and told him, 'We have found the Messiah' (that is, the Christ). And he brought him to Jesus" (John 1:40-41). The key is always authentic friendship. To repeat, the key word is friendship. Jesus' primary ministry was one-to-one relationships.

Some studies conclude that more than half the people who come to Jesus in the United States come through this style. This has certainly been true in my ministry.

Our friends know and accept us. Jesus said, "Anyone who accepts your message is also accepting me. And anyone who rejects you is rejecting me" (Luke 10:16 NLT). This teaching indicates that we need to befriend people so they are able to receive Jesus' message of Good News. If we are conscious of Jesus living through us, those who the Spirit is calling will be drawn to Jesus in us. (Gal. 2:20).

For the invitational approach to be effective, churches need to have services at which the unchurched feel comfortable and the Gospel is presented in a way they can understand. Unchurched friends should not fear that they will be put on the spot or in some way embarrassed. To become disciples the newcomes need to be linked to a mentor who will walk with him.

Gentle persistence in a loving manner communicates to the unchurched that we care. When Elwood, a new believer, went to a church conference, someone asked him why he started coming to church. He said, "Because Pastor Dave kept inviting me, he wouldn't give up." I had gone to his home and visited with him and his family many times. I called occasionally and prompted others in the church to do the same. This is how we "compel" them to come. (Luke 14:23).

Lord Jesus, give me eyes to see people who are open to an invitation to come to you. Give me gentle boldness to extend that invitation. Amen.

Vision

Isaiah 35:7

Christians are people with vision. On the birthday of the church Peter quoted the prophecy of Joel, "Your sons and daughters will prophesy, your young men will see visions, your old men will dream dreams" (Acts 2:17).

"Then will the eyes of the blind be opened and the ears of the deaf unstopped. Then will the lame leap like a deer and the mute tongue shout for joy. Water will gush forth in the wilderness and streams in the desert. The burning sand will become a pool, the thirsty ground bubbling springs" (Isaiah 35:5-7).

"Delight yourself in the Lord and he will give you the desires of your heart. Commit your ways to the Lord; trust in him and he will do this; He will make your righteousness shine like the dawn, the justice of your cause like the noonday sun" (Psalm 37:4-6).

As a church consultant, I have worked with many churches that are dying for lack of vision. Those that have a few remaining youth, I encourage to invite these youth to the leadership meetings and hear their concerns. Empower the youth in your congregation. Spot their gifts and encourage them. It's amazing what God will do through them. Remember the disciples were young, very young. Jesus could have picked mature people—he wanted people with a vision.

If you have lost your vision, cry out to God for a fresh vision. We need people with sanctified imagination, which is another way of defining vision. Vision is really faith. Is your faith becoming stronger? Forget those traditions that are no longer producing fruit and ask God to give you a new vision.

Let the fire of God's presence consume you, give you a vision. Your vision won't be fulfilled overnight; it may not be fulfilled in your lifetime. God will test you as he tested Abraham by asking you to slay your Isaac to see if your vision is more important than your love for him.

Lord, give me your vision for my life and for your church. Amen.

Heal Our Land

II Chronicles 7:14

"If my people, who are called by my name, will humble themselves and pray and seek my face and turn from their wicked ways, then will I hear from heaven, and will forgive their sin and will heal their land" (II Chron. 7:14).

God asks four things of his people: (1) humility, (2) prayer, (3) seeking his face, and (4) turning from their wicked ways. Then he will respond: (1) He will hear from heaven, (2) forgive their sin, and (3) heal their land.

Are you and I humbling ourselves before the Lord? Are we saying an unconditional "Yes" to Jesus in every area of our lives? If there is one "little" area where we have not given over to the Lordship of Jesus, we grieve his Spirit and lose his power.

Are you and I praying people? Ask the Lord to send a spirit of prayer into your life. (Zechariah 12:10). Ask him to teach you how to pray. Until we make prayer a priority in our life and in our churches we will be ineffective and fruitless. Paul writes, "Prayer is essential in this ongoing warfare. Pray hard and long. Pray for your brothers and sisters. Keep each other's spirits up so that no one falls behind or drops out" (Eph. 6:18 Msg.).

Are we seeking his face? The Amplified Bible translates "seek my face" as: "crave and require of necessity my face." "As the deer pants for streams of water, so my soul pants for you, O God. My soul thirsts for God, for the living God" (Ps. 42:1-2).

Are we turning from our wicked ways—repenting? There is a difference between repentance and forgiveness. Repentance is a resolve to turn and do God's will. It a step beyond forgiveness our life is now transformed. (Gal. 5:16-21).

When we do this God has promised to (1) hear from heaven, (2) forgive our sin, and (3) heal our land.

Lord God, our land needs healing. We are so far from you. Forgive our sin. Give me grace and strength to cast aside my selfish and sinful ways. Come into my life with the fullness of your Holy Spirit and use me to be an instrument of healing. Amen.

Jesus Is Coming Again

Acts 1:4-8

Just before Jesus ascended to heaven he said: "Do not leave Jerusalem, but wait for the gift my Father promised. . . . John baptized with water, but in a few days you will be baptized with the Holy Spirit." So when they met together, they asked him, "Lord, are you at this time going to restore the kingdom to Israel?" He said to them: "It is not for you to know the times or dates the Father has set by his own authority. But you will receive power when the Holy Spirit comes on you; and you will be my witnesses in Jerusalem, and in all Judea and Samaria and to the ends of the earth" (Acts 1:4-8).

Too often Christians get caught up in the debate concerning the date of the Lord's return. As pastor I, have had persons in my congregation who were "sure" the Lord had to return in a particular year because of their understanding of a prophecy and its "perfect" fit with today's world scene.

There is something far more important than the date of Jesus' return, that is sharing the Good News in "Jerusalem" i.e. at work, school or across your street, then in the neighboring towns and state and finally around the world. While the return of our Lord is a central doctrine of the Christian faith, the date is not for us to know. It is known only by the Father. (Mark 13:32 and Acts 1:7). Don't get trapped into arguing over the date. Point people to Jesus and the necessity of knowing him so they can experience eternal life and be ready for the Lord's return. (John 17:3).

It took persecution for the apostles to take Jesus' command seriously. They spread the Good News in Jerusalem, Samaria, Ethiopia and throughout the known world. Many died because of their witness.

Cardinal Francis George said, "I will die in bed, my successor will die in prison, his successor will die in the town square as a martyr and his successor will gather up the shards of a broken civilization and put them back together again as has been the pattern throughout history."

Lord Jesus, enable me to focus on being a faithful witness for you. Amen.

July 6

What's for Dinner?

Isaiah 55:1-2

"Come, all you who are thirsty, come to the waters; and you who have no money, come buy and eat! Come buy wine and milk without money and without cost. Why spend money on what is not bread, and your labor on what does not satisfy? Listen . . . eat what is good, and your soul will delight in the richest of fare" (Is. 55:1-2).

When tempted, Jesus said to the Devil: "It takes more than bread to stay alive. It takes a steady stream of words from God's mouth" (Matt. 4:4 Msg.). "Do not work for food that spoils, but for food that endures to eternal life" (John 6:27). "Do not worry about your life, what you will eat or drink . . . Is not life more important than food? Look at the birds of the air . . . your heavenly Father feeds them. Are you not much more valuable than they?" (Matt. 6:25-26).

"My food is to do the will of him who sent me and to finish his work . . . Open your eyes and look at the fields! They are ripe for harvest. Even now the reaper draws his wages, even now he harvests the crop for eternal life, so that the sower and the reaper may be glad together" (John 4:32-36). The joy of sharing Jesus will feed your soul with such enthusiasm that you will forget about eating lunch. This is true fasting.

Many people live to eat. Let's learn to eat so we can live. After church services I hear people asking, "Which restaurant shall we go to?" Many will spend more for their Sunday noon meal than they drop into the offering basket to extend God's Kingdom. Around the table will their conversation be about football, the stock market or about the pastor's message and how it relates to their life?

"I have often told you before . . . many live as enemies of the cross of Christ. Their destiny is destruction, their god is their stomach, and their glory is in their shame. Their mind is on earthly things. But our citizenship is in heaven. And we eagerly await a Savior from there, the Lord Jesus Christ" (Phil. 3:18-20).

Father, I want to know you more than I want my daily food. Amen.

Grace, the Core of the Christian's Life

I Corinthians 15:9-10

The acrostic for G-R-A-C-E = God's Riches At Christ's Expense. Grace is at the very core of Christ's Kingdom, a clear characteristic of Christ. "The grace of the Lord Jesus be with you" (I Cor. 16:23). The Message reads: "Our Master Jesus has his arms wide open for you."

When I think of grace I think of the simple but profound fact that God loves me. I don't deserve his love. As Paul says, "I am less than the least of all God's people, this grace was given me; to preach to the Gentiles the unsearchable riches of Christ" (Eph. 3:8). Again he writes: "For I am the least of the apostles and do not even deserve to be called an apostle, because I persecuted the church of God. But by the grace of God I am what I am, and his grace to me was not without effect" (I Cor. 15:9-10).

Grace was expressed daily in the life of our Lord. He chose to relate to ostracized women (John 4 & 8), he touched those with leprosy (Luke 5:13), he ate with sinners like Levi (Luke 5:29) and Zacchaeus (Luke 19:7). He welcomed the defiant (Luke 15:20). He highly praised the generosity of the stranger, the Good Samaritan, (Luke 10:33), he showed concern for the children and forgave those who crucified him. (Matt. 5:44). Jesus is a grace person.

Life for the Christian begins with grace and ends with grace. The more we mature the more we grow in grace. Let his grace make you strong in Christ Jesus. We are called to grow in grace. (II Peter 3:18). Paul says, "I'm not about to let his grace go to waste. Haven't I worked hard trying to do more than any of the others? Even then, my work didn't amount to all that much. It was God giving me the work to do, God giving me the energy to do it" (I Cor. 15:9-10 Msg.). (Zechariah 12:10).

Lord Jesus, all that I am, and all that I have is a gift from you. Your grace is the center of my life. My desire is to grow in grace. Because of your grace I will love and serve you with all my heart. Amen.

A New Wardrobe

Colossians 3:5-17

Paul describes moving from the old life to a new life as changing our wardrobe.

He begins by informing us to kill (put off) everything connected with the way of death: "sexual promiscuity, impurity, lust, doing whatever you feel like whenever you feel like it, and grabbing whatever attracts your fancy. That's a life shaped by things and feelings instead of by God. It's because of that kind of thing that God is about to explode in anger. It wasn't long ago that you were doing all that stuff and not knowing any better. But you know better now, so make sure it's all gone for good; bad temper, irritability, meanness, profanity, dirty talk . . .

"Don't lie to one another. You're done with that old life. It's like a filthy set of ill-fitting clothes you've stripped off and put in the fire. Now you're dressed in a new wardrobe. Every item of your new way of life is custom-made by the Creator, with his label on it. All the old fashions are obsolete. Words like Jewish and non-Jewish, religious and irreligious, insider and outsider, uncivilized and uncouth, slave and free, mean nothing. From now on everyone is defined by Christ, everyone is included in Christ.

"So chosen by God for this new life of love, dress in the wardrobe God picked out for you; compassion, kindness, humility, quiet strength, discipline. Be even-tempered, content with second place, quick to forgive an offense. Forgive as quickly and completely as the Master forgave you. And regardless of what else you put on, wear love. It's your basic, all-purpose garment. Never be without it . . .

"Let the peace of Christ keep you in tune with each other, in step with each other. None of this going off and doing your own things. And cultivate thankfulness. Let the Word of Christ—the Message—have the run of the house. Give it plenty of room in your lives. Instruct and direct one another using good common sense. And sing, sing your hearts out to God! Let every detail in your lives—words, actions, whatever—be done in the name of the Master, Jesus, thanking God the Father every step of the way" (Col. 3:5-17 Msg.).

Father, by your grace I will wear my new wardrobe. Amen.

Can We Answer Jesus' Prayer?

John 17:21-22

Jesus prayed: "The goal is for all of them to become one heart and mind— just as you, Father, are in me and I in you, so they might be one heart and mind with us. Then the world might believe that you, in fact, sent me. The same glory you gave me, I gave them, so they'll be as unified and together as we are—I in them and you in me" (John 17:21-22 Msg.).

"A new command I give you; Love one another. As I have loved you so you must love one another. By this all men will know that you are my disciples, if you love one another" (John 13:34-35).

There are well over 300 denominations in the United States. With the rise of independent churches there seems to be more divisions than ever.

Our unity is found in Jesus. Paul gives us what I believe to be the core absolutes on which we can base our unity. "I want to remind you of the gospel I preached to you, which you received and on which you have taken your stand. By this gospel you are saved, if you hold firmly to the word I preached to you. Otherwise, you have believed in vain. For what I received I passed on to you as of first importance: that Christ died for our sins according to the Scriptures, that he was buried, that he was raised on the third day according to the Scriptures, and that he appeared to Peter, and then to the Twelve. After that, he appeared to more than five hundred of the brothers at the same time" (I Cor. 15:1-6).

These verses are foundational for our unity. Be open to listening to others who differ with you on "interpretations" realizing that you may not agree with them. Hopefully we can work together and fellowship together setting aside our personal preferences, subjective opinions and feelings. I believe it is possible to do this without compromising our convictions.

Lord, forgive us for our disunity with all our divisions. Enable me to focus on the supreme values of Jesus who is the way, the truth and the life. Bring us together. Amen.

Compassion

Matthew 9:36

Jesus loved people deeply. When I consider that he was sinless but constantly surrounded by sinful people, his love amazes me. (Mark 2:15). There was injustice, envy and hate on every side. He had every right to condemn the sinner, to take a moral stand, form protests and attack individuals. Yet when he saw the crowds he had compassion on them because they had no hope, wandering like lost sheep without a shepherd.

Rather than being filled with disdain, he was filled with love. He laid down his life for these lost sheep. We need new eyes to see people as Jesus saw them. The more we grow in our walk with Jesus the more we have Jesus' attitude for the lost sheep we meet each day. Jesus' love showed through him so that sinners were drawn to him. His life set forth the clear statement that the more spiritually mature I am, the more approachable I should be to people who are hurting and who are outside God's Kingdom. Our approachability increases as we become more like Christ.

As "Jesus looked out over the crowds, his heart broke. So confused and aimless they were, like sheep with no shepherd. 'What a huge harvest!' he said to his disciples. 'How few workers! On your knees and pray for harvest hands'" (Matthew 9:36-38 Msg.).

Today a man walked five miles to come to our church. He had come six months ago for two Sundays but then dropped out. He said, "I tried many churches but this is where I feel loved." Let's ask ourselves: "Are those outside the faith drawn to us?" It's heart breaking to see that the self-righteous, judgmental religious people of Jesus' day despaired and even hated Jesus. Are any of those elements in your heart? Are they in your church? Are sinners drawn to you and to your church? Do you spend more time praying for the lost or for physical needs? Are you praying for more workers to enter the harvest? Are you training your children to love the lost?

Lord, give me a passion for the lost; to love as you loved—pray as you prayed. Amen.

We Need Each Other

Romans 1:11-12

We need each other. "I long to see you so that I may impart to you some spiritual gift to make you strong—that is that you and I may be mutually encouraged by each other's faith" (Ro. 1:11-12). I'm tempted to think that Paul was so advanced in the Lord that he did not need others. Listen to the following scriptures from his pen.

"When Timothy comes back, he can cheer me up by telling me how you are getting along" (Phil. 2:19 NLT). "I was glad when Stephanas, Fortunatus and Achaicus arrived, because they have supplied what was lacking from you. For they refreshed my spirit and yours also. Such men deserve recognition" (I Cor. 16:17-18).

"May the Lord show mercy to the household of Onesiphorus, because he often refreshed me and was not ashamed of my chains" (II Tim. 1:16).

"Let's see how inventive we can be in encouraging love and helping out, not avoiding worshiping together as some do but spurring each other on, especially as we see the big Day approaching" (Heb. 10:24-25 Msg.).

From the opening chapters of the Bible God made it clear that it was not good for us to be alone. (Genesis 2:18). Christianity must be expressed in community. There is no such thing as a Christian choosing to live in isolation. Every time the Lord's Supper is mentioned in scripture it is always in the context of community. In participating in baptism and the communion service we promise not only to be faithful to our Lord but we promise to be in a loving relationship with each other. We need each other. A Christian who chooses to isolate him or herself will develop a warped faith. We need to not only hear from the Holy Spirit ourselves but we need to hear what the Spirit is saying to our brothers and sisters. Peter records that God says, "I will pour out my Spirit on all people" (Acts 2:17). There are seventeen one-another admonitions in the New Testament. We need each other.

Lord, our culture has taught us to be individualistic and independent. Enable me to love and encourage others and to be encouraged by them. Amen.

Jesus and the Holy Spirit

John 5:19

Jesus told the disciples that he said only what the Father told him to say and he did nothing except what he saw the Father doing. (John 5:19, 12:49-50). How is that possible? Jesus was tuned into the Holy Spirit.

We have the same Holy Spirit. Are we aware of the Holy Spirit? Pray continually for the Holy Spirit to fill you. Was Jesus always full of the Holy Spirit? Luke records, "Jesus, full of the Holy Spirit, returned from the Jordan and was led by the Spirit in the desert" (4:1). After the temptation "Jesus returned to Galilee in the power of the Spirit" (Luke 4:14). I believe even in Jesus' life there were times when the power of the Holy Spirit was more intense than other times. For example, "The power of the Lord was present for him to heal the sick" (Luke 5:17). Several times the Gospels report that there was power to heal. This implies that the fullness of the Spirit was present with Jesus in various degrees. If Jesus needed to be filled with the Spirit, so do we.

We need to be more conscious of God's Holy Spirit. We need his Spirit for everything, especially for witnessing. (Acts 1:8).

The Father cut off every branch in Jesus that did not bear fruit and prunes those branches that are bearing fruit so they will bear more fruit. (John 15:2). If Jesus had to be cut and pruned how much more do we need to be cut and pruned so we can bear more fruit? Jesus also had to learn obedience: "Although he was a son, he learned obedience from what he suffered" (Hebrews 5:8). If Jesus needed to learn obedience how much more do we need to learn to be obedient? Are your thoughts pleasing to God? Are you wasting time on things that do not build your faith? Is your money and time extending God's Kingdom or your king-dom?

Jesus, help me to learn obedience through the things I suffer. Help me not to complain when you remove the parts of my life that are not bearing fruit and pruning the parts that are bearing fruit so they will be more fruitful. Amen.

Methods That No Longer Work

Matthew 23:5

"Everything the Pharisees do is done for men to see" (Matt. 23:5).

Jesus is straight forward to those who hang onto their traditions that are not effective in transforming lives. Jesus addresses these religious hypocrites in Matthew 23: "You're hopeless! What arrogant stupidity!" (Message Bible). They were blind. They were "orthodox" but spiritually dead. Is this true of your church? Do you and your church do things over and over without seeing any fruit?

A church that uses methods that no longer work is being unfaithful to Christ. If your employer trains you to complete a task using a new approach and you insist on continuing using the traditional method, you are unfaithful. You will lose your job to someone who is willing to use the method prescribed by the employer.

Are you willing to experiment with new forms of worship or are you stuck in your traditions and rituals? Which is more important, our comfort or our love for the lost? Which is more important, our traditions, our likes, our preference or the salvation of our youth who are going to other churches or not going anywhere?

Check your attitudes toward youth who are committed to Jesus but want to change things. What are our attitudes towards other congregations that are making disciples who make disciples? Do you raise questions about their approach or methods in a condemnatory spirit or do you rejoice with them? Are you willing to learn from them?

Be humble enough to learn from others. Let's cry out to Jesus to open our eyes to new ways that we can reach out to the lost in our community. Paul says, he becomes all things to all people to win them to Christ. (I Cor. 9:22). Let's adopt this verse as our marching order. This will not be easy but it will bring great rewards. If you are not taking any risks for Jesus, it means you are not exercising your faith. Without faith you cannot please God. (Hebrews 11:6).

Lord Jesus, help me to be humble and flexible, to learn from others who are making disciples. Teach me Lord to follow your Holy Spirit through all these changes. Amen.

Are You Conscious of the Holy Spirit?

Acts 2

Why was the early church so effective in spreading the Gospel? They depended on the Holy Spirit. The Holy Spirit is mentioned more than forty times in the book of Acts. Too often we have neglected to talk about the Holy Spirit because Christians have different interpretations concerning manifestations of the Spirit today.

Jesus said to the disciples after the resurrection: "'Peace be with you! As the Father has sent me, I am sending you.' And with that he breathed on them and said, 'Receive the Holy Spirit. If you forgive anyone his sins, they are forgiven; if you do not forgive them, they are not forgiven'" (John 20:21-23). Are you aware that you are sent under the anointing of the Holy Spirit?

In Jesus' longest prayer recorded in the Gospels just before the cross, Jesus prays for unity of the believers so the world will be drawn to the Gospel. (John 17). It's this unity among Christians that is a power-drawing card for the work of God's Kingdom. Unfortunately divisions often occur over the very power that should unite us.

Jesus simply said, "receive the Holy Spirit." We don't need to argue or split hairs over such terms as the baptism of the Holy Spirit, the anointing of the Holy Spirit, the second work of grace or whatever. Ask Jesus to make your heart and spirit open to receiving more of his Holy Spirit. When you receive the Spirit you will walk in newness of life, (Ro. 8:1-4) you will have power for witnessing, (Acts 1:8) and Jesus says you will forgive or withhold forgiveness (John 20:23).

We have no power to change the heart of another person. That's the work of the Holy Spirit. We do what we can; pray, model and speak words the Spirit gives us but the conviction of sin comes from the Holy Spirit. God created each person with a free will. We can't choose for them. They must make that choice.

Father, I am helpless without your Spirit. Enable me to be a Christian model, sharing the Good News in the power of your Spirit. Amen.

We Are as Sick as Our Secrets

Psalm 139:23-24

Psychologists tell us we spend enormous amounts of emotional energy guarding our secrets. We think: "If people really knew me they would reject me."

"Nothing in all creation is hidden from God's sight. Everything is uncovered and laid bare before the eyes of him to whom we must give account" (Hebrews 4:13).

David the man after God's own heart, (Acts 13:22) prayed: "Search me, O God, and know my heart; test me and know my anxious thoughts. See if there is any offensive way in me, and lead me in the way everlasting" (Ps. 139:23-24). Pray David's prayer. Confess and repent of any sins that come to your mind. "If we claim to be without sin, we deceive ourselves and the truth is not in us. If we confess our sins, he is faithful and just and will forgive us our sins and purify us from all unrighteousness. If we claim we have not sinned, we make him out to be a liar and his word has no place in our lives" (I John 1:8-10).

For your psychological and emotional wellbeing name your sins. Don't hide your sins. Take them to the cross, i.e. repent. Carrying sin is a slap in the face of our Lord because you are saying that his work on the cross was not sufficient for you. Picture Jesus taking each sin and forgiving it. See him giving his life's blood to wash you clean and make you pure. He paid the debt for your sins. You are forgiven.

If you still do not feel forgiven go to a mature Christian whom you can trust to keep confidences. "Confess your sins to each other and pray for each other so that you may be healed" (James 5:16). The mature Christian will assure you that you are forgiven. Their forgiveness will assist you in accepting your forgiveness from God. The freedom you experience will change your outlook on life. Jesus said, "If the Son sets you free, you will indeed be free" (John 8:36 NLT). Thank Jesus for setting you free! Dying to self (Gal. 2:20)—not just being united with him or merged into him but being made one with him, you will be free indeed. You have died. It is his life lived through you.

Jesus, I confess my sins to you. I want to be one with you. Amen.

Family and Hometown

Luke 4:24-29

Jesus said, "No prophet is accepted in his hometown. I assure you that there were many widows in Israel in Elijah's time, when the sky was shut for three and a half-years and there was a severe famine throughout the land. Yet, Elijah was not sent to any of them, but to a widow in Zarephath in the region of Sidon. And there were many in Israel with leprosy in the time of Elisha the prophet, yet not one of them was cleansed—only Naaman the Syrian. All the people in the synagogue were furious when they heard this. They got up, drove him out of the town, and took him to the brow of the hill on which the town was built, in order to throw him down the cliff" (Luke 4:24-29).

Why were the hometown people so furious at Jesus? They were all speaking well of him (v. 22) but immediately things changed 180 degrees from praise to fury. They could not imagine that God would love people who were not like them. They believed God loved only Jewish people. When you witness and bring people to Jesus and to your church, the church may not always give you or the new people a warm welcome.

Evangelists are often the least appreciated persons in our older traditional congregations. They bring the "wrong" people to church. Jesus said, "Count yourself blessed every time people put you down or throw you out or speak lies about you to discredit me. What it means is that the truth is too close for comfort and they are uncomfortable. You can be glad when that happens ... For though they don't like it, I do! And all heaven applauds. And know that you are in good company. My prophets and witnesses have always gotten into this kind of trouble" (Matt. 5:10-12 Msg.).

The most segregated hour of the week is Sunday 10:00 AM. Until that changes the church will not impact our culture. Learn to know persons who are different than you. Invite them for a backyard cookout, to a Thanksgiving or Christmas dinner. Their perspective on the Scriptures will enrich your understanding of God at work in the world. You will be enriched. At Capital Christian we had 20 or more nationalities worshipping together. It was a foretaste of heaven.

Father, enable me to be faithful in witnessing even though others may be critical. Amen.

Foolishness of the Cross

I Corinthians 1:21

"Since the world in all its fancy wisdom never had a clue when it came to knowing God, God in his wisdom took delight in using what the world considered dumb—preaching, of all things!—to bring those who trust him into the way of salvation" (I Cor. 1:21 Msg.).

Remember that preaching in the New Testament was used to describe the Christians' communication to non-Christians. Preaching is proclaiming the Good News! Teaching is the term used for communicating with other Christians. This means every Christian is called to preach or proclaim the Good News. It's amazing how God uses this method in our modern hi-tech world to change lives for eternity.

"God chose the foolish things of the world to shame the wise; God chose the weak things of the world to shame the strong. He chose the lowly things of this world and the despised things—and the things that are not—to nullify the things that are, so that no one may boast before him" (Verses 27-28).

Unless the Holy Spirit has softened the hearts of unbelievers and is drawing them to Jesus they will see your sharing the Good News as foolishness or as stupidity.

You may find it difficult to consider yourself a preacher in the New Testament sense. When you share the Good News with the prebeliever you are a preacher. Accept your New Testament title and make your boast in Jesus Christ. (v. 31).

When you share Christ Jesus be sure to take people to the cross. To the world the cross is just another story. To the Christian the cross is central. It's the only plus sign that makes things add up. It is more important than all the empires of history.

Our preaching may be interesting but it will not transform or translate lives from the kingdom of darkness to the kingdom of Jesus Christ unless it includes an awareness of the price Jesus paid for our sin. (Col. 1:14).

Jesus, thank you for paying the price for my sin. Enable me to keep the cross foundational and central in my life especially as I share the Good News. Amen.

Global Positioning System (GPS)

Romans 8:14

Global Positioning Systems are common. No more getting lost. Parents can track their children. When you don't follow instructions the GPS recalculates. If you think you know better than the GPS and take a different turn, it recalculates. One fellow commented, "I got so tired of hearing it recalculating that I turned it off."

Liken the GPS to the Holy Spirit. The Holy Spirit is our guide. "Those who are led by the Spirit of God are sons of God" (Ro. 8:14). "Live by the Spirit, and you will not gratify the desires of the sinful nature." "Since you live by the Spirit, let us keep in step with the Spirit" (Gal. 5:16 and 25).

The Spirit led the apostles. "Paul and his companions traveled throughout the region of Phrygia and Galatia, having been kept by the Holy Spirit from preaching the word in the province of Asia. When they came to the border of Mysia, they tried to enter Bithynia, but the Spirit of Jesus would not allow them to" (Acts 16:6-7).

We grieve the Spirit when we do not follow his leading. (Eph. 4:30). The Spirit recalculates calling us back to God's path, calling us to repent and be empowered for service. (Hebrews 10:29). When we do not repent the Spirit is there to discipline us. (Acts 5:3).

Jim Denison quotes the great Baptist preacher Charles Spurgeon: "Without the Spirit of God we can do nothing. We are as ships without wind or chariots without steeds. Like branches without sap, we are withered. Like coals without fire, we are useless. . . . It is not enough simply to believe that the Holy Spirit lives in us. Many a poor man has had an oil well on his farm and didn't know it." In the parable of the Prodigal Son the Father says to the older brother, "Everything I have is yours" (Luke 15:31). We have an oil well but don't realize it. We have God in us. (Ro. 8:9). Walk in the power and presence of the Spirit and the supernatural will become natural. Soar with the eagles.

Lord Jesus, you know every detour, every hill and valley, every curve in my path. Thank you for guiding me through each day. Amen.

A Heart Issue

Matthew 15:18-20

"The things that come out of the mouth come from the heart, and these make a man 'unclean.' For out of the heart comes evil thoughts, murder, adultery, sexual immorality, theft, false testimony, slander. These are what make a man 'unclean'" (Matt. 15:18-20).

"The heart is deceitful above all things and beyond cure. Who can understand it?" (Jer. 17:9). "People will be lovers of themselves, lovers of money, boastful, proud, abusive, disobedient to their parents, ungrateful, unholy, without love, unforgiving, slanderers, without self-control, brutal, not lovers of the good, treacherous, rash, conceited, lovers of pleasure . . . having a form of godliness but denying its power" (II Tim. 3:1-5). "See to it that none of you has a sinful, unbelieving heart that turns away from the living God" (Heb. 3:12).

Jesus says: "Blessed are the pure in heart, for they will see God" (Matt. 5:8). The Message reads: "You're blessed when you get your inside world—your mind and heart—put right. Then you can see God in the outside world."

God comes to our rescue. He gives us a new heart. Through Jesus' death and resurrection he atones and forgives all who come to him in repentance no matter what sins they have committed. (I John 1:9). "All have sinned and fall short of the glory of God, and are justified freely by his grace through redemption that came by Christ Jesus" (Ro. 3:23-25).

How is your inside world? The good news is that Jesus can cleanse your heart. Jesus is a high priest who, "meets our need—one who is holy, blameless, pure, set apart from sinners, exalted above the heavens" (Heb. 7:26). "If we confess our sins, he is faithful and just to forgive us our sins and purify us from all unrighteousness" (I John 1:9). What a gift! Such love demands my soul, my life and my all. Hallelujah!

Father, I thank you that even though I have a wicked heart, Jesus the perfect, sinless priest gives me a pure heart, one that seeks to honor and follow you. Amen.

Efficient or Effective?

II Corinthians 13:5-6

We want to be effective Christians. Peter Drucker says, "Efficiency is doing things right. Effectiveness is doing the right things." So often our lives are full of activities but our productivity is low. The same is true for many churches. God wants your life and your church to be effective and productive.

"Test yourselves to make sure you are solid in the faith. Don't drift along taking everything for granted. Give yourselves regular checkups. You need firsthand evidence, not mere hearsay, that Jesus Christ is in you. Test it out. If you fail the test, do something about it" (II Cor. 13:5-6 Msg.). (Psalm 139:23-24).

Examine your heart but also examine your effectiveness. Jesus said, "When you are joined with me and I with you, the relation intimate and organic, the harvest is sure to be abundant" (John 15:5 Msg.). "This is to my Father's glory, that you bear much fruit" (John 15:8).

In John 15, Jesus links effectiveness and productiveness with prayer. "If you remain in me and my words remain in you, ask whatever you wish, and it will be given you" (John 15:7). This verse removes much of the mystery of how Jesus remains in us. He says if my words remain in you, your prayers will be answered and you will produce a large harvest. (v. 8).

Let's not skirt around this or try to make excuses for a poor crop. Cry out to Jesus in prayer claiming this wonderful promise. In prayer, if we listen we discover what God wants. "Be still and know that I am God" (Psalm 46:10). In prayer we call and he will show us great and mighty things. (Jer. 33:3). If his word is not remaining in you, then ask him for a love for his word as David. He states that he meditates on God's name all night. "My soul is starved and hungry, ravenous!—insatiable for your nourishing commands" (Ps. 119:55 & 20 Msg.). (Col. 3:16-17).

Lord Jesus, I want my roots to go down deep into your word. I will feast on your word. By your power working in me, I will produce an abundant harvest. Amen.

No Grumbling or Arguing

Philippians 2:14-16

"Do everything without complaining or arguing. So that you may become blameless and pure, children of God without fault in a crooked and depraved generation, in which you shine like stars in the universe as you hold out the word of life" (Phil. 2:14-16).

One study indicates that five percent of people were born dissenters. It's natural to complain, it's supernatural to experience God controlling your tongue. No one likes to be around a person who is always complaining and arguing. In several churches that I coached, nearly every meeting someone was complaining. Arguing and complaining brings unnecessary frustration and stymies the advancement of God's work.

Paul writes: "Do not let any unwholesome talk come out of your mouths, but only what is helpful for building others up according to their needs, that it may benefit those who listen. And do not grieve the Holy Spirit of God. . .. Get rid of all bitterness, rage, and anger, brawling and slander, along with every form of malice. Be kind and compassionate to one another, forgiving each other, just as in Christ, God forgave you" (Eph. 4:28-32).

No man can tame the tongue. (James 3:8). Out of our heart comes evil speech. (Matt. 15:19). "If anyone considers himself religious and yet does not keep a tight rein on his tongue, he deceives himself and his religion is worthless" (James 1:26). "We demolish arguments and every pretension that sets itself up against the knowledge of God, and we take captive every thought to make it obedient to Christ" (II Cor. 10:5).

When you allow complaining, bitterness, anger, and slander to come out of your mouth you grieve the Holy Spirit. Confess that you cannot control your tongue and claim the Holy Spirit's power to give you a clean mouth to speak only what is wholesome for the building up of others.

Jesus, forgive me for complaining. Cleanse my heart, mind and mouth. I want to say only what you want me to say so I can build others up. Amen.

Everything I Have Is Yours

Luke 15:25-32

The parable of the lost son was given for the purpose of turning the spotlight on the older brother. The Father said, "My son, you are always with me, and everything I have is yours. But we had to celebrate and be glad, because this brother of yours was dead and is alive again; he was lost and is found" (Luke 15:31-32).

The older brother's resentment of his younger brother who squandered his inheritance in a wild and irresponsible lifestyle is like the attitude repeated throughout the scriptures: Jonah with the people of Nineveh, the disciples' attitude toward the woman at the well, or the Pharisees' attitude toward the Gentiles. Not surprising it is the same attitude we often find among God's people today.

All that the father owned was available to the sons. The older brother was blind to what was his. Unless we realize what God has given us, our attitude will be the same as the older brother. Notice the Father's attitude when the rebellious son confesses, "Father, I have sinned against heaven and against you. I am no longer worthy to be called your son" (v. 21). "The father said, 'bring the best robe . . . a ring for his finger and sandals for his feet. Bring the fatted calf and kill it. Let's have a feast and celebrate. For this son of mine was dead and is alive again, he was lost and is found.' So they began to celebrate" (vv. 22-24).

The father's love included both brothers. Examine your heart to see if you love the rebels in your community. Those who come to Jesus after leading notoriously sinful lives are often held in suspicion. Let's rejoice like the angels in heaven when they repent and turn to God. Like our Father we need to accept repentant sinners wholeheartedly and give them the support and encouragement they need to become disciples. "Accept each other just as Christ has accepted you so that God will be given glory" (Ro. 15:7).

Jesus, give me the heart of the Father to accept others just as Christ Jesus has accepted me. Amen.

"I Am The Way"—Jesus

John 14:6

Today the clear majority even of those who call themselves evangelical Christians believe there are many ways to heaven. Jesus and the New Testament writers state clearly that Jesus is the only way. If there are many ways to heaven there is no need for missionaries. Even those who have never heard the Good News, believe there is a supreme being who will have mercy on us if we do enough good works. The problem is no one has ever discovered how many good words are enough. Jesus presents the only way to heaven.

"For God so greatly loved and dearly prized the world that He [even] gave up His only-begotten (unique) Son, so that whoever believes in Him—who cleaves to him, trusts Him and relies on Him—may not perish, but have eternal life and [actually] live forever!" (John 3:16 AMP).

Jesus told Thomas, "I am the way, the truth and the life. No one can come to the Father except through me" (John 14:6). "God wants everyone to be saved and to understand the truth. For there is only one God and one Mediator who can reconcile God and people. He is the man Christ Jesus. He gave his life to purchase freedom for everyone" (I Tim. 2:4-6 NLT).

"Salvation is found in no one else, for there is no other name under heaven given to men by which we must be saved" (Acts 4:12).

"Some godless people have wormed their way in among you saying that God's forgiveness allows us to live immoral lives. The fate of such people was determined long ago, for they have turned against our only Master and Lord, Jesus Christ" (Jude 4).

"All glory to him who alone is God our Savior through Jesus Christ our Lord" (Jude 25 NLT).

Father, thank you that you loved us so much that we have the only way to heaven. Amen.

What About Those Who Never Heard? (Part I)

Psalm 19:1-4

There are more than two billion people who have never heard the Good News of salvation through Jesus Christ. God speaks through his creation, through our conscience, through his miracles and through his people.

First, God speaks through his creation. "Lift your eyes and look to the heavens: Who created all these? He brings out the starry host one by one, and calls them each by name" (Is. 40:26). "The heavens declare the glory of God; the skies proclaim the work of his hands. Day after day they pour forth speech; night after night they display knowledge. There is no speech or language where their voice is not heard. Their voice goes out into all the earth, their words to the ends of the world" (Ps. 19:1-4).

Since God's creation points to a Creator we should know intuitively not to worship the created things but rather the Creator. The Creator is greater than his creation. God's creation points everyone to his power and divinity.

"The wrath of God is being revealed from heaven against all the godlessness and wickedness of men who suppress the truth by their wickedness, since what may be known about God is plain to them, because God has made it plain to them. For since the creation of the world God's invisible qualities—his eternal power and divine nature—have been clearly seen, being understood from what has been made, so that men are without excuse. For although they knew God, they neither glorified him as God nor gave thanks to him, but their thinking became futile and their foolish hearts were darkened . . . God gave them over in the sinful desires of their heart to sexual impurity for the degrading of their bodies with one another. They exchanged the truth of God for a lie, and worshipped and served created things rather than the Creator . . ." (Ro. 1:18-25).

God has revealed himself plainly to all people through his creation. They suppress this obvious truth to go their own way. Since they know the truth they will have to endure the consequences of their choice.

Father thank you for your revelation in your creation all around us. Amen.

Those Who Have Never Heard (Part II)

John 1:9

Second, God not only speaks through nature he speaks through our conscience. We are born with a conscience. "The true light coming into the world—the genuine, perfect, steadfast Light—that illumines every person" (John 1:9 AMP). No one lives up to what they know is right. We all know it is wrong to push grandma into the path of an oncoming train or to kill innocent people especially children. When people deny God long enough their conscience is seared. (I Tim. 4:2). We are born with a desire for justice because we are born in the image of God. (Gen. 1:27).

"When outsiders who have never heard of God's law follow it more or less by instinct, they confirm its truth by their obedience. They show that God's law is not something alien, imposed on us from without, but woven into the very fabric of our creation. There is something deep within them that echo God's yes and no, right and wrong. Their response to God's yes and no will become public knowledge on the day God makes his final decision about every man and woman" (Ro. 2:14-15 Msg.). On the Judgment Day they will see that they did not follow their conscience but chose to say "no" to God's way.

"We are not godly. We are constant sinners so your anger is heavy on us. How can people like us be saved? We are all infected and impure with sin. When we proudly display our righteous deeds, we find they are but filthy rags . . . Yet no one calls on your name or pleads with you for mercy. Therefore you have turned away from us and turned us over to our sins" (Isaiah 64:5b-8).

God never sends anyone to hell; he makes it hard for anyone to go there. We have no excuse. He speaks through our conscience. We see his handiwork every day—in every tree, flower, bird, the stars and the birth of a baby, but we deny the obvious.

"Without faith it is impossible to please God, because anyone who comes to him must believe that he exists and that he rewards those who earnestly seek him" (Heb. 11:6).

Father, thank you for my conscience. Help me to line it up with your word. Amen.

What About Those Who Never Heard? (Part III)

Acts 17:26-27

God Speaks Through Miracles

Cornelius knew about God but not about Jesus. God sent Peter to explain the Gospel to him. (Acts 10). Frequently God sends missionaries to those seeking God. At other times God reveals himself via dreams, appearances of angels, etc.

We need missionaries because even though those who believe there is a God, live with guilt since they do not know how their sin can be removed. Missionaries explain that sin brings the curse of death but Jesus took the curse upon himself. (Gal. 3:10, 13). He did more than lift the curse, he became the curse and in doing so, allowed us to live a life as victors through him. (I Cor. 15:57). We are not under condemnation. (Ro. 8:1). What Good News!

"From one man God made every nation of men . . . he determined . . . the exact places where they should live. God did this so that men would seek him and perhaps reach out for him and find him, though he is not far from each one of us. (Acts 17:26-27).

Rather than asking, What about those who have never heard of salvation through Jesus, ask why they haven't heard. Jesus gave us a clear mandate to take the Gospel to them. Paul writes: "Everyone who calls on the name of the Lord will be saved. How can they call on the one they have not believed in? And how can they believe in the one of whom they have not heard? And how can they hear without someone preaching to them?" (Ro. 10:13-14).

People need to hear how they can have a personal relationship with God. "He who has the Son has life; he who does not have the Son of God does not have life" (I John 5:12). Knowing that God exists is not enough. People must learn that God is loving and that he sent his Son to demonstrate his love for us. (Ro. 5:8). Will you share the Good News with someone today?

Father, we pray for more workers to take the Good News to those who have never heard. Amen.

Pure Eyes

Job 31:1

Job made a covenant with his eyes not to look lustfully on a woman. (Job. 31:1). Jesus said, "Anyone who looks at a woman lustfully has already committed adultery with her in his heart." (Matt. 5:28). The New Testament talks more about sexual immorality than any other sin. It is nearly always the first sin listed in the 17 catalogues of sin in the New Testament. The porn industry is a $12 billion industry. The majority of Americans see nothing wrong with porn. Since sex is their god it's only a matter of time for America to come under God's judgment.

Douglas Weiss says, "Wherever I am . . . and no matter what the denomination, at least half of the men in the church admit to being sexually addicted. The clergy doesn't differ that much from the general population—between a third and half." (Jane Lampman—Staff writer of the *Christian Science Monitor*.)

Jesus said, "The eyes are windows into your body. If you open your eyes wide in wonder and belief, your body fills up with light. If you live squinty-eyed in greed and distrust, your body is a dank cellar. If you pull the blinds on your windows, what a dark life you will have!" (Matt. 6:22-23 Msg.). Jesus also said, "If your eye causes you to sin pluck it out" (Matt. 18:9 NLT). Jesus is saying nothing less than a radical commitment to him will deliver you from sexual sin. Do whatever you need to do for victory including humbling yourself before God and before an accountability group of other mature men or women. The Holy Spirit will enable you to bring every thought captive so you can live with a pure life. (I Cor. 10:5).

There is no lasting victory apart from Jesus. The Good News is that he is greater than any temptation you can imagine. Only he can give you the power to live above sin. You will never be a fulfilled, joyful Christian unless you allow Jesus to give you pure eyes and heart. Surrender to Jesus and he will give you deliverance.

Lord Jesus put a guard over my physical eyes and over the eyes of my mind and heart. Cleanse me and make my heart pure. Amen.

Fishing for People

Matthew 4:19

"As Jesus was walking beside the Sea of Galilee, he saw two brothers, Simon called Peter and his brother Andrew. They were casting a net into the lake, for they were fishermen. 'Come, follow me,' Jesus said, 'and I will make you fishers of men.' At once they left their nets and followed him. Going on from there, he saw two other brothers, James son of Zebedee and his brother John. They were in a boat with their father Zebedee, preparing their nets. Jesus called them, and immediately they left the boat and their father and followed him" (Matt. 4:18-22).

Many Christians today say, just love people because they are God's creation. That's no excuse for not sharing the Good News. Jesus certainly loved people but he loved people for the purpose of inviting them into his Kingdom. Jesus came to seek and save those who were lost. (Luke 19:10). We don't want to manipulate people or make them our project. However, Jesus gives us dozens of commands, many of them in parables, to share the Good News. (John 17:18). Jesus makes it clear we are called to fish for people. That is our motive. God is not willing that any perish. As the Spirit flows through you to persons who are prebelievers you don't need to pressure them. It is God's Spirit that draws them to himself. You are simply the tool he has chosen to use.

We love our children unconditionally. Whatever they do they will always be our child and we will go on loving them. However we do all we possibly can to be sure they know God's purpose and passion for their life. As Moses says, we are to teach them throughout the day, when we eat, work, play and at night before bedtime. (Deut. 6:7). John writes: "I have no greater joy than to hear that my children are walking in the truth" (III John 4). Jude writes that we are to snatch people from the fire. (v. 23). Jesus said we are to compel them to come to the banquet. (Luke 14:23).

Father, search me. See if there are any impure motives. Forgive me and enable me to love people as you love them. May I be an instrument in your hands to bring them to Jesus. Amen.

Check Your Motives

I John 4:18

"There is no fear in love. Perfect love drives out fear, because fear has to do with punishment" (I John 4:18).

When I was a kid I invited Jesus into my life primarily because I was afraid of going to hell. I did not comprehend the great love of God in providing Jesus as the atoning sacrifice for my sin. The prodigal son did not return home primarily because he fully understood the Father's heart of love but because he was starving. (Luke 15).

Your Heavenly Father loved you first. (I John 4:19). "Even before he made the world, God loved you and chose you in Christ to be holy and without fault in his eyes" (Eph. 1:4 NLT). You owe everything to your Father. Thank God for his indescribable gift. (II Cor. 9:15).

"Give thanks to the Lord, for he is good! His faithful love endures forever . . . Give thanks to him who alone does mighty miracles. His faithful love endures forever . . ." (Ps. 136:1-4 NLT). David assures us that God's love is endless, unconditional and unchanging. "For the Lord is good, His unfailing love continues forever and his faithfulness continues to each generation" (Ps. 100:5 NLT).

No wonder Paul prayed for the Christians in Ephesis: "I pray that out of his glorious riches he may strengthen you with power through his Spirit in your inner being, so that Christ may dwell in your hearts through faith. And I pray that you, being rooted and established in love, may have power, together with all the saints to grasp how wide and long and high and deep is the love of Christ and to know this love that surpasses knowledge—that you may be filled to the measure of all the fullness of God" (Eph. 3:16-19). Thank God daily for his gift of love.

God's very essence is love. (I John 4:8). God is also just. If we reject his love, i.e. if we do not obey his commandments the wrath of God abides on us. (Eph. 2:1-5)

Lord, I want to grow in love for you—to love you with all my heart, soul, mind and strength. Amen.

Reluctant Jonah

Jonah 1:2-3

If God can use Jonah he can use you! "The Lord told Jonah: 'Get up and go to the great city of Nineveh! Announce my judgment against it because I have seen how wicked its people are . . .' But Jonah got up and went in the opposite direction in order to get away from the Lord. He went down to the sea coast, to the port of Joppa, where he found a ship leaving for Tarshish. He bought a ticket and went on board, hoping that by going away . . . he could escape from the Lord" (Jonah 1:2-3 NLT).

Why was Jonah so adverse to seeing the Ninevites coming to God? Nineveh was a wicked city known for its atrocities, the ISIS of their day. The Ninevites were the enemy. Jonah was sucked into the religious self-righteous culture of his time.

Why are so few of us ministering in our prisons? Are we willing to see our enemies come to Jesus and enter our homes and churches? Why are Christians often reluctant to welcome the unchurched into their church family? Are we afraid our children will adopt their lifestyle? Whenever those thoughts enter our minds we are saying, "Our God is anemic. He is not adequate to keep us." In the Jonah account the people of Nineveh repented. They changed. The Holy Spirit is in the business of changing people's lives today.

Have you been like Jonah, going in the opposite direction to what God wants? Have you lived beside your neighbor for years or worked beside your peers and never took the opportunity to share your faith? Have you sat beside an unsaved friend in class for a semester and never prayed for them or shared your faith with them? Do they know you are a follower of Jesus? Jesus commissioned us to share the Good News. We have a responsibility to not only live our faith but to proclaim our faith in word and deed. We know it's God's will that none perish and that all come to repentance. (II Peter 3:9). We can ask in faith knowing he will help us share the Good News. God used reluctant Jonah and he will use you. Allow the Holy Spirit to bring the results.

Lord, like Jonah I have turned my back to my "enemies." Enable me to be your faithful and effective witness today. Amen.

I'd Rather Be a Sailor Than Be Jonah

Jonah 1:5, 12-14

"All the sailors were afraid and each cried out to his own god. And they threw the cargo into the sea to lighten the ship. But Jonah had gone below deck, where he lay down and fell into a deep sleep" (Jonah 1:5).

The sailors in desperation cried out to their god(s), even throwing their cargo into the sea! Often God has to allow us to face impossible situations to wake us up. After the 9-11-2001 crisis when more than 3,000 died in the falling towers, church attendance soared but only for a few weeks. There was no true repentance. We returned to a self-centered lifestyle and our gods of materialism.

The sailors asked Jonah, "Tell us, who is responsible for making all this trouble? What do you do? Where do you come from? From what people are you?" (1:8). After Jonah informed them who he was and who his God was, the sailors cried out to the Lord. They even tried to keep from throwing Jonah overboard. Jonah said, "Pick me up and throw me into the sea and it will become calm. I know that it is my fault that this great storm has come upon you. . . ." Instead, the men did their best to row back to land . . . The sailors cried to the LORD, "O Lord, please do not let us die for taking this man's life. Do not hold us accountable for killing an innocent man, for you, O Lord, have done as you pleased" (1:12-14).

Jonah in his stubbornness was willing to die rather than say "yes" to God's call to go to Nineveh. Jesus said, "Woe to you, teachers of the law and Pharisees, you hypocrites! You shut the kingdom of heaven in men's faces. You yourselves do not enter nor will you let those enter who are trying to" (Matt. 23:13-14). These sailors had a greater fear of God than Jonah.

I'd rather be a sailor, open to God's will, than a Jonah who knew God's will but rejected it. We know we are called to bring the living water to thirsty sailors. Have we like Jonah become self-absorbed and put a wall around God's love.

Lord, give me courage to share your love to the unchurched around me. Give me your compassion like Jesus who did not exclude anyone. Amen.

Lord, I Do Not Want to Be Like Jonah

Jonah 1:1 & 4:1-2

When Jonah shared God's message and they obeyed, "Jonah was furious, he lost his temper. He yelled at God, 'God! I knew it—when I was back home, I knew this was going to happen! That's why I ran off to Tarshish! I knew you were sheer grace and mercy, not easily angered, rich in love, and ready at the drop of a hat to turn your plans of punishment into a program of forgiveness!'" (Jonah 4:1-2 Msg.).

In Luke 4 the Jewish people were ready to kill Jesus when he announced in his hometown synagogue in Nazareth that the Good News was for everyone, even to the Gentiles.

When those who worked all day during the heat received the same amount of wages that those received who only worked one hour they began to grumble against the landlord even though they received what was promised. (Matt. 20:11).

Jesus said, "I have not come to call the righteous but sinners" (Luke 5:32). The Pharisees were angry when Jesus ate with the tax collectors but Jesus said, "It is not the healthy who need a doctor, but the sick" (Mark 2:17). When the prodigal son returned home the older brother was angry. "You never gave me a banquet or had a celebration for me" (Luke 15:28-30).

How do I insure that I do not become the Jonah, older brother, or the Pharisees?

Go back to the cross and see again the love that drove Jesus. See the Father giving his Only Son. See Jesus coming to live in sinful humanity. See the great cloud of witnesses who have been faithful, many of them giving their lives for the cause of the Good News. Experience the joy of obedience and faithfulness. Know that all heaven rejoices over one sinner who repents. Experience the peace of Christ. Finally, pray over your Jerusalem as Jesus prayed and wept over those who were lost.

Father, forgive my apprehension when people come to you who are different from my culture, traditions, opinions and preferences. Remove the "Jonah spirit" from me. Give me your heart of compassion. Amen.

Discipline Is Critical

II Timothy 2:5

"If anyone competes as an athlete, he does not receive the victor's crown unless he competes according to the rules" (II Tim. 2:5). "Train yourself for spiritual fitness" (I Tim. 4:7 NLT).

Athletes exercise long hours, forcing their bodies to endure pain. They practice, practice, practice. They watch their diet. They get adequate sleep. Their social life is often cut to a minimum. Some travel, living away from family and friends in order to compete to win a victor's crown. They memorize the rules so they know them without thinking twice.

Jesus gave us guidelines. If we break them they will break us. His basic guideline is to love God with all our heart, soul, mind and strength and to love our neighbor as we love ourselves. (Matt. 22:37-39). Beginning in chapter three of Genesis we decided we will not follow God's rules. There is something about our old nature that resists being told what is best for us. We are not sure anyone, including God, knows better than we do.

"A man reaps what he sows. The one who sows to please his sinful nature, from that nature will reap destruction; the one who sows to please the Spirit, from the Spirit will reap eternal life" (Gal. 5:8). Jesus said, "If you hold to my teaching you are really my disciples. Then you will know the truth, and the truth will set you free" (John 8:32).

"The Lord is the Spirit, and where the Spirit of the Lord is, there is freedom" (II Cor. 3:17). God's rules are not burdensome. (I John 5:3). They are liberating. Paul writes, "Through Christ Jesus the law of the Spirit of life set me free from the law of sin and death" (Ro. 8:2). Exercise your freedom by serving God, not by doing wrong. (I Peter 2:16). "I say, live by the Spirit, and you will not gratify the desires of the sinful nature" (Gal. 5:16).

Lord Jesus, I discipline my body by the power of your Spirit. With your grace I will say no to the desires of the flesh and yes to the law of life in Christ Jesus. Amen.

Work Hard

II Timothy 3:6

"The hardworking farmer should be the first to receive a share of the crops" (II Tim. 3:6). This is the third example describing a disciple of Jesus. The first is a soldier who does his best to please his commander, the second is the athlete who competes according to the rules of the game and the third is a farmer who works hard.

Farmers get up early and work to sunset. I grew up on a farm. The cows have to be milked at least twice a day usually 5:30 AM and 5:30 PM. This means getting up early and staying up late. There is field work. Weeds and pests are a constant battle. The risk is great. If there is no rain or too much rain often the crops are lost. Just as a farmer must work hard and take risks the same is true in our Christian life.

Peter admonished us to make every effort to add to our faith goodness, knowledge, self-control, perseverance, godliness, and love. They will keep you from being ineffective and unproductive. (II Peter 1:5-8). "Work hard to prove that you really are among those God has called and chosen. Doing this, you will never stumble or fall away. And God will open wide the gates of heaven for you to enter into the eternal Kingdom of our Lord and Savior Jesus Christ" (vv. 10-11). A few verses later Peter says, "I will work hard to make these things clear to you. I want you to remember them long after I am gone" (v. 15). "Make every effort to live a pure and blameless life" (3:14). "Work hard at living in peace with others" (I Peter 3:15 NLT).

We are to train ourselves for spiritual fitness. (I Tim. 4:7). "I forget what is behind and strain forward to what is ahead and press toward the goal" (Phil. 3:13-14).

While salvation is a gift we show our love for Jesus by obeying his commandments. "He has created us anew in Christ Jesus, so that we can do the good things he planned for us long ago" (Eph. 2:10 NLT). We want to make every effort to please him.

Lord Jesus, forgive my laziness and lethargy. Fill me with your Spirit of enthusiasm and zeal. I will serve you with my whole heart. Amen.

Come and See

John 1:45-46

"Philip found Nathaniel and informed him they found Jesus of Nazareth, the son of Joseph. He said, 'Nazareth? You've got to be kidding.' But Philip said, 'Come and see for yourself'" (John 1:45-46 Msg.).

One church has a large sign, "Come and See!" (John 1:46). Is anything happening in my church that compels me to invite my unchurched neighbors to "come and see?"

Many Christians are embarrassed to invite their friends to church because they know their friends would not feel comfortable. Our uneasiness about their level of comfort often comes not from a confrontation of sin or the offense of the cross but feeling they may be unable to relate to traditional worship that is second nature to us.

While the message of the Gospel never changes, the methods we use to bridge the message to the people must change with every generation. I have the Pennsylvania State Farmers Degree but in the last sixty years farming has changed so drastically that I know nothing about farming. Yet many churches want to preserve the past, even though the past rituals and traditions are not meaningful to the unchurched.

Jesus said, "No one sews a patch of unshrunk cloth, on an old garment, for the patch will pull away from the garment, making the tear worse. Neither do men pour new wine into old wineskins. If they do, the skins will burst, the wine will run out and the wineskins will be ruined. No, they pour new wine into new wineskins, and both are preserved" (Matt. 9:16-17). We need to accept the style of worship that younger people can appreciate and adapt to the new wine that Jesus has for us. God loves all types of music that reverences God and exalts our Lord Jesus Christ.

When we keep doing the same things over and over and there are no baptisms of adults we need to ask, "Is it time to change wine skins?"

Lord, forgive our stubbornness. Give us wisdom to understand our church culture and the courage to make the changes we need to make so our unchurched neighbors can be brought to Christ and become his disciples. Amen.

217

Not a False Bone

John 1:47-49

"When Jesus saw Nathanael he said, 'There's a real Israelite, not a false bone in his body." Nathanael said, 'Where did you get that idea? You don't know me.' Jesus answered, 'One day, long before Philip called you here, I saw you under the fig tree.' Nathanael explained, 'Rabbi! You are the Son of God, the King of Israel!'" (John 1:47-49 Msg.). What a compliment from Jesus: "Not a false bone!"

David was transparent. He was guilty of a multitude of sins: adultery, deceit, pride and lies. But whenever he sinned and became aware of his sin he came running to God in sincere repentance, confessed his sin and was forgiven. Relationship with God was restored. This did not mean that he did not suffer the consequences of his sin. When he committed adultery with Bathsheba he prayed and fasted for seven days but the child died. (II Samuel 12:19). Like Adam and Eve we try to hide our sin. "The heart is deceitful above all things and beyond cure. Who can understand it?" (Jeremiah 17:9). God hates falsehood. (Rev. 21:8, 22:15).

The Lord says, "These are the things you are to do. Speak the truth to each other, and render true and sound judgment in your courts; do not plot evil against your neighbor, and do not love to swear falsely. I hate all this,' declares the Lord" (Zechariah 8:16-17). "Put off falsehood and speak truthfully to your neighbor, for we are all members of one body" (Eph. 4:25).

Honesty is a foundation principle necessary for mutual relationships. Today only 19 percent of millennials believe you can trust people. Ninety percent of engineering students are willing to cheat. Many children don't trust their parents. Many parishioners don't trust their pastor. "Run up and down every street in Jerusalem," says the Lord. "Look high and lo, search throughout the city! If you can find even one person who is just and honest, I will not destroy the city" (Jeremiah 5:1 NLT).

"Investigate my life, O God, find out everything about me; Cross-examine and test me, get a clear picture of what I'm about; See for yourself whether I've done anything wrong then guide me on the road to eternal life" (Psalm 139:23-24 Msg.).

Help Hasten Jesus' Return

Matthew 24:14

Jesus said, "The gospel of the kingdom will be preached ... to all nations, (Greek = ethnic groups), and then the end will come" (Matt. 24:14). There are more than 6,000 unreached ethnic groups; that's one-fourth of our world's population. We are not sure to what degree of penetration of the Gospel Jesus has in mind before he will return. He is Lord, he can return anytime. We must be ready because we do not know the day or the hour of Christ's return. (Matt. 24:36).

We send very few missionaries to these unreached groups. Jesus said, "The harvest is plentiful but the workers are few. Ask the Lord of the harvest to send out workers into the harvest field" (Matt. 9:37-38).

A family was active in their church. Whenever missionaries came to speak they served as host. They gave generously to support missionaries. However when their son said, "I want to be a missionary," the parents were upset. "You're putting your life in danger and passing up a good job opportunity here."

If you knew the solution to curing cancer and didn't share it, you would be guilty of a criminal offense. We have the answer to life's problems. It is not right to withhold Good News from those who, according to Jesus, are going to hell without faith in Him.

If all that you gained from your salvation is something that you could hold on to without passing it on, then it is not Good News. If Christ is your life sharing the Good News is as natural as breathing. Peter and John said, "We cannot help but speak about what we have seen and heard" (Ac. 4:19-20).

We have lost our passion. Too often sports, television, Iphones, moonlighting, newer cars and vacations, are more important to us than the mandate of the Great Commission. Fall in love with Jesus so you overflow with his love. (John 7:38).

Father, you gave your Son. Jesus, you gave your life. I give you my life. Amen.

Fight the Good Fight of Faith

II Timothy 6:12

"It's impossible to please God apart from faith. Why? Because anyone who wants to approach God must believe both that he exists and that he cares enough to respond to those who seek him" (Hebrews 11:6 Msg.).

Faith is more than mental assent to Biblical truths. Many Christians poo-poo a faith that prays for a parking place or lost car keys or for help on a test. These prayers are appropriate if we sincerely ask God to forgive our carelessness and request his help to be more disciplined. Christians must have heart-faith and childlike trust in the risen Christ—a faith that affects the mundane and all of life.

Do we have a form of godliness but lack the power, the faith to see it operate in our daily life? (II Tim. 3:5). Believing—prayer is the life-line to God's power. Do I have a form of prayer but lack the faith to see it operate with power?

God can revive our faith through his Word. "Faith comes from hearing the message, and the message is heard through the word of Christ" (Ro. 10:17). Let your roots go down into Christ so you grow in faith. (Col. 2:7). There is only one fight in life—the fight of faith. (I Tim. 6:12).

Paul planted the church in Thessalonica in only three weeks, and then he was forced to leave. Paul . . . sent Timothy to strengthen and encourage them in their faith. (I Thess. 3:2). Paul sent to find out about their faith. Timothy brought good news about their faith. Paul and his companions were encouraged because of their faith. He prayed that they would see the Thessalonians again and supply what is lacking in their faith. (vv. 5 - 10).

"The fundamental fact of existence is that this trust in God, this faith, is the firm foundation under everything that makes life worth living. It's our handle on what we can't see" (Hebrews 11:1 Msg.). Faith is a muscle. No matter how small it is Jesus reminds us that even mustard seed faith can removed mountains. Exercise your faith and it will grow stronger. (Matt. 17:20).

Jesus, I want to exercise my faith so I can serve you more effectively. Amen.

Can You Amaze Jesus?

Luke 7:9 & Matthew 9:29

When Jesus told the Roman centurion he would go to his house to heal his servant the centurion said he was not to come but simply speak the word of healing, Jesus was amazed at his great faith. (Luke 7:9).

When the hometown people did not believe, Jesus was amazed at their lack of faith. "Jesus said, 'Only in his hometown among his relatives and in his own house is a prophet without honor.' He could not do any miracles there, except lay his hands on a few sick people and heal them. He was amazed at their lack of faith" (Mark 6:4-7). "Jesus could have done greater miracles but he chose not to because of their unbelief. The miracles he did had little effect on the people. They did not believe he was from God so Jesus looked elsewhere seeking those who would respond to his message" (Life Application Bible).

We cannot please God without faith. (Heb. 11:6). Exercise your faith. Claim the promises in God's word but don't pull them out of context. For example: "Ask anything you wish and it will be done for you" (John 14:13-14). What we ask must line up with God's will. (John 14:14, I John 5:14). Timing is also a major factor. I am often impatient for God to act.

God tests our faith to make us stronger. It grows best in cloudy days. "Consider it pure joy whenever you face trials . . . because you know that the testing of your faith produces perseverance" (James 1:1-2). Shadrach, Meshach and Abednego were men of faith. When the king threatened to throw them in the furnace they said, "God is able to deliver us . . . but even if he does not, we want you to know that we will not serve your gods" (Daniel 3:17-18).

Our faith is built up as we hear his word presented as the very words of God. (I Peter 4:10). Faith is built up as people give testimonies of God working in their lives. It is build up as we worship in songs of praise with thankful hearts. (Eph. 5:19-20).

Lord, thank you for the gift of faith. Enable me to exercise the faith you have given me. Amen.

Exercise Faith in God

Isaiah 29:13

"The Lord says: 'These people come near to me with their mouth and honor me with their lips, but their hearts are far from me. Their worship of me is made up of rules taught by men'" (Isaiah 29:13).

Some Christians teach that you cannot admit that you are sick, poor or have problems because that is a negative confession or lack of faith. Some on their death bed claim they are getting better physically as they are dying. Others naively claim prosperity while over extending themselves in charge-card debts.

A Christian does not deny reality or play mind games. God wants hearts of integrity and authenticity.

When we are battling anger, envy, pride, jealousy, pornography, alcohol, nicotine, drug addiction or poor health, etc. we need to be honest. If there is sin we confess lack of faith and ask God's forgiveness. True faith comes from an honest heart. We need to confess: Lord, I am helpless in myself. Purify my heart. You alone can give me the victory over this sin. Give me strength to say no. Sustain and bring healing to my body in your time and way. I submit to your schedule knowing you will never forsake me. Thank you Jesus.

The fight of faith is claiming the promises of Christ's sufficiency. We no longer need to struggle alone in our own strength. With Christ we can go through every situation victoriously. (Phil. 4:13). God promises to supply our needs. (Phil. 4:19). Since the Lord is our Shepherd we will not lack anything! (Psalm 23:1). Lord, I will trust your Holy Spirit to guide me.

Apart from God's grace and his power in me, I am nothing. I've been a Christian for seventy years but the old nature is still there. I don't try harder to overcome sin, I run to the cross for his cleansing blood and his resurrection power! Hallelujah! Soar with the eagles.

Lord, I thank you for your cleansing blood and resurrection power! They are just as powerful today as the day you raised Jesus from the tomb. Amen.

Who Directs Your Steps?

Matthew 16:24-25

"Don't I have rights?" Jesus said, "Anyone who intends to come with me has to let me lead. You're not in the driver's seat, I am" (Matt. 16:24-25 Msg.). It is not in man to direct his steps. (Jeremiah 10:23). "The steps of a good man are ordered by the Lord" (Ps. 37:23 KJV). Frequently I find God is directing my steps as I need to talk with someone and at just the right time God brings our paths together.

"If any of you wants to be my follower you must put aside your selfish ambition, shoulder your cross, and follow me . . . But if you give up your life for me, you will find true life" (Luke 9:23-24 NLT). If there is anything that you are unwilling to take to the cross you make the cross of no effect in your life. Jesus calls you to abandon any rights, your independence and self-will. He's in charge! He is LORD! We are his servants (Greek = slaves or servants). "You have been set free from sin, and have become slaves to righteousness" (Ro. 6:18). A slave has no rights.

What have you that God has not given you? (I Cor. 4:7). It is often the good things that are not God's best for us. If the Lord removes your dream can you still rejoice?

If we put his Kingdom first he will take care of your dreams, your career. (Matt. 6:33). Your vocation is to follow his path. Joy is found not in your career but in doing God's will. God will order your steps if you give him first place. God is more concerned about your heart than your ministry. Keep your heart on fire and he will take care of your ministry. Passion grows out of a heart and a life of prayer.

We must lay everything on the altar. With Paul we can then say: "I have learned how to get along happily whether I have much or little. I know how to live on almost nothing or with everything. I have learned the secret of living in every situation whether it is with a full stomach or empty, with plenty or little. For I can do everything with the help of Christ who gives me the strength I need" (Phil. 4:11-13 NLT).

Lord, I give you all my "rights." You are Lord, I am your servant. Guide my steps, I'll go and do whatever you say. Amen.

Keep Up-to-Date and Do Not Grieve the Holy Spirit

Ephesians 4:30-32

"Do not quench (suppress or subdue) the Holy Spirit" (I Thess. 5:19 AMP). "Do not grieve the Holy Spirit of God, with whom you were sealed for the day of redemption" (Eph. 4:30). How do we grieve the Spirit: "Let all bitterness and indignation and wrath (passion, rage, bad temper) and resentment (anger, animosity) and quarreling (brawling, clamor, contention) and slander (evil speaking, abusive or blasphemous language) be banished from you, with all malice (spite, ill will or baseness of any kind. Become useful and helpful and kind to one another, tenderhearted (compassionate, understanding, loving-hearted), forgiving one another [readily and freely], as God in Christ forgave you" (Eph. 4:31-32 AMP).

The voice of the Spirit comes as a gentle whisper. (I Kings 19:12). In the rush of living it is hard to hear a gentle whisper. We need to keep up-to-date intimacy with Jesus to hear his gentle whisper. Just as the Father told Jesus what to say and how to say it, we too can hear the Spirit's gentle whisper telling us what to say and how to say it. (John 12:49). "Since we live by the Spirit, let us keep in step with the Spirit" (Gal. 5:24).

We grieve the Spirit not only by what we say or do but by sins of omission. "Any person who knows what is right to do but does not do it, to him it is sin" (James 4:17 AMP). What is God asking you to do that you have not done? If we know we should send a text or email to encourage someone and don't do it we grieve the Spirit. If God asks you to help your neighbor who just had surgery, you grieve the Spirit if you don't help them. If we waste time we grieve the Spirit. Is the Spirit nudging you to encourage a woman whose husband has just left her and her children? Is the Spirit nudging you to invite your co-workers to a backyard barbeque to build relationships? Be aware of the Holy Spirit guidance throughout your day.

Lord Jesus I thank you for your Spirit. Forgive me for not paying attention to your gentle voice. Enable me to keep in step with your Spirit. Amen.

Make the Most of Every Opportunity

Ephesians 5:15-17

"Watch your step. Use your head. Make the most of every chance you get. These are desperate times! Don't live carelessly, unthinkingly. Make sure you understand what the Master wants" (Eph. 5:15-17 Msg.).

"Be wise in the way you act toward outsiders; make the most of every opportunity. Let your conversation be always full of grace, seasoned with salt, so that you may know how to answer everyone" (Col. 4:5-6).

"If you are asked about your Christian hope, always be ready to explain it. But you must do this in a gentle and respectful way. Keep your conscience clear. Then if people speak evil against you they will be ashamed when they see what a good life you live because you belong to Christ" (I Peter 3:15-16 NLT).

For Peter and Paul every encounter with those both inside and outside God's Kingdom was an opportunity to share Jesus. Are you consciously asking the Holy Spirit to prompt you to speak for the Lord? The time is short; therefore we need to make the most of every opportunity. We don't know when our last opportunity will be to share the Good News or for them to hear the Good News.

Peter reminds us to be gracious. What we say should be salty or tasty. Hopefully it will arouse curiosity. Use the "AA" approach, i.e. arouse curiosity and answer questions. When we are walking in the Spirit many doors will open. We will sense when people have a need. Their need is a door to reaching them. It's usually appropriate to mention that you will be praying for them. Then check back to see how things are developing letting them know you have been praying for them. Showing love will hopefully build a positive relationship to continue your witness for Jesus.

If you are enthusiastic about what Jesus has done for you, praying for the Holy Spirit to draw others to the Savior opportunities will be there.

Lord Jesus, enable me to be tuned into your Spirit so I can use every opportunity to share the Good News with others. Amen.

The Isaac Factor

Genesis 22

"God tested Abraham, He said to him, 'Abraham!' 'Here I am,' he replied. Then God said, 'Take your son, your only son, Isaac, whom you love, and go to the region of Moriah. Sacrifice him there as a burnt offering on one of the mountains I will tell you about.' Early the next morning Abraham got up and saddled his donkey. He took with him two of his servants and his son Isaac" (Genesis 22:1-3).

God was testing Abraham. Isaac was Abraham's heart and soul! He had waited 13 years for God to miraculously give him the son of promise. Abraham told the servants, "Stay here with the donkey while I and the boy go over there. We will worship and then we will come back to you" (v. 5). WE will come back. Abraham believed God would provide another sacrifice or raise Isaac from death.

Has God asked you to take your most precious possession and place it on the altar? What are you hanging onto? Is he asking you to move so you can serve him in another location, perhaps help plant a church or serve in foreign missions? Is he asking you to move to help care for your aging parents? Is he asking you to give up your more than adequate salary with great benefits? Is he asking you to stay in your marriage even though you want out? For some of you the greatest test you will face is to either stay with your church or to move to another congregation. God may be asking you to give up your present ministry and move to a less appealing situation.

In my fifty years of ministry the two most difficult situations I encountered resulted in the best experiences of my life. When doors closed he opened other doors. God had better things than I could envision.

Whatever God is asking you to give up, respond like Abraham: "Early the next morning Abraham got up and saddled his donkey . . ." No rebuttal, no argument, no asking "why."

Lord, I lay everything on the altar. Whatever you say or wherever you ask me to go, I will obey. Amen.

False Hope

Matthew 7:21-23

"Not everyone who says to me, 'Lord Lord,' will enter the kingdom of heaven, but only he who does the will of my Father who is in heaven. Many will say to me on that day, 'Lord, Lord, did we not prophesy in your name, and in your name, drive out demons and perform many miracles?' Then I will tell them plainly, 'I never knew you. Away from me, you evildoers!'" (Matt. 7:21-23).

The Message Bible reads: "Knowing the correct password—saying 'Master, Master,' for instance—isn't going to get you anywhere with me. What is required is serious obedience—doing what my Father wills. I can see it now—at the Final Judgment thousands strutting up to me and saying, 'Master, we preached the Message, we bashed the demons, our God-sponsored projects had everyone talking.' And do you know what I am going to say? 'You missed the boat. All you did was use me to make yourselves important. You don't impress me one bit. You're out of here.'"

Jesus said, "False Christ's and false prophets will appear and perform great signs and miracles to deceive even the elect—if that were possible" (Matt. 24:24).

Paul writes: "The coming of the lawless one will be in accordance with the work of Satan displayed in all kinds of counterfeit miracles, signs and wonders" (II Thess. 2:9). (Rev. 13:13; 16:14; 19:20 and Exodus 7 and 8).

Not everyone who claims to know Jesus knows him. There are satanic and demonic powers that can do amazing miracles but they do not obey the Lord. At the judgment they will be greatly disappointed as Jesus says, "Depart, I never knew you." We must search the word of the Lord to see if teachers are teaching the truth and bearing fruit that lasts for eternity. Don't be fooled by false claims even when they are backed up with miracles. Check to see if the fruit remains faithful to the teaching of our Lord.

Lord, help me to be discerning when I become aware of people performing various signs and miracles. Enable me to walk my talk—to be obedient to you in all things. Amen.

Angels

Hebrews 1:14

"Are not all angels ministering spirits sent to serve those who will inherit salvation?" (Hebrews 1:14). "He ordered his angels to guard you wherever you go. If you stumble, they'll catch you; their job is to keep you from falling" (Ps. 91:11-12 Msg.).

How blessed we are that God not only provides his Holy Spirit to dwell in us but he also sends his angels to minister to us. They proclaim God's message. (Rev. 14:6-12). They execute God's judgment. (Acts 12 and Rev 20). They brought the law to Moses. (Gal. 3:19 and Hebrews 2:2). However, they are created beings and we are not to worship them. (Col. 2:18). The angels longed to understand salvation but they were not able to comprehend that Jesus would come and provide this great redemption. (I Peter 1:12).

"See that you do not look down on one of these little ones. For I tell you that their angels in heaven always see the face of my Father in heaven" (Matt. 18:10). Certain angels are assigned to watch over the children. While many are not delivered or spared from accidents nevertheless angels are with them to comfort them.

Peter was sleeping in prison facing a trial the next morning. An angel came and delivered him. (Acts 12:7-10). How often have you been spared from accidents or evil and been unaware of the angel's deliverance? I was traveling on the interstate late one night while it was pouring down rain. My car hydroplaned heading directly into the rear of a tractor-trailer. I shouted "Jesus! Jesus! Jesus!" Just before I hit I heard a thump. Immediately I was aware an Angel pushed my car over several feet so I missed the truck.

The angel of the Lord shut the mouths of the lions so that Daniel was not harmed. (Daniel 6:22). An angel stood by Paul and informed him that he and all the people on the ship would be spared. (Acts 27:23). "The angel of the Lord encamps around those who fear him, and he delivers them" (Ps. 34:7).

Lord Jesus, I thank you for the ministry of angels. Thank you for delivering me from harm many times. You are so wonderful! Amen.

The Mature Christian

Romans 8:29 & Psalm 34

"Those God foreknew he also predestined to be conformed to the likeness of his Son" (Ro. 8:29). The goal is clear: Be like Jesus.

Two of the mature saints, David and Paul were honest in sharing the highs and lows in their life. In Psalm 34, David's faith is very high. He says that God will deliver us from fear, (v. 4), save us out of our troubles, (v. 6), guard and deliver us, (v. 7), show us goodness, (v. 8), supply our needs, (v. 9), listen when we talk to him, (v. 15), and redeem us, (v. 22). Wow! What promises!

David reminds us in the same Psalm we must seek him, (vv. 4 & 10), cry out to him, (vv. 6 & 17), trust him, (v. 8), fear him, (vv. 7 & 9), refrain from lying, (v. 13), turn from evil, do good and seek peace, (v. 14), be humble (v. 18) and serve him. (v. 22).

Other times David writes: "O Lord, heal me, for my bones are in agony. My soul is in anguish. How long, O Lord, how long?" (Ps. 6:2-3). I am worn out from groaning; all night long I flood my bed with weeping and drench my couch with tears. My eyes grow weak with sorrow; they fail because of all my foes" (Ps. 6:6-7).

Paul explicitly expounds: "We were crushed and completely overwhelmed, and we thought we would never live through it. In fact, we expected to die. But as a result, we learned not to rely on ourselves, but on God who can raise the dead. And he did deliver us from mortal danger" (I Cor. 1:8-10 NLT). We are "dying and yet we live on; beaten, and yet not killed; sorrowful, yet always rejoicing; poor, yet making many rich; having nothing, and yet possessing everything" (6:10). From prison Paul writes, "Be joyful always; pray continually; give thanks in all circumstances" (I Thess. 5:16-18).

Mature Christians can go through the valleys or ride on the mountaintops as they learn to rejoice in the sufficiency of Jesus.

Jesus, thank you for your grace that reaches out to me when I do not fully attain or live up to your will for me. Enable me to move on to maturity in Christ Jesus. Amen.

August 17

Boundaries or Center Focus

John 12:32

"When I am lifted up on the cross, I will draw everyone to myself" (John 12:32).

Many view the Christian faith with Christ at the center but then see all kinds of fences or boundaries in relationship to Christ. An example of boundaries might be the implication that a person couldn't be a Christian if they live a materialistic lifestyle, if they are covered with tattoos, or drink alcohol, etc.

Rather than set up those artificial boundaries let's think of Jesus as the center and see people coming to him from every arena of life and life styles. He said, "But I, when I am lifted up from the earth, I will draw all men to myself" (John 12:32). Setting up boundaries inevitably leads to legalism. Jesus is in the business of tearing down walls. (Eph. 2:11-22). Legalistic attitudes rob us of our joy. We live with guilt because we can never keep all the standards.

Paul has a helpful word. (Gal. 5:13-21). "You, my brothers, were called to be free. But do not use your freedom to indulge the sinful nature; rather, serve one another in love. The entire law is summed up in a single command: 'Love your neighbor as yourself.' If you keep on biting and devouring each other, watch out or you will be destroyed by each other."

Nevertheless there are boundaries. "So I say, live by the Spirit, and you will not gratify the desires of the sinful nature. For the sinful nature desires what is contrary to the Spirit, and the Spirit what is contrary to the sinful nature . . . (We are a walking civil war.) But if you are led by the Spirit, you are not under law.

"The acts of the sinful nature are obvious: sexual immorality, impurity and debauchery, idolatry and witchcraft; hatred, discord, jealousy, fits of rage, selfish ambition, dissensions, factions and envy, drunkenness, orgies, and the like. I warn you, as I did before, that those who live like this will not inherit the kingdom of God."

Lord Jesus, enable me to live by your Spirit and never to use my freedom to gratify my sinful nature. Amen.

Worthless Fasting

"Shout . . . Tell my people of their sins! Yet they act so pious! They come to the Temple every day and seem delighted to hear my laws. You would almost think this was a righteous nation that would never abandon its God. . . . 'We have fasted before you!' they say. 'Why aren't you impressed? We have done much penance, and you don't even notice it!'" (Isaiah 58:1-3 NLT).

Isaiah shouts to get their attention. He is talking with "nice church people" who gather to sing the right words, hear the good sermons and return next week for worship. They have a form of Godliness but no power. (II Tim. 3:5).

"I will tell you why! It's because you are living for yourselves even while you are fasting. You keep right on oppressing your workers. What good is fasting when you keep on fighting and quarreling? . . . You humble yourselves by going through the motions of penance, bowing your heads like a blade of grass in the wind . . . Do you really think this will please the Lord?" (Is. 58:3-5 NLT).

Too often our theology is not matched with our sociology: Our worship doesn't translate into life, and our Sunday doesn't carry over into Monday. They were sowing wild oats during the week and going to church praying for a crop failure. We must practice what we preach and preach what we practice or no one would be saved.

"The kind of fasting I want calls you to free those who are wrongly imprisoned and to stop oppressing those who work for you. Treat them fairly and give them what they earn . . . Share your food, . . . welcome poor wanderers into your homes. Give clothes to those who need them, and do not hide from relatives who need your help. If you do these things, . . . your healing will come quickly. . . Then when you call, the Lord will answer . . ." (vv. 6-9).

Jesus said when you fast, not if you fast. Unless prayer/fasting become more important than your food, you will not experience revival in your life or in your church.

Jesus help me to practice your true fast. Amen.

Full Joy

John 15:11

"I have told you this so that my joy may be in you and that your joy may be complete" (John 15:11).

Some said, "You Christians seem to have a religion that makes you miserable." Perhaps they were baptized in lemon juice. What a poor advertisement! The joy of the Lord does not radiate from them. A smile would greatly help their countenance. Is it because they have deep hurts that were never healed? Is it because they are carrying heavy burdens? Is it because they believe God doesn't want us to enjoy life?

Joy or joyful is mentioned hundreds of times in the Bible. "The Kingdom of God is . . . righteousness, peace and joy in the Holy Spirit" (Ro. 14:17). "Ask and you will receive, and your joy will be complete" (John 16:23). "Always be full of joy in the Lord. I say it again—rejoice!" (Phil. 4:4 NLT). "Our hearts ache but we always have joy" (II Cor. 6:10 NLT). To the persecuted Christians, "You believe in Jesus and are filled with inexpressible and glorious joy. For you are receiving the salvation of your souls" (I Peter 1:8-9). "The joy of the Lord is your strength" (Nehemiah 8:10). "In your presence is fullness of joy" (Psalm 16:11 KJV). That's straight forward. We live in his presence. (James 4:8, John 14:23).

The source is Jesus. Joy is the evidence of the Holy Spirit living in you. (Gal. 5:22). If you obey his commands your joy will be full! (John 15:9-11). His command is to make disciples. When he sent the disciples the first time (Luke 10:1ff) they returned with joy because they were successful. Jesus tells them that they are not to rejoice in successful service but to rejoice because of their relationship with him.

Joy comes when we have an intimate relationship with the risen Christ. All authority has been given to me . . . make disciples and your joy will be complete. Do I trust the Holy Spirit to use me to bring people to Jesus?

Lord Jesus I will obey your powerful Holy Spirit. May your joy be my strength. Amen.

Grow in Knowledge

II Peter 3:18

"Grow in the . . . knowledge of our Lord and Savior Jesus Christ" (II Peter 3:18 NLT).

The word "knowledge" is experiential knowledge. There is a different Greek word for factual or cognitive knowledge. God's truth is hidden to those who will not obey him. Jesus prays: "O Father, Lord of heaven and earth thank you for hiding the truth from those who think themselves so wise and clever, and for revealing it to the childlike. Yes, Father, it pleased you to do it this way!" (Matt. 22:25-26 NLT). Knowledge was hidden because of their pride. They suppress the obvious truth which is in creation—in them and all around them.

Obedience is the key to opening God's truth. We don't come to understand God in the abstract or through philosophy but through a relationship. Having a personal relationship comes as we live and walk in the light of God's truth. "If we walk in the light, as he is in the light, we have fellowship with one another and the blood of Jesus, his Son, purifies us from all sin" (I John 1:7). When we are cleansed from sin we are born into his Kingdom. That means God is our Father. Jesus is our brother and his Holy Spirit lives within us. We can experience a vital, dynamic and intimate relationship with Jesus. He lives in us. (Gal. 2:20). We abide in him. (John 15:4). The supernatural becomes natural.

Studying about God with no intention to know him is an intellectual exercise. It is dead works. (Hebrews 6:1). Obedience brings understanding. Peter admonished us to grow in our love, friendship and obedience to God. We must be willing to do the will of the Father. Then we will know the truth and the truth will set us free.

As we walk in obedience the truth opens up to us. Paul writes, "I pray you may be active in sharing your faith, so that you will have a full understanding of every good thing we have in Christ" (Philemon 6). As you are obedient in sharing your faith, both in word and deed your understanding of Christ will grow.

Lord, enable me to walk in obedience so I can grow in experiencing more and more of your love and grace. Amen.

I'm Not So Bad

Matthew 22:10 & 7:1-5

"The servants went out into the streets and gathered all the people they could find, both good and bad, and the wedding hall was filled with guests" (Matt. 22:10).

Christians often see themselves as being good and the people of the world as bad. The Greek word "bad" is at times translated "evil" or "wicked." A minister read a long list of sins from Galatians 5 and said, "I want everyone here to stand up if you have committed any of these sins." One man stood, than another and another until nearly everyone stood. A man attending the church for the first time said, "These are my kind of people. I will be at home here." He gave his life to the Lord.

We all sin and fall short of God's standard. (Ro. 3:23). We all inherited the sin nature. Some people have suffered more and experienced less of the grace and love of God because they have not learned to cast their care on him. This makes it more difficult for them to understand God's grace and to accept the forgiveness and power Jesus has provided for them.

Hurting people tend to hurt others. No matter how offensive one's actions, we all need God's mercy. I have experienced more of God's love than many who were not raised in a Christian family. Therefore I have more responsibility to show God's love and mercy to those who have not experienced his love. This helps me see myself on the same level as those whose actions seem more obviously evil than mine.

By God's grace I have been forgiven, but I have the same sin issues as everyone, no matter how repulsive their action and sin. When we critically judge others it points to a lack of understanding our sin nature.

There's freedom in letting God be the judge and simply holding up the grace of Jesus. The key for Christians is to remember that God loves us all. Our part is to repent of our sins and accept his love and forgiveness. (John 3:16-17).

Jesus, thank you for saving me from sin. Help me to love others as you loved me. Amen.

Both Mission and Ministry

John 17:18

You have a mission and a ministry. What's the difference? You may find it helpful to think in terms of mission as your service outside the congregation while your ministry is within Christ's body.

Our ministry is to, "Serve one another in love" (Gal. 5:13). Jesus says in referring to the Father: "In the same way that you gave me a mission in the world, I gave them a mission in the world" (John 17:18 Msg.). We, like Jesus, are sent into the world. (Jh. 17:18 and 20:21). Jesus understood his mission. At age 12 he said, "I must be about my Father's business." Since we are the body of Christ, his mission is our mission. He came to seek and save the lost. We must do the same.

In ministry we serve (Gal. 5:13), honor (Ro. 12:10), accept (Ro. 15:7), instruct (Ro. 15:14), carry burdens (Gal. 6:2), bear with (Eph. 4:2), submit (Eph. 5:12), encourage (I Thess. 5:11), pray (James 5:16) and love one another (John 13:34).

Many Christians who have been in church all their lives, even in small groups for years, still do not have a vibrant, contagious faith. For a vibrant contagious faith we need a ministry and a mission. Unless our biological families give birth we will die. Unless our churches have an outward focus we will die even though we have an inward ministry. Every member needs to have a vital part in not only a ministry but also a mission in the world.

You can be committed to church without being committed to Christ but you cannot be committed to Christ and not be committed to the church. Jesus died for his bride, the church. Don't let people try to tell you the church is not important. It's not perfect but it's the best we will ever have.

Some may be physically unable to serve in mission but they can pray and witness. If they understand their inside church ministry is directly helping the mission of the church this hurdle can be overcome. Jesus calls us to be involved both in ministry and mission, an inward focus and an outward focus.

Lord Jesus, enable me to be faithful in both ministry and mission. Amen.

From Enemies to Friends

II Corinthians 5:18

"Christ changed us from enemies into his friends and gave us the task of making others his friends also" (II Cor. 5:18 TEV).

In an apocrypha story, Jesus is talking with an angel. The angel asked him how things were going on earth. He said, "Many people are coming to new life. The Kingdom of God is expanding but we have a long way to go." Looking concerned the angel questioned, "What is your strategy for reaching the others?" Jesus said, "It's for each Christian to invite others to enter my Kingdom." The angel asked, "What if that plan doesn't work?" Jesus said, "I have no plan B!"

We are sent to speak for Jesus. "God put the world square with himself through the Messiah, giving the world a fresh start by offering forgiveness of sins. God has given us the task of telling everyone what he is doing. We're Christ's representatives. God uses us to persuade men and women to drop their differences and enter into God's work to making things right between them. We're speaking for Christ himself now: Become friends with God; he's already a friend with you" (I Cor. 5:18-20 Msg.).

Elisha turned enemies into friends. The King of Aram was at war with Israel. King Aram was frustrated because someone was telling the Israelites exactly where the his army would attack next. The King discovered it was Elisha who was causing his defeat so he sent an army to capture him. When Elisha's servant got up he saw this huge army surrounding them. Elisha said, "Don't be afraid! . . . For there are more on our side than on theirs!" (II Kings 6:16 NLT). Elisha prayed and the servant's eyes were opened and he saw the hillside filled with horses and chariots of fire. (v. 17).

Then Elisha prayed for the enemy army to be blinded. He led them to Samaria and after their eyes were opened he prepared a huge feast and sent them home. They were no longer enemies. "If your enemies are hungry, feed them. If they are thirsty, give them something to drink, and they will be ashamed of what they have done to you. . . . Conquer evil by doing good" (Ro. 12:20-21 NLT).

Lord, help me to do good to my enemies. Amen.

Pray Specifically

Luke 11:9-13

"Ask and it will be given to you; seek and you will find; knock and the door will be opened to you. For everyone who asks receives; he who seeks finds; and to him who knocks, the door will be opened. Which of you fathers, if your son asks for a fish will give him a snake instead? Or if he asks for an egg, will give him a scorpion? If you then, though you are evil, (since you have an evil nature) know how to give good gifts to your children, how much more will your Father in heaven give the Holy Spirit to those who ask him!" (Luke 11:9-13).

Praying in generalities is much easier than praying specifically. Praying specifically takes faith. Prayers without faith are nothing more than dead ritual. General prayers are not wrong such as, Lord bless our nation, our President and our church. There are times when God places a burden on you for a world leader, a nation, or a church when you only have a general idea of the needs of that situation.

In specific prayers you are expressing your desire, your burden for a person so name that person. When people are in small groups instead of praying for specific people their prayers are often in generalities or in categories such as praying for the lost, for the teachers in your school, for missionaries or for the governments of the world.

It is helpful to pray for persons by name unless you can't trust others to keep the situation in confidence. If you know the situation mention specific needs, e.g. their marriage, their health or their finances. The more specifically you pray the more obvious it is when the answer comes. Answered prayer builds faith and is an encouragement to everyone.

Prayer is like putting your car in gear. Don't pray unless you are willing to take action. God may want to use you to answer your prayer.

Lord Jesus, help me to sincerely ask in faith knowing that you are more willing to answer our requests than earthly fathers are to answer the requests from their children. Amen.

When You Can't Sleep

John 10:3 & Psalm 23

When you can't sleep don't count sheep, talk to the Shepherd. Meditate on some of your favorite Scriptures. How can you remember Scripture? It's helpful to know that when Jesus quoted from the Old Testament he sometimes did not quote verbatim but the essence of Scripture. Many of you know Psalm 23, the Shepherd Psalm. God knows our thoughts and the contents of our hearts. He loves when you meditate on his word. Some Scriptures I often use for meditation are:

When we are in Christ we are a new creation, the old is gone and the new has come. (II Cor. 5:17).

God raised me up seated me with Jesus in the heavenly realms. (Eph. 2:6).

"I have been crucified with Christ and I no longer live, but Christ lives in me. The life I live in the body I live by faith in the Son of God, who loved me and gave himself for me" (Gal. 2:20).

"God who is able to do immeasurably more than all we ask or imagine, according to his power that is at work within us, to him be glory in the church and in Christ Jesus . . . for ever and ever! Amen" (Eph. 3:20-21).

"In all these things we are more than conquerors through him who loved us. For I am convinced that neither death nor life, neither angels nor demons, neither the present nor the future . . . nor anything else in all creation, will be able to separate us from the love of God" (Ro. 8:37-39).

"He gives strength to the weary and increases the power of the weak. Even youths grow tired and weary, and young men stumble and fall; but those who hope in the Lord will renew their strength. They will soar on wings like eagles; they will run and not grow weary, they will walk and not be faint" (Is. 40:29-31).

Lord, I love your word. It is a lamp for my feet and a light for my path. I will meditate on it day and night. Amen.

The Life-Giving Way

Hebrews 10

Can you imagine going to worship with your animals, the very best of the herd, then seeing your animal killed with the blood being sprinkled over the altar and sprinkled over you?

Notice the tremendous contrast in the New Testament. The blood of Jesus Christ cleanses us from all sin. (I John 1:7). What a precious gift of life Jesus gives us! "By one sacrifice, Jesus has made perfect forever those who are being made holy. The Holy Spirit also testifies to us about this. First he says: 'This is the covenant I will make with them after that time, says the Lord. I will put my laws in their hearts and I will write them on their minds.' Then he adds: 'Their sins and lawless acts I will remember no more'" (Heb. 10:14-17).

"So, friends, we can now—without hesitation—walk right up to God, into 'the Holy Place.' Jesus has cleared the way by the blood of his sacrifice acting as our priest before God. . . . So let's do it—full of belief, confident that we're presentable inside and out. Let's keep a firm grip on the promises that keep us going. He always keeps his word. Let's see how inventive we can be in encouraging love and helping out not avoiding worshiping together as some do but spurring each other on, especially as we see the big Day approaching" (Heb. 10:19-25 Msg.).

There is no deliverance from the sins that trip us up apart from the cross. It's in him alone that we have redemption through his blood. (Eph. 1:7). We can read self-help books, apply the latest psychology and use every ounce of will power all to no avail. When we come to the cross and receive his cleansing he gives us a new heart and a new mind. We are new people in Christ Jesus. (II Cor. 5:17).

Come to Jesus the life-giving way today and let him live his life through you. (Gal. 2:20).

Father, I come through Jesus the life-giving way. I want Jesus to live through me today. Amen.

Victory in Pain

Hebrews 13:5

God's discipline is one cause of pain. The writer of Hebrews states: "Do not lose heart when he rebukes you, because the Lord disciplines the one he loves, and he chastens everyone he accepts as his son" (12:5-6). The King James Version says, "He chastens and scourges every son he receives."

Contrast this with Jesus' words, "Are not two sparrows sold for a penny? Yet not one of them will fall to the ground outside our Father's care. And even the very hairs of your head are all numbered. So don't be afraid. . ." (Matt. 10:29-30). God's love is always there for the sparrow even though the sparrow may freeze to death in the winter. God's unconditional love is with those who are suffering and being martyred. Nothing can separate us from his love: "Trouble or hardship or persecution or famine or nakedness or danger or sword? As it is written: 'No, in all these things we are more than conquerors'" (Ro. 8:35). Since God is for us no person or demonic force can overcome us. (v. 31).

My wife, Helen, has lived with increasing pain from Erosive Osteo Arthritis, Macular Degeneration, Oral Lichen Planus, Peripheral Neuropathy, and a rare blood cancer, Waldenstrom's Macroglobulinemia. She has learned to cast her cares on Jesus. She says, "As long as I am praising God, I'm ok. Thank God his mercies are new every morning and great is his faithfulness" (Lamentations 3:22-23). She walked into physical therapy and they greeted her: "Here comes inspiration." She finds Jesus sufficient enabling her to smile and give a powerful witness for the Lord.

God said, "I will never leave you or forsake you; never will I forsake you" (Heb 13:5). To capture the fuller meaning of the Greek the Amplified reads: "God himself has said, I will not in any way fail you nor give you up, nor leave you without support. [I will] not, [I will] not, [I will] not in any degree leave you helpless, or forsake you, let [you] down, [relax my hold on you]—Assuredly not!' So we take comfort and are encouraged and confidently and boldly say, 'The Lord is my Helper, I will not be seized with alarm—I will not fear or dread or be terrified. What can man do to me?'" (vv. 5-6).

Father, you are always with us in our pain. Your presence sustains us. Amen.

Privilege or Responsibility

Ezekiel 3:17-20

"Son of man, I've made you a watchman for the family of Israel. Whenever you hear me say something, warn them for me. If I say to the wicked, 'You are going to die,' and you don't sound the alarm warning them that it's a matter of life or death, they will die, and it will be your fault. I'll hold you responsible. But if you warn the wicked and they keep right on sinning anyway, they'll most certainly die for their sin, but you won't die. You'll have saved your life" (Ezekiel 3:17-20 Msg.).

You are the only Christian some people know. Your mission is to share Jesus with these people. It is a privilege to share Jesus with them: "God has given us the privilege of urging everyone to come into his favor and be reconciled to him" (II Cor. 5:18 LB).

If your neighbor had a deadly disease and you knew the cure it would be inexcusable to withhold that information. But it is worse to keep secret the way to forgiveness and eternal life. We have the greatest news in the world, and sharing it is the greatest kindness you can show to anyone.

Persons who have been Christians for a long time often forget how hopeless it felt to be without Christ. No matter how contented or successful people appear to be, without Christ they are hopelessly lost and headed for eternal separation from God. Jesus is the only One who can save people. (Acts 4:12). Everybody needs Jesus.

Why did God let us here after we accepted him? In heaven we can worship, fellowship, sing, pray and hear God's Word, but we won't be able to win people for Jesus and make disciples. Nothing you do is more important than helping people find Jesus. It's a matter of life and death. Your work, your friendship, your finances will all be gone in a few years. The consequences of your mission will last forever.

It's urgent. Jesus said: "As long as it is day, we must do the work of him who sent me. Night is coming, when no one can work" (John 9:4).

Jesus, thank you for the privilege of sharing the Good News. Amen.

Neighbors

John 17:15 & I Corinthians 6:17

"I'm not asking you to take them out of the world, but to keep them safe from the evil one." The Message reads, "I'm not asking that you take them out of the world but that you guard them from the Evil One" (John 17:15 Msg.).

"Leave the corruption and compromise; leave it for good," says God. "Don't link up with those who will pollute you. I want you all for myself" (I Cor. 6:17 Msg.).

Here we have contrasting scriptures. When it comes to neighbors do you desire Christian neighbors or do you want nonbelievers to move close to you so you can win them to Jesus? Christians naturally desire for other Christians to move beside them because their values are similar.

Might there be a better approach when it comes to neighbors? My wife, Helen, prays for the new family that will be moving into an empty house. If they are Christians she prays that they will be active in extending God's Kingdom. If they are not Christians she prays that she will be able to faithfully share Jesus with them.

Helen expressed her delight in meeting a new neighbor and mentioned she had been praying for them. The lady said, "How could you pray for us when you didn't know who was moving in? I'm a Christian, but I never thought about praying for new neighbors."

Paul writes in Ephesians 4:15 that we are to make the most of every opportunity. Let's not separate ourselves from the world by isolating ourselves with those who do not believe as we do. Let's be the salt, the light and the leaven that Jesus desires for us to be. (Matt. 5:13-16).

Lord, forgive me for too often being exclusive and desiring to live where others already are Christians. Help me to get out of the salt shaker and into the world bringing the life of your salvation to others. Amen.

God Is Eternal (Part I)

Genesis 1:1

There are many things we can't understand. "In the beginning God created the heavens and the earth" (Gen. 1:1). We think everything must have a beginning. But God always was. "The secret things belong to the Lord our God, but the things revealed belong to us . . . that we may follow all the words of this law" (Deut. 29:29).

"Before the mountains were born or you brought forth the earth and the world, from everlasting to everlasting you are God" (Ps. 90:2). "Do you not know? . . . The Lord is the everlasting God, the Creator of the ends of the earth . . . His understanding no one can fathom" (Is. 40:28).

God says, "My thoughts are not your thoughts, neither are your way my ways, declares the Lord. As the heavens are higher than the earth, so are my ways higher than your way and my thoughts than your thoughts" (Isaiah 55:8-9).

"In the beginning the Word already existed. He was with God, and he was God. He was in the beginning with God. He created everything there is. Nothing exists that he didn't make. Life was in him, and his life gives light to everyone" (John 1:1-5 NLT).

Eternity is like numbers. Begin with zero and go positive or negative. You will never get to the end. There is always one more number either positive or negative. "God has planted eternity in the human heart" (Eccl. 3:11 NLT). What comes before the cosmos? God! And what was before God? God! Understand it? No. We are finite and the infinite baffles us.

God said to Moses, "I AM WHO I AM . . . Say to the Israelites: I AM has sent me to you" (Exodus 3:14). "Am" means to exist, to be. We all need air, food, etc. but God is self sufficient and self existent. He always has existed and always will exist. God breathed into Adam the breath of life but Adam sinned and death came. "The whole creation has been groaning . . . not only so but we ourselves groan inwardly . . . for the redemption of our bodies" (Ro. 8:22-23).

Jesus, thank you for providing eternal life with you. Amen. (John 14:1-2).

You Are Eternal (Part II)

II Peter 3:10-14

"What is your life? You are a mist that appears for a little while and then vanishes" (Ja. 4:14). "Don't boast about tomorrow, for you do not know what a day may bring forth" (Prov. 27:1). The short span of our life is so minuscule compared to eternity that it should impel us to live as faithful fully committed disciples of Christ.

During this short span we are on probation. How we live will determine our future destiny for billions of years and beyond. Jesus said, "I tell you that men will have to give account on the Day of Judgment for every careless word they have spoken. For by your words you will be acquitted, and by your words you will be condemned" (Matt. 12:36-37). The Message reads: "Every one of these careless words is going to come back to haunt you. There will be a time of Reckoning. Words are powerful, take them seriously. Words can be your salvation. Words can also be your damnation." "Let those who thoughtlessly consider the brevity of life remember the length of eternity." (Thomas Kent). "If we fully comprehend the brevity of life, our greatest desire would be to please God and serve one another." (James Dobson).

You are eternal. God picked you out, chose you before the foundation of the world. (Eph. 1:4). This means in God's eyes you always were. It means you are living in eternity now. Jesus said, "If you believe in me you will never die" (John 11:26). You will live eternally.

"Everyone who has this hope of Christ's return purifies himself, just as he is pure" (I John 3:3). "Since everything will be destroyed . . . you ought to live holy and godly lives as you look forward to the day of God and speed its coming. That day will bring about the destruction of the heavens by fire, and the elements will melt in the heat. But in keeping with his promise we are looking forward to a new heaven and a new earth, the home of righteousness. Since you are looking forward to this, make every effort to be found spotless, blameless and at peace with him" (II Peter 3:10-14).

Lord, we don't understand infinite and finite. We humbly bow in grateful thanks for bridging the gap to bring us to yourself for eternity. Amen.

A Fresh Start

II Corinthians 5:17-20

"Anyone united with the Messiah gets a fresh start, is created new. The old life is gone; a new life burgeons! (flourishes rapidly). Look at it! All this comes from the God who settled the relationship between us and him, and then called us to settle our relationships with each other. God put the world square with himself through the Messiah, giving the world a fresh start by offering forgiveness of sins. God has given us the task of telling everyone what he is doing. We're Christ's representatives, God uses us to persuade men and women to drop their differences and enter into God's work of making things right between them" (II Cor. 5:17-20 Msg.).

Can you imagine a greater message than this—guaranteed a fresh start! The old life is gone, we think differently. We see things from God's perspective. We have new desires. The things of the world have lost their attraction and their power over us.

Has God changed the things that really matter to you? If you still desire and long for the old ways go to the cross and lay the old desires on the altar. You know deep down you had nothing to do with this change except give yourself to God. He did the changing for you. Your desires changed, your love for him became predominate. It's impossible to describe other than to say, it is God's life in me. Paul explains it: "I have been crucified with Christ and I no longer live, but Christ lives in me. The life I live in the body, I live by faith in the Son of God who loved me and gave himself for me" (Gal. 2:20). It's more than a changed life it is an exchanged life!

If you haven't experienced this change—throw yourself once again at the foot of the cross and say, "Lord, I give you not only my time, money and service. I give you my heart. All that I am, all that I have I give to you. Use me to extend your Kingdom." What joy, peace and power await you!

Thank you Lord Jesus, for translating me from the kingdom of darkness to the Kingdom of your beloved Son. Use me to persuade men and women to drop their differences and enter into God's work of making things right between them. Amen.

Is There Time to Retire?

Revelation 2:2-5

"I know all the things you do. I have seen your hard work and your patient endurance. I know you don't tolerate evil people . . . You have patiently suffered for me without quitting. But I have this complaint against you. You don't love me or each other as you did at first. Look how far you have fallen from your first love! Turn back to me again and work as you did at first. If you don't, I will come and remove your lampstand from its place among the churches" (Rev. 2:2-5 NLT).

At a retired pastor's conference we talked about the decline of the American church. The general consensus was that they did their part. Where do we read in Scripture that there is a retirement time for the Christian? "They shall bear fruit in old age they will stay fresh and green, proclaiming, 'The Lord is upright; he is my Rock and there is no wickedness in him'" (Ps. 92:14-15). "Though outwardly we are wasting away, yet inwardly we are being renewed day by day. For our light and momentary troubles are achieving for us an eternal glory that far outweighs them all" (II Cor. 4:16-17).

Have you lost your first love? "Never be lazy in your work, but serve the Lord enthusiastically" (Ro. 12:11 NLT). Can you imagine Paul retiring? While it is appropriate to turn the leadership over to younger Christians, you never retire.

Jesus heard that John the Baptist was killed. He tried to get alone but the crowds surrounded him. He healed their sick. He fed the multitude. When he finally gets alone what does he do? He prays and then teaches the disciples on the Sea of Galilee a dramatic lesson at three in the morning. What a model! (Matt. 14:13-25).

"Be strong and steady, always enthusiastic about the Lord's work, for you know that nothing you do for the Lord is ever useless" (I Cor. 5:58 NLT). "So don't get tired of doing what is good. Don't get discouraged and give up, for we will reap a harvest of blessing at the appropriate time. Whenever we have the opportunity, we should do good to everyone" (Gal. 6:9-10 NLT). "Never tire of doing good" (II Thess. 3:13).

Lord Jesus, help my Spiritual temperature to stay red hot until the day you call me home. Amen.

Work Is Not a Curse

Genesis 2:15

"The Lord God took the man and put him in the Garden of Eden to work it and take care of it" (Genesis 2:15).

Work is a blessing, not a curse. God worked: "By the seventh day God had finished the work he had been doing; so on the seventh day he rested from all his work. And God blessed the seventh day and made it holy, because on it he rested from all the work of creating that he had done" (Genesis 2:2-3).

Jesus said, "My Father is always at his work to this very day, and I, too am working" (John 5:17). Jesus is preparing a place for us. (John 14:2).

Even before the fall, Adam and Eve were given the privilege of working in the Garden of Eden. Imagine how boring life would be if we had no work. Perhaps it helps to think of it this way: Find God's purpose for yourself and you will never have to work again. Why, because when we are doing what God wants us to do, the work is usually satisfying, fulfilling and rewarding.

Who is your employer? "Slaves, obey your earthly masters in everything you do. Try to please them all the time not just when they are watching you. Serve them sincerely because of your reverent fear of the Lord. Work willingly at whatever you do as though you were working for the Lord rather than for people. Remember that the Lord will give you an inheritance as your reward and that the Master you are serving is Christ" (Col. 3:22 NLT).

Paul has to remind some Christians, if you don't work you don't eat. (II Thess. 3:10).

Do you dread going to your present job/work? Ask God to change your attitude. If you really believe you need to change jobs to be fulfilled, ask God to open the door and explore other options. If the door stays closed ask God to give you grace so you can begin to enjoy your work.

Lord Jesus, thank you for my job. Help me to remember I am working for you more than my earthly employer. Amen.

Use Your Gifts

I Corinthians 12:1, 7, 11

"I write about the special abilities the Holy Spirit gives to each of us . . ." (I Cor. 12:1 NLT). "A spiritual gift is given to each of us as a means of helping the entire church" (I Cor. 12:7 NLT). "It is the one and only Holy Spirit who distributes these gifts. He alone decides which gift each person should have" (I Cor. 12:11 NLT). "God has given gifts to each of you from his great variety of spiritual gifts" (I Peter 4:10 NLT).

It's clear you have several gifts. Don't ever feel you are insignificant. Your gift is to be used to build up the body of Christ and extend God's Kingdom. The next readings will highlight how your spiritual gifts operate.

Ignorance of spiritual gifts may be at the root of much of the frustration and guilt that plagues many Christians and stymies their ministry and mission. Too often we try to do things that we do not enjoy: We try to teach because the church needs a teacher, we sing in the choir because the director needs more tenors even though we don't enjoy singing. We try to show mercy to mental patients but are exhausted no matter how much we pray.

When we function in areas where we are not gifted we become frustrated and burn out. Others will eventually see that we are serving out of obligation. This is not a good advertisement for the body of Christ.

If we are to bear fruit that remains it's helpful to find and operate in our gift(s). As a Christian you love the Lord and endeavor to serve him. One way I have found to discover your gift(s) is to ask: If time, energy and finances were no hindrance, what would you really like to do with your life? What makes you fulfilled? What brings you deep joy and satisfaction? What would you like to hear at your memorial service?

These questions get at the heart of our gift(s). Pray and search your heart to discover what brings you deep joy and closer to Jesus. This is where your gifts lie.

Lord Jesus open my eyes to the gifts you have given me and I will joyfully serve you. Amen.

Gifts or Roles

Romans 12 & I Corinthians 12

"I can do everything through him who gives me strength" (Phil. 4:13). "With my God I can scale a wall" (Psalm 18:29).

There are times when you will be in a situation where people need help but you feel you are not gifted to help them. In these situations God gives grace so that even though you are uncomfortable, God provides the ability to minister effectively. This is exercising your role as a Christian rather than operating from your gift-mix.

What were Jesus' primary gift(s)? I believe Jesus had all the gifts. In one sense I believe we have all the gifts, too. As we mature in our Christian life we will find ourselves being called to sometimes serve in areas other than our giftedness. We can grow and develop in those areas. We don't train a dog to fly or a bird to dig up bones. Our primary focus should be in areas where we are gifted. At the same time when there is a need in the body of Christ for certain gifts we pray for the Lord to send people with those gifts. Until the prayer is answered, God will provide grace for you to meet those needs.

You are held accountable to God to develop each of your gifts to your potential. Discern where you best fit. Is it through prophesying, serving, teaching, encouraging, contributing, leading, showing mercy (Romans 12:6-8) or is it in other gifts? One list of gifts is mentioned in First Cor. 12 and elsewhere. We will consider these in the days ahead. When you serve within you gift-mix you will find spontaneous joy overflowing from your heart.

It is very important to remember that the fruit of the Spirit takes priority over the gifts of the Spirit. (Gal. 5:22-23). The primary characteristic of the Christian is love. Spiritual fruit deals with relationships and the quality of our living. Spiritual gifts relate to our function and our calling. Gifts are task-oriented and fruit is character-oriented. Fruit is eternal while gifts are temporal.

Lord Jesus, thank you for the gifts you have given me. Help me to develop all my gifts but most importantly enable me to grow in love for you and for others. Amen.

Discovering God's Will

Romans 12:1-6

"I urge you . . . to offer your bodies as living sacrifices, holy and pleasing to God—this is your spiritual act of worship. Do not conform any longer to the patterns of this world, but be transformed by the renewing of your mind. Then you will be able to test and approve what God's will is—his good, pleasing and perfect will. For by the grace given me I say to every one of you: Do not think of yourself more highly then you ought, but rather think of yourself with sober judgment, in accordance with the measure of faith God has given you. Just as each of us has one body with many members, and these members do not all have the same function, so in Christ we who are many form one body, and each member belongs to all the others. We have different gifts, according to the grace given us" (Romans 12:1-6).

In vv. 1 and 2 God wants us to offer our lives to him and not to follow the patterns of the world. Doing this does not always make clear what specifically God wants for us to do. In vv. 4-6 we learn we are given faith to discern what function we are to play in building God's Kingdom. Think soberly—be realistic about the faith God has given you. Then discern which of the gifts described in verses 3-8 or in First Corinthians 12 you enjoy doing. You will discover how these gifts fit your personality and passion. Functioning in your gifts assists you in finding the will of God for your life.

Volunteer to serve in a wide variety of situations. It will soon become apparent that you are more comfortable in certain contexts rather than in others. God often uses your past experience to equip and point you in the direction where you can serve him most effectively.

In the following readings we will focus on the characteristics of individual gifts. This too should assist you in discovering joy and fulfillment as you serve where God designed you to serve.

Lord Jesus open my eyes to see how I can best use the gifts you have given me to bear fruit that lasts for eternity. Amen.

Importance of Cooperation

I Corinthians 12:14-17

"The body has many different parts, not just one part. If the foot says, 'I am not a part of the body because I am not a hand,' that does not make it any less a part of the body. And if the ear says, 'I am not part of the body because I am only an ear and not an eye,' would that make it any less a part of the body? Suppose the whole body were an eye—then how would you hear? Or if your whole body were just one big ear, how would you smell anything?" (I Cor. 12-14-17 NLT).

Our differences are a blessing. Imagine a church in which everyone wanted to be the worship leader and no one was able to play an instrument. Would you enjoy going to class if no one had the gift of teaching or no one had the gift of help so that the church was never clean?

Give each person a different piece of baseball equipment and tell them to play alone. What a frustrating experience. The pitcher would have no catcher. It takes all nine players plus another team to play. We need each other!

Ultimately the gifts are not given for the individual's use; they are given for the benefit of the church family. "Each one should use whatever gift he has received to serve others, faithfully administering God's grace in its various forms" (I Peter 4:10-11 NLT).

Too often in our churches we develop programs and then try to find people to work in those programs. It's best to first discover the gifts of the people and the vision they have for a particular ministry and encourage them to utilize their gifts in that ministry. Encourage them and empower them to try their wings. Faith is spelled R-I-S-K. Experiment with sanctified imagination. Step out in faith. Pray and move ahead. God will either open or close the door. Develop ministry groups to serve others both within the church and in the community. Empower these persons to use their gifts within the vision of the church. This energizes the group and makes for an effective church.

Father, thank you for giving me gifts. Help me to use them most effectively to build up your body for your glory. Amen.

The Teaching Gift

Luke 1:1-4

Teaching is the gift of acquiring and imparting spiritual truth so that others learn and profit by their instruction. Notice how Luke begins his Gospel. "Many have undertaken to draw up an account of the things that have been fulfilled among us, just as they were handed down to us by those who from the first were eyewitnesses and servants of the word. Therefore, since I myself have carefully investigated everything from the beginning, it seemed good also to me to write an orderly account for you, . . . so that you may know the certainty of the things you have been taught" (Luke 1:1-4).

Teaching is the most universal gift in the New Testament. The Greek word, "didasko," to teach, appears more than 200 times. It's far more predominant than preaching. Most churches want preachers. This is one reason the American church is anemic. Teachers give lessons and expect results. Too often we just listen to preachers' messages but there is little if any accountability.

Teachers are curious persons: Luke "carefully investigated everything." They go into detailed explanations. They present truth in a systematic sequence. Luke wrote an "orderly account." Teachers may say, "If people are just taught the truth everything will be fine." Teachers like to know the source of the materials. Word meanings are important. They move from the word to the people. They prefer Biblical illustrations as compared to contemporary illustrations.

To further identify this gift ask, Am I a curious person? Do I enjoy Bible study? Can I put together a Bible outline? Can I sum up the important points or principles of the Bible study? Do my students ever tell me how I have helped them? Do I enjoy teaching? Am I asked to teach?

Some of the most important people in my life have been teachers. Even if you don't have the gift of teaching you need to exercise your role as a teacher to your children. Paul encouraged the Christians at Rome to be competent to teach each other. (Ro. 15:14).

Lord, enable me to use and develop my gift of teaching. Amen.

The Gift of Knowledge

John 4:16-19

"'Go, call your husband and come back.' 'I have no husband,' she replied. Jesus said to her, 'You are right when you say you have no husband. The fact is, you have had five husbands, and the man you now have is not your husband. What you have just said is quite true.' 'Sir,' the woman said, 'I can see that you are a prophet'" (John 4:16-19).

The person with the gift of knowledge has the ability to receive divine revelation that builds up the body of Christ. While praying for others, the Holy Spirit frequently imparts "secrets" to the intercessor so they find themselves praying for specific things.

Notice this knowledge comes from the Holy Spirit not from human intelligence. There is no direct relationship with a person's IQ. The gift is frequently exercised in a counseling situation. This is illustrated in the above scripture as Jesus encountered the woman at the well. Jesus told Nathaniel, I saw you while you were still under the fig tree before Philip called you. (John 1:48). Nathaniel was so impressed he declared: "Rabbi, you are the Son of God; you are the King of Israel" (John 1:49).

"Previous to President Kennedy's trip to Dallas, Billy Graham called the White House and told them he felt that something dreadful was going to happen to the President. Mr. Graham asked that President Kennedy postpone his trip. The White House thanked the evangelist for his concern, but the trip was not cancelled." The President was killed. (See Rick Yohn's book, *Discover Your Spiritual Gift and Use It.*)

Brother Yun, in his book *Living Waters*, tells of persecuted Christians in China meeting unannounced as the Holy Spirit directed them to a secret place in the middle of the night to avoid being arrested by the secret police.

My wife, Helen, has this gift. People come to her with questions about what direction to take. Do you find yourself with insights before others? Are your insights accurate? Is it evident to you that the only explanation for your insight is God's Holy Spirit?

Lord Jesus, help me to use the gift of knowledge. Amen.

The Gift of Wisdom

Acts 15:2 & 12-21

After a sharp dispute between the apostles and the Pharisees, James said, "Listen to me" (v. 12). "It is my judgment . . . that we should not make it difficult for the Gentiles who are turning to God. Instead we should write to them, telling them to abstain from food polluted by idols, from sexual immorality, from the meat of strangled animals and from blood" (Acts 15:19-20). They all agreed.

The person with the gift of wisdom has the ability to receive divine revelation that speaks to a specific need in the body of Christ. Knowledge is truth about the situation. Wisdom is the application of knowledge for a particular situation.

This person has the ability to listen to diverse points of view and come up with a solution that satisfies everyone. Have you been in a group where there were several sides to an issue? You wondered how the group could possibly be united after this. Then God spoke through a word of wisdom. You think: "That was so simple. Why didn't I think of that?"

As with the gift of knowledge there is no direct relationship with one's IQ. The word of wisdom is what we might often call common sense. It's a practical, almost "simple" solution. Solomon had a simple solution to a complex situation. (I Kings 3:16-28). People with this gift see problems as opportunities.

Do people who need advice come to you? Do members of a committee look your way before the final decision? Do you foresee the results of a particular course of action? Can you share insights so they are acceptable to others?

James writes: "If any of you lacks wisdom, he should ask God who gives generously to all without finding fault, and it will be given to him. But when he asks, he must believe, because he who doubts is like a wave of the sea, tossed by the wind. That person should not think they will receive anything from the Lord" (James 1:5-8).

Lord, help me to see others with this gift. Enable me to listen to your voice so I can receive your wisdom. Amen.

The Gift of Exhortation

Colossians 1:28-29

"We proclaim him, admonishing and teaching everyone with all wisdom, so that we may present everyone perfect in Christ. To this end I labor, struggling with all his energy, which so powerfully works in me" (Col. 1:28-29).

The exhorter is one who can speak words of comfort, admonition, and encouragement to motivate Christians toward maturity in Christ. So intense is Paul that he struggles with all Christ's energy to bring this about. The word for struggle here is the same word used to describe Jesus' experience in Gethsemane when he sweat, as it were, drops of blood in prayerful agony for our redemption.

The exhorter is motivated to discover where you are so they can help you move to maturity. They ask questions: "What is God teaching you in your prayer life? What did you learn in your devotions today? Where do you want to be a month from now?"

Present-day counselors are usually more passive than the exhorter. We are often too shy to admonish one another. Paul was constantly urging, warning and pleading with men and women to grow in Christ. (Col. 3:16).

The exhorter has the ability to visualize spiritual progress in the life of others and then use that vision to motivate them to take step-by-step action. Exhorters can see the potential God has given you. They desire for you to move to a new level of maturity.

"I want you to know how much I am struggling for you and for those in Loadicea, for all who have not met me personally. My purpose is that they may be encouraged in heart and united in love, so that they may have the full riches of complete understanding, in order that they may know the mystery of God, namely, Christ, in whom are hidden all the treasures of wisdom and knowledge" (Col. 2:1-3).

The exhorter is comfortable ministering to strangers. He or she likes to work one-on-one. The gift can operate with groups but it is more difficult to present step-by-step solutions since individuals are at different places in their maturity.

Lord, enable me to encourage others in moving toward a new level of maturity. Amen.

The Gift of Service

Hebrews 6:10-12

"God is not unjust; he will not forget your work and the love you have shown him as you have helped his people and continue to help them. We want each of you to show this same diligence to the very end, in order to make our hope sure. We do not want you to become lazy, but to imitate those who through faith and patience inherit what has been promised" (Heb. 6:10-12).

"The Son of Man did not come to be served, but to serve" (Mark 10:45). The person with the gift of service has the ability to sense community needs and utilize community resources for the advancement of the Kingdom. They notice what others overlook; e.g. a broken book shelf, the lack of coat hangers, the lawn mower not cutting cleanly, or the dripping faucet. If you are setting up and taking down chairs they cannot resist offering to help.

Wherever the need these persons step up to the plate. Even if they are not especially gifted in music they will try to help out. Do you need a teacher or an administrator—they will often be the first to fill in until others more gifted come on the scene.

They tend to feel unqualified for spiritual leadership. Empower and affirm them so they do not feel like second-class citizens. When other people thank them help them to respond with statements like: "God has been so good to me. I want to pass some of his love along to others."

Servers are often turned off with long-range goals. Visionaries need to break down the three- to five-year-goals into smaller short-range projects. Then those with the gift of service will work night and day to complete the task.

Sometimes the person with the gift of service tends to neglect his or her family needs in caring for the needs of other people. Do you usually sense what needs to be done? Do you often go ahead and do it. Is it easier for you to accept a work assignment than to lead out in directing others? If so, you have the gift of service.

Lord, enable me to be a faithful servant today. Amen.

The Gift of Helps

"When Barnabas and Saul arrived at Salamis, they proclaimed the word of God in the Jewish synagogues. John Mark was with them as their helper" (Acts 13:5).

The person with the gift of helps has the ability to help other members of the Body of Christ so they can more effectively utilize their gift(s) in serving Christ. They receive a sense of fulfillment in helping others to minister more effectively. They are not as focused on completing the project as they are on freeing others to do ministry.

These people often remember the little idiosyncrasies or likes and dislikes of the person they are serving. They express God's love by being sensitive to others' needs and pleasing them. They along with those with the gift of service tend to neglect or disregard their own or their families' needs to help others. One church secretary was so dedicated she took work home with her. I was often concerned that she did not neglect her family.

Onesiphorus was a helper who exercised much effort in searching for Paul while in Rome. He helped Paul in many ways, refreshed his spirit and was not ashamed of his chains. (II Tim. 1:16-17).

"Those parts of the body that seem to be weaker are indispensable, and the parts that we think are less honorable we treat with special honor" (I Cor. 12:22-23). These people are glad to work behind the scenes. They may be insulted if you insist on paying them. They like to volunteer.

Do you find fulfillment in helping others so they are free to minister more effectively? Do you exercise initiative asking if you can do something specifically for them? The person with this gift usually has a specific project in mind when they offer to help, rather than asking, "Can I be of help to you?" They enjoy helping indefinitely as long as they know their service is needed and others are not taking advantage of them.

Lord, I thank you for the many people who have helped me. Enable me to help others as well. Amen.

The Gift of Hospitality

Matthew 25:23, 35

"Do not forget to entertain strangers, for by so doing some people have entertained angels without knowing it" (Hebrews 13:2).

The person with the gift of hospitality has the ability to entertain others, including strangers so they feel at ease. Food is a leveler. Everyone likes to eat. Luke pictures Jesus eating in eight of his 24 chapters. Hospitality means "love of strangers." Entertaining places the focus on the host as Martha demonstrated, while Biblical hospitality focuses on the guest as Mary demonstrates. (Luke 10:38-42). The person with the gift of hospitality serves others in a way they like to be served. The guests feel they are not imposing and so are free to return at a later time.

Church leaders must have this gift. (Titus 1:8; I Tim. 3:2). Until our attitudes change whereby we include new persons into our circle of friends we will not reach the unchurched. Hospitality is the most important gift in extending God's Kingdom!

The most frequent questions asked by first time people who come to church are: "Will I be accepted" or "Will I fit in?" Take the initiative to talk with people moving into your community. Smile and introduce yourself. Ask their name and assure them "It's great to have you. May I show you around?" But remember there is a million miles between being friendly or becoming a friend.

Hospitality overcomes the walls that separate "insiders" and "outsiders." Too often the longer a congregation has been in existence the higher the walls. Groups have a window of about four months to gain new members. We must show hospitality or form new groups to provide for their acceptance and inclusion or they will leave.

Open your home to others. One in every three or four persons in the U.S. admits to having no close friends. What an opportunity to extend friendship! Invite new people to your home for a barbeque or have a house warming party for new people.

Lord, enable me to show hospitality in my community and church. Amen.

The Gift of Giving

Acts 9:36

"In Joppa there was a disciple named . . . Dorcas, who was always doing good and helping the poor" (Acts 9:36).

The person with the gift of giving knows that nothing they possess is their own. They find fulfillment in giving generously, sacrificially and cheerfully. (II Cor. 9:7). They are good stewards of their finances and resources in order to give to the Lord's work. They often give to unglamorous projects as for example when the church discovers their sewer line is in need of repair. They joyfully give far more than their tithe.

They do not pressure or appreciate the pastor saying publically, "We need $10,000. Who will give me $1,000?" They like to give anonymously. They are tuned into what God wants them to give.

The gift of giving is not tied to how much wealth one possesses. The poor widow who gave her two pennies had the gift of giving. (Mark 12:43-44). The Corinthian Church gave sacrificially out of their poverty. (II Cor. 8:2-7). On the other hand Joseph gave from his abundance. (Luke 23:50-53).

As a pastor visiting in the home of someone with the gift of giving it was almost impossible to leave without them sharing something with me. I had to learn that I was blessing them by graciously receiving their gift.

They have a clear belief in the principle of reciprocity however this belief is not their primary motivation for giving. They give not to receive but to advance the Kingdom of God. They have a desire to use their gift to motivate others to give. "I showed you that by this kind of hard work we must help the weak, remembering the words the Lord Jesus himself said, 'It is more blessed to give than to receive'" (Acts 20:35).

Would you rather meet another's need than your own need? Do you give consistently and systematically to causes that you know you can trust? Do you receive joy in giving?

Lord, help me to be a cheerful giver. Amen.

The Gift of Voluntary Poverty

Mark 14:3-9 & Acts 2:44-45

"Some of those present were saying indignantly to one another, 'Why this waste of perfume? It could have been sold for more than a year's wages and the money given to the poor.' And they rebuked her harshly'" (Mark 14:4-5).

The person with the gift of voluntary poverty gives most of his/her material possessions for the cause of Christ. They give sacrificially but the word sacrifice doesn't enter their minds. They often neglect their own needs in order to meet the needs of others. They live simply so others can simply live. Perhaps they drive an older car, live in a house that does not have the latest conveniences or do not dress in up-to-date attire.

These persons give a high percentage, far more than the tithe, of their income to the work of God's Kingdom. Most people would complain if they had to live on the level of their lifestyle. John Wesley left a well-worn coat and two silver teaspoons in his estate; but during his lifetime he gave $150,000 to the Lord's work. George Muller was poor all his life, yet he gave $180,000 to the Lord's work. Orie Miller, founder of Mennonite Central Committee, a relief agency, gave ninety percent of his income to the Lord. A college president, Elmer Neufeld, my personal friend lived a frugal life so he could advance the cause of Christ.

Persons with the gift of voluntary poverty may be tempted with the sin of gift projection. Gift projection is taking a gift that we have and projecting it on others, expecting them to operate the way we do.

They may say, "People tell me that I give sacrificially but I don't see it that way at all. I enjoy giving. I have enough to meet my basic needs and that's all I care to have. I have no desire to accumulate wealth or possessions." If more Christians lived as they live imagine what could be accomplished in feeding the hungry, educating the unlearned or sending missionaries around the world.

Lord, help me to live sacrificially so I can bless others. Amen.

The Gifts of Leadership and Administration

Titus 1:5 & Exodus 18:17-27

The gift of leadership is the ability to direct others in such a way that they want to voluntarily participate in a project and feel blessed in their participation. The gift of administrator is the ability to delegate responsibility in such a way that the goal is accomplished and the Body of Christ is built up. Moses and Joseph were leaders but their responsibilities grew so that they had to become administrators. (Gen. 41:41ff. and Ex. 18:17-27).

When Paul mentored Titus he was using his gift of leadership but when he instructed him to appoint elders he was exercising the gift of administration. "I left you at Crete to straighten out what was unfinished and appoint elders in every town, as I directed you" (Titus 1:5).

The leader is more person-oriented. The administrator is goal-oriented. The administrator delegates responsibility. The leader can usually work directly with all the people in accomplishing the tasks while the administrator will find this impossible because of the size and complexity of the task.

Leaders are self-starters with vision and urgency. They anticipate the progression of events and move the process forward to completion. They utilize resources to overcome hurdles. The administrator makes organizational and time charts. They appoint others to take care of the details in order to attend to the whole so the project is completed on schedule. Every parent must function as a leader and an administrator if they are to have a healthy family.

Notice how Jesus used these two gifts: "OK team your goal is to go into all the world and make disciples but wait until the Holy Spirit comes who will provide all the power you need to be witnesses here at home and then continue going to the ends of the earth. Remember I will be with you every day until I return" (Matt. 28:18-20 free translation).

Lord, help me to be a faithful leader and to delegate responsibilities so the Body of Christ can impact my community and surrounding areas. Amen.

The Gift of Pastor/Shepherd

John 10:11-14

"I am the good shepherd. The good shepherd lays down his life for the sheep. The hired hand is not the shepherd who owns the sheep. So when he sees the wolf coming, he abandons the sheep and runs away. Then the wolf attacks the flock and scatters it . . . I am the good shepherd; I know my sheep and my sheep know me" (John 10:11-14).

The person with the gift of pastoring has the God-given ability to assume responsibility for the spiritual welfare of a group of believers over a long period of time. Since the shepherd knows his sheep intimately he cannot care for a large number of people. As the church grows the pastor needs to have his elders, ministry team leaders, or small group leaders serve as pastors to the people. He moves from shepherd to administrator and vision-caster.

Every follower of Jesus is to love and care for others. They will spend long hours with those who are hurting whether physically, emotionally, mentally or spiritually.

The exhorter will move people to Christ by outlining a plan of action. The prophet will speak words of admonition. The giver will give a gift to help. The server will perform a service. The teacher will state the truth. The administrator will organize a plan to help. The shepherd/pastor will be there over the long term for the maturing of the sheep. The pastor is a true friend. He or she will lay down their life for the sheep. There is a definite intimacy that exists between the shepherd and the sheep.

Although the shepherd is patient he/she corrects the sheep. This may be difficult since shepherds have a compassionate heart. They must learn to speak the truth in love.

Do you have the ability to develop friendships that last? Have you been used of the Lord to move people toward maturity in their walk with Jesus? You are a shepherd.

Lord, I want to be a good shepherd. Give me your heart of love for those who are hurting and need healing. Amen.

The Gift of Mercy

"Blessed are the merciful, for they will be shown mercy" (Matthew 5:7).

"The Samaritan, as he traveled, came where the man was; and when he saw him, he took pity on him. He went to him and bandaged his wounds. Then he put the man on his own donkey, took him to an inn and took care of him" (Luke 10:33-34).

The person with the gift of mercy feels compassion especially towards those with emotional, mental, or physical needs and ministers to those needs with ease. The recipient feels God's love.

Persons with this gift often have difficulty ministering discipline. They don't want to see others hurt. After disciplining their children they may feel they need to apologize because they were too harsh. If another disciplines they may come to the disciplined persons and say, "John didn't really mean that. John is a kind person." The truth may be that John did mean what he said. The person with the gift of mercy must learn that God disciplines people to teach them lessons they need to learn. (Hebrews 12:7-10).

Surveys show that at least half of the people have this gift. If your gift is mercy, Paul says, "Do it cheerfully" (Ro. 12:8). The word for cheerfully only occurs twice in the New Testament: the Lord loves a cheerful giver (II Cor. 9:7) and here when showing mercy. The Greek word means with hilarity or with joy.

Mercy can read people's feelings and feel deeply with their pain. They can detect friction in a group. They have great difficulty coping with our violent culture.

If your gift is mercy be on your guard if someone corrects you or offers constructive criticism lest you feel discouraged and even become depressed. Be especially careful with your tone of voice when you correct a person with the gift of mercy because they tend to be oversensitive.

Lord Jesus, thank you for your mercy and the mercy I feel from others. Forgive me when I take correction or criticism too seriously so that I feel depressed. Help me to forgive myself and to remember to extend mercy to others. Amen.

The Gift of Evangelism

II Timothy 4:5 & Acts 21:8

"Do the work of an evangelist" (II Tim. 4:5). Although Timothy's primary gift was not evangelism Paul encouraged him to share the Good News. Jesus did not give the Great Commission as a possible option or suggestion. The Great Commission is for everyone. When Jesus sent out the 72, five or ten of the men did not say, "Evangelism is not my gift." Every one of the 72 obeyed Jesus. (Luke 10:1-12).

The Holy Spirit empowers us to obey the Great Commission. "You will receive power when the Holy Spirit comes on you; and you will be my witnesses (martyrs) in Jerusalem, (at home) and . . . to the ends of the earth" (Acts 1:8).

Why are we intimidated? Have we forgotten it is Good News? Are we turned off because others have used a wrong approach and embarrassed us? Is it because we believe one's faith is too personal? Is it because we don't know how to share our faith? Perhaps we believe the non-Christian would not feel at home in our church.

The evangelist enjoys meeting new people. He or she is able to share Jesus with unbelievers in such a way that many become disciples of Christ and active members in the local body of believers. Every new person they meet is another possible opportunity for them to share Jesus. (Acts 8:35).

The evangelist moves the conversation toward spiritual truths, presents Jesus and expects a decision in the foreseeable future. To the evangelist, sharing the Good News and not asking for a decision is like a car salesman telling you all about a car but not asking for a sale. The evangelist has a holy boldness. Paul asked the Christians to pray for him to be fearless in presenting the Gospel. (Eph. 6:19-20).

The person with the gift of evangelism is often a loner in a congregation that is nurture-oriented. If the congregation has little concern for the lost and new people are simply tolerated rather than loved and accepted the evangelist will either become discouraged and bury his gift or move to another congregation.

Lord, help me to be obedient to your command to share the Good News. Amen.

September 21

The Gift of Prophecy

Romans 12:6

"If a man's gift is prophesying, let him use it in proportion to his faith" (Ro. 12:6).

The gift of prophecy is the ability God gives to speak an authorative word concerning a particular situation. These people have an inner compulsion to speak the truth when confronted with sin. The prophet's motivation is to warn of the consequences of sin. They think: "That's what happens when you don't follow God's instruction." Their motto is: "The truth will set you free" (John 8:32). Fathers with the gift of prophecy need to heed the instruction: "Fathers, do not exasperate your children . . ." (Eph. 6:4).

Prophets tend to be blunt and therefore are often misunderstood. They usually see issues as either "white or black"—"right or wrong." They are especially turned off by hypocrisy and dishonesty or when someone takes advantage of the underdog. Prophets are willing to suffer for the truth. Jeremiah risked his life. He was misunderstood and persecuted. The prophet often uses his own sin as an example to teach others. Prophecies, especially in the New Testament, are to be tested by the congregation. (I Cor. 14:29 and I Thess. 5:20-21). In the New Testament the claim to be infallible is not permissible but the claim to inspiration is permissible.

Some have the mistaken notion that prophets cannot control what is said when the Holy Spirit speaks through them. This is not the case: "The spirit of the prophets is subject to the control of prophets. For God is not a God of disorder but of peace" (I Cor. 14:32-33).

Prophets find it relatively easy to stand alone on an issue. A prophet quotes scripture to support his or her message. They expect immediate results. Since they have received a word from the Lord they often have trouble fitting into institutional structures.

It's easy for prophets to be straightforward in a group on an issue even though they know others do not agree. Do people come to you later and thank you for your admonition even though it was difficult for them to hear you at the time?

Lord, enable me to be bold for you when people are going their own way. Amen.

The Gift of Faith

Hebrews 11

"Faith is being sure of what we hope for and certain of what we do not see" (Hebrews 11:1). "If I have faith and can move mountains but do not have love, I am nothing" (I Cor. 13:2).

All Christians must have faith to be saved. (Eph. 2:8). "Without faith it is impossible to please God, because anyone who comes to him must believe that he exists and that he rewards those who earnestly seek him" (Hebrews 11:6). The person with the gift of faith can discern with confidence the will of God and accomplish great things.

The gift of faith is the ability to "dream" God's "dreams" and move forward amidst great obstacles. People of faith can take ridicule and criticism. Elijah stood alone in faith on Mt. Carmel surrounded by hundreds of false prophets. (I Kings 18).

George Muller had the gift of faith. He prayed to God and fed over 2,000 orphans without asking for money. Those with this gift tend to tackle big things. Jesus said in Mark 11:23 if we have faith and do not doubt we can move mountains.

The late Bill Bright writes: "It is my strong conviction that it's impossible to ask God for too much if our hearts are pure and we pray according to the Word and will of God. It's a basic spiritual principle that whatever we vividly envision, ardently desire, sincerely believe and enthusiastically act upon will come to pass assuming that there is spiritual authority for it. It is this principle that is the foundation of praying supernaturally."

The fruit of a tree comes at the end of the limb where it's vulnerable. We like to abide by the trunk but there is no fruit. Step out in faith and you will be fruitful.

Has God given you specific goals of what you might accomplish for Him? Are you frustrated when your ideas are slowed by bureaucracy? Are you ready to step out in faith and put everything you have on the line to see God's vision become reality?

Lord, I thank you for the gift of faith. Help me to grow in mountain-moving faith. Amen.

The Gift of Intercession

Luke 6:12

"Jesus went to the mountains to pray, and spent the night praying to God" (Luke 6:12). The gift of intercession is the special ability the Holy Spirit gives to certain individuals to pray for extended periods of time for others resulting in God's moving in obvious ways.

The person with the gift of intercession knows that the effectiveness of another's ministry depends on his/her prayers. Daniel was convinced of this as he interceded for the people of God (Daniel 9). Note the length of his prayer (vv. 4-19). Samuel knew that if he did not pray for Israel he would be sinning. "As for me, far be it from me that I should sin against the Lord by failing to pray for you" (I Samuel 12:23).

The intercessor's focus is for others not for themselves. Jesus taught us to pray for others by using the plural pronouns in what we call the "Lord's prayer" Our Father, not my Father. (Matt. 6:9-14). We cannot pray the Lord's prayer without praying for others.

Jesus got up early in the morning to pray. (Luke 4:42). He withdrew from the people to pray (5:16). Luther spent a couple hours each day in prayer. It is obvious by the poor attendance in prayer meetings that we need more people with this gift.

Intercessors pray with passion. The Greek word which we translate agonize, anguish or struggle describes this person well. Paul writes, "I want you to know how much I am struggling for you and for those at Loadicea, and for all who have not met me personally" (Col. 2:1). Paul was praying fervently for people he had never met. "Epaphras is wrestling in prayer for you" (Col. 4:12).

Do you spend extended periods of time in prayer? Do you enjoy praying even though it is physically exhausting? Do you have a prayer list? Do you experience regular and specific answers to your prayers? Do others come to you requesting you to pray for them? Do you find it relatively easy to "pray continually?" (I Thess. 5:16).

Lord, help me to develop the gift of intercession. Raise up more intercessors. Amen.

September 24

The Missionary Gift

Romans 10:15

"How can they preach unless they are sent? As it is written, 'How beautiful are the feet of those who bring good news!'" (Ro. 10:15).

"This man is my chosen instrument to carry my name before the Gentiles and their kings and before the people of Israel" (Acts 9:15). "When this gospel is preached to all the world then the end will come" (Matt. 24:14).

The person with the missionary gift shares the Gospel and ministers effectively to those in a different culture. They enjoy the challenge of working with different cultures. Language study, new food, a different climate and new customs do not intimidate them, in fact, it energizes them.

They don't mind moving from one place to another. They are home away from home. They are willing to die and be buried in their new home. They don't talk about going back home in the sense they long to return to their childhood culture. They miss their families but find it relatively easy to cope with separation from loved ones. They replace the need for family by finding new "brothers" and "sisters." They love to make new friends.

Nearly two billion people have never heard of Jesus. We need missionaries!

What has happened to our missionary zeal? Many churches believe acts of service fulfills their role as a missionary. We serve but neglect the proclamation of the Good News. Are you encouraging your children to serve as missionaries? There are more missionaries coming to the United States than we are sending out to evangelize the world. Jesus said that the harvest is ripe and plentiful. He reminds us to pray for workers. Are you praying for workers to enter the harvest? (Luke 10:2).

Do you enjoy meeting and working with people from other cultures? Do you have a burden for lost people in other countries or for persons who come to your community from other cultures?

Lord, enable me to be a missionary to those of another culture in my community. Amen.

The Gift of Martyrdom

Acts 5:41-42

"The apostles went out of the High Council overjoyed because they had been given the honor of being dishonored on account of the Name. Every day they were in the Temple and homes, teaching and preaching Christ Jesus, not letting up for a minute" (Acts 5:41-42 Msg.). "About midnight Paul and Silas were praying and singing hymns to God, and the other prisoners were listening to them" (Acts 16:25).

The person with the gift of martyrdom is joyful while being persecuted. Paul and Stephen were praying and rejoicing in their persecution. (Acts 7:60). Peter knowing that James was just martyred fell asleep even though he was next in line. (Acts 12:6).

The gift of martyrdom is a special ability God gives to members of the body of Christ to suffer victorious facing death. The Greek word "martures" appears 173 times in the New Testament and is usually translated "witness" or "testimony." A "martyr" or a "witness" in the New Testament sense is one who is willing to testify about Christ even to the point of being persecuted unto death.

There are times when foreign workers are encouraged to flee the country because it is unsafe. Those with this gift will want to remain. That does not mean they are any more spiritual or more committed to the cause of Christ than those who leave.

Those with this gift have a holy boldness. Multitudes of Christians who live in countries where they suffer persecution find this gift necessary every day. Reports estimate that more than 100,000 Christians die for their faith each year. The Voice of the Martyrs ministers to persecuted Christian in 68 countries. (Read *Martyrs Mirror* by J. Van Braght for the individual accounts of 4,000 martyrs.)

Do you find yourself identifying with persecuted Christians? Are you praying for those being persecuted? Can you face criticism and physical torture with confidence? Can you risk your reputation in your loyalty to Christ without feelings of self-pity?

Lord, give grace and strength to those who are suffering for you. Help me to be faithful to pray for them. Enable me to be both sensitive and bold in my witness. Amen.

The Gift of Discernments of Spirits

Acts 5:1-11

"Peter said, 'Ananias, how is it that Satan has so filled your heart that you have lied to the Holy Spirit and have kept for yourself some of the money you received for the land? Didn't it belong to you before it was sold? And after it was sold, wasn't the money at your disposal? What made you think of doing such a thing? You have not lied to men but to God.' When he heard this, he fell down and died'" (Acts 5:3-5).

Jesus said, "Stop judging by mere appearances, and make a right judgment" (John 7:24). The false cults and their use of modern media make it necessary to practice daily discernment. Christians are admonished to discern good and evil, truth and error. (Hebrews 5:14). For every gift there is a counterpart. It looks real but is not. The innocent and gullible will often be deceived by these unscrupulous religious wolves in sheep's clothing that infiltrate our churches and attract many to their group. We need the gift of discernment to counteract these counterfeits.

Paul in his farewell address to the Ephesian Church says, "I know that after I leave, savage wolves will come in among you and will not spare the flock. Even from your own number men will arise and distort the truth in order to draw away disciples after them" (Acts 20:29-31). Both Peter and Jude spoke of those who are unfaithful infiltrating their communion table. (II Peter 2:13; Jude 12).

Satan often appears as an angel of light. (II Cor. 11:14-15). Demon activity is prevalent in many countries. As the U.S. becomes more ungodly many more persons are influenced by demonic activity. Those with the gift of discernment need to help us discern the motives of those who are teaching or making appeals for money. Some have turned their backs to the truth. (I Tim. 6:5). Too many make appeals for funds to feed the hungry and the poor but at the same time live extravagant lifestyles. How true is this today!

Do people consult with you about matters involving interpersonal relationships? Does your track record indicate that the persons you spotted as phonies are truly phonies?

Lord, I need your Holy Spirit to enable me to make right judgments. Amen.

The Gift of Celibacy

I Corinthians 7:7

"Since there is so much immorality, each man should have his own wife, and each woman her own husband. The husband should fulfill his marital duty to his wife, and likewise the wife to her husband. . . . I wish that all men were as I am. But each man has his own gift from God; one has this gift, another has that" (I Cor. 7:2-7).

The person with the gift of celibacy has the ability to enjoy singleness without suffering undue sexual temptations. Celibacy is another spiritual gift that clearly illustrates the difference between a role and a gift. All of us must exercise the role of celibacy at various times. Those who are not married and widows and widowers all must exercise the role of celibacy. Those who are married must exercise the role of celibacy when they are separated from their spouse.

God has promised, "No test or temptation that comes our way is beyond the course of what others have had to face. All you need to remember is that God will never let you down; he'll never let you be pushed past your limit; he'll always be there to help you come through it" (I Cor. 10:13 Msg.). Again he says: "My grace is sufficient for you, for my power is made perfect in weakness" (II Cor. 12:9).

One of the main purposes of celibacy is that you have more time to serve the Lord. "I would like you to be free from concern. An unmarried man is concerned about the Lord's affairs—how he can please the Lord. But a married man is concerned about the affairs of this world—how he can please his wife—and his interests are divided. An unmarried woman or virgin is concerned about the Lord's affairs: Her aim is to be devoted to the Lord in both body and spirit. But a married woman is concerned about the affairs of this world—how she can please her husband" (I Cor. 7:32-34).

There are many examples of single persons who have made a great impact on God's Kingdom. Singles are not second-class citizens.

Lord, help me, whether single or married, to always love you and serve you with all my heart. Amen.

The Gift of Craftsmanship

Exodus 31:1-11

"The Lord said to Moses, 'I have chosen Bezalel . . . and I have filled him with the Spirit of God, with skill, ability and knowledge in all kinds of crafts—to make artistic designs for work in gold, silver and bronze, to cut and set stones, to work in wood, and to engage in all kinds of craftsmanship . . . and also the woven garments . . .'" (Exodus 31:1-11).

God gave Oholiah the ability to teach others these skills of designers, embroiderers in blue, purple and scarlet yarn and fine linen and weavers. (Exodus 35:30-35). Dorcas used her sewing skills to spread God's love. (Acts 9:36).

These scriptures help us see that God's spirit is equipping people for all crafts and trades. The person with the gift of craftsmanship has the ability to use their skills to advance God's Kingdom. God gifts people with skills in technology to operate our audio and visual aids department. Others blog or use facebook and media of all kinds to advance the Good News of Jesus. People check out church websites before they come to visit a church. A friend makes hundreds of toy cars, trucks, etc. and gives them to the church to distribute at Christmastime.

"Whatever you do, whether in word or deed, do it all in the name of the Lord Jesus, giving thanks to God the Father through him" (Col. 3:17). Jesus was a carpenter until he launched his public ministry at age thirty. (Mark 6:3 and Luke 3:23).

If you have the gift of craftsmanship, don't ever walk around with inferior feelings and think: "I'm just a carpenter; I'm just a factory worker." Use your gifts to develop relationships between yourself and your peers. You don't need the gift of evangelism to witness for Jesus Christ—you can open doors and build close friendships with the gift of craftsmanship. Every congregation needs men and women with this gift!

Father, thank you that Jesus graced the wood shop with his presence and skills. Thank you for gifting people in all kinds of craftsmanship today. Help me to develop my gifts in these areas and to use them for your glory in advancing your Kingdom. Amen.

The Gifts of Music and Writing

I Kings 4:32

The Hebrews concentrated on music and writing since painting was basically prohibited with the second commandment. (Exodus 20:4). "Solomon spoke three thousand proverbs and his songs numbered a thousand and five" (I Kings 4:32). We can't imagine how difficult it would be to read our bibles apart from the gift of writing. It's hard to imagine a worship service without music. Many believe more people come to salvation through music than through the spoken word.

These persons have a special ability God gives to sing, compose, write, or play music well. The Old Testament records several expressions of these gifts: (1) There were the instrumentalists—"skilled in playing musical instruments" (II Chron. 34:12). (2) The singers, Heman, Asaph and Ethan. (I Chron.15:19). (3) David and Asaph are listed as lyricists or composers of music. (II Chron. 29:30). (4) Choir directors or conductors. (Nehemiah 12:46). (5) Instructors. (I Chron. 15:22) and (6) those who made instruments. (II Chron. 7:6; and 29:26-27).

Paul admonishes us to speak to one another in psalms, hymns and spiritual songs. (Eph. 5:19, Col. 3:16). Those who came to worship came having composed a hymn or received a word, revelation, or an instruction from the Lord. (I Cor. 14:26).

The person with the gift of music or writing is in touch with his/her emotions. This is one reason the book of Psalms is one of the most appreciated books of the Bible. David expresses a wide range of feelings in Psalm 119: e.g. "My soul is consumed with longing for your laws" (v. 20); "See how hungry I am for your counsel" (v. 40 Msg.); "My soul faints with longing for your salvation" (v. 81); The person with these gifts is one who's endowed with great imagination and emotion as e.g. weeping day and night (Psalm 42:3), as well as extolling the Lord continuously (34:1).

Do words flow from your pen? Are you a creative person often dressing in bright colors? Do you usually appreciate the new rather than the traditional? Form letters, assembly lines, or stereotypes are not your forté?

Lord, enable me to develop the gifts of writing and music. Amen.

273

The Gifts of Music (Part II)

Philippians 2:3

"In humility consider others better than yourself" (Phil. 2:3).

Since there are more "wars" fought over music styles and since some believe music is more influential in reaching unbelievers than sermons, I am allotting a second reading to the subject of music.

Music speaks to our heart more easily than the spoken word. In *Breaking the Missional Code*, Ed Stetzer and David Putman write: "Scripture teaches that we are to 'consider others better than yourselves' (Phil. 2:3). This includes the truth that our preferences should never become more important than what our church needs to be and do missionally. For that matter, the church's focus should not be the preferences of other church members either. A truly biblical church will ask, 'What will it take to transform this community by the power of the Gospel' not how many hymns do we have to sing to make everybody happy."

If our focus is on transforming the community by the power of the Gospel, we will have solved the music issue and many others as well. God loves all kinds of music when sung from a pure heart. Does our music connect people with God's presence?

We can broaden our appreciation for various styles of music, but it isn't easy. Here are four options: (1) Maintain the status quo if you are reaching the unchurched and lives are being transformed for Christ. (2) Offer two services: one with contemporary music and one with traditional music. (3) A transitional model: No one wants to be told they have to adjust to another style of music. (4) A blended model: Many congregations are using this approach of traditional hymns accompanied with a worship band and contemporary praise music. The blended model may be the best solution for most traditional churches. Whatever approaches that appeal to the unchurched is the one the church needs to seriously consider since the purpose of the church is to fulfill the great commission of our Lord.

Lord, help me to remember it is not my preferences that are important but to accept and appreciate the model that brings people to new life in Christ. Amen.

The Gifts of Healing

I Corinthians 12:9, 28, 30

"To each one the manifestation of the Spirit is given for the common good . . . to another gifts of healings by that one Spirit . . . (I Cor. 12:7-9, also 28 and 30).

Persons with the gifts of healing have the ability by God's Holy Spirit to cause another person to be healed apart from natural means. In the Greek New Testament we have the plural term, "gifts of healing." (I Cor. 12:9, 28 and 30). This may indicate that a separate enabling of the Holy Spirit is given for each individual affliction. Another possible explanation is that the Spirit uses different approaches for different situations: Sometimes Jesus laid hands on the sick, sometimes he spoke, sometimes he spat and made clay; and sometimes he sent them to wash. (Mark 6:5; John 4:50; Mark 7:33; John 9:7).

During Jesus' passion it is clear he was in charge even though they beat, scourged, jeered, tortured and crucified him. God's grace was sufficient for Jesus. His grace will be sufficient for us in our pain and suffering if we, like him, submit to the Father's will. Both Paul and Peter instruct us to have this same attitude that Jesus had during his trial. (Phil. 2:5-8 and I Peter 2:21-3:1). Peter and Paul had special gifts of healing (Acts 5:15 and 19:11) but were at other times not given this gift. (II Tim. 4:20; 5:23; Gal. 4:13-16; Phil. 2:26-27). Why did Jesus tell the Christians to visit the sick in Matt. 25:36 and at other times to heal the sick as in Luke 10:9? In James 5:13-20 we are instructed to have elders anoint the sick with oil in the name of the Lord and we will be healed. If there is sin involved it needs to be confessed and forgiven for healing to take place. (I Cor. 11:30).

Visit the sick, anoint them with oil and pray for their healing. The prayers of a righteous person are powerful and effective. (James 5:16).

Father, I thank you for healing me many times, and for answering my prayers for healing others whether physical or emotional healing. Pour out your grace on those who are ill and suffering. We praise you for our new body at your return. Amen.

The Gift of Miracles

John 14:12

The gift of miracles is the special ability God gives to certain members of the Body of Christ to perform works that alter the course of natural law. "I tell you the truth, anyone who has faith in me will do what I have been doing. He will do even greater things than these, because I am going to the Father" (John 14:12).

Some teach that the day of miracles is past. Jeremiah writes 32:20, "You performed miracles, signs and wonders in Egypt and have continued them to this day, both in Israel and among all mankind, and have gained the renown that is still yours." The time from deliverance in Egypt to Jeremiah's time was 850 years.

Many times God has spared my life. I am a walking miracle. A fire was sweeping across the land in Illinois getting closer to a church. Two young men on their knees cried out to God and the winds changed immediately.

My father-in-law, in Honduras, was flying in a small plane. When they took off it was clear, but the clouds soon engulfed them. The gas tank was almost empty and the runway located in the mountain village was nowhere to be seen. There were no electronic instruments. He prayed, "God open the clouds just like you parted the Red Sea." A small opening appeared and they saw a small patch of earth—the runway. No one was around the small airport. They knew a plane could not land because of the heavy cloud cover.

Watchman Nee in his book, *Sit, Walk, Stand* preached for days in China with little effect. A new Christian who was with Nee's group asked the people why they didn't respond. They informed him that their god was adequate because he kept the rain away on their holy day for 286 years. The young Christian said to the crowd, "It will rain on that day." It flooded! The Chinese set another date. The Christians said it will rain on that day. It poured! The God of Elijah was again manifesting his mighty power and many turned to Christ. When we walk with Jesus the supernatural becomes natural!

Lord, thank you for the abundance of miracles we experienced today. Amen.

The Gifts of Tongues and Interpretation of Tongues

I Corinthians 14

The gift of tongues and interpretation of tongues is the special ability that God gives to members of the body of Christ to speak in a language that they have never learned or to interpret the utterances of unknown languages.

"I am grateful to God for the gift of praying in tongues that he gives us for praising him, which leads to wonderful intimacies we enjoy with him. I enter into this as much or more than any of you" (I Cor. 14:18 Msg.).

"If messages or prayers are offered in tongues, two or three's the limit, and then only if someone is present who can interpret what you're saying. Otherwise, keep it between God and yourself. And no more than two or three speakers at a meeting ... Take your turn ... so each speaker gets a chance to say something special from God, and you all learn from each other. If you choose to speak, you're also responsible for how and when you speak" (I Cor. 14:27-32 Msg.).

The speaking in tongues is in operation today in millions of Christians worldwide. This gift was operative: (1) The Day of Pentecost. "All 120 disciples were filled with the Holy Spirit and began to speak in other tongues as the Spirit enabled them" (Acts 2:4). (2) When Peter and John placed their hands on the Samaritans they received the Holy Spirit. Simon wanted to buy the ability to impart the gift. (Acts 8:4-18). (3) At Paul's Conversion. (Acts 9:1-19). Ananias baptized Saul and scales fell from his eyes. (v. 18). Either at this time or later Paul received the gift of tongues. "I thank God I speak in tongues more than you all" (I Cor. 14:18). (4) The House of Cornelius. (Acts 10:1-46) and (5) The Ephesian Pentecost. (Acts 19:1-6).

Paul orders that speaking with tongues should not be forbidden. (I Cor. 14:39). It is a means of building up the believer. (I Cor. 14:4 and I Cor. 12:10).

Lord, I thank you for the gift of tongues that enables people to speak a language they have never learned and for the ability to praise you using this gift of your Holy Spirit. Amen.

October 4

Faithful Minority

Deuteronomy 1:22

"You all came to me (Moses) and said, 'First, let's send out scouts to explore the land for us. They will advise us on the best route to take and which towns we should enter'" (Deut. 1:22 NLT).

The scouts were not sent to determine whether they should enter the land. They were to decide the best strategy to enter the land. God made it clear they were to enter and that he would give their enemies into their hands. But only two of the twelve, Joshua and Caleb had faith to believe they should enter the land. The others were intimidated by the walled cities and the giants. They were never allowed to enter the good land because of their lack of faith. (1:35).

God called Gideon to deliver his people but he was afraid. God granted him a couple signs until he finally went. (Judges 6 and 7). How many signs does God have to give us before we share the Good News? We hear our friend has terminal cancer, or another friend is depressed even suicidal, another was in a car accident and needs hope and another couple is heading toward divorce. How loud does God have to speak before we say, "Yes?"

God promises he will be with us. The spies regretted their actions. We too pay the price for not being obedient to the Great Commission. The price is stale Christianity, dead churches and many regrets.

The family line dies out when babies are not born into our biological family. That's what is happening to thousands of churches in the U.S. More than half of our churches have not baptized a born again Christian this past year. Young people are leaving the organized churches in droves.

Father give me the passion like you had when you sent Jesus to live and die for us. Jesus give me the passion you demonstrated as you left your Father and worked as a carpenter, despised and rejected by your people and finally crucified. Holy Spirit give me your passion for the lost that you demonstrated as you left heaven and came to dwell in my sinful heart, now being made holy by your transforming grace. Amen.

Renting or Owning the Scriptures

John 14:19

Jesus said, "I will not leave you orphaned. I'm coming back. In just a little while the world will no longer see me, but you're going to see me because I am alive and you're about to come alive" (John 14:19 Msg.).

"You're about to come alive." Do you have days when you don't feel very much alive? The vibrancy and joy of life is nowhere to be found. On those days we are not a good advertisement. We are not contagious. On those days we still believe the Scriptures—at least intellectually but we are not living them or owning them, we are merely renting them. Jesus says, when the Spirit comes you will come alive!

Paul owned God's promises. "If you only look at us, you might well miss the brightness. We carry his precious Message around in the unadorned clay pots of our ordinary lives. That's to prevent anyone from confusing God's incomparable power with us. As it is, there's not much chance of that. You know for yourselves that we're not much to look at. We've been surrounded and battered by troubles, but we're not demoralized, we're not sure what to do, but we know that God knows what to do, we're been spiritually terrorized, but God hasn't left our side, we've been thrown down, but we haven't been broken. What they did to Jesus, they do to us—trial and torture, mockery and murder, what Jesus did among them, he does in us—he lives! . . .while we are going through the worst we're getting in on the best" (II Cor. 4:7-12 Msg.).

Paul was alive even in his worst days. Only as Jesus is in you can you come alive on those days. Claim David's promise: "The Lord delights in a man's way, he makes his steps firm: though he stumbles, he will not fall, for the Lord upholds him with his hand" (Psalm 37:23-24). Remember Jesus' words, "Because I am alive you are about to come alive." He promised to never forsake you or abandon you so let him live his life through you.

Lord Jesus, some days I'm sinking. Help me, especially on those days to own the Scriptures and allow you to live through me. Come alive in me. Amen.

"Be Still and Know That I Am God"

Psalm 46:10

"Step out of the traffic! Take a long, loving look at me, your High God, above politics, above everything" (Psalm 46:10 Msg.). This is a difficult admonition for me and for many in our time-conscious, action packed U.S. culture. I am an activist. I come to God with my agenda and my schedule. His agenda may not be what I think is important. I am learning to be still. Saint Francis of Assisi prayed so appropriately:

> Lord, make me an instrument of your peace.
> Where there is hatred, let me sow love;
> where there is injury, pardon;
> where there is doubt, faith;
> where there is despair, hope;
> where there is darkness, light;
> and where there is sadness, joy.
>
> O Divine Master, grant that I may not so much seek
> to be consoled as to console;
> to be understood as to understand;
> to be loved as to love.
> For it is in giving that we receive;
> it is in pardoning that we are pardoned;
> and it is in dying that we are born to eternal life. Amen.

In learning to communicate with God we need to understand that God chooses the time and the topic! His desires must trump ours. He is God, not me! Let him set the agenda. God may not always want to discuss the same topic as I do. I may want to talk about my occupation. He may want to check my attitude about my occupation. I may want to discuss my future. He may want to strengthen my faith and talk future later. I may want a WHY and he may just want me to TRUST! I may want OUT of what he wants me IN!

There are times when you want to talk, while he just wants you to be quiet. God always reserves the right to remain silent. He may just want you to sit and wait in quietness. He may just want you to BE!—To love him and worship and adore him. Let him "rejoice over you with singing" (Zephaniah 3:17).

Lord, help me to "Be still and know that you are God." Amen.

Header navigation

Night and Day Difference

I Peter 2:9

You are chosen by God "to do his work and speak out for him to tell others of the night and day difference he made for you" (I Peter 2:9 Msg.). Witnessing is all about sharing the night and day difference Jesus makes in your life. You are not to argue your case or try to prove you are right. You're not an attorney. You're a witness. You report what happens in your life and how things are changing.

Share your story. Stories attract attention. Your story is unique. You have no exact duplicate. Only you can share it. If you don't, it will be lost forever. Your story is exactly that—your story. People have to accept it or they have to write you off. If your character is consistent they cannot write you off easily. We remember people's stories longer than our doctrines. There will be times the Spirit brings your story to their remembrance. The Holy Spirit will take your testimony and use it to convict people of their need for Jesus.

Your story is more authorative than a sermon. Many unchurched see pastors as professional salespersons, but the unchurched see you as one who has voluntarily chosen to follow Jesus. This gives you credibility. Share what life was like before you met Jesus, how you met him, and what happened when you met him. Share what difference he is making in your life today. "Make the most of every opportunity because the days are evil" (Col. 5:16).

Many people today don't accept the authority of the Bible but they will listen to your God moments. Paul told his experiences. (Acts 22-26). The believers went everywhere sharing Jesus. I'm sure they shared how Jesus changed their life.

If you have not experienced a night and day difference, cry out to God. He will meet you and give you a fresh victory and joy so that like Peter and John you can't help but share your story with others.

Lord, give me a boldness to share the night and day difference you make in my life. Amen.

See Others as God Sees Them

Matthew 9:36

"When Jesus looked over the crowds, his heart broke. So confused and aimless they were, like sheep with no Shepherd" (Matthew 9:36 Msg.). Jesus saw people, looked into their souls, and grieved over their condition. He saw them through the eyes of eternity. He saw them as his brothers and sisters created in his own image. He longed to relate to them. Seeing people as God's creation will help you love them.

We need eyes to see as Jesus sees. We see our work peers, classmates, neighbors, the bank teller, the checkout woman, the barber, the postman, and others—without ever considering their spiritual condition. Why don't we have compassion for them as Jesus does?

Time is a factor but learn to relate to those you meet in the flow of life. It's amazing how God opens the door if we are tuned into his Spirit. Could you clear your calendar one night a week to intentionally relate to your unchurched peers.

Over my nearly fifty years of pastoral ministry I usually reserved Saturday afternoon for visiting non-members. After visiting three or four families I could often tell that I would have one new family present. That had an impact on the morning worship service. The people were encouraged and the message and music became more vibrant.

Be a model to your congregation. When they see the joy in persons who find new life in Jesus they will want to invite others to Jesus too. The people you associate with in church are going to heaven—at least I hope so! When will you leave the 99 and help the lost one.?Find the evangelists in your church and elicit their help to relate to the unchurched. Jesus said: "I will make, (i.e. mold, shape, form), you to be fishers of men" (Matt. 4:19).

Lord, help me to see the people I meet each day as you see them—sheep without a shepherd. Enable me to love them enough to take the time and effort to build a relationship and share the Good News. Amen.

Today—Better Than Yesterday— Tomorrow Better Than Today

II Cor. 3:18 & 4:16-18

"The Lord is the Spirit, and where the Spirit of the Lord is, there is freedom. We, who with unveiled faces all reflect the Lord's glory, are being transformed into his likeness with ever-increasing glory, which comes from the Lord, who is the Spirit" (II Cor. 3:18).

"The path of the righteous is like the first gleam of dawn, shinning ever brighter till the full light of day" (Prov. 4:18).

"For our light, momentary affliction (this slight distress of the passing hour) is ever more and more abundantly preparing and producing and achieving for us an everlasting weight of glory—beyond all measure excessively surpassing all comparisons and all calculations, a vast and transcendant glory and blessedness never to cease! Since we consider and look not to the things that are seen but to the things that are unseen; for the things that are visible are temporal (brief and fleeting), but the things that are invisible are deathless and everlasting" (II Cor. 4:17-18 AMP).

We are to be renewed day by day. (II Cor. 4:16). Some days I am like David who often shouts expressing his joy to the Lord. One pastor said, "I would be delighted if some of my people would be renewed year by year." We are to reflect the Lord's glory—shining brighter and brighter until we are called home.

Beware of anything that distorts Jesus' reflection in your life. Good things are often the enemy of the best. Don't let your goals, your desires, your work, your hobbies, your friends, even your family crowd out your relationship with God. Keep short accounts. If you are doing something that you are not sure God is pleased with, confess it and move on in the power of the Holy Spirit. "He who conceals his sins does not prosper, but whoever confesses and renounces them finds mercy" (Prov. 28:13).

Guard against a hurried lifestyle so you do not crowd out the voice of the Lord and friendship of others. God is more concerned about your "being" than your "doing."

Lord Jesus, I love you. Enable me to give you first place. Amen.

October 10
Don't Buy the Lies
John 8:44

"When he lies, he (Satan) speaks his native language, for he is a liar and the father of lies" (John 8:44). Satan will whisper lies to keep you from sharing the Good News: "You really don't know those people well enough." "They are too busy." "Now is not the time." "Just build relationships a little longer." "They need to see Jesus in you before you can talk to them." "If you share the Gospel they will reject you and Jesus." "Your life is not consistent with your message anyway." "They won't believe you."

Paul says, "We work urgently with everyone we meet to get them ready to face God. God alone knows how well we do this but I hope you realize how much and deeply we care. (Why does Paul work urgently?) Sooner or later we'll all have to face God, regardless of our conditions. We will appear before Christ and take what's coming to us as a result of our actions, either good or bad. That keeps us vigilant, you can be sure. It's no light thing to know that we'll all one day stand in the place of judgment" (II Cor. 5:10-11 Msg.).

A vivacious second grade teacher was gloriously saved. She came into my study and said, "I don't understand what is wrong with me. In the teachers' lounge I can talk about anything but when it comes to sharing Jesus I clam up." The devil would tell you they don't want your witness. Don't buy his lies!

Jesus' brother Jude didn't buy Satan's lies. He writes that we must snatch our friends from the fire and save them. (v. 23). We take witnessing seriously because it is a matter of life and death. Our unsaved friends, no matter how good, need Jesus. We must snatch them from the fire.

Jesus said, "All men will hate you because of me" (Matt. 10:22). Remember, "Greater is he who is in you than he who is in the world" (I John 4:4).

Lord Jesus, give me the courage I need to follow your Spirit in boldly sharing Jesus. Amen.

Remember Those in Prison and Those Mistreated

Hebrews 13:3

"Remember those in prison as if you were their fellow prisoners, and those who are mistreated as if you yourselves were suffering" (Hebrews 13:3). Jesus says: "I was sick and you stopped to visit, I was in prison and you came to me" (Matt. 25:36 Msg.).

It's estimated that 100,000 persons have been martyred for Christ each of the past ten years. Voice of the Martyrs with its fifty years of history is ministering to these prisoners and their families in sixty-eight countries. We who live in "Christian freedom" have a responsibility to pray for and support those who are persecuted. Many have said, "Don't pray for our deliverance, pray that we be faithful."

In the U.S. we have two million prisoners plus another million in our parole system. Crime escalates. Many are enslaved to drugs and substance abuse. Their families are suffering. Do you or your church visit and minister to those in prison? Be diligent to work through "red tape" to minister behind those prison doors. Many will be receptive to the love of Jesus. In visiting them we are visiting Jesus! (Matt. 25:44-45).

The church has been negligent in assisting those who are in prison or have served their time. Some feel their efforts are useless since the majority return back to their destructive lifestyle and are soon back in prison. This doesn't negate God's command to visit those in prison. What an opportunity for churches to provided counseling and rehab programs so this cycle can be stopped.

For some the recovery will be short but for most it will take months or even years. Your efforts will be greatly rewarded as they become fully devoted followers of Jesus. They in turn will be effective in assisting others who are caught in this deadly web. A friend of mine drives 100 miles each month to encourage and disciple a prisoner he led to the Lord.

Father, raise up workers to minister to those in prison and for those who are persecuted for your name sake. Amen.

October 12

Remember

Deuteronomy 5:15

"Remember that you were slaves in Egypt and that the Lord your God brought you out of there with a mighty hand and an outstretched arm" (Deut. 5:15). "Remember" or one of its forms appears nearly 300 times in the Bible. In Moses' final sermon recorded in Deuteronomy, 16 times he tells the people to remember. The New Testament tells us to remember at least 55 times. I try to be future focused. (Phil. 3:13). But I need roots. I would not be here without parents or have a future without my past. I would have no hope except faithful witnesses passed the message to me.

Jesus in the upper room with his disciples, "took bread, gave thanks and broke it, and gave it to them, saying, 'This is my body given for you; do this in remembrance of me'" (Luke 22:19).

Our faith is rooted in events recorded in Scriptures as well as in our history. God revealed himself in many ways (Heb. 1:1) but supremely in his Son, the Lord Jesus. We must go back to those facts for the foundation of our faith.

When I left home my parents said, "Remember who you are" i.e. remember what you have been taught and act appropriately. God is saying the same thing over and over in the Scriptures. Paul writes, "There's nothing like the written Word of God for showing you the way to salvation through faith in Christ Jesus. Every part of Scripture is God-breathed and useful one way or another—showing us truth, exposing our rebellion, correcting our mistakes, training us to live God's way. Through the Word we are put together and shaped up for the tasks God has for us" (II Tim. 3:15-17 Msg.).

Paul reminds us to remember we too were separated from Christ, without hope and without God. (Eph. 2:12-13). Remembering our past without Jesus will help us appreciate the new life we have in Christ.

Lord Jesus, thank you for parents and others who passed on the way of salvation through faith in Jesus. Help me to pass on this faith to others. Amen.

Who Is Jesus?

John 6:24-38

Who does Jesus say he is? Jesus identified himself in John's Gospel.

First, Jesus is the bread of life. "Don't be so concerned about perishable things like food. Spend your energy seeking eternal life that the Son of Man can give you . . . I am the bread of life whoever comes to me will never be hungry again. Whoever believes in me will never be thirsty" (John 6:24-38 NLT).

Second, Jesus is the light of the world. "I am the light of the world. If you follow me, you won't have to walk in darkness, because you will have the light that leads to life" (John 8:12 NLT).

Third, Jesus is the gate for the sheep. (John 10:7). He is the only way into God's eternal kingdom. Sheep are vulnerable and helpless. We are helpless to save ourselves from eternal death but Jesus opens the gate for us.

Fourth, Jesus is the Good Shepherd. "I am the good shepherd. The good shepherd sacrifices his life for the sheep. A hired hand will run when he sees a wolf coming . . . I am the good shepherd; I know my own sheep, and they know me" (John 10:14 NLT).

Fifth, Jesus is the resurrection and the life. "I am the resurrection and the life. Anyone who believes in me will live, even after dying. Everyone who lives in me and believes in me will never ever die" (John 11:25-26 NLT).

Sixth, Jesus says, "I am the way, and the truth, and the life. No one comes to the Father (God) except through me" (John 14:6).

Seventh, Jesus is the true vine. "Those who remain in me and I in them will produce much fruit. For apart from me you can do nothing" (John 15:1-5 NLT).

Jesus you are more than I could ever want. What an honor it is to serve you. Amen.

October 14

Boldly Face the Future

John 14:27

"Peace I leave with you; my peace I give to you. I do not give to you as the world gives. Do not let your hearts be troubled and do not be afraid" (John 14:27). We do not need to fear the future! Jesus concludes his commission to us: "I am with you all the days, perpetually, uniformly and on every occasion—to the [very] close and consummation of the age" (Matt. 28:20b AMP) "You will keep in perfect peace all who trust in you, whose thoughts are fixed on you! Trust in the Lord always, for the Lord God is the eternal Rock!" (Isaiah 26:3 NLT).

The foundations are shaking. We are not sure what is good or evil, right or wrong or even if there is a right or wrong. Our universities teach that each person is their own god. This is not new. (Isaiah 5:20). The history of our world is one of continual turmoil. Fear robs us of faith. "It's impossible to please God apart from faith. And why? Because anyone who wants to approach God must believe both that he exists and that he cares enough to respond to those who seek him." (Heb. 11:6 Msg.).

John writes: "You are of God—you belong to Him—and have [already] defeated and overcome [the agents of antichrist], because He Who lives in us is greater (mightier) than he who is in the world" (I John 4:4 AMP). "God has said, I will not in any way fail you nor give you up nor leave you without support. I [will] not, [I will] not, [I will] not in any degree leave you helpless, nor forsake nor let [you] down, [relax my hold on you], Assuredly not!" (Heb. 13:5b AMP).

"Do not let your heart be troubled. Trust in God; trust also in me. In my Father's house are many rooms . . . I am going there to prepare a place for you . . . I will come back and take you to be with me that you also may be where I am" (John 14:1-3). We have a future so wonderful we will not remember the trials of this life. Hallelujah!

Lord I will trust you until the day you call me home to be with you. (Is. 12:2). Amen.

Google, Your Best Teacher?

Psalm 106:43

"Over and over God rescued them, but they never learned—until finally their sins destroyed them" (Psalm 106:43 Msg.). "Lord, teach me lessons for living so I can stay the course" (Psalm 119:33 Msg.).

Moses had many years to think as he tended sheep before God called him. (Ex. 3:1). Today "Google" does much of our thinking for us. Do you take time to think and meditate on Scripture? Jesus spent forty days of intense meditation in the wilderness and changed history. Paul after his Damascus Road conversion spent three years in meditation before he began his public ministry. (Gal. 1:17-18).

David was meditating as he watched sheep. Seven times he refers to meditation in Ps. 119. His focus is on God's word and God's works. "Blessed is he whose delight is in the law of the Lord, and who mediates on his law day and night!" (Ps. 1:2). "On my bed I remember you; I think of you during the watches of the night" (Ps. 63:6).

Is experience the best teacher? It is only if we reflect or meditate and learn from our experiences. "Over and over God rescued the Israelites, but they never learned—until finally their sins destroyed them" (Ps. 106:43 Msg.). We can learn from other's experiences if we meditate and apply what we learn. That's why teachers have an important role. "A wise friend's timely reprimand is like a gold ring slipped on your finger" (Prov. 25:12 Msg.).

Jesus is thinking about our thoughts. "I am he who searches hearts and minds and I will repay each of you according to your deeds" (Revelation 2:23). As Christians we have the mind of Christ. (I Cor. 2:16). Focus and meditate on Jesus. "May the words of my mouth and the meditation of my heart be pleasing in your sight, Lord, my Rock and my Redeemer" (Ps. 19:14).

Lord Jesus, forgive me for meditating on worldly pleasures. Enable me to meditate on your word and works so I can be all that you want me to be. Amen.

October 16

Remove Rough Edges

II Corinthians 12:10

Peter's final words: "Grow in the grace and knowledge of our Lord and Savior Jesus Christ. To him be glory both now and forever! Amen" (II Peter 3:18).

How do we grow in grace? Elam Stauffer, missionary to Africa, now with the Lord, said: "No need—no grace, much need—much grace." I need God's grace to make James 1:2 become more alive in my life. James says that we are to "consider it wholly joyful whenever you are enveloped in or encounter trials of any sort, or fall into various temptations" (1:2 AMP).

Paul wrote to the Corinthians who were challenging his apostleship: "Because of the extravagance of those revelations and so I wouldn't get a big head, I was given the gift of a handicap to keep me in constant touch with my limitations. Satan's angel did his best to get me down; what he in fact did was push me to my knees. No danger then of walking around high and mighty! At first I didn't think of it as a gift, and begged God to remove it. Three times I did that, and then he told me: 'My grace is enough; it's all you need. My strength comes into its own in your weakness.' Once I heard that, I was glad to let it happen. I quit focusing on the handicap and began appreciating the gift. It was a case of Christ's strength moving in on my weakness. Now I take limitations in stride, and with good cheer, these limitations that cut me down to size—abuse, accidents, opposition, bad breaks. I just let Christ take over. And so the weaker I get, the stronger I become" (II Cor. 12:7-10 Msg.).

God's grace is all I need. Have you learned that truth? If we can't thank God for the "thorn in the flesh" or the difficulties of life then we need to grow in grace. We grow in grace as we admit to the Lord that we are helpless to help ourselves. We ask for grace to accept our situation knowing he never makes a mistake or causes us a needless tear.

Lord, I am your jewel, keep knocking the rough edges off my life. Help me to see my weaknesses and my needs as opportunities to grow in grace so you can shine brightly through my adversity. Amen.

World-Class Christian or Worldly Christian

Psalm 67:2 & Matthew 24:14

Worldly Christians are self-centered. They see God as primarily there for their personal fulfillment. They go to church if it is convenient. Vacation, school activities, moonlighting are given priority while the church is pushed aside. When they go it's because they want to meet their friends. You will not find them in a small group that demands any accountability and certainly not at mission conferences. They're just not interested. They seek God's blessings, approval and comfort but have no desire to make him Lord. They want a ticket to heaven. As Rick Warren says, "They want to use God for their purposes instead of being used for his purposes."

Laodicea had this situation: "I know your deeds, that you are neither cold nor hot. I wish you were either one or the other! So because you are lukewarm—neither hot or cold—I am about to spit you out of my mouth. You say, 'I am rich; I have acquired wealth and do not need a thing.' But you do not realize that you are wretched, pitiful, poor, blind and naked" (Rev. 3:15-17).

On the other hand, world-class Christians know they are saved to serve. They know they are sent by Jesus to be the salt and light of the world. "Send us around the world with the news of your saving power and your eternal plan for all mankind" (Psalm 67:2 LB). They know they are ambassadors representing Jesus their leader, Lord and King. They are the only fully alive people. They have a confidence, joy and enthusiasm that is contagious. They wake up each morning expecting God to use them to make a difference in the people around them.

God invites you to be a world-class Christian. We can make a difference around the world by praying and using the internet. Hasten the day of Jesus' return by seeing people come to Christ in every nation on earth. "This Gospel of the kingdom will be preached in the whole world as a testimony to all nations, and then the end will come" (Matt. 24:14).

Lord Jesus, make me a world-class Christian. Amen.

Can Belief and Obedience Be Separated?

Hebrews 11:6

The devil believes but is not obedient. Faith and obedience are couplets that we must never separate. (Heb. 11:6). Belief and actions must go together. Jesus said, "Not all people who sound religious are really godly . . . The decisive issue is whether they obey my Father. On judgment day many will tell me, 'Lord, Lord, we prophesied in your name and cast out demons in your name . . .' But I will reply, 'I never knew you. Go away'" (Matt. 7:21-23 NLT).

"The King will . . . say, 'Away with you, you cursed ones, into the eternal fire prepared for the Devil and his demons. For I was hungry . . . I was thirsty, and you didn't feed me or give me anything to drink. I was a stranger, and you didn't invite me into your home. I was naked, and you gave me no clothing. I was sick and in prison and you did not visit me.' They will reply, 'Lord, when did we ever see you . . . and not help you?' And he will answer, 'When you refused to help the least of these my brothers and sisters you were refusing to help me. And they will go away into eternal punishment, but the righteous will go into eternal life'" (Matt. 25:41-45 NLT).

God "will judge all people according to what they have done. He will give eternal life to those who persist in doing what is good . . . But he will pour out his anger and wrath on those who live for themselves, who refuse to obey the truth and practice evil deeds" (Ro. 2:6-8 NLT).

"All the churches will know that I am the one who searches out the thoughts and intentions of every person. And I will give to you whatever you deserve" (Rev. 2:23 NLT). "The dead were judged by what they had done . . ." (Rev. 20:12).

While works are important it's God who gives us the will and the power to do them so we can't take any credit for good deeds. "Be careful to put into action God's saving work, obeying God with deep reverence and fear. For God is working in you giving you the desire to obey and the power to do what pleases him" (Phil. 2:12-13 NLT).

Jesus, enable me to put my faith in action serving you with a pure heart. Amen.

Today—the Best Time to be Alive

Matthew 6:33

Today is the best time to be alive! Christianity is growing faster today than ever before. There are 170,000 baptisms every day: 34,000 in Latin America, 30,000 in China, 25,000 in Africa, and 15,000 in India. Thirty-five hundred churches open every week. Papua New Guinea's government mandates the Bible being taught in every school. The world's religions growth percentiles: Buddhists 1.7%, Nominal Christians 2.2%, Hindus 2.3 %, Muslims 2.7%, Non-religious 2.8% and Bible-believing Christians 6.9%.

After 70 years of oppression in the Soviet Union, Christians number about 100 million – five times the number of the Communist Party at the height of its popularity. More than 15,000 public school teachers are teaching morals from the Bible in their classes. Studies show Biblical orthodoxy is winning converts while churches that have lost their biblical moorings languish. (The above is compiled from "wwwthetravelingteam.org/growth of the church.")

America is on a moral skid? We have 350,000 churches. The "gospel" is preached daily over 100's of Christian radio stations and scores of Christian TV stations. Today much theology is a watered-down version of Biblical Christianity. We live no differently from our unchurched neighbors. Sin is not recognized. Grace is cheap.

Dietrich Bonhoeffer writes: "Cheap grace is the preaching of forgiveness without requiring repentance, baptism without church discipline, communion without confession, absolution without personal confession. Cheap grace is grace without discipleship, grace without the cross, grace without Jesus Christ, living and incarnate... Bonhoeffer calls us to 'costly grace' which "is costly because it cost a man his life, and it is grace because it gives a man the only true life" (Jim Denison's blog January 17, 2017).

What a contrast from Christianity today. We see ourselves as good lawabiding citizens. We go to work, we go to church occasionally, we don't harm anyone, and we help our neighbor when it's convenient. Whenever there is a conflict with church activities, sports, school, etc. too often we teach our children by placing God and his church at the bottom of our priorities. There is little sensing of seeking first the Kingdom of Heaven. (Matt. 6:33). We think because we are "good" we are godly.

Lord, forgive our lethargy. We repent. Empower us through your Holy Spirit. Amen.

October 20

Ezekiel Speaks to America

Ezekiel 33:31

"My people come to you,... then sit before you to listen to your words, but they do not put them into practice. With their mouths they express devotion, but their hearts are greedy for unjust gain." (33:31). God's people rejected God and ignored his decrees. (5:6). The sins of the leaders, elders and prophets were especially evident. God saw their sexual sins and their greed. (22:1-12).

God called Ezekiel to be a "watchman." "Whenever you hear a word from my mouth, you shall give them warning from me" (3:17). We are blind to the coming judgment of God. Where are the Watchmen? Daily we learn of wars, the overuse of drugs, suicides, violence, pornography, and government corruption. Human trafficking is one of the fastest growing criminal enterprises soon to surpass the drug trade. Two and one/half million people around the world are in forced labor at any given time. In a recent survey 70% of people today believe that God accepts the worship of all religions, including those that believe in many gods. Sixty percent agree that everyone will eventually go to heaven.

The good news: God is ready to forgive everyone willing to repent and turn from their sinful ways. "You will know that I am the Lord, O people of Israel, when I have honored my name by treating you mercifully in spite of your wickedness." (20:44).

You are called to be watchmen. Watchmen warn the people of danger – yes even of God's anger and wrath, words that appear fifty-six times in this book. "God has not given us a spirit of timidity, but a spirt of power, of love and of self-discipline" (II Tim. 1:7). We will be held accountable if we fail to warn our family, friends and neighbors. "If the watchman sees the enemy coming and doesn't sound the alarm to warn the people, he is responsible for their captivity. They will die in their sins, but I will hold the watchman responsible for their deaths." (33:6). Will you be a faithful watchman?

Lord, you have not given us a spirit of fear but of power, love and discipline. Enable me to be a faithful watchman. Amen.

Success Without a Successor Is Failure

II Timothy 2:2

Someone has said, "Success without a successor is failure."

"The things you have heard me say in the presence of many witnesses entrust to reliable men who will also be qualified to teach others" (II Tim. 2:2).

Notice the passion of these Biblical writers: Moses writes: "These are all the commands, laws, and regulations that the Lord your God told me to teach you so you may obey them . . . and so you and your children and grandchildren might fear the Lord your God as long as you live. . . . You must love the Lord your God with all your heart, all your soul and all your strength. . . . Repeat them again and again to your children. Talk about them when you are at home and when you are away on a journey, when you are lying down and when you are getting up again. Tie them to your hands as a reminder, and wear them on your forehead. Write them on the doorposts of your house and on your gates" (Deuteronomy 6:1-9 NLT).

The Psalmist Asaph writes: "I will teach . . . stories our ancestors handed down to us. We will not hide these truths from our children but will tell the next generation about the glorious deeds of the Lord. We will tell of his power and the mighty miracles he did . . . He commanded our ancestors to teach them to their children, so the next generation might know them . . . that they in turn might teach their children. So each generation can set its hope anew on God, remembering his glorious miracles and obeying his commands. Then they will not be like their ancestors—stubborn, rebellious, and unfaithful, refusing to give their hearts to God" (Ps. 78:2-8 NLT).

"O God, you have taught me from my earliest childhood, and I have constantly told others about the wonderful things you do. . . . Let me proclaim your power to this new generation, your mighty miracles to all who come after me" (Ps. 71:17-18 NLT).

Lord, my faith is precious to me. Enable me to pass it on to the next generation. Amen.

Declaring God's Glory All Day Long

Psalm 71

"O Lord, you alone are my hope. I've trusted you . . . from childhood. Yes, you have been with me from birth; from my mother's womb you have cared for me. No wonder I am always praising you! My life is an example to many, because you have been my strength and protection. That is why I can never stop praising you. I declare your glory all day long . . . I will praise you more and more. I will tell everyone about your righteousness. All day long I will proclaim your saving power, for I am overwhelmed by how much you have done for me." David continues . . .

"I will praise your mighty deeds, O Sovereign Lord. I will tell everyone that you alone are just and good. O God, you have taught me from my earliest childhood, and I have constantly told others about the wonderful things you do. Now that I am old and gray, do not abandon me, O God. Let me proclaim your power to this new generation, your mighty miracles to all who come after me. Your righteousness, O God, reaches to the highest heavens. You have done such wonderful things. Who can compare with you, O God? You have allowed me to suffer much hardship, but you will restore me to life again and lift me up from the depths of the earth. You will restore me to even greater honor and comfort me once again . . .

"Then I will praise you with music on the harp, because you are faithful to your promises . . . I will sing for you with a lyre . . . I will shout for joy and sing your praises, for you have redeemed me. I will tell about your righteous deeds all day long . . ." (Psalm 71:5-24 NLT).

David's life was focused on praising God continually (71:6, 8, 24) to everyone (vv. 15, 16). Even in his old age he asks God to help him proclaim his power to the new generation. (v. 18). His life is an example to many. (v. 7). He is a witness to everyone using musical instruments and his voice as he sings and shouts praises to the Lord who redeemed him. (vv. 22-24).

Lord, I want to be like David, praising you continually. Amen.

Eliminating Walls

John 4:3-7

"Jesus left Judea to return to Galilee. He had to go through Samaria on the way. He came to the Samaritan village of Sychar . . . Jesus, sat wearily beside the well about noontime. Soon a Samaritan woman came to draw water and Jesus said to her, 'Please give me a drink'" (John 4:3-7 NLT). Jesus chose to go through Samaria to break down walls.

Jesus was not provincial. He came to remove walls. "He has broken down the wall of hostility that used to separate us. By his death he ended the whole system of Jewish law that excluded the Gentiles. His purpose was to make peace between Jews and Gentiles by creating in himself one new person . . ." (Eph. 2:14-16 NLT).

"God so loved the world that he gave his only Son, so that everyone who believes in him will not perish but have eternal life . . ." (John 3:16 NLT). David writes, "May your ways be known throughout the earth, your saving power among people everywhere. May the nations praise you, O God. Yes, may all the nations praise you . . . You direct the actions of the whole world" (Excerpts from Psalm 67 NLT).

We tend to build walls—walls between husband and wife, parents and children, extended family walls, walls with our neighbors, walls with Christians in other congregations, walls with people of other cultures. Jesus came to do away with walls.

He touched the lepers. He spoke with women and treated prostitutes with respect. He ate with the tax collectors who were looked upon as traitors. He healed Roman citizens. He associated with the poor and the rich, the religious and those who claimed no religion or a different religion. There were no walls with Jesus.

He chose Simon the Zealot whose passion was to eliminate the Romans. Jesus chose Levi the tax collector who cooperated with the Romans. With his great love and wisdom he was able to help them to forget their differences so they could work together. What wall do you need to remove today?

Lord, enable me to remove the walls I have allowed to be in my life. Amen.

October 24

You Have to Have It to Share It

Acts 4:20

"Why don't we share our faith?" Less than fifteen percent of the population goes to church each week in any given community. Maybe we don't know the unchurched or feel we need more training. Training is helpful but that is not the most critical reason. Are we afraid people may reject us? Maybe we don't share our faith because we don't have it to share. You have to have it to share it! Apostles Peter and John had it and they couldn't help but share it. "There's no question—we can't keep quiet about what we've seen and heard" (Acts 4:20 Msg.).

Many Muslims are anxious to share their faith. Why, because they believe their way is the only way to heaven. They say, "We accept your Jesus, why can't you accept our Mohammad. He is more recent than Jesus."

Have you lost your zeal to share your faith because you are not sure that Acts 4:12 is true: "Salvation is found in no other name under heaven given to men by which we must be saved." If we truly believe Acts 4:12 we will find that we can't keep quiet about our faith. (Acts 4:20). Jesus said, "I am the way, the truth and the life. No one comes to the Father except through me" (John 14:6). "There is one God and one mediator between God and men, the man Christ Jesus" (I Timothy 2:5). "I am the Lord and there is no other; apart from me there is no God" (Isaiah 45:5).

As a young man, Billy Graham, like all of us, had doubts about the authority of Scripture. He told the Lord that he accepts the Scripture by faith as His divine Word. From that moment forward he had a new confidence and power.

If all that you gained from salvation is something you can keep to yourself then it is not Good News. Because of God's Good News you will want to share it with others.

Lord Jesus, I accept the authority of your Word. Restore to me the excitement of a renewed faith in you so I am compelled to share it. Amen.

Jesus—Yes; Church—No!

Hebrews 10:25

The belief in "solo" Christianity or "lone ranger" Christianity is every-where: "Anyone knows you can be a Christian and not go to church." That's the same as saying, "I want to be a football player but I'm not interested in joining the team." There is no such thing as being an effective Christian in isolation. We hear: My faith is personal; it's none of your business what I believe; I have my own personal walk with God.

The church needs to be a hospital for sinners not a rest home for saints. Churches need to be a place of acceptance, love and healing. People go to the bar to find acceptance and understanding. Accepting people does not mean you take sin lightly. You don't see a beer commercial with one person drinking alone.

Many surveys state clearly that going to church is healthy and results in longevity and quality of life. The more we isolate ourselves the more we fight discouragement and depression. God designed us to be social.

Stress is linked to most every major disease we encounter. Surveys show women who attend religious services more than once a week have a 33 percent lower risk of death than women who never attend worship. Those who did not attend church at all were twice as likely to die pre-maturely as those who attend.

Church gives us a sense of purpose, a positive outlook and compassion for others. The remedy for stress is not found in our fallen culture but in our risen Lord. The early church turned the world upside down. We are called to do the same. (Acts 17:6).

"Let's see how inventive we can be in encouraging love and helping out, not avoiding worshiping together as some do but spurring each other on, especially as we see the big Day approaching" (Hebrews 10:23-25 Msg.).

Lord, enable my church to become a community loving and serving people. Amen.

Who Has Your Heart?

Matthew 22:37-39

"Jesus replied, 'You must love the Lord your God with all your heart, all your soul, and all your mind.' This is the first and greatest commandment. A second is equally important; 'Love your neighbor as yourself.' All the other commandments and all the demands of the prophets are based on these two commandments" (Matt. 22:37-40 NLT).

In our culture production is everything. The bottom line is what counts. We tend to prove our love for God and for people by our works and by serving them. If a husband wants to prove his love for his wife, what does he do? He often tries to prove his love by serving and working for her. He can give her money, things, and even his time. While this is good she wants more. She wants a relationship. She wants his heart. Jesus said we must give him all our heart, soul, mind and strength. The key is the little word: "All." We seek his Kingdom first not second. (Matt. 6:33).

We all have observed a marriage breakup that caught us unaware. We thought things were great. He provided for her, what more could she want? She fell in love with another man who showed her affection by listening to her heart and spending time with her. He won her heart. She was drawn to his ability to understand and accept her. Relationship takes precedence over service. Pray for God's Holy Spirit to give you a heart of passion for him which naturally overflows in a life of self-less love and service to others.

When Jesus summarized the law and the prophets he said that love from your heart is a must. We find it much easier to serve or work for Jesus than to develop an intimate relationship with him. Mary chose to sit at Jesus' feet while Martha was focused more on service. (Luke 10:38-42). We cannot truly serve Jesus until we know him and love him. Paul's deepest desire was to know Christ. (Phil. 3:10).

Lord, enable me to love spending time with you, learning to know you, listening to your voice and walking in obedience in your will for me. Amen.

Ordinary Days

Isaiah 40:31

Jesus promised, "He will never leave us nor forsake us" (Heb. 13:5-6). "Even though I walk through the valley of the shadow of death I will fear no evil, for you are with me" (Psalm 23:4). "The Lord waits for you to come to him so he can show you his love and compassion. For the Lord is a faithful God. Blessed are those who wait for him to help them" (Isaiah 30:18 NLT).

"They that wait on the Lord (or hope in the Lord) will find new strength. They will fly high on wings like eagles. They will run and not grow weary. They will walk and not faint" (Isaiah 40:31 NLT). How do we fly high or soar on eagle's wings? Habakkuk says, "Even though the fig trees have no blossoms, and there are no grapes on the vine, even though the olive crop fails, and the fields lie empty; even though the flocks die in the fields . . . yet I will rejoice in the Lord. I will be joyful in the God of my salvation. The Sovereign Lord is my strength! He will make me as surefooted as a deer, and bring me safely over the mountains" (Habakkuk 3:17-19 NLT).

Can you soar like an eagle over the mountaintops when there are ordinary days of endless routine and daily grind? We all have wills that the Holy Spirit will empower if we ask. We must will to do what we know God wants us to do, not what we feel like doing. Habakkuk says, "I will rejoice . . . the Sovereign Lord is my strength . . . He will bring me safely over the mountains." We must fight the good fight of faith by putting on the armor of God. (Eph. 6:10-18).

Paul admonishes Timothy to discipline himself to be godly. (I Tim. 4:7). "Everyone who competes in the games goes into strict training . . . I beat my body and make it my slave so that after I have preached to others, I myself will not be disqualified for the prize" (I Cor. 9:25-27).

Lord, enable me to soar like an eagle and rejoice in you amidst the ordinary routine of life. Amen.

Repentance—the Foundation of the Christian Life

II Corinthians 7:10

Repentance is being remorseful; changing both your mind and your actions. "Godly sorrow brings repentance that leads to salvation and leaves no regret, but worldly sorrow brings death" (II Cor. 7:10). Judas was remorseful when he betrayed Jesus but not repentant. Repentance means to make a 180 degree turn.

Jesus said, unless you repent you will perish. (Luke 13:3-4). "If we claim to be without sin, we deceive ourselves . . ." (I John 1:8). There is no forgiveness without repentance since anything short of repentance is claiming we are innocent before God. We avoid repentance because it is death to our ego.

John the Baptist burst on the scene shouting, "Repent, for the kingdom of heaven is near . . . Produce fruit in keeping with repentance . . . I baptize you with water for repentance" (Matt. 3:2, 8 and 11).

Jesus began his public ministry, "Repent, for the kingdom of heaven is near" (Matt. 4:17). "I have not come to call the righteous, but sinners to repentance" (Luke 5:32). Jesus sent his disciples and "they went out preaching that people should repent" (Mark 6:12). Jesus says, "I tell you . . . there will be more rejoicing in heaven over one sinner who repents than over the ninety-nine who need no repentance" (Luke 15:7).

Before Jesus ascended to heaven he said to his disciples, "This is what is written: 'The Christ will suffer and rise from the dead on the third day, and repentance and forgiveness of sins will be preached in his name to all nations'" (Luke 24:46-47).

At Pentecost Peter stood up and declared, "God has made this Jesus, whom you crucified, both Lord and Christ. When the people heard this, they were cut to the heart and said . . . 'Brothers, what shall we do?' Peter replied, 'Repent and be baptized, every one of you, in the name of Jesus Christ for the forgiveness of your sins. And you will receive the gift of the Holy Spirit'" (Acts 2:36-38). "Repent and turn to God so that your sins may be wiped out" (Acts 3:19).

Father, I repent of all my sins. Amen.

Praise

Psalm 34:1

"I will praise the Lord at all times. I will constantly speak his praises" (Ps. 34:1 NLT). "My tongue will speak of your righteousness and of your praises all day long" (Ps. 35:18). David was continually praising the Lord.

Praise is sometimes translated "Hallelujah." George Frederick Handel in composing "The Messiah" repeats the word "Hallelujah" approximately 150 times. When he finished composing he wept because he'd seen the face of God. Praise puts us into the presence of God. The Lord inhabits the praises of his people. (Ps. 22:3 KJV).

David's final Psalm (150) includes eleven commands to praise the Lord. He says we are to praise him for his acts of power, and his surpassing greatness. We praise him with the trumpet, harp, lyre, tambourine, strings, and symbols. We praise him with the dance. Everything that has breath is instructed to praise the Lord.

When we come to Jesus for salvation we want to praise him for his unspeakable gift. As time passes we tend to lose our first love. We need to discipline ourselves to praise him. To live in his presence we need to praise him. David says, "I will constantly speak his praises." Praise affects our attitude. Attitude affects our relationships and productivity. Let's offer a sacrifice of praise. (Heb. 13:15).

Praise and thanksgiving propels us into God's presence. When you are filled with God's Spirit praise will come naturally. (Eph. 3:18-19; I Thess. 5:16-17). You will wake up in the morning praising God. (Lamentations 3:22; Isaiah 50:4). Learn to praise God in times of adversity. You will discover a new level of joy, your joy will be full. There will be times when you don't feel like praising God. Don't go by feelings. Offer a sacrifice of praise.

Praise invites Jesus' presence—into seemingly impossible situations. He puts your situation in a totally different perspective. Praise gets us ready for heaven!

Lord Jesus, you are worthy to be praised, I choose to praise you continually. Amen.

303

October 30

Weeds

Hebrews 12:1-2

"Let us throw off everything that hinders and the sin that so easily entangles, and let us run with perseverance the race marked out for us. Let us fix our eyes on Jesus, the author and perfecter of our faith, who for the joy set before him endured the cross, scorning its shame, and sat down at the right hand of God" (Hebrews 12:1-2).

When working in the garden or lawn you deal with weeds. You can let them grow and spread, cut them off, spray them to hopefully kill them, or uproot them.

In dealing with sin you have several options as well although only one truly works. You can resist sin by re-doubling your determination to have more willpower to overcome it. You can take the advice of a psychologist who coaches you to relax and let go of your moral scruples that's causing your guilt. After all, you will be told, you are basically a good person, not nearly as bad as many others . . . And the psychologist may ask, "Who can live up to such high expectations?" There's no need to be neurotic. Just do what brings you fulfillment and works . . .

However, only Jesus can truly transform us! He gives us a new birth—a fresh start through his resurrection. (I Peter 1:4). Come to Him in genuine repentance. He'll forgive your sins so you can live in his resurrection power. He replaces hate with love, resentment with forgiveness, worry with peace and death with life. Jesus gets at the root of the problem. (Gal. 2:20).

Although Jesus purifies us from all unrighteousness, temptation is still there. The winds of the world blow weed seeds into our minds. We must decide what we'll do with those weed seeds. Paul asks, "We died to sin; how can we live in it any longer?" (Ro. 6:2). Does this mean we never sin? "If we claim to be without sin, we deceive ourselves and the truth is not in us. If we confess our sins, he is faithful and just and will forgive us our sins and purify us from all unrighteousness" (I John 1:8-9).

Lord, forgive me and enable me to live in your resurrection power today. Amen.

Dynamic Power

Acts 1:8

The word "power" appears 120 times in the New Testament. The Greek word is "dumanis." In some contexts it is translated, miracle or mighty work. Just before Jesus' ascension he said, "You will receive power when the Holy Spirit comes on you; and you will be my witnesses in Jerusalem, and in all Judea and Samaria, and to the ends of the earth" (Acts 1:8). With the power or dynamic of the Holy Spirit we move about in the world. Since you have the Holy Spirit this power and boldness is in you! May the Lord open your eyes and hearts to operate from this position. Solomon says the righteous are as bold as lions. (Prov. 28:1).

Consider interpreting Acts 1:8 as: You will witness Jesus being at work everywhere; in Jerusalem ... and to the ends of the earth. Jesus is already present in the people with whom we will be witnessing.

Doesn't that make it much easier? This is basically saying we work with Jesus since he is already there, more than working for Jesus. Pray to see how Jesus is already working preparing hearts for his entrance. This not only makes it easier to witness, it raises our faith level, increasing our confidence and boldness.

Our spiritual eyes can become 20/20. We begin to see people as Jesus sees them. Jesus saw people as sheep that had been bruised, beaten and confused. Rather than being filled with distain, he was filled with love. "When he saw the crowds, he had compassion on them, because they were harassed and helpless, like sheep without a shepherd" (Matt. 9:36).

As you mature, your love and your approachability increases. You will grow in your love for others and your willingness to open your hearts and arms to hurting people.

Lord, I thank you that wherever I go you are already present preparing hearts to receive you. Give me eyes to perceive you at work and boldness to declare the Good News. Amen.

You Have Resurrection Power! (Part I)

Ephesians 1:27-31

Jesus said, "I am going to send you what my Father has promised; but stay in the city until you have been clothed with power from on high" (Luke 24:49). Then he added these final words: "You will receive power when the Holy Spirit comes on you, and you will be my witnesses in Jerusalem . . . and to the ends of the earth" (Acts 1:8).

Paul prays for the Christians in Ephesis to understand God's power within them: "I keep asking that God . . . may give you the spirit of wisdom . . . so that you may know him better . . . and may know the hope to which he has called you . . . and his incomparably great power for us who believe. That power is like the working of his mighty strength which he exerted in Christ when he raised him from the dead and seated him at his right hand in the heavenly realms, far about all rule and authority, power and dominion . . . not only in the present age but also in the one to come" (Eph. 1:17-21).

If ever there was a time when God's power was put to the test it was when Jesus lay in the tomb. This same power that God used to raise Jesus abides in us. We must admit our inability to change ourselves, seek God's forgiveness and walk in freedom. I meet with men enslaved with addictions: sexual addictions, alcohol, those attempting suicide, and those wasting themselves on drugs. God's power will break the chains of these addictions. God uses his church to love and hold each of us accountable to aid in overcoming these addictions.

Jesus came to release the captives and the oppressed. (Luke 4:18). "No test or temptation that comes your way is beyond the course of what others have had to face. God will never let you down; he'll never let you be pushed past your limit; he'll always be there to help you come through it" (I Cor. 10:13 Msg.). "Those who become Christians become new persons. They are not the same anymore, for the old life is gone. A new life has begun" (II Cor. 5:17 NLT).

Lord, open my eyes to your resurrection power. Amen.

You Have Resurrection Power!
(Part II)

II Timothy 1:7

Timothy was a shy young pastor. Paul reminded him: "God has not given us a spirit of timidity, but a spirit of power, of love and of self-discipline (or self-control)" (II Tim. 1:7). Notice how love and self-discipline are connected with God's dynamic power. Self-discipline means I do exactly what I know I should do, i.e. I do what God planned for me to do. It's only the Holy Spirit's power in us that we experience self-control.

How could Paul go to the wicked city of Rome, the capital of the world, with confidence? He says, "I am not ashamed of the gospel because it is the power of God for the salvation of everyone who believes, first for the Jews, then for the Gentiles" (Ro. 1:16). Paul knew God's power within him would overcome every demonic force he would face in Rome.

"Everything . . . is worthless when compared with the priceless gain of knowing Christ Jesus my Lord. I have discarded everything else, counting it all as garbage, so that I may have Christ and become one with him . . . I trust Christ to save me. For God's way of making us right with himself depends on faith. As a result, I can really know Christ and experience the mighty power that raised him from the dead . . ." (Phil. 3:8-10 NLT). You too can know his resurrection power!

This resurrection power made it impossible for death to keep Jesus in the tomb. (Acts 2:24). "If the Spirit of him who raised Jesus from the dead is living in you, he who raised Christ from the dead will also give life to your mortal bodies because of his Spirit who lives in you" (Ro. 8:11). Every Christian has God's Holy Spirit so we have no excuse for questioning his power in us. (Ro. 8:9). Keep in step with the Spirit. (Gal. 6:25). "May the God of hope fill you with all joy and peace as you trust in him, so the you may overflow with hope by the power of the Holy Spirit" (Ro.15:13).

Father, enable me to experience your resurrection power to overcome all temptations. Amen.

Passion for God

Ephesians 3:17-19

"God is love" (I John 4:16). "Go after a life of love as if your life depends on it" (I Cor. 14:1 Msg.). "Faith, hope and love remain, but the greatest of these is love" (I Cor. 13:13). God measures our lives by how we love.

"I pray that out of God's glorious riches he may strengthen you with power through his Spirit in your inner being, and that Christ may dwell in your hearts through faith. I pray that you being rooted and established in love may have power . . . to grasp how wide long, high and deep is the love of Christ, and to know his love that surpasses knowledge—that you may be filled to the measure of all the fullness of God" (Eph. 3:16-19).

"Be imitators of God as dearly loved children and live a life of love, just as Christ loved us and gave himself up for us . . ." (Eph. 5:1-2). Don't let your love grow cold. Pray for God to open your eyes to his extravagant love. Bask in the reality that God loves you to the extent that he laid down his life for you. "Greater love has no one than this, that he lay down his life for his friends" (John 15:13).

"Love one another as I have loved you" (John 13:34). Love God with all your heart. Just as your heart is the key to understanding your spouse so your heart is the key to understanding God's love. To grow in love with your spouse you spend time together. Put your spouse ahead of your own desires. "Believe in the Lord Jesus, and you will be saved" (Acts 16:31). Intellectual belief is not sufficient. You must know him. The Greek word for believe is an action word. Believe means that we trust in, cling to and rely upon the Lord Jesus. Grow in the fullness of God's love. (Eph. 3:17-19).

Paul prays for the church to grasp the indescribable love of God. God delights in you! You love him because he first loved you. (I John 4:19).

Lord Jesus open my eyes anew to your love for me. Amen.

Who's Coming to Dinner?

"By this time . . . men and women of doubtful reputation were hanging around Jesus, listening intently. The Pharisees and religious scholars were not pleased. . . . They growled, 'He takes in sinners and eats meals with them, treating them like old friends'" (Luke 15:1 Msg.).

"Jesus saw Levi at his tax collection booth and said, 'Follow me!' That night Levi invited Jesus and his disciples to be his dinner guests, along with his fellow tax collectors and many other notorious sinners. (There were many people of this kind among the crowds that followed Jesus.) But when some . . . Pharisees saw him eating with people like that they said to his disciples, 'Why does he eat with such scum?' Jesus told them, 'Healthy people don't need a doctor—sick people do. I have come to call sinners not those who think they are already good enough'" (Mark 2:15-27 NLT).

What was it about Jesus that intrigued sinners to come and listen to his teachings? Was it because they felt he understood and accepted them? Jesus was comfortable with sinners. He came: to seek and save the lost. (Luke 19:10). He came not to call the righteous but sinners. (Mark 2:17). That was his life's purpose and it must be ours. We accept unbelievers because Jesus accepted them. (John 3:17).

Jesus did not condone their sin. He accepted them, related to them by entering into their life, talking and eating with them. (Matt. 19:5).

We must take Jesus wherever we go. For salt to do its work it has to get out of the salt shaker. We will not win people for Jesus by staying in our Christian ghettos. Jesus instructs us to let our light shine for people to see our good works.

Paul wrote, "I have become all things to all men so that by all possible means I might save some" (I Cor. 8:22). Will you intentionally reach out to someone who doesn't know Jesus?

Jesus, enable me to love sinners and build bridges to them. Amen.

What Was Jesus' Most Prominent Subject? (Part I)

Matthew 6:9-21

Jesus spoke more about money than any other subject. Today there is an imbalance in much preaching overemphasizing God's promises of material blessings. Jesus said, "Life does not consist in an abundance of possessions" (Lk.12:14). While God blesses materially, multitudes of poor Christians die who are sincere followers of Jesus. Jesus was a refugee. (Matt. 2:13-15). He had no place to lay his head. (Lk.9:58). He died owning no property except the clothes on his back.

"You know how full of love and kindness our Lord Jesus Christ was. Though he was very rich, yet for your sakes he became poor, so that by his poverty he could make you rich" (II Cor. 8:9). Paul wrote, "We are poor but make many rich" (II Cor. 6:10).

"Don't store up treasures here on earth ... Store your treasures in heaven where they will never become moth-eaten or rusty and be safe from thieves. Wherever you treasure is there your heart and thoughts will also be" (Matt. 6:9-21 NLT).

"When the rich young ruler wanted to follow Jesus, Jesus said, 'Sell everything you have and give to the poor and you will have treasure in heaven. Then come, follow me'" (Mark 10:21). Wealth had captured his heart. "Jesus said to his disciples, 'It's hard for a rich man to enter the kingdom of heaven. Again, I tell you, it's easier for a camel to go through the eye of a needle than for a rich man to enter the kingdom of God'" (Matt. 19:23-24).

"Zacchaeus, unlike the rich ruler had a change of heart. He said, 'Lord! ... I give half of my possession to the poor and if I have cheated anybody I will pay back four times the amount.' Jesus said, 'Today salvation has come to this house'" (Luke 19:9).

Jesus said for some "the deceitfulness of wealth and the desire for other things come in and choke the word, making it unfruitful" (Mk. 4:18-19).

Lord, all that I have, I received from you. It's all yours! Amen.

What Was Jesus' Most Prominent Subject? (Part II)

Luke 6:38 & 14:12-14

"Give and it will be given to you. A good measure pressed down, shaken together and running over, will be poured into your lap. For with the measure you use it will be measured to you" (Luke 6:38). Sow sparingly and reap sparingly, sow generously reap generously . . . God loves a cheerful giver. (II Cor. 9:6-7).

Don't love this evil world or lust for everything you see. Possessions are temporal. David prays, "Do not inflict me with the love for money" (Ps. 119:36 NLT).

Today the average Christian gives about two percent. All we have comes from the hand of God. Before you spend money on things that are not necessary ask for God's permission. You'll be amazed how great a financial advisor he is.

Excel in the grace of giving. (II Cor. 8:7). Using hyperbole, Jesus states you are not to invite your families or anyone who can invite you back like your rich neighbors; rather invite the poor, the crippled, the lame and the blind. (Luke 14:12-14). In the parable of the banquet the master sent his servants to invite a real estate owner, a man who bought new farm machinery (oxen) and a man who just got married. They refused to come . . . The master was angry and told the servants to bring in the poor, the crippled, the blind and the lame. (Luke 14:15-24).

The more we possess the more we tend to place our security in things. We live as if we don't need God. If we're sick we go to the doctor. If we're hungry we go to the food bank. If we need somewhere to stay we find a friend or a homeless shelter. Are we putting our trust in God or in our resources?

"Has not God chosen those who are poor in the eyes of the world to be rich in faith . . . Is it not the rich who are exploiting you? . . . Are they not the ones who are slandering the noble name of him to whom you belong?" (James 2:5-7).

Father, all that I have I cheerfully give to you. Amen.

November 7

Harvest Time Is Now!

John 4:35-36

"Now is the time of God's favor, now is the day of salvation" (I Cor. 6:2).

Jesus commands his disciples: "The harvest is plentiful, but the workers are few. Ask the Lord of the harvest, therefore, to send out workers into his harvest field. Go! I am sending you out like lambs, among wolves" (Luke 10:2-3).

Now is the time to pray for workers. "Do not say, 'Four months more and then the harvest.' I tell you, open your eyes and look at the fields! They are ripe for harvest. Even now the reaper draws his wages, even now he harvests the crop for eternal life, so that the sower and the reaper may be glad together" (John 4:35-36).

Ed Steltzer writes, "We've jazzed up the music, spiced up the sermons, and spruced up the buildings but the wheat still isn't harvesting itself." How true! Jesus says we are to pray for more workers. The problem is not the harvest. The harvest is everywhere. We bump into the harvest every time we go to the supermarket, service station, dental office, post office, or a football game. The harvest is work peers or classmates. Be conscious of the harvest every time you see the U-haul truck in your neighborhood, every time a new house is being built. God loved the people of the world so much he sent Jesus to give eternal life. We are called to give our lives, too.

Ask the Lord to give you his passion 24/7 like Moses and Paul: "I have a great sorrow and unceasing anguish in my heart. For I could wish that I were cursed and cut off from Christ for the sake of my brothers" (Ro. 9:2 and Exodus 32:32). Pray for the Lord to open your eyes to the harvest all around you. How blessed we are to have the privilege of introducing people to the Good News of eternal life through Jesus Christ our creator and savior. Who will you share Jesus with today?

Lord, help me to remember that today is the day of salvation. Give me your passion to share the Good News to those I meet. Amen.

Why Don't I Do What I Know Is Right?

Romans 7:14-8:2

"I know all of God's commands are spiritual but I'm not . . . I'm full of myself . . . I decide one way, but then I act another, doing things I absolutely despise . . . I obviously need help! . . . I can will it, but I can't do it . . . I'm at the end of my rope . . . He (Jesus) acted to set things right in this life of contradictions where I want to serve God with all my heart and mind, but am pulled by the influence of sin to do something totally different. With the arrival of Jesus . . . that fateful dilemma is resolved. Those who enter into Christ's being-here-for-us no longer have to live under a continuous, low-lying black cloud. A new power is in operation. The Spirit of life in Christ, like a strong wind, has magnificently cleared the air, freeing you from a fated lifetime of brutal tyranny at the hands of sin and death" (Ro. 7:14-8:2 Msg.).

We are a walking civil war. Paul writes: "Be on your guard; stand firm in the faith; be courageous and strong" (I Cor. 16:13). "We do not fight with weapons of the flesh. We use God's weapons for the destruction of Satan's fortresses" (II Cor. 10:3-4).

"We put on the full armor of God so that we can stand against the devil's schemes. For our struggle is not against flesh and blood, but against the rulers, against the authorities, against the powers of this dark world, and against the spiritual forces of evil in the heavenly realms. Therefore put on the full armor of God, so that when the day of evil comes, you may be able to stand your ground, and after you have done everything, stand . . . . In addition, take up the shield of faith, with which you can extinguish all the flaming arrows of the evil one. Take the helmet of salvation and the sword of the Spirit, which is the word of God" (Eph. 6:11-18, I Thess. 5:8). Fight the good fight of faith. (I Tim. 6:12).

We need Jesus' Holy Spirit's power to empower our wills so we do his will.

Father, thank you that through Christ Jesus and his Holy Spirit dwelling in me you have set me free from the law of sin and death. Hallelujah! Amen. (Ro. 8:1-2).

313

You're in a Victory Parade

II Corinthians 2:14-16

"In the Messiah, in Christ, God leads us from place to place in one perpetual victory parade. Through us, he brings knowledge of Christ. Everywhere we go people breathe in the exquisite fragrance. Because of Christ, we give off a sweet scent rising to God, which is recognized by those on the way to salvation—an aroma redolent with life" (II Cor. 2:14-16 Msg.).

What an optimistic view of life. "God leads us from place to place in one perpetual victory parade," (Msg.). The NIV reads: "Thanks be to God, who always leads us in triumphal procession in Christ and through us spreads everywhere the fragrance of the knowledge of him."

This is life on the higher plane. In the next verse he says, "But those on the way to destruction treat us more like the stench from a rotting corpse" (v. 16 Msg.). Paul lived with the realization that many others despised his presence and tried to kill him.

The parade Paul refers to is the procession of victorious soldiers returning from the battle. Picture yourself with Jesus marching and leading this triumphal procession as you radiate the aroma of Jesus.

How could Paul be victorious?

First: He knew he was crucified and risen with Christ. (Gal. 2:20).
Second: He was filled with the Holy Spirit. (Eph. 5:18)
Third: He believed in the power of the resurrection. (Col. 3:1)
Fourth: He believed in the power of prayer. (Col. 2:1)
Fifth: He thought good and helpful things. (Phil 4:8)
Sixth: He wore the full armor of God. (Eph. 6:10-18)
Seventh: He had a passion for others. (Ro. 9:1-2 and 10:1)
Eighth: He anticipated heaven. (II Tim. 4:7)

Lord Jesus, enable my life to be a sweet perfume to those I meet today. Amen.

Start at Home

"You must love the Lord you God with all your heart, all your soul, and all your strength. And you must commit yourselves wholeheartedly to these commands . . . Repeat them again and again to your children. Talk about them when you are at home . . ." (Deuteronomy 6:5-7 NLT). Husbands and wives submit to one another out of reverence for Christ. (Eph. 5:21).

Living our faith must begin at home. We can witness at work but if we are not faithful in living for Jesus at home we have lost the battle. We can be successful in business, in the community and in church but if our home is in disrepair we have failed. "If anyone does not know how to manage his own family, how can he take care of God's church?" (I Tim. 3:5).

I was blessed to have parents who were not perfect but who lived their faith at home. Mottos adorned our walls that impacted my life. I repeat them here: "Your life will soon be past only what's done for Christ will last" and "Say nothing you would not like to be saying when Jesus comes. Do nothing you would not like to be doing when Jesus comes, and go nowhere you would not want to be when Jesus comes."

My mother read the Bible each evening before we went to bed and made sure I said my prayers. More importantly I observed my parents kneeling beside their bed in prayer before they retired for the night. They taught me by modeling the value of prayer. Even though my dad has been deceased for many years I can still hear my Dad whistling hymns as he worked. Let's bring whistling back.

When there was a needy family, especially among relatives who lost a mate, my parents offered assistance. One farmer was short on hay so my Dad delivered a wagon load of hay. That was 40 years ago but the farmer talks about it to this day.

Lord, enable me to be a faithful disciple expressing love to my spouse, children and those I meet. Amen.

November 11

Don't Hide Your Light . . . Let It Shine

Matthew 5:14-16

"You are the light of the world. A city on a hill cannot be hidden. Neither do people light a lamp and put it under a bowl. Instead they put it on a stand, and it gives light to everyone in the house. In the same way, let your light shine before men, that they may see your good deeds and praise your Father in heaven" (Matt. 5:14-16).

"God is not unjust; he will not forget your work and the love you have shown him as you have helped his people and continue to help them" (Hebrews 6:10). Go public with your good deeds. Tell people what you are up to. Don't be arrogant or a braggart but as the Message Bible says, "bring out the God-colors in the world." When people see your acts of kindness many will thank you. Point them to God with statements like, "God has been good to me, I enjoy sharing his love with you." Or "God has blessed me I want to share his blessings by helping whenever I can. I enjoy passing his blessings around."

As the Spirit directs, use these statements as a spring board to a conversation about faith in God. You may ask if they have faith in God. Or you might say, "After what you have been through perhaps God seems pretty distant." Their need provides a bridge to walk across to introduce them to a life transformed by Jesus.

You are not to hide your good deeds. Sometimes Christians allow the devil to spoof them into keeping their mouth shut by whispering: "Talking about your works is bragging." If you know that everything you do is because of Jesus living his life through you, that's not being proud. Paul puts it well: "I can do everything through him who gives me strength" (Phil. 4:13).

It will be a great day when Christians are known for good works rather than for what they are against.

Lord, enable me to hear your Holy Spirit's voice so I know what to say and what you want me to do. Shine through me! Amen.

Barnabas the Encourager

Acts 4:36-37

"There was Joseph, the one the apostles nicknamed Barnabas (which means 'Son of Encouragement') . . . He sold a field he owned and brought the money to the apostles for those in need" (Acts 4:36-37). Barnabas is an encourager.

When Paul arrived in Jerusalem following his conversion, the believers thought his story was a trick for him to capture and kill more Christians. Barnabas convinced them otherwise. Barnabas encouraged Mark to go on Paul's first missionary journey. Partway through the journey Mark left for home. Later Paul was upset with Mark. On his next missionary trip, Paul refused to take Mark. Instead Barnabas encouraged and took Mark with him. Later Mark wrote one of the Gospels. (Acts 15:36-41).

"Encourage one another daily, as long as it is called Today, so that none of you may be hardened by sins' deceitfulness" (Heb. 3:13). Ask God to open your eyes and give you wisdom to discern how to help and encourage people.

Growing up on a dairy farm it was understood that I would not have time to participate in after school sports. I was needed to help milk cows. I was a stuttering kid with an inferiority complex. During my freshmen year the junior varsity team was not doing well. The coach approached me about coming to practice. While I was not able to join the team the coach will never know how much he encouraged me.

Paul writes: "Encourage each other and build each other up. (I Thess. 5:11, 14 NLT). While I was in seminary I received an anonymous gift of money which greatly encouraged me.

"May our Lord Jesus Christ himself and God our Father, who loved us and by his grace gave us eternal encouragement and good hope, encourage your hearts and strengthen you in every good deed and word." (II Thess. 2:16-17).

Father, thank you for your eternal encouragement. Enable me to encourage someone today. Amen.

Why Is the Blood of Jesus Crucial?

I John 1:7

Blood is the red cord that runs from Genesis to Revelation. Blood is central to God's plan of redemption. When Adam and Eve sinned they covered their nakedness with fig leaves but God killed an animal to clothe them with garments of skin. (Gen. 3:21). The life is in the blood. (Leviticus 14:11). "Without the shedding of blood there is no forgiveness" (Heb. 9:22).

"The life of a creature is in the blood, and I have given it to you to make atonement for yourselves; it is the blood that makes atonement for one's life" (Lev. 17:11). Blood sacrifice is innate in most every tribe throughout history.

Jesus gave his life's blood for the sins of the world. This is the reason we will see Jesus' nail prints when we get to heaven. "He (Jesus) was pierced for our transgressions, he was crushed for our iniquities; the punishment that brought us peace was upon him, and by his wounds we are healed" (Is. 53:5).

When Noah landed the Ark, he offered blood sacrifices to God. Abraham had to learn that Isaac, the son of promise, could be truly surrendered to God only by death. (Gen. 22:1-18). But God provided a ram as a substitute for Isaac. Jesus is our substitute.

For God's people to be delivered from slavery they had to kill a lamb and sprinkle the blood on the doorpost so the death angel would not destroy the oldest son in the household. This was the beginning of the Passover which we celebrate as Holy Communion, a service of thanksgiving for Jesus giving his life's blood as the Lamb of God sacrificed to cover and remove our sin.

The cross is central. It is the most recognized symbol in the world. Paul says, "I resolved to know nothing while I was with you except Jesus Christ and him crucified" (I Cor. 2:2). There is no salvation apart from the cross. "If we are living in the light of God's presence, just as Christ is, then we have fellowship with each other and the blood of Jesus, his Son, cleanses us from every sin" (I John 1:7 NLT).

Lord, thank you for covering my sin with your precious blood. Amen.

318

In the Name of Jesus

John 14:14

"You can ask for anything in my name, and I will do it, because the work of the Son brings glory to the Father. Yes, ask anything in my name and I will do it!" (John 14:13-14).

"You did not choose me, but I chose you and appointed you to go and bear fruit. . . . Then the Father will give you whatever you ask in my name" (John 15:16). Sincerely praying in Jesus' name connects us to the heart of God. It is so easy to allow this phrase, "In the Name of Jesus" to become mechanical. Never use Jesus' name as a magical formula. There is a fragrance in Jesus' name that appeals to the Father.

If you go to a bank and give them a check in your name they will cash it as long as you have the money in your account. If my account is depleted they will not cash it. If a wealthy depositor gives you a signed check they will cash it. If you go to your Father in heaven it's like going to the bank of heaven and asking in Jesus' name. Jesus has unlimited credit. He wants you to use it!

". . . He will give you" (John 16:23). Jesus said that because of my name my Father will respond to your prayers. By praying in the name of Jesus the Father sees us and honors us the same as he does his son. The challenge is to remain in Jesus, to be one with him, so our requests are in line with the thought, motives and desires of Jesus. These prayers the Father will answer in his time and way.

All things were created by him and for him and by him all things hold together. (Col. 1:16-17). There is truly power in the name of Jesus.

When David Yonggi Cho spoke to American clergy they asked him the secret of his huge church? He said you pray and obey, later they asked again and he gave the same answer. They asked a third time. He wept saying you just don't get it.

Jesus, thank you for the privilege of asking in your name, knowing your bank is more than adequate for withdraws in line with your will. Amen.

A Bondservant of Jesus

Galatians 2:20

"I have been crucified with Christ and I no longer live, but Christ lives in me. The life I live in the body, I live by faith in the Son of God, who loved me and gave himself for me" (Gal. 2:20).

"I identified myself completely with him. Indeed I have been crucified with Christ. My ego is no longer central. It is no longer important that I appear righteous before you or have your good opinion, and I am no longer driven to impress God. Christ lives in me. The life you see me living is not 'mine,' but it is lived by faith in the Son of God, who loved me and gave himself for me. I am not going to go back on that" (Gal. 2:20 Msg.).

Your independence and rights are gone. It's not your goals, your life; it is Jesus' life and his alone. Surrender your life to him. No one can do this for you. You must decide this yourself. This is a daily decision. Jesus said we must deny our self and take up our cross daily and follow him. (Luke 9:23). The Message Bible states (vv. 23-24): "Anyone who intends to come with me has to let me lead. You're not in the driver's seat—I am. Don't run from suffering, embrace it. Follow me and I'll show you how . . . Self-sacrifice is the way, my way to finding yourself, your true self."

Say to Jesus, "Whatever you want to do with me is fine, I want your will above everything else." If I need to go through the valley of the shadow of death to be broken before you, that is what I want. You know what I need so I can be crucified with you. When you reach that point immediately the supernatural identification with Jesus takes place in you. The passion of Christianity comes from knowingly and intentionally signing away your own rights and becoming a bondservant of Jesus Christ. Until you become a bondservant the supernatural will not become natural.

Lord, give me a vision of what you want me to do with my life, then enable me to carry it out moment by moment. Amen.

Don't Be Lured Away

II Corinthians 11:2-4

We need to have God's passion burning within us. (Jer. 20:9). In order for Paul to compare his own ministry with the false teachers who invaded the church at Corinth, he had to speak about himself. He has God's passion burning within him.

"The thing that has me so upset (divinely jealous) is that I care about you so much—this is the passion of God burning inside me! I promised your hand in marriage to Christ, presented you as a pure virgin to her husband. And now I'm afraid that exactly as the Snake seduced Eve with his smooth patter, you are being lured away from the simple purity of your love for Christ" (II Cor. 11:2-4 Msg.).

Paul led the Corinthians to Christ. He promised them to Christ, the bridegroom and now they are opening their hearts to another groom. Their new groom was the legalism of Judaistic teaching. These false teachers brought a spirit of bondage, fear and worldliness instead of freedom, love, joy, peace and power. It was a different gospel which was no gospel at all. It was bad news, not good news.

As Paul was divinely jealous so you too need to be upset when those who claim to be Christians turn and follow a different gospel. Just as you need to be direct and confront your children when they take a path that leads to death you must be direct with those who walk down the path of legalism or any other false teaching. Paul reminded the Corinthians how he brought the Gospel to them without remuneration. Now they are turning their backs on him and following those who impose burdens on them. "If one of you should wander from the truth and someone should bring him back, remember this: Whoever turns a sinner from the error of his way will save him from death and cover over a multitude of sins" (James 5:19-20).

Lord, may your passion burn within me, your divine jealousy motivate me to do all I can to bring back those who are being seduced by Satan to follow another gospel. Enable me to warn them with your Spirit of truth and grace. Amen.

Water

John 4:13-14

"Water" appears 700 times in the Bible. We can only live a few days without water. Jesus said, "Whoever drinks the water I give him will never thirst . . . the water I give him will become in him a spring of water welling up to eternal life" (John 4:13-14).

Jesus is picturing a vigorous fountain—water leaping up. Other versions read: a perpetual spring, living water or an artesian spring within, or a gushing fountain of endless life. Jesus uses water as a symbol of the Holy Spirit and the vigorous, abundant life. (John 7:39, 10:10). You overflow with this endless source of love, joy and peace, etc. (Gal. 5:22). This river passes through you to others. Jesus said, "If anyone is thirsty, let him come to me and drink. Whoever believes in me . . . streams of living water will flow from within him" (John 7:37-38). (John 4:10). When people "bump" against you a little of God's love, joy and peace will be splashed on them.

If you find that the fountain of life is not springing up from within you blessing the lives of others—something is blocking the flow. Could it be that you are like the Dead Sea producing nothing of life? The flow has stopped because like the Dead Sea you are not passing it on. If you are keeping it to yourself it will dry up.

If you are not living in the Spirit, God has so much more for you! Stay true to him. Be obedient in every detail and you will experience the water that becomes a spring gushing up and overflowing to others. Pay attention to the source. Remain in Jesus and you will bear much fruit. (John 15:5). No one can block a river indefinitely. It will overcome every obstacle. Others may throw rocks in its path or try to dam it up but it will overflow.

This Spring of Water will become a river not only here (John 7:37-39) but God's river of water bringing life will continue in heaven as well! (Rev. 22:1-2; 17).

Father, I thank you for your Holy Spirit. Thank you that I never need to be thirsty again. Enable your Spirit within me to overflow to many thirsty people around me. Amen.

Love the Wine, Not the Wineskins

Matthew 9:16-17

"I'm announcing the new salvation work" (Isaiah 42:9 Msg.)

Jesus said, "No one sews a patch of unshrunk cloth on an old garment, for the patch will pull away from the garment, making the tear worse. Neither do men pour new wine into old wineskins. If they do, the skins will burst, the wine will run out and the wineskins will be ruined. No they pour new wine into new wineskins, and both are preserved" (Matt. 9:16-17).

Many churches think if they just keep doing the things they have been doing they will fulfill God's design for the church. Are you fulfilling the Great Commission if your church hasn't baptized a new adult believer for a year or two? We can't keep doing the same thing over and over and expect different results.

Doing new things usually means dropping the old things. Someone stated: "Everyone is in favor of new things as long as they are exactly like the old things." Many congregations are afraid of trying new things. They are more comfortable staying the same size even though they know Jesus calls us to fish for people. They would rather give to missions in another part of the world than give to reach their neighbors across the street. Your church is seriously in trouble if you are not reaching anyone in the community. If the Lord calls you to be a witness to your congregation, that's your mission. However, if year after year they do not hear your cry to pray for and give priority to reaching the lost around your church, you need to shake the dust off your feet and move to where the Spirit is moving. We need to love the wine and not the wine skins.

The harvest is ripe. The Holy Spirit has not lost his power. Jesus said, if we abide in him we will be fruitful, faithful yes, but also fruitful. (John 15:5, 15).

Lord Jesus, give me the courage to live in the powerful wind of your Holy Spirit. Amen.

How Did Jesus Keep the Disciples on Track?

Matthew 10:2-4

Can you imagine Matthew the tax collector and Simon the zealot tolerating each other in Jesus' small group? The animosity was intense. How could Jesus keep Simon from killing Matthew? The zealots degenerated into a body of assassins. They couldn't tolerate Rome. Matthew on the other hand was considered a traitor since he cooperated with the Romans to collect taxes. Tax collectors were hated by all the Jews, especially the Pharisees. The tax collectors were free to charge whatever they chose as long as Rome got its share. Many overcharged for the animal offerings.

Imagine having these two men in your same small group. The difference between Republicans and Democrats is no comparison. Maybe a terrorist and a conservative politician is a better comparison. How did Jesus keep Simon and Matthew on the same team?

Jesus' presence was so powerful and his mission so focused and intense that they were caught up in the vision of helping him build a Kingdom that would outlast the Roman Kingdom. Jesus' words gripped their hearts and changed their philosophy: "If anyone would come after me, he must deny himself and take up his cross daily and follow me. For whoever wants to save his life will lose it, but whoever loses his life for me will save it. What good is it for a man to gain the whole world, and yet lose or forfeit his very self? If anyone is ashamed of me and my words, the Son of Man will be ashamed of him when he comes in his glory . . ." (Luke 9:23-26).

They took Jesus seriously when he said, "If you forgive men, when they sin against you, your heavenly Father will also forgive you. But if you do not forgive men their sins, your Father will not forgive your sins" (Matt. 6:14-15). "Love your enemies . . ." (Ro. 12:9-14). If we take God's word seriously our focusing on Jesus most disagreements will go out the window and the world will take notice.

Lord, enable me to forgive those who disagree with me. Use me to bring healing to broken relationships so your Kingdom can expand. Amen.

Overflow with Hope

Romans 15:13

"May the God of hope fill you with all joy and peace as you trust in him, so that you may overflow with hope by the power of the Holy Spirit" (Ro. 15:13). Prisoners were forced to move piles of dirt only to have them replace the dirt. After some time with this repetition many of them became suicidal. Prisoners can endure indescribable suffering as long as they have hope.

Those who don't know Jesus, Paul says are "without hope and without God in the world" (Eph. 2:12).

The Scriptures give us hope: "For everything that was written in the past was written to teach us, so that through endurance and the encouragement of the Scriptures we might have hope" (Ro. 15:4). Let the Scriptures build you up and give you hope. Meditate on Psalm 23, or 9:18, 25:3,119:43, I Cor. 6:14, and 15:19.

C. S. Lewis wrote: "We try to be our own masters as if we had created ourselves. Then we hopelessly strive to invent some sort of happiness for ourselves outside of God, apart from God. And out of that hopeless attempt has come human history . . . the long, terrible story of man trying to find something other than God which will make him happy."

"We who have run for our very lives to God have every reason to grab the promised hope with both hands and never let go." (Hebrews 6:18 Msg.).

Edward Mote wrote this Gospel song in 1834: My hope is built on nothing less than Jesus' blood and righteousness. I dare not trust the sweetest frame, but wholly lean on Jesus' name. When he shall come with trumpet sound, oh, may I then in him be found, dressed in his righteousness alone, faultless to stand before the throne. On Christ the solid rock, I stand; all other ground is sinking sand.

Father, I overflow with hope through the power of your Holy Spirit. Amen.

November 21

O Mighty Warrior!

Judges 6:12

"The angel of God appeared to Gideon and said, 'God is with you, O mighty Warrior!'" (Judges 6:12 Msg.).

When God called Gideon he was unwilling to listen. He questioned God's presence. The Israelites were hiding in caves and dens for fear of Midian. Gideon asked, "Where are all the miracles our fathers told us about?" God said, "Go in the strength that is yours. Save Israel from Midian. Haven't I just sent you?" (6:14 Msg.). Gideon responded, "Me, my master? How and with what could I ever save Israel? Look at me. My clan's the weakest in Manasseh and I'm the runt of the litter" (v. 15 Msg.).

After the Lord gave Gideon several miraculous signs of his presence, "God's Spirit came upon Gideon" (v. 34). With God's Spirit he defeated the enemy.

You have God's Spirit. "If anyone does not have the Spirit of Christ, he does not belong to Christ" (Ro. 8:9). Jesus' final words were, "You will receive power when the Holy Spirit comes on you; and you will be my witnesses . . ." (Acts 1:8).

God has commissioned you: "Just as the Father sent me, I send you" (John 20:21 Msg.). "In the same way you gave me a mission in the world, I give them a mission in the world" (John 17:18 Msg.). (Matt. 28:18-20).

With God's Spirit in us we will overcome the enemy. "The Spirit in you is far stronger than anything in the world" (I John 4:4 Msg.). "God did not give you a spirit of timidity, but a spirit of power, of love and of self-discipline" (II Tim. 1:7).

Jesus' Spirit lives in his children. You will overcome the enemy. "'Not by might, not by power, but by my Spirit,' says the Lord Almighty" (Zechariah 4:6).

Lord Jesus, enable me to remember who I am in you. Since you are in me and commissioned me, I will conquer the enemy through the power of your Spirit. Amen.

Enjoying Life

John 10:10

"I came that they may have and enjoy life, and have it in abundance—to the full, till it overflows" (John 10:10 AMP). "The Lord is my shepherd; I have everything I need" (Ps. 23:1). "My health may fail, and my spirit may grow weak, but God remains the strength of my heart; he is mine forever" (Ps. 73:26 NLT). "Our present sufferings are not worth comparing with the glory that will be revealed in us" (Ro. 8:18).

"Moses chose to be mistreated along with the people of God rather than to enjoy the pleasures of sin for a short time" (Heb. 11:24-25). The world offers short-lived pleasure. Compare this, "You have made known to me the path of life; you will fill me with joy in your presence, with eternal pleasures at your right hand" (Ps. 16:11).

"Relax with what you have. Since God assured us, 'I'll never let you down, never walk off and leave you,' we can boldly quote, 'God is there, ready to help; I'm fearless no matter what. Who or what can get to me?'" (Hebrews 13:5-6 Msg.).

Jesus makes all the difference. You are chosen by God and adopted as his child. (Eph. 1:3-8, John 1:23). You're forgiven and live in right standing with God. (Ro. 5:1). You're free of condemnation. (Ro. 8:1). You're confident that God will complete the good work he started in you. (Phil. 1:6). You're a citizen of heaven. (Phil. 3:20). The evil one cannot touch you. (I John 5:18). Jesus is your friend. (John 15:14). "Godliness with contentment is great gain" (I Tim. 6:6).

"His divine power has given us everything we need for life and godliness through our knowledge of him" (II Peter 1:3).

Jesus will give you wisdom to understand global problems as poverty, starvation, AIDS, human trafficking, global warming, racism, sexism, disease, war, and drugs empowering you to do what you can to alleviate them. (Matt. 6:10).

Lord Jesus, thank you that you came to live within me and provide all I need for life and godliness. Amen.

God Can Use Anyone

Judges 11:1

"Jephthah the Gileadite was one tough warrior. He was the son of a whore" (Judges 11:1 Msg.). Jephthah was kicked out of his father's family so he would have no part in the inheritance. Time passed. When the Ammonites began fighting Israel, his half-brothers remembered Jephthah being a mighty warrior. They approached him asking him to lead them into battle. Jephthah agreed provided they promised to make him their leader. (v. 9).

Jephthah tried to reason with the Ammonites but they refused to listen to a word that he said. "God's Spirit came upon Jephthah . . . God gave them to him. He beat them soundly" (vv. 29 & 32).

Look at a few of Jesus' ancestors. Tamar deceived Judah in retaliation for his neglect in giving her his third son, Shelah, for a husband. Rahab was a prostitute. David was a murderer and adulterer. Rehoboam abandoned the worship of God and allowed idolatry to flourish. Asa responded with rage when confronted about his sin. Uzziah tried to perform priestly duties in direct disobedience to God. Ahaz sacrificed some of his children in Baal worship. Manasseh sacrificed his children to idols.

God works through people whom we are inclined to reject. If you feel like a failure, remember Jephthah. Many in Jesus' lineage were people of poor reputation. No matter what your background, God can use you. It doesn't matter where you were born, who your parents and ancestors were, God can use you.

Welcome seekers and walk together with them as they become disciples. I like the question, "Is your next pastor saved yet?" Do you have faith to believe that God will transform prebelievers into believers who are being discipled and can become workers and leaders in the church? That needs to happen.

Lord, thank you for accepting me with my background. Enable me to accept everyone you accept. Amen. (Ro. 15:7).

Tolerance—America's Idol

John 8:11

Tolerance is one of America's idols. There are many things Jesus did not tolerate. Jesus came not to call the (self) righteous but sinners. (Luke 5:32). Jesus loved the rich young ruler but left him walk away because he was not willing to sell his possessions. (Mark 10:21-23). He did not condemn the woman caught in adultery but told her, "Go now and leave your life of sin" (John 8:11).

Jesus says, "Do you suppose that I have come to bring peace to the earth. I did not come to bring peace (tolerance) but a sword. For I have come to turn a man against his father, a daughter against her mother, a daughter-in-law against her mother-in-law. . . . Anyone who loves his father or mother more than me is not worthy of me; anyone who loves his son or daughter more than me is not worthy of me; and anyone who does not take his cross and follow me is not worthy of me" (Matt 10:34-38).

Jesus said, "Do not give dogs what is sacred; do not throw your pearls to pigs" (Matt. 7:6). He called Herod a fox. (Luke 13-32). "Small is the gate and narrow the road that leads to life, and only a few find it. Watch out for false prophets" (Matt. 7:14-15). "Not everyone who says to me, 'Lord, Lord,' will enter the kingdom of heaven, but only he who does the will of my Father who is in heaven . . ." (Matt. 7:21-23).

When Jesus heard the disciples rebuking those who brought their children to Jesus, he was indignant. (Mark 10:14). He scolded the disciples for their little faith. (Mark 4:40). Paul's long list of sins in many of his letters states that those who do these things will not enter God's Kingdom. (Gal. 5:19-21).

Don't let people intimidate you when they call you intolerant or bigoted. Jesus reminds us, "All men will hate you because of me" (Mark 13:13). Jesus' exercised intolerance toward the sinfulness and wickedness of men and women. On the other hand he offers forgiveness to everyone who comes to him in repentance and faith.

Lord, give me wisdom to know how to love persons who are deliberately living in sin. Amen.

Are You Thankful?

Philippians 4:6-7

David writes, "O Lord my God, I will give you thanks forever" (Ps. 30:12). "Let them give thanks to the Lord for his unfailing love and his wonderful deeds for men . . ." (Ps. 107:8-9). "Give thanks to the Lord; his love endures forever" (Ps. 118:29). "At midnight I rise to give you thanks for your righteous laws" (Ps. 119:62). "I will awaken the dawn" (Ps. 108:2). "Enter his gates with thanksgiving and . . . praise him, give thanks and praise his name" (Ps. 100:5).

Do you enter church with thanksgiving or do you stay up Saturday night and fill your mind with the garbage on TV? Discipline yourself to get a good night's sleep so you can truly worship. (I Tim. 4:7).

I often wake up in the morning with a hymn or Gospel song I learned as a youth. When we are filled with the Spirit we have a song in our heart. Ephesians 5:20 reminds us we are to always give thanks to God the Father for everything in the name of our Lord Jesus Christ. Couples who exhibit thankfulness tend to be more committed to each other and are more likely to remain in their relationships. Thankfulness turns despair to faith. "Give thanks in all circumstance, for this is God's will for you" (I Thess. 5:18).

Paul writes from prison: "Be thankful. Let the word of Christ dwell in you richly as you sing . . . with gratitude in your hearts to God. Whatever you do, do it all in the name of the Lord Jesus, giving thanks to God the Father through him" (Col. 5:15-17). Thankfulness takes the sting out of adversity. Overcome discontent with a spirit of thankfulness.

Jesus healed the ten lepers. But only one returned to thank him. (Luke 17:11-19). How often are we part of the nine who forget to thank God for his blessings? Thankfulness brings peace and contentment. "Don't be anxious about anything, but in everything, by prayer with thanksgiving, present your requests to God. And the peace of God . . . will guard your hearts and your minds in Christ Jesus" (Phil. 4:6-7).

Jesus, I thank you for the gift of yourself, making it possible for me to be thankful. Amen.

Triumph Over Sin

Mark 5

"When Jesus got out of the boat, a man with an evil spirit came from the tombs to meet him. This man lived in the tombs, and no one could bind him anymore, not even with a chain. He had often been chained hand and foot, but he tore the chains apart and broke the irons on his feet. No one was strong enough to subdue him. Night and day among the tombs and in the hills he would cry out and cut himself with stones" (Mark 5:2-5).

After Jesus healed the man, freeing him of the evil spirits, he begged to go with Jesus but Jesus sent him to witness to the people who knew him. (vv. 18-20).

Jesus can break any bondage. Paul explains how deliverance can be real. "If God himself has taken up residence in your life, you can hardly be thinking more of yourself than of him. . . . He dwells in you—even though you still experience all the limitations of sin—you yourself experience life on God's terms. It stands to reason . . . that if the alive and present God who raised Jesus from the dead moves into your life, he'll do the same thing in you that he did in Jesus. . . . When God lives and breathes in you (and he does, as surely as he did in Jesus), you are delivered from that dead life. With his Spirit living in you, your body will be as alive as Christ's! . . .

". . . We don't owe this old do-it-yourself life one red cent. There's nothing in it for us. . . . The best thing to do is give it a decent burial and get on with your new life. . . . This resurrection life you received from God is not a timid, grave-tending life. It's adventurously expectant, greeting God with a childlike 'What's next, Papa?' . . . We know who he is, and we know who we are; Father and children. And we know we are going to get what's coming to us—an unbelievable inheritance! . . . If we go through the hard times with him, then we're certainly going to go through the good times with him!" (Ro. 8:8-17 Msg.).

Father, thank you for your resurrection life in me delivering me from sinful habits and giving me an unbelievable inheritance. Amen.

What Keeps Things from Flying Apart?

Colossians 1:15-17

Is your world flying apart? "Jesus is the image of the invisible God. . . . For by him all things were created: things in heaven and on earth, visible and invisible, whether thrones or powers or rulers or authorities, all things were created by him and for him. He is before all things, and in him all things hold together" (Col. 1:15-17). Jesus created all things and keeps them from flying apart.

With the electron microscope biological scientists have discovered the protein molecule laminin. There are up to 60,000 protein molecules in the human body. Laminin is like the rebar you place in cement to hold it together making it strong. Laminin is the steel in the human body. The fascinating thing about the molecule laminin is that it is shaped in the form of a cross. Amazing! Jesus who holds everything together created this protein molecule, laminin to hold things together in your body, creating it in the shape of a cross.

There are more than a million heavenly bodies larger than our earth for every person who has ever lived on our planet. "God determined the number of the stars and calls them each by name" (Ps. 147:4). God is in control of each one so that astronomers can project the path of these heavenly bodies and where they will be years from now. On the other end of the spectrum is the microcosm with its atoms, and neutrons, that God holds together.

The Lord foils the plans of the nations; he thwarts the purposes of the people. But the plans of the Lord stand firm forever, the purposes of his heart through all generations. . . . The Lord sees all mankind; from his dwelling place. He, who forms the hearts of all, watches everything we do. (Ps. 33:6-15).

The answer for all our brokenness is to trust in Jesus. It's through him that all things hold together. God works it out for our good. (Ro. 8:28). If God is for us who can be against us? (Ro. 8:19-37).

Father, our world is broken. Thank you for holding all things together. Amen.

Bible: A Mirror for USA?

Roman 1:18-32

Perhaps the most accurate Scripture describing our nation is Romans 1:18-32: "The wrath of God is being revealed from heaven against all the godlessness and wickedness of men who suppress the truth by their wickedness since what may be known about God is plain to them, because God has made it plain to them. For since the creation of the world God's invisible qualities—his eternal power and divine nature—have been clearly seen being understood from what has been made, so that men are without excuse . . .

"Even their women exchanged natural relations for unnatural ones. In the same way the men also abandoned natural relations with women and were inflamed with lust for one another . . .

"Furthermore, since they did not think it worthwhile to retain the knowledge of God, he gave them over to a depraved mind, to do what ought not to be done . . . They are full of envy, murder, strife, deceit and malice. They are gossips, slanderers, God haters, insolent, arrogant and boastful; they invent ways of doing evil, they disobey their parents; they are senseless, faithless, heartless, ruthless. Although they know God's righteous decree that those who do such things deserve death, they not only continue to do these very things but also approve of those who practice them."

According to Jim Denison, Denison Forum, Oct. 4, 2016, "Organized movements are seeking to advance polygamy in our country. Zoophilia (sexual relations between people and animals) is becoming more accepted. It's easy to think that the culture is sliding into a moral abyss from which there is no return and for which there is no hope." As it was in Noah's time so it will be before Jesus returns. (Matt. 24:37). The people in Jeremiah's day did not even blush at their loathsome acts. (Jer. 6:13-15). But we never give up on God. Jesus' world was immoral—from pagan idolatry to emperor worship to mystery cults and bestiality. Then Jesus began the mightiest spiritual movement in human history. What our Lord did then, he can do today!

Lord, I choose to put on the full armor of God to overcome the immoral culture. Amen.

November 29

Revival

I John 1:7

"If we walk in the light as he is in the light, we have fellowship with one another, and the blood of Jesus, his Son, purifies us from all sin" (I John 1:7).

"Walking in the light means an altogether new sensitiveness to sin, calling things by their proper name of sin, such as pride, hardness, doubt, fear, self-pity, which are often passed over as merely human reactions. It means a readiness to 'break' and confess at the feet of Him who was broken for us, for the Blood does not cleanse excuses, but always cleanses sin, confessed as sin; then revival is just the daily experience of a soul full of Jesus and running over. Revival is the life of the Lord Jesus poured into human hearts." (*The Calvary Road* by Roy Hession, p. 6.)

"His power is boundless. And we, on our part, have only to get into a right relationship with Him, and we shall see His power being demonstrated in our hearts and lives and service, and His victorious life will fill us and overflow through us to others. That is Revival in its essence." (p. 13)

To come into the light our wills must be broken. This is painful, and humiliating but mandatory. It is no longer I but Christ. Our "I", (ego) must bend and become a "C" which means Christ is in me and I am conformed to him.' (Gal. 2:20).

Revival implies that we lost the fire of the Holy Spirit burning brightly in us. Let the Holy Spirit blow through you, cleaning you from all sin.

Keep short accounts. As soon as you sense you displeased the Lord, confess it immediately. "Whoever conceals their sins does not prosper, but the one who confesses and renounces them finds mercy" (Prov. 28:13). "Blessed is the one whose transgressions are forgiven whose sins are covered" (Ps. 32:1).

Revival will come as we recognize and admit our sin to God, trust God's willingness to forgive and accept God's forgiveness. Go forth in the power of the Holy Spirit serving him with joy and delight.

Father I confess my sin, forgive me, cleanse me and empower me to serve you. Amen.

Boring or Refreshing

Acts 3:19-20

"Repent ... and turn to God, so that your sins may be wiped out, that times of refreshing may come from the Lord, and that he may send ... Jesus" (Acts 3:19-20). Jesus brings continual and eternal refreshment to life. He is the God of surprises. Staleness is a sign that we are not lined up with God. Anytime we are bored we are not receiving his life lived through us.

When Paul says, be filled with the Holy Spirit he is, according to the Greek, saying, keep on be filled. (Eph. 5:18). It's like eating. We are full but in a few hours we need to eat again. We need to be filled again and again because we leak, we forget, we let things of the world crowd out a consciousness of God's presence in us.

"Whatever you do, work at it with all your heart, as working for the Lord, not for men, since you know that you will receive an inheritance from the Lord" (Col. 3:23-24).

Brother Lawrence did not like kitchen work, yet for 15 years, he found fulfillment in this work. He was determined to do everything for God asking for grace to do his work. He learned to submit to God. He was willing to work anywhere, always glad to be able to do little things for God. (*The Practice of the Presence of God*, p. 12.)

How could Paul rejoice in the Lord in the midst of all his trials, sufferings and persecutions? Listen to First Thess. 5:16-24 AMP, "Be happy [in your faith] and rejoice and be glad-hearted continually—always. Be unceasing in prayer—praying perseveringly; Thank [God] in everything—no matter what the circumstances may be, be thankful and give thanks ... Test all things [until you can recognize] what is good; [to that] hold fast. Abstain from evil—shrink from it and keep aloof from it. And may the God of peace Himself sanctify you through and through—that is, separate you from profane things and wholly consecrated to God—and may your spirit, soul and body be preserved sound and complete [found] blameless at the coming of our Lord."

Wherever you find yourself ask for grace to be refreshed. God will meet you there.

Father, thank you for meeting me in the mundane, routine chores of life. Amen.

Open your Eyes

I John 10:10

Lift up your heads! Open your eyes! God has so much more for you than we can imagine. Taste and see that the Lord is good. (Ps. 34:8). Hear these superlatives.

I soar on eagle's wings. (Isaiah 40:31).

I have fullness of joy, joy inexpressible and glorious joy. (I Peter 1:8).

I have peace that passes all understanding. (Phil. 4:7).

I am more than a conqueror. (Romans 8:37).

I am given unsearchable, inexhaustible riches in Christ. (Eph. 3:8).

I can scale a wall. (II Samuel 22:30).

I can do all things through Christ who strengthens me. (Phil. 4:13).

I can do more through Christ than I can ask or imagine. (Eph. 3:20-21).

I rejoice in suffering. (James 1:1-3).

I have abundant life—life to the full. (John 10:10).

I cast my cares and worries on the Lord. (I Peter 5:7).

I have rivers of living water flowing from me. (John 7:38).

I am overcome with joy and gladness. (Isaiah 35:10).

I shout praises to the Lord. (Psalm 98:4).

I give thanks in all circumstances. (I Thessalonians 5:18).

I have the feet of a deer. (Habakkuk 3:19).

Why is there so much discouragement, depression, Christians with no smile, or no song in their heart? Few Christians experience these promises. They don't go far enough or deep enough to experience God's joy. They have no concept of sitting with Christ in a heavenly place, soaring on eagle's wings. Christ is not their life.

God has greater things for you! Keep in step with his Holy Spirit. Become who God says you are.

Father enable me to become all that you say I am. Amen.

Take Your Seat

Ephesians 2:6

"You are seated with Christ." Does it sound ridiculous?

"God raised us from the dead along with Christ, and we are seated with Christ in the heavenly realms all because we are one with Christ Jesus" (Eph. 2:6 NLT).

Paul suffered horrendous persecution: five times beaten with thirty-nine lashes, beaten with rods three times, stoned, shipwrecked, often without food and water . . . and yet he writes from prison that God has raised him up to sit beside Christ.

Paul prays for the Christians in Ephesis to have their eyes open to see where they are seated: "I pray that you will begin to understand the incredible greatness of his power for us who believe. This is the same mighty power that raised Christ from the dead and seated him in the place of honor at God's right hand in the heavenly realms. Now he is far above any ruler or authority or power or leader or anything else in this world or in the world to come" (Eph. 1:19-21 NLT).

If you understand where you are seated you can conquer through Jesus any ruler, authority, power, or situation now or in your future. No situation you face can remove you from your seat beside Jesus.

Have you recently lost a loved one or a family member? You may be battling cancer, pain, disappointment, depression or a spirit of criticism. Ask God to open your eyes to see where you are seated. You are beside Messiah Jesus above every situation!

The Hebrew root word for "to heal" is "relax." If you learn to relax in Jesus' presence you will experience peace and joy beyond your imagination. Ask Jesus to open your eyes to see the victory that is yours sitting beside King Jesus.

Father, thank you for a place to rest and relax especially in troubling times. God, I praise you for the power you provide for me to live above every situation. Amen.

A Fresh Start for Everyone

Ephesians 2:12-21

Walls and fences are everywhere; some are high, some last for centuries. Most of the 57 wars that our world is currently experiencing are because of economics, religion and race. Do you know your neighbors? Is your backyard fence a wall? Do you have walls in your family? Do you have friends who are poor? Who are you keeping out of your life or your church? Sunday morning is the most segregated time of the week.

Remember you were without hope and without God. (v. 12). "Because of Christ—dying that death, shedding that blood –you who were once out of it altogether are in on everything. . . . Jesus tore down the wall we used to keep each other at a distance. . . . Instead of continuing with two groups of people separated by centuries of animosity and suspicion, he created a new kind of human being, a fresh start for everybody. Christ brought us together though his death on the Cross . . . . He treated us as equals, and so made us equals. Through him we both share the same Spirit and have equal access to the Father. . . . You're no longer strangers or outsiders. You belong here, with as much right to the name Christian as anyone. . . . God is fitting you . . . stone by stone with Christ Jesus as the cornerstone that holds all the parts together" (Eph. 2:13-21 Msg.).

We are all one—all part of his building. Now we fit in with others just as one stone fits with another because we are building on Jesus Christ our foundation stone. Stones were not formed by a mold. Every stone is different and has to be fit into place.

As his born-again children we have the same Holy Spirit as Jesus has and the same access to our Father. The ground at the cross is level. Jesus died for everyone. Jesus will remove walls. We are no longer on the out-side without God and without hope because we are part of Jesus' body—the church.

Jesus enable me to help remove walls in families, churches and our world. With your Spirit's help I will remove all walls that I have erected. Amen.

Boasting Is OK

Romans 11:13-14

No one likes a person who constantly calls attention to themselves. Paul boasts in his weakness because it magnifies Christ. (II Cor. 12:9). "It is because of God that you are in Christ Jesus who has become for us . . . righteousness, holiness and redemption. Therefore, as it is written: 'Let him who boasts, boast in the Lord'" (I Cor. 1:30-31). "I can do everything through Christ who gives me strength" (Phil. 4:13).

In describing his ministry to the Gentiles Paul writes, "I make much of my ministry in the hope that I may somehow arouse my own people to envy and save some of them" (Ro. 11:13-14). Paul is determined to see as many people as possible enter God's kingdom. "I lay great stress on my ministry and magnify my office, in the hope of making my fellow Jews jealous—in order to stir them up to imitate, copy and appropriate and thus managing to save some of them" (AMP).

Do you make much of your ministry or do you tone down or belittle your ministry so no one can accuse you of being proud? Don't be afraid to glory in the cross, to publicly magnify Jesus and the fulfilling and abundant life he gives to you.

"Let not the wise man gloat in his wisdom, or the mighty man in his might, or the rich man in his riches. Let him boast in this alone: that they truly know me and understand that I am the Lord who is just and righteous, whose love is unfailing and that I delight in these things. I, the Lord, have spoken!" (Jer. 9:23-24 NLT). "My soul will boast in the Lord; let the afflicted hear and rejoice. Glorify the Lord with me; let us exalt his name together" (Ps. 34:2-3).

Even though, "fig trees may no longer bloom, or vineyards produce grapes, and harvest time a failure, sheep pens may be empty, and cattle stall vacant—I will still celebrate because the Lord God saves me" (Habakkuk 3:17-18 CEV).

Father, I celebrate the joy of knowing you. I will lift you up so others will be drawn to you. Amen. (John 12:32).

Overcoming Spiritual Dullness

Hebrews 6:10-12

"For God is not unfair. He will not forget how hard you have worked for him and how you have shown your love to him by caring for other Christians . . . Our great desire is that you will keep right on loving others as long as life lasts. . . . Then you will not become spiritually dull and indifferent. Instead, you will follow the example of those who are going to inherit God's promises because of their faith and patience" (Heb. 6:10-12 NLT).

"The more you grow . . . the more you will become productive and useful in your knowledge of our Lord Jesus Christ . . . Work hard to prove that you really are among those God has called and chosen. Doing this you will never stumble or fall away. And God will open wide the gates of heaven for you to enter into the eternal Kingdom of our Lord and Savior Jesus Christ" (II Peter 1:8-11 NLT).

Working hard at caring for others removes dullness from our life. God will reward us by opening wide the gates of heaven. On the other hand, carnal, self-centered Christians don't work hard for the Lord and don't reproduce. Their works will be burned up. "If any man builds on this foundation (Jesus Christ), using gold, silver, costly stones, wood, hay or straw, his work will be shown for what it is, because the Day will bring it to light. It will be revealed with fire, and the fire will test the quality of each man's work. If what he has built survives he will receive his reward. If it is burned up, he will suffer loss; he himself will be saved, but only as one escaping through the flames" (I Cor. 3:12-15).

"I discipline my body like an athlete, training it to do what it should. Otherwise, I fear that after preaching to others, I myself might be disqualified" (I Cor. 9:27 NLT).

Live in God's love. (John 15:9). It's only God's pure self-less love flowing through you that can overcome spiritual dullness.

Lord, by your grace I choose to show love to everyone. May your joy and love flow through me to others today. Amen.

The Greatest Virtue

Colossians 3:12-14

"As God's chosen people, holy and dearly loved, clothe yourselves with compassion, kindness, humility, gentleness and patience. Bear with each other and forgive whatever grievance you may have against one another. Forgive as the Lord forgave you. Over all these virtues put on love, which binds them together" (Col. 3:12-14).

"Love keeps no record of the wrongs" (I Cor. 13:7). "Be patient, bearing with one another in love" (Eph. 4:2). True forgiveness holds no grudges. We may remember past injustices but in Christ they are forgiven and their sting is under the blood, forgiven and healed.

Bitterness robs you of being an effective Christian. A church decided to split. It began at a banquet when an elder was served a smaller piece of ham than the person beside him. While it is hard to keep from either laughing or crying it is all too true that the smallest slights can begin a root of bitterness and even a church split.

Some people do not last long in a small group; they can't discuss controversial issues in a rational, level-headed manner. They find it impossible to work with a committee because they have hurts which rise to the surface evidenced in their tone of voice. Their root of bitterness was never healed.

One writer suggests that Christians have more trouble with this than secular people because we have high moral standards but are short on grace. Learn to extend grace to yourself and others. As God forgave you forgive others and yourself. "If you do not forgive men their sins, your Father will not forgive your sins" (Matt. 6:15).

When there are deep unhealed wounds we take vengeance. Vengeance belongs to God. He will take care of the avenger. (Ro. 12:19). Vengeance causes the avenger to commit the greater evil. Confess your hurts, your faults, to God and to each other so you can be healed. (I John 1:9 & James 5:16). Come to Jesus for healing.

Father, forgive me for carrying hurts in my heart. I bring them to you for healing. Amen.

Holy Compassion

Philippians 3:18

When a group of international persons left America to return home they were asked what memories they will take with them. Their response was the many obese people and all the food that is thrown into the garbage. Is our stomach our God? Do we glory in our gourmet dinners? Jesus said, "I have food to eat that you know nothing about" (John 4:32). Until we make prayer more important than our food we will not soar like eagles.

"As I often told you before and now say again even with tears, many live as enemies of the cross of Christ. Their destiny is destruction, their god is their stomach, and their glory is in their shame. Their mind is on earthly things. But our citizenship is in heaven. We eagerly await a Savior from there, the Lord Jesus Christ" (Phil. 3:18-20).

Paul says he told the Christians repeatedly with tears. . . . Why the tears, because the destiny of these people is destruction. Their god is their stomach. All they think about is earthly things. Are you more concerned about getting to the restaurant following a church service than spending time in fellowship: praying and encouraging each other?

A Christian was concerned about his young banker who did not know the Lord. For eighteen months, every time he went to the bank he asked the young man to meet with him so they could study the Bible together. To get him off his back the young man finally agreed. They studied together. The young man gave his life to Christ. Today this banker has a dramatic testimony and is as zealous as the Christian who led him to the Lord.

"I have treasured the words of his (God's) mouth more than my daily bread" (Job. 23:12). "How sweet are your words to my taste, yes sweeter than honey to my mouth!" (Ps. 119:103 KJV). Jesus said natural bread is not sufficient. We must feed on God's word. (Matt. 4:4).

Lord Jesus, forgive me when my stomach is more important than my desire to pray and share the Good News so others will not go to destruction. Amen.

Are You in the Coast Guard?

James 5:19-20 & Matthew 18:12-14

Join the coast guard for Jesus. "Brothers and sisters, we urge you to warm those who are lazy. Encourage those who are timid. Take tender care of those who are weak. Be patient with everyone" (I Thess. 5:14 NLT). "My dear friends, if you know people who have wandered off from God's truth, don't write them off. Go after them. Get them back and you will have rescued precious lives from destruction and prevented an epidemic of wandering away from God" (James 5:19-20 Msg.).

Note the urgency—"go after them," "rescue them from destruction." First pray. Talk to God about them before you talk to them about returning to God. Second, check your love level. Do they know you really care? Third, build a friendship. If the wanderer refuses to hear you take another brother who everyone respects and try to win them back. (Matt. 18:16).

When you do this Jesus says, "You prevent an epidemic of people wandering off!" We never know the influence of one person. One person's change of direction can impact a church and even a multitude. Who has the greater influence, Billy Graham, or the person that led Billy to faith in Jesus?

Jesus said, "If a shepherd has one hundred sheep, and one wanders away and is lost, what will he do? Won't he leave the ninety-nine others and go out into the hills to search for the lost one? And if he finds it, he will surely rejoice over it more than over the ninety-nine that didn't wander away! In the same way, it is not my heavenly Father's will that even one of these little ones should perish" (Matt. 18:12-14 NLT).

God has called you to be a rescuer of wanderers. Hopefully most people in your congregation have a good foundation. But as happens in every congregation some grow cold and wander away. Jesus is asking you to rescue and save them from destroying others in the process. Ask the Lord to give you eyes to see those who are in need of encouragement.

Lord Jesus, enable me to be a rescuer for those who are wandering, an encourager for those who are timid and patient with everyone. Amen.

December 9

God Is Sovereign

Psalm 33:8-19

"With my great power and outstretched arm I made the earth and its people and the animals that are on it, and I give it to anyone I please" (Jer. 27:5). Jehoshaphat prayed: "O Lord God you rule over all the kingdoms of the nations. Power and might are in your hand, and no one can withstand you" (II Chron. 20:5-6).

"The king's heart is in the hand of the Lord; he directs it like a watercourse wherever he pleases" (Prov. 21:1). God humbled Nebuchadnezzar until he "acknowledged that the Most High God is sovereign over the kingdoms of men and sets over them anyone he wishes" (Daniel 5:21c; 4:25).

"The nations are as a drop in a bucket, and are counted as the small dust of the balance. All nations before Him are as nothing, and they are counted by Him as less than nothing and meaningless. It is he who sits upon the circle of the earth, and the inhabitants are as grasshoppers, who stretches out the heavens as a curtain, and spreads them out as a tent to dwell in. He brings the princes to nothing; He makes the judges of the earth meaningless. Scarcely shall they be planted; . . . when he will also blow on them, and they will wither, and the whirlwind will take them away as stubble." (Excerpts from Isaiah 40:15-24).

"Let all the earth fear the Lord; let all the people of the world revere him. For he spoke, and it came to be; he commanded, and it stood firm. The Lord foils the plans of the nations; he thwarts the purpose of the people. But the plans of the Lord stand firm forever, the purposes of his heart through all generations. Blessed is the nation whose God is the Lord; the people he chose for his inheritance. From heaven the Lord looks down and sees all mankind; he watches all who live on earth—he who forms the hearts of all, who considers everything they do. No king is saved by the size of his army; no warrior escapes his great strength" (Ps. 33:8-19).

Lord, what a great God you are! I trust you. You are my Lord and King. Amen.

Christians and Culture— Swimming Upstream

Romans 12:2

How should Christians act when their nation is in turmoil? As citizens of heaven our first allegiance is to God's Kingdom. (Acts 4:19-20, 5:29). Pharaoh ordered the midwives to kill all the baby boys. "Because the midwives feared God, they refused to obey the king and allowed the baby boys to live." God rewarded them. (Exodus 1:17 NLT). Shadrach, Meshach and Abednego refused to bow to the king's statue and God delivered them. (Daniel 3).

Jim Denison's blog May 18, 2017, quotes a second-century letter describing how early Christians distinguished themselves from their culture: "Christians are indistinguishable from other men either by nationality, language, or customs. They do not inhabit separate cities, or speak a strange dialect . . . . they follow the customs of whatever city they happen to be living in . . . (I Cor. 8:22)

"They live in their own countries as though they were only passing through. They play their full role as citizens, but labor under all the disabilities of aliens. Any country can be their homeland, but for them their homeland . . . is a foreign country. Like others, they marry and have children, but they do not [kill] them. They share their meals, but not their wives. They live in the flesh, but they are not governed by the desires of the flesh. They pass their days upon earth, but they are citizens of heaven. Obedient to the law, they yet live on a level that transcends the law . . . . To speak in general terms, we may say that the Christian is to the world what the soul is to the body. As the soul is present in every part of the body, while remaining distinct from it, so Christians are found in all the cities but cannot be identified with the world."

Are you conscious of being different in attitudes and demeanor, in language, in showing forgiveness and love? Do you sow peace and security? (Col. 3). "Don't copy the behavior and customs of this world but let God transform you into a new person . . ." (Ro. 12:2 NLT).

Father, thank you that I am a new creation because of Jesus living in me. Amen.

A Major Myth

Acts 12:2

Our culture bought into the myth that everyone goes to a better place when they die. If you doubt this just recall the last few funerals you attended. This myth negates the need for eternal salvation. Why bother to rescue people from eternal suffering if we are not sure Jesus really meant what he said about hell or even if hell exists?

The Apostles and the early church believers were passionate for our Lord. "King Herod had James, the brother of John, put to death with the sword" (Acts 12:2). The disciples all died for their faith. Often we are quiet because it will strain our relationship with those who don't know Jesus.

Our culture decided that Jesus is only one path among many paths to get to heaven. We live as if people have far more pressing needs than coming to know Jesus. If that is true then Jesus' Great Commission is not a priority.

The result is many Christians focus on delivering people from physical suffering. We feed the hungry, provide clean water for the thirsty, clothe the shivering, eradicate diseases which is what Jesus taught us to do. However, these works often take precedence over sharing the Gospel, even to the point of forgetting why we minister to human suffering.

Jesus met both physical and spiritual needs. For many Christians it is much easier to meet the physical needs of people than to minister to their spiritual needs. Physical needs are temporal. Spiritual life is eternal. The early church went everywhere sharing the Gospel. (Acts 8:2). In Mark 2:5 Jesus met the spiritual need before he met the physical need. Both are important but don't forget the spiritual dimension.

The apostles died sharing their faith. Are we willing to risk straining a relationship with our unchurched friends to bring them to Jesus? We are giving them the opportunity to spend eternity with our Lord rather than with the devil and his angels.

Lord, help me not only to meet temporal needs but to share the Good News even when I sense it may strain a relationship. Amen.

A Slippery Slope

I John 2:15

Many today have lost a sense of awe, wonder and reverence. This attitude has infiltrated the church. Have you lost your reverence for Almighty God? Satan loves to have us get on the slippery slope of light-hearted living and light-hearted worship.

We have lost the urgency of fervent prayer. Bob Pierce prayed, "Lord, break my heart with the things that break the heart of God." John Knox prayed, "Give me Scotland or I die." David Brainered prayed, "Lord, let me make a difference for you that is utterly disproportionate to who I am. God has designed us to depend on his Word to lead his people in ways that are utterly disproportionate to who we are." John Wesley said, "God will do nothing but in answer to prayer."

Christians living under repressive governments learn how to pray in desperation. "Hearts of Fire" depicts persecuted women from eight different countries who were imprisoned and tortured. When they're released they are more zealous than ever. Many returned to prison for not being quiet about their faith.

In *Screwtape Letters* C. S. Lewis (Chapter 12) depicts the slippery slope from zeal to indifference. Satan usually begins not by tempting us with overt sins of murder, drunkenness, adultery, etc. Once a person decides to follow Jesus, Satan sidetracks us with "little" things." Little things like wasting our time—hours spent on the internet, facebook, Iphone, being preoccupied with sports, winning the lottery, staying in fashion, or anything to get our minds off Jesus. Materialism is Satan's major weapon. Vacations are more important than the church's missions.

"Don't conform to the patterns of this world, but be transformed by the renewing of your mind" (Ro. 12:2). Remember, "We have the mind of Christ" (I Cor. 2:16). "Your attitude should be the same as that of Christ Jesus: . . . he humbled himself and became obedient to death—even death on a cross! Therefore God exalted him to the highest place and gave him the name that is above every name" (Phil. 1:5-9).

Lord, it's so easy to slide down the slippery slope of carnality. Restore to me the passion that loves you with all my heart, soul, mind and strength. Amen.

Suffering for Our Lord

I Peter 4:1

"Since Christ suffered in his body, arm yourselves also with the same attitude, because he who has suffered in his body is done with sin" (I Peter 4:1). Brother Yun in his book, *Living Water*, Zondervan 2008, pp. 42-43 says that for many years in China the Christians sang this song:

From the time the church was birthed on the day of Pentecost
The followers of the Lord have willingly sacrificed themselves
Tens of thousands have died that the Gospel might prosper
As such they have obtained the crown of life

CHORUS:
To be a martyr for the Lord, to be a martyr for the Lord
I am willing to die gloriously for the Lord.
Those apostles who loved the Lord to the end
Willingly followed the Lord down the path of suffering

John was exiled to the lonely isle of Patmos
Stephen was stoned to death by an angry crowd
Matthew was stabbed to death in Persia by a mob
Mark died as horses pulled his two legs apart
Doctor Luke was cruelly hanged
Peter, Philip and Simon were crucified on a cross
Bartholomew was skinned alive by the heathen
Thomas died in India as five horses pulled his body apart
The apostle James was beheaded by King Herod
Little James was cut in half by a sharp saw
James the brother of the Lord was stoned to death
Judas was tied to a pillar and shot by arrows
Matthias had his head cut off in Jerusalem
Paul was a martyr under Emperor Nero
I am willing to take up the cross and go forward
To follow the apostle down the road of sacrifice
That tens of thousands of precious souls can be saved
I am willing to leave all and be a martyr for the Lord.

Can anything be called a sacrifice if the reward is greater than the sacrifice?

Everyone Did As They Pleased

Judges 17:6

During the 50's and 60's the most frequent Scripture verse quoted by college youth was John 3:16 KJV, "God so loved the world that whoever believes in him will not perish but have everlasting life." During the 90's it was Matthew 7:1, "Do not judge, or you too will be judged." Today it's not a verse but the philosophy that people can do "whatever they feel like doing." (Judges 17:6 Msg.).

When people persist in turning their backs on God "their foolish hearts are darkened" (Ro. 1:21). "They become hopelessly confused. Their minds are full of darkness; they wander far from the life God gives because they have closed their minds and hardened their hearts against him.... They live for lustful pleasure and eagerly practice every kind of impurity" (Eph. 4:17-20).

When you talk about sin they feel judged. Jesus said, "Do not judge others, and you will not be judged" (Matt. 7:1). However verse 6 says we are not to give dogs what is sacred or cast pearls to swine. In v. 15 we are to be aware of false prophets. Jesus also said, "judge fairly and rightly" (John 7:24 AMP). Learn to recognize the "dogs, swine and false prophets." We do not judge them, we show love. (John 3:16-17).

Jesus instructs us concerning other Christians: "Why do you look at the speck of sawdust in your brother's eye and pay no attention to the plank in your own eye? ... You hypocrite, first take the plank out of your own eye, and then you will see clearly to remove the speck from your brother's eye" (Matt. 7:3-5). Look at your own life first. Extend love and grace. Our judgment must match God's. "Everything is permissible for me but not everything is beneficial.... I will not be mastered by anything" (I Cor. 6:12). God placed in everyone a sense of right and wrong. We know murder, stealing, and adultery are wrong. Tolerance is not king. Christians need to be clear that sin is sin.

Lord, enable me to remove the plank from my own life first so I can extend love and grace to others . . . to hate what is evil and cling to the good. Amen. (Ro. 12:9).

Hearing God's Call

Psalm 37:23

"The steps of a good man are ordered by the Lord and he delights in his way" (Ps. 37:23 JKV).

"In all your ways acknowledge him and he shall direct your paths" (Prov. 3:6 JKV). Take care of your passion for Christ and he will take care of your ministry. Focus on your vocation (serving the Lord) and he will take care of your career.

How do you know God's will for your life?

First, seek first God's Kingdom. (Matt. 6:33).

Second, study the Scriptures to see how God works in the lives of people in scripture. "By your words I can see where I'm going: they throw a beam of light on my dark path" (Ps. 119:105 Msg.).

Third, there is wisdom in Godly counselors. "Without good direction, people lose their way; the more wise counsel you follow, the better your chances" (Prov. 11:14 Msg.).

Fourth, what energizes you? What have you enjoyed doing in the past? What do you clearly desire to do? "Delight yourself in the Lord and he will give you the desires of your heart" (Ps. 37:4).

Fifth, what experiences have you had that prepare you to serve God presently? "The Lord who delivered me form the paw of the lion and the paw of the bear will deliver me from the hand of this Philistine" (I Samuel 17:37).

Sixth, where has God placed you presently? Your situation may be the door God is opening for you to walk through. God frequently uses circumstances to guide us. "Joseph's brothers pulled Joseph out of the cistern and sold him to the Ishmaelites who took him with them down to Egypt" (Genesis 37:28 Msg.).

Seventh, learn to hear his voice. "Jesus' sheep follow him because they know his voice" (John 10:4). "If anyone hears my voice and opens the door, I will come in and eat with him and he with me" (Rev. 3:20).

Finally, stay close to Jesus. He will give you his peace. (John 14:27).

Lord Jesus, I desire to be close to you; to be obedient in all things. Guide me. Amen.

Think Positively

Philippians 4:8

From prison Paul wrote, "Summing it all up, friends . . . fill your minds and meditate on things true, noble, reputable, authentic, compelling, gracious—the best, not the worst; the beautiful, not the ugly; things to praise, not things to curse" (Phil. 4:8 Msg.).

How could Paul fill his mind with good thoughts in prison? Paul understood the importance of thinking pure thoughts: "For as a person thinks in his heart, so is he" (Prov. 23:7 KJV). He had learned that positive thoughts are more profitable and God honoring than negative thoughts. Studies have shown that negative thoughts linger longer and make a deeper impression in our minds than positive thoughts. It's a good practice before giving a negative statement to another person to precede it with several positive compliments. God offers grace before he gives instruction. He delivered Israel from slavery before he gave the 10 commandments. (Ex. 20:2ff).

"Blessed are the pure in heart (mind)" (Matt. 5:8). "We have the mind of Christ" (I Cor. 2:16). Jesus said to the Pharisees, "They had minds like a snake pit! How do you suppose what you say is worth anything when you are so foul-minded? It's your heart, not the dictionary that gives meaning to your words" (Matt. 12:34-35 Msg.). Be transformed by the renewing of your mind. (Ro. 12:2).

"No one can know God's thoughts except God's own Spirit. God has given us his Spirit (not the world's spirit) so we can know the wonderful things God has freely given us" (I Cor. 2:11-12 NLT).

The more you think negative thoughts about a person the more you have trouble loving them. Remember they were created in God's image. Sometimes we hear we are to love the sinner and hate the sin. Is that possible? Thinking positive thoughts about people help us to love them. We begin to see them through God's eyes.

Jesus, I pray with David, "Search me, O God, and know my heart; test me and know my anxious thoughts. See if there is any offensive way in me, and lead me in the way everlasting" (Ps. 139:23-24).

351

Welcome One Another

Romans 15:5-9

"May our dependable steady and warmly personal God develop maturity in you so that you get along with each other as well as Jesus gets along with us all. Then we'll be a choir—not our voices only, but our very lives singing in harmony in a stunning anthem to the God and Father of our Master Jesus! So reach out and welcome one another to God's glory. Jesus did it; now you do it! Jesus, staying true to God's purposes, reached out in a special way to the Jewish insiders so that the old ancestral promises would come true for them. As a result, the non-Jewish outsiders have been able to experience mercy and to show appreciation to God" (Ro. 15:5-9 Msg.).

Church consulting takes me to different churches. I entered the church and received a program. There was no recognition that I was new. This was a small congregation of 75 people, so everyone knew everyone else. I had to ask where the Sunday School classes met. No one informed me where the restrooms were located. There were refreshments in the basement, where some had already gathered, but no one made any effort to inform me.

I picked a class and sat down in a circle of twenty chairs, ten were occupied. The teacher made no attempt to welcome me. I have experienced cold shoulder treatment in other churches as well.

"Love cares more for others than for self" (I Cor. 13:4 Msg.). Someone said, "A church not reaching out, passes out." Our churches must become places of warm fellowship reaching out to those we don't know. "So reach out and welcome one another to God's glory. Jesus did it; now you do it" (Ro. 15:7 Msg.).

Jesus left heaven to welcome us. Learn to intentionally and naturally reach out to others to welcome them. To stay in our own little cliques is inexcusable. God's Kingdom will never expand unless we have love in our hearts that intentionally reaches out to others.

Lord, help me to be sensitive to new people so they can experience God's unconditional love and respond in worship to him. Amen.

When I Am Weak, Then I Am Strong

II Corinthians 12:9

The Lord said to Paul, "My gracious favor is all you need. My power works best in your weakness" (II Cor. 12:9 NLT).

God gave Paul a thorn in the flesh to keep him from being proud. Three times he begged God to remove it. God told him, "My grace is enough; it's all you need. My strength comes into its own in your weakness" (v. 9 Msg.). Then Paul responds: "Once I heard that, I was glad to let it happen. I quit focusing on the handicap and began appreciating the gift. It was a case of Christ's strength moving in on my weakness. Now I take limitations in stride, and with good cheer, these limitations have cut me down to size—abuse, accidents, opposition, bad breaks. I just let Christ take over! And so the weaker I get, the stronger I become" (II Cor. 12:9-10 Msg.).

All we need is God's grace! Life by its very nature has times of discouragement and bad news. Do I take bad news in stride? Jesus was not caught off guard. He knew about it before I heard about it. Paul learned to glory in tribulation. (Ro. 5:3 KJV). Whatever the situation is, Jesus is sufficient. People are drawn to the Savior when they see his sufficiency in us as the light of Christ shines brighter and brighter in our life.

How do we reach this level of maturity? We deny ourselves, take up our cross and follow Christ. (Matt. 16:24). We surrender ourselves to him. No matter what he asks we have one answer: "YES Lord!" "Anyone who intends to come with me has to let me lead. You're not in the driver's seat; I am. Don't run from suffering, embrace it. Follow me and I'll show you how. Self-help is no help at all. Self-sacrifice is the way, my way, to finding yourself, your true self" (Matt. 16:24-25 Msg.).

Lord, when bad news and disappointments come, I choose to trust in you. In faith I thank you realizing you are in control. In my weakness you are strong. Teach me the lessons I am to learn and use me for your glory. Amen.

Cut Out the Word "Impossible"

Matthew 19:16-26

Jesus said, "With man this is impossible, but with God all things are possible" (Matt. 19:26). "Jesus looked hard at them and said, 'No chance at all if you think you can pull it off yourself. Every chance in the world if you trust God to do it'" (Msg.).

A young ruler came to Jesus and asked, "What good thing must I do to get eternal life?" Jesus responded . . . "Why do you call me good? No one is good except God alone. If you want to enter life, obey the commandments."

The ruler declared he already kept the commandments. He asked, "What do I still lack?" Jesus replied, "If you want to be perfect, go, sell your possessions and give to the poor and you will have treasure in heaven. Then come follow me." He went away very sad, because he was a man of great wealth. Jesus said, "How hard it is for the rich to enter the Kingdom of God." In fact Jesus explained that it's easier for a camel to go through the eye of a needle than for a rich man to enter the kingdom of God. The disciples responded, "Who then can be saved?" Jesus looked at them and said, "With man this is impossible, but with God all things are possible" (Matt. 19:26).

With God everyone who humbles themselves and turns to Christ can be saved no matter how far they are from God. I related closely to a man who is on his seventh marriage, another who was head of Satan's Angels and hired a hit man to kill his wife, child molesters, drug pushers and alcoholics. Those who have repented and are following Jesus will be in heaven. Unless you and I repent we will likewise perish. (Luke 13:1-5).

Take the word impossible out of your vocabulary. God has a purpose for your life, find it. Don't focus on what you don't have. Focus on what you have and use it.

"Nothing is impossible with God" (Luke 1:37 NLT).

Lord Jesus, thank you that with you all things are possible since I am in you and you are in me. Amen.

Help Your Pastor

Ephesians 6:19-20

"Don't forget to pray for me. Pray that I'll know what to say and have the courage to say it at the right time, telling the mystery to one and all, the Message that I, jailbird preacher that I am, am responsible for getting out" (Eph. 6:19-20 Msg.). "Brothers, pray for us" (I Thess. 5:25).

There is always a need for more workers, pastors and congregational leaders. How can you support them?

Pray. Prayer is of upmost importance. Pray for wisdom, strength and God's grace to empower the pastor and his family!

Encourage the pastor to delegate responsibilities. Offer to help wherever there is need. Pastors often try to do everything.

Encourage others in carrying out their ministry.

Take training to increase your ministry skills.

Be assertive in asking the pastors how you can assist them.

Affirm your pastor by verbal and written notes of appreciation. Point out specific things you appreciated in their messages.

Be a listening ear for the pastor.

Be a friend to the pastor and the pastor's family.

Offer to help with household tasks.

Surprise the pastor and family with an occasional gift.

Encourage your pastor to follow Ephesians 4:11-13 Msg., "He handed out gifts of apostle, prophet, evangelist and pastor-teacher to train Christians in skilled servant work, working within . . . the church, until we're all moving . . . graceful in response to God's Son, fully mature adults alive like Christ." The Scripture is clear: Everyone has gifts to help build up the body of Christ. (Ro. 12:4-6).

Father, I pray for our pastor and his family. I pray for wisdom and physical strength but more importantly, strength of character. I pray that others will use their gifts to assist in building up the church so we can grow to maturity in making disciples.

December 21

Enter Their World

I Corinthians 9:19-22

"I have voluntarily become a servant to any and all in order to reach a wide range of people: religious, nonreligious, meticulous, moralists, loose-living immoralists, the defeated, the demoralized—whoever. I did not take on their way of life. I kept my bearings in Christ—but I entered their world and tried to experience things from their point of view. I've become just about every sort of servant there is in my attempts to lead those I meet into a God-saved life" (I Cor. 9:19-22 Msg.).

Many community people have no idea what goes on inside the church. They see the church as irrelevant. To be irrelevant is irreverent. Jesus gave us the opposite picture of who we are to be: the light that can't be hid and the salt that changes the flavor of the community. (Matt. 5:14-16). The prebelievers were drawn to Jesus.

When I ask congregations what the purpose of the church is, they usually respond by saying, "worship and fellowship." These are good answers but the main purpose of the church is the same purpose Jesus had, namely, to seek and save the lost and to make disciples. (Luke 19:10 and Matt. 28:18-20).

How do we build bridges to our communities? We help meet community needs. We participate in community activities: sports teams, school programs, hosting block parties, etc. We meet people's needs: feed the hungry and provide after school programs or volunteer in the hospital, schools or library.

Jesus was conscious of his culture. On different occasions he slipped through the crowd because his attire was no different than theirs. Forty-five of Jesus' parables were presented in the marketplace. All but ten of his conversations recorded in the Gospel were outside the Temple. We need to understand the culture in which we live. (I Chronicles 12:29). Jesus' language was understood by adults and children. Everyone knew the importance of good soil, candlelight, flowers, birds and the signs in the sky.

Lord, enable me to build relationships with the unchurched so I can be an effective witness for you. Amen.

Does God Heal?

Corinthians 4:16

God heals either now or when we enter heaven. "Before I was afflicted I went astray, and now I obey your word" (Ps. 119:67, 71, 75 and 92). Jesus healed everyone who came to him. (Luke 6:19). In John 5:1-9 there apparently were dozens of sick but Jesus healed only one lame man. In Luke 10 Jesus sent the 72 disciples out to heal the sick but later in his ministry he says we are to visit the sick. (Matt. 25: 36, 39, 43 and 44).

"We groan inwardly as we wait eagerly for our adoption to sonship, the redemption of our bodies" (Ro. 8:23). "Outwardly we are wasting away, yet inwardly we are being renewed day by day" (II Cor. 4:16). "Epaphroditus was ill even at the point of death, but God had mercy on him . . . but also on me to spare me sorrow upon sorrow. . ." (Phil. 2:27-30). If Paul could deliver healing he would not have to be concerned about Epaphroditus' illness. By way of contrast in Acts 19:11-12, "God did extraordinary miracles through Paul, so that even handkerchiefs and aprons that had touched him were taken to the sick and their illnesses were cured and the evil spirits left them." The circumstances and situation made all the difference, God does what is best. (Acts 28:7-9).

Paul advises Timothy, "Stop drinking only water, and use a little wine because of your stomach and your frequent illnesses." (I Tim. 5:23). He left Trophimus sick in Miletus. (II Tim. 4:20). "It was because of an illness that I first preached the gospel to you" (Gal. 4:13). Paul was given a thorn in the flesh from Satan to torment him and to keep him from being proud. God said, "My grace is sufficient for you for my power is made perfect in weakness" (II Cor. 12:7-9).

Thank God for the thousands of times he answers our prayers for healing. Yet there are other times when God says, "My grace is sufficient." Daily, God heals multitudes of people physically often utilizing medicine or through his direct miraculous touch.

Father thank you for physical healing but more importantly, for eternal healing. Amen.

Persistence in Prayer

Luke 11:9-13

Persistence is an indication of faith. If you are to do great things for God you must persist. When your prayers are not answered in the way you desire, God wants you to continue to cry out to Jesus. "Anyone who comes to him must believe that he exists and that he rewards those who earnestly seek him" (Hebrews 11:6). Sometimes God does not answer our prayers as we desire. But if we are praying according to God's will we will receive his best. As you intently look into the face of God consistently, diligently seeking his will and his power he will answer. "You will seek me and find me when you seek me with all your heart" (Jeremiah 29:13).

Jesus said, "I say to you, Ask and keep on asking, and it shall be given to you; seek and keep on seeking and you shall find; knock and keep on knocking, and the door shall be opened to you. For everyone who asks and keeps on asking receives, and he who seeks and keeps on seeking finds, and to him who knocks and keeps on knocking the door shall be opened . . . . If you then, evil-minded as you are, know how to give good gifts . . . to your children, how much more will your heavenly Father give the Holy Spirit to those who ask and continue to ask him!" (Luke 11:9-13 AMP).

Jesus told a parable of the persistent widow who came to the judge. The judge finally gave her what she asked for. Jesus concludes that God will surely answer those who cry out for him day and night. Then he asks: "When the Son of Man comes, will he find faith on the earth?" (Luke 18:7-8). Our faith is tested when answers to our prayers do not come in our timing. The challenge is to persist in faith even when we don't understand what God is doing. He has bigger things in mind than the answer to our immediate prayer.

The early church devoted themselves to prayer. (Acts 2:42). Jesus said, "My house will be called a house of prayer" (Matt. 21:13). We should always pray and not give up. (Luke 18:1). "Do not be anxious about anything, but in everything, by prayer and petition, with thanksgiving, present your requests to God" (Phil. 4:6).

Lord, enable me to persist in prayer. Amen.

Dead Church

Revelation 3:1-3

"I see right through your work. You have a reputation for vigor and zest, but you're dead, stone dead. Up on your feet! Take a deep breath! Maybe there's life in you yet. But I wouldn't know it, by looking at your busywork; nothing of God's work has been completed. Your condition is desperate. Think of the gift you once had in your hands, the Message you heard with your ears—grasp it again and turn back to God" (Rev. 3:1-3 Msg.).

Some churches are busy but dead. There is no fruit—no baptisms, only casual prayer. Their fatigue is from doing church work, not the work of the church. Activities are focused inward. When our knowledge of God's truth no longer translates into our life for the lives of others we die. We need to stir up ourselves and overcome our fears.

"I remind you to fan into flame the gift of God, which is in you through the laying on of my hands" (II Tim. 1:6-7). The Amplified Bible reminds us to rekindle the embers, fanning the flame and keeping the inner fire burning. (v. 6). We do this by sincerely praying the prayer I have suggested before: "Father give me your passion—the passion of giving your only Son for this lost world, Jesus give me your passion— the passion you had when you died on the cross for this lost world. Holy Spirit give me your passion—the passion you had in leaving heaven in all its splendor and coming to dwell in sinful humanity, now being made holy by your work.

"For God did not give us a spirit of timidity—of cowardice, of craven and cringing and fawning fear—but [He has given us a spirit] of power and of love and of a calm and well-balanced mind and discipline and self-control" (v. 7 AMP). Paul pleeds, "agonize with me by praying to God or me." (Ro. 15:30).

These verses will transform your life and the life of your church. You will be an instrument to move people from doubt to faith, from busy-work to fruitful work, from death to eternal life.

Lord, enable me to stir into flame the gifts you have given me—to move from fear to power, from death to life. Amen.

Good Tidings of Great Joy —for Whom?

Luke 2 (Christmas Day)

"The angel of the Lord appeared to the shepherds, and the glory of the Lord shone around them, and they were terrified. But the angel said to them, 'Do not be afraid. I bring you good news of great joy that will be for all the people. Today in the town of David a Savior has been born to you; he is Christ the Lord'" (Luke 2:8-11).

This good news of great joy is for everyone. But read the following from, www.thetravelingteam.org: "If everyone is obeying God's 'calling' to be a missionary, God is calling 99.9995% of people to work among the 45% of the world population that already has the gospel, and calling virtually no one (.0005%) to relocate among the other 54% of the world population that are not Christians. You have a better chance of being in a plane crash than being one of the few missionaries to the unreached out of the total 2 billion Christians in the world.

"In light of God's word, this seems unfathomable and it appears to be almost complete disobedience on the part of the Church to go make disciples of all the nations. Financially, we are hoarding 99.99% of our income for ourselves.

"The current status quo is to do virtually nothing to reach the unreached people groups of the world. The percentages of man-power and money focused on Unresearched People Groups are almost undetectable they are so small."

Many millions this Christmas Day have never heard the name of Jesus—the Good News of great joy. Paul writes, "I want you to know how strenuously I am exerting myself for you and for . . . all those who never met me . . ." (Col. 2:1). The same Greek word is used to describe Jesus' agony in the Garden as he prayed and sweat drops of blood for us. (Luke 22:44). Jesus agonized for our salvation. Paul agonized for those he did not know. Lord, forgive me for my lack of passion for the lost.

Father, send workers to the two billion who have never heard the Good News. I commit myself to pray and fast for the millions who are eternally lost. Amen.

My All for His Glory

Philippians 1:20-21

"For I live in eager expectation and hope that I will never do anything that causes me shame, but that I will always be bold for Christ, as I have been in the past, and that my life will always honor Christ, whether I live or I die. For to me, living is for Christ, and dying is even better" (Phil. 1:20-21 NLT).

"We will all feel very much ashamed if we do not yield to Jesus the areas of our lives He has asked us to yield to Him . . . To reach that level of determination is a matter of the will, not of debate or of reasoning. It is absolute and irrevocable surrender of the will. An undue amount of thought and consideration for ourselves is what keeps us from making that decision, although we cover it up with the pretense that it is others we are considering . . . Shut out every other thought and keep yourself before God in this one thing only—my utmost for His highest. I am determined to be absolutely and entirely for Him and Him alone." (Oswald Chambers, *My Upmost for his Highest*, January 1 Daily Devotional Reading.)

Paul had settled the commitment issue. It no longer matters if I live or die. In fact it would be far easier to die than to stay here. (v. 21). The Moravian missionaries sold themselves as slaves to reach the unreached slaves for Christ. There were others who did not pack suitcases but built coffins to pack their things knowing they may never return to their homeland.

God said to Abram, "Leave your native country, your relatives, and your father's family, and go to the land that I will show you . . . So Abram departed as the Lord had instructed" (Gen. 12:1-4). No arguments, no "buts" but instant obedience. Later God asked him to take his son of promise, Isaac, and offer him on the altar. Again he was obedient. God honored his faith by providing a substitute offering. Abraham is the father of the faithful.

If there is any area of your life that you have determined to keep for yourself, you will be ashamed both today and at the Judgment Day. Give yourself completely to him.

Lord, I surrender my all to you. Do with me what you desire. I will obey you. Amen.

Don't Be a Stumbling Block

I Corinthians 10:32-33

"So whether you eat or drink or whatever you do, do it all for the glory of God. Do not cause anyone to stumble, whether Jews, Greeks or the church of God—even as I try to please everybody in every way, so that they may be saved" (I Cor. 10:32-33). You can never say, "God I want to do what I want." We are to do everything not for our selfish glory but for the glory of God.

Paul lived to glorify God in everything. Why? So people could come to salvation in Jesus. Paul was always conscious that the unsaved were watching him. I try to silently pray for wisdom as I meet people. It still amazes me how God answers that prayer. The supernatural becomes natural. I want to say and do only what the Lord wants me to say and do, so they can be saved. That was the purpose of Jesus' life and it must be our purpose.

"Make it your ambition to lead a quiet life, to mind your own business and to work with your hands, just as we told you, so that your daily life may win the respect of outsiders" (I Thess. 4:12). Our daily life's work needs to be above reproach as a witness to everyone.

"Slaves (servants) must obey their masters and do their best to please them. They must not talk back or steal, but they must show themselves to be entirely trustworthy. Then they will make the teaching about God our Savior attractive in every way . . . We are instructed to turn from godless living and sinful pleasures. We should live in this evil world with self-control, right conduct and devotion to God . . ." (Titus 3:9-12 NLT).

"We are God's aroma of Christ among those who are being saved and those who are perishing. To the one we are the smell of death; to the other, the fragrance of life" (II Cor. 2:15-16).

Make Jesus attractive by how you live so others will want to become his disciples.

Lord Jesus, help me to live faithfully obeying you in everything at home, at work and in my community so others will be attracted to you and become your child. Amen.

You Want to Change?

Philippians 4:11-13

Prayer changes you. The purpose of prayer is to know God, not merely to get things from God. Prayer changes us. My will is bent to God's will.

John Wesley prayed [using modern English], "I am no longer my own but yours. Do to me what you will, rank me with whoever. Let me be employed for you or laid aside for you. Let me be full, let me to empty. Let me have all things, let me have nothing. I freely and heartily yield all things to your approval and disposal. . . . Amen."

Most North Americans believe they are entitled to a happy life. We hear that message through commercials and in the "prosperity gospel." We believe we can control our destiny. Our tendency is to think, oh yeah, God, I need you, too. God desires for us to grow into doing his will.

While Paul says he has not attained perfection (Phil. 3:12) he also says, "I have learned to be content whatever the circumstances. I know what it is to be in need, and I know what it is to be in plenty. I have learned the secret of being content in any and every situation, whether well fed or hungry, whether living in plenty or in want. I can do everything through him who gives me strength" (Phil. 4:11-13).

God loves you. Yes, you will be tested. God knows what is best and how to move you to maturity. "Endure hardship as discipline" (Heb. 12:6-7). Consider the life of the eleven disciples being faithful unto death. Consider the accounts of the Voice of Martyrs working in 68 different countries. God is a loving God which means he disciplines his children. We do the same with our children because we love them.

Parents, teach your children to pray as soon as they can talk. Tell them, "God loves you!" Do they know that Jesus is there when the lights go out? Do they see you praying? Are they conscious that Jesus is with them all the time because they know he is with you 24/7?

Lord, I put myself at your disposal. I want your will more than anything in life. Amen.

December 29

False Teachers, Money Hungry

II Corinthians 2:17

Jude was eager to write about the wonderful salvation we share but he also had to deal with church problems. He writes, "Certain men whose condemnation was written about long ago have secretly slipped in among you. They are godless men, who change the grace of our God into a license for immorality and deny Jesus Christ . . ." (Jude 3-6). Sexual license has permeated our culture. Too often it is in the church. It's the most frequent sin listed in the Bible. God loves everyone but he will not tolerate unrepentant sinners. We must not allow their false doctrine.

Paul warns the elders in Ephesis, "I know that after I leave, savage wolves will come in among you and will not spare the flock. Even from your own number men will arise and distort the truth in order to draw away disciples after them" (Acts 20:29-31). Paul instructs Titus to silence and rebuke sternly those men who rebel against right teaching and engage in useless talk, deceiving people. They only want your money. (Titus 1:10-14). We live in a time of tolerance. It is unacceptable in many churches to talk about false teaching and those who beg for money. The teachers in their greed make up clever lies to get hold of your money. (II Pet. 2:3). Paul writes, "We are not like those hucksters—and there are many of them—who preach just to make money" (II Cor. 2:17 NLT). The Greek word means "hawking"—a con man or swindler who preys on unsuspecting victims.

Jesus says, "Watch out for false prophets. They come to you in sheep's clothing, but inwardly they are ferocious wolves. By their fruit you will recognize them" (Matt. 7:15-16). Ezekiel 33:31, "They come pretending to be sincere and sit before you listening. But they have no intention of doing what I tell them. They express love with their mouths, but their hearts seek only after money" (NLT).

Jesus, enable me to discern pure teaching and not be deceived by those who are using the Gospel for their own gain to make money. Amen.

Heaven, the Christian's Eternal Home (Part I)

Revelation 7:14-17

"No eye has seen, no ear has heard, no mind has conceived what God has prepared for those who love him" (I Cor. 2:9).

"We know that when he comes we will be like him, for we will see him as he really is. And all who believe this will keep themselves pure, just as Christ is pure" (I John 3:2-3 NLT). "While you are waiting for Christ's return to happen, make every effort to live a pure and blameless life. And be at peace with God" (II Pet. 3:14 NLT).

We'll know each other in heaven. Jesus took Peter, James and John to the mountain where he was transfigured. "Suddenly, Moses and Elijah appeared and began talking with Jesus. Peter blurted out, 'Lord, this is wonderful!'" (Matt. 17:2-4 NLT).

Paul was forbidden to tell what he experienced when he was caught up to paradise. (II Cor. 12:4). He was eager to get there: "I desire to depart and be with Christ which is better by far . . ." (Phil. 1:23). "Though outwardly we're wasting away, yet inwardly we are being renewed day by day. For our light and momentary troubles are achieving for us an eternal glory that far outweighs them all" (II Cor. 4:16-18). "Our citizenship is in heaven. And we eagerly await a Savior from there, the Lord Jesus Christ, who . . . will transform our lowly bodies so that they will be like his glorious body" (Phil 3:20-21).

"These have come out of the great tribulation; they have washed their robes and made them white in the blood of the Lamb. Therefore, they are before the throne of God and serve him day and night in his temple . . . Never again will they hunger, never again will they thirst. The sun will not beat upon them, nor any scorching heat. For the Lamb at the center of the throne will be their shepherd; he will lead them to springs of living water. God will wipe away every tear from their eyes" (Rev. 7:14-17).

Thank you for our wonderful future. Amen.

Will You Be in Heaven? (Part II)

Revelation 21:3-8

"The home of God is now among his people! He will live with them. . . . There will be no more death or sorrow or crying or pain for the old world and its evils are gone forever. And the one sitting on the throne said, 'Lord, I am making all things new!' And then he said to me . . . 'To all who are thirsty I will give the springs of the water of life without charge! All who are victorious will inherit all these blessings, and I will be their God, and they will be my children. But cowards who turn away from me, and unbelievers, and the corrupt and murderers, and the immoral, and those who practice witchcraft, and idol worshipers, and all liars—their doom is in the lake that burns with fire and sulfur'" (Rev. 21:3-8). "Anyone who does what is shameful or deceitful will not enter, but only those whose names are written in the Lamb's book of life" (Rev. 21:27).

"The Water-of-Life River . . . flowed from God's throne; . . . the Tree of life planted on each side of the River, producing twelve kinds of fruit, a ripe fruit each month. The leaves of the Tree are for healing the nations. Never again will anything be cursed. The throne of God and of the Lamb is at the center. His servants will . . . look on his face, their foreheads mirroring God. Never again will there be any night. No one will need lamplight or sunlight . . . And they will rule with him forever" (Rev. 22:1-5 Msg.).

"We shall be like him for we shall see him as he is" (I John 3:2; Phil. 3:21). We . . . will be imperishable raised in glory and in power. (I Cor. 15:42-43). We are co-heirs with Christ. (Ro. 8:17). Our inheritance will never perish, spoil or fade. (I Pet. 1:4). We rest from our work and our deeds will be rewarded. (Rev. 14:13).

Will you be in heaven? "He who has the Son has life; he who does not have the Son of God does not have life" (I John 5:12).

Lord, thank you for our tremendous future with you. Come quickly! Amen.

Jesus is Our Righteousness, Holiness and Redemption.

I Cor. 1:30-31

"God placed us in Christ Jesus, who has become for us wisdom from God – that is, our righteousness, holiness and redemption. Therefore, as it is written, 'Let him who boasts, boast in the Lord'" (I Cor. 1:30-31). "It is from God that you have your life in Christ Jesus, whom God made our wisdom from God, [that is, revealed to us a knowledge of the divine plan of salvation previously hidden, manifesting itself as] our Righteousness and thus making us upright and putting us in right standing with God; and our consecration – making us pure and holy, and our redemption – providing our ransom from eternal penalty for sin" (AMP).

The Message puts it this way: "Everything we have – right thinking and right living, a clean slate and a fresh start - comes from God by way of Jesus Christ." Let's boast about Jesus!

God put us in Christ. We are in Christ or Christ is in us. We must belief and live knowing this is true. Because we are in Christ we have a right standing with God, we are pure and holy, (in his eyes) and our ransom for sin is paid. The Message reminds us: Everything we have – right thinking and right living comes from God.

It is only because God put you in Jesus that you are righteous, holy and redeemed. That is how God sees us. Do you see yourself as God sees you? Seeing yourself as God sees you will encourage and enable you to walk in righteousness and holiness as a new creation in Christ.

Many are content to be "good" people when God wants us to be "Godly" people. "Whenever you turn to the right or to the left, you will hear a voice saying, 'This is the road! Now follow it'" (Isaiah 30:12 CEV).

Ask God to open your spiritual eyes, (eyes of faith) to see yourself as God sees you. Thanking God for your standing in Jesus will enable you to thank God for your position as righteous, holy and redeemed and allows his supernatural life to be expressed in your daily life.

Lord, thank you that you are my righteousness, holiness and redemption. Amen